A Bird-Finding Guide to Ontario

CLIVE E. GOODWIN

A Bird-Finding Guide to Ontario

Revised Edition

UNIVERSITY OF TORONTO PRESS
Toronto Buffalo London

© University of Toronto Press Incorporated 1995
Toronto Buffalo London
Printed in Canada

ISBN 0-8020-6904-5

Printed on acid-free paper

Canadian Cataloguing in Publication Data

Goodwin, Clive E.
  A bird-finding guide to Ontario

  Rev. ed.
  Includes index.
  ISBN 0-8020-6904-5

  1. Bird watching – Ontario – Guidebooks.   I. Title.

  QL685.5.05G64 1995   598'.07234713   C94-932474-4

University of Toronto Press acknowledges the financial assistance to its publishing program of the Canada Council and the Ontario Arts Council.

Contents

Maps

Preface

Ontario is one of the major destinations for bird watchers on the continent. It is rewarding in every season; from the landbirds sheltering in the dense cedars on Point Pelee in early May, to Merlins hunting shorebirds on the beaches of Presqu'île in September; and from the golden flash of a Prothonotary Warbler in the sun-dappled summer sloughs of Rondeau, to a Gyrfalcon gracing the grain elevators in the Thunder Bay winter. There is birding to suit every level of activity, from sitting by the fire watching the flow of finches at one's feeder, to hiking the tundra of Hudson Bay in search of arctic nesters. And there is birding to challenge every level of skill, from sorting out the bright throng of spring warblers in a city park, to distinguishing between the gulls in the milling flocks above Niagara Falls.

But the province is vast, and the birding locations are not listed in the travel brochures. This book aims to provide the necessary guide to birding in the province, defining where to go and how to get there. The popularity of its first edition attests to the need for such information.

This second edition not only gives an opportunity to update that material – now over ten years old – but also to make the book much more useful. In particular there was a need to provide more information on the status of individual species, and the tables of the first edition are now replaced by a full systematic list. The site numbering system used previously proved exasperating to use, so a new approach to site identification has been adopted, with the original chapters subdivided to make them more manageable.

We have had some requests to handle the directions as a series of 'tours,' following the pattern of the pioneering Lane guides. Our own experience with such tours, however, is that they can be awkward to use for persons not following the prescribed route. As Ontario's birding spots are widely dispersed and birders can arrive from many directions, we have chosen to maintain a more generalized approach to describing the selected locations.

A second area of debate was the degree to which we should cover sewage lagoons. These can vary widely in their attractiveness to birds, but as there was little information available on their quality when the first edition was written, almost all were included. There is still a lack of information on many of them, and as even less productive lagoons can still be among the better locations in an area for waterbirds, in the end relatively few have been dropped from this edition.

No book of this kind can be complete. There are a multitude of good places to watch birds in Ontario; it is only possible to offer a selection of the most popular and productive localities. We have covered the major locations in some detail, but also attempted to provide the birder with choices of places that should yield good birding across the province.

The original scope of the second edition was to adopt a 'no news is good news' approach, and revise only those areas we knew (or had been told) were in need of revision. We soon discovered this laissez faire approach was not working, and in the end we revisited most of the major areas. We were also fortunate (and very grateful) to receive enthusiastic assistance from the persons acknowledged below. Their collective input on those parts of the province with which we are less familiar has made this edition enormously stronger than its predecessor.

The information here came from a multitude of sources, but particular thanks are due to the following, who made major contributions for the areas noted: G. Bellerby (Niagara); A.D. Brewer (Guelph, Luther Marsh, and Mountsberg); C.A., D.L., and J.L. Campbell (Pelee Island, Cambridge, and Kitchener/

Waterloo); W.R. Clark (Pembroke and area); B.M. and Laurie DiLabio (chapter 14); D.H. Elder (chapter 18); N.G. Escott (chapter 17); J. McCracken and Long Point Bird Observatory (chapter 7); J. Nicholson (Sudbury and Manitoulin); M. Parker (chapter 5); R. Pittaway (Lake Simcoe, Carden Plain, Haliburton and Algonquin); D. Paleczny (Cochrane); D. Rupert (chapter 4); R.D. Tafel (North Bay); R. Tozer (Algonquin Provincial Park); R.D. Weir (chapter 13); P. Allen Woodliffe (Walpole Island and Rondeau) and R. Yukich (Sault Ste Marie). Many others have provided valuable information, suggestions, and assistance in a variety of ways, including R.F. Andrle, D. Asquith, M. Bain, G. Bennett, R. Bowles, G. Carpentier, A. Chartier, M. Coteau, A. Dawe, P. Deacon, C. Dersch, R. Falconer, G.M. Hamilton, P. Harper, T. Hince, P. Holder, J.W. Johnson, A.H. Kelley, T. Lang, E.W. Lewis, C.J. MacFayden, R.D. McRae, J. McClure, A. Mills, L. Nichols, B. Parker, S. Peruniak, A. Rider, D.C. Sadler, A. Sandilands, M. Scholz, R. Smith, M. Smout, J. Wallace, and M.C. Williams. I apologize to anyone whom I have overlooked, and indeed much of the information has been gathered over many years, with the willing help throughout that time of birders across the province.

I have chosen not to include a full listing of citations for the distributional information provided, with apologies to those whose published material was drawn on with inadequate citation. My defence is that, in spite of appearances, brevity in a book of this kind is vital, and a full list of citations would only lengthen both the book and its publication time enormously. Neither would it greatly enhance it: those looking for scholarly treatises will inevitably search elsewhere. Accuracy, however, is important; and special gratitude is due to R.D. James and R.D. Weir, who willingly undertook the tedious and demanding task of reading critically the systematic list. Both made many valuable suggestions and pointed out inaccuracies and ambiguities. Ron Ridout kindly provided valuable additional material.

Thanks also to G.D. Boggs and T. Beechey of the Ministry of Natural Resources' Parks Planning Section for allowing access to their files, and to B. Hogarth of the Pollution Control Branch of the Ministry of the Environment for making available the tabulation of major municipal sewage lagoons used in the first

edition. The Maitland Valley and Lakehead Region Conservation Authorities provided useful information. J. Satterly and
G.K. Peck provided information initially for my *A Birdfinding
Guide to the Toronto Region*, used again here. All the information
supplied has been modified to harmonize with the rest of the
text, and responsibility for any errors or omissions is mine alone.

Finally, this book is again a joint effort in all but name. My
wife, Joy, has been an active participant in the book's preparation at every stage, from recording distances in the field to
proofreading the final effort. It would not have been written
without her support and contributions.

Works of this kind date quickly, and there are bound to be
mistakes. We urge and welcome suggestions for corrections,
and additions for a future revision.

CEG
Cobourg, December 1994

A Bird-Finding Guide to Ontario

MAP 1   Southern Ontario showing provincial counties, districts, regional and district municipalities.

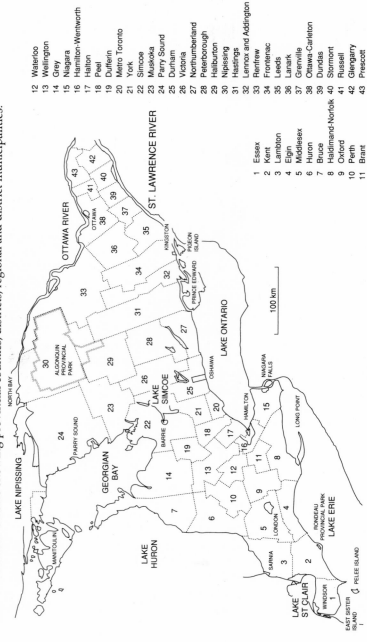

1	Essex
2	Kent
3	Lambton
4	Elgin
5	Middlesex
6	Huron
7	Bruce
8	Haldimand-Norfolk
9	Oxford
10	Perth
11	Brant
12	Waterloo
13	Wellington
14	Grey
15	Niagara
16	Hamilton-Wentworth
17	Halton
18	Peel
19	Dufferin
20	Metro Toronto
21	York
22	Simcoe
23	Muskoka
24	Parry Sound
25	Durham
26	Victoria
27	Northumberland
28	Peterborough
29	Haliburton
30	Nipissing
31	Hastings
32	Lennox and Addington
33	Renfrew
34	Frontenac
35	Leeds
36	Lanark
37	Grenville
38	Ottawa-Carleton
39	Dundas
40	Stormont
41	Russell
42	Glengarry
43	Prescott

1 How to Use This Book

This chapter presents the plan of the book. There are four main sections. The first gives general information on Ontario birds and their status in the province, the next (chapters 3–18) contains the regional accounts and forms the major body of the text, and the last two chapters contain information for visitors and a systematic list of species.

If you are unfamiliar with the province, first read chapters 2 and 19. Chapter 2 starts with a general picture of the province as a whole, the habitats it contains, and the common breeding birds one can expect to encounter. There are notes for each season on weather conditions, the kinds of birding that can be most productive, and the commoner birds that will be seen as the season progresses. The objective of the chapter is to avoid constant repetition of habitat descriptions and lists of birds throughout the text, and it should give you a good overview of what to expect, and when and where. The systematic list also may have general comments about the patterns of occurrence of some of the major species groups, such as hawks or shorebirds. Chapter 19 has other information that should be useful to a naturalist new to the province.

If you are interested in a specific locality, first check the index; the location may be mentioned, in which case you can turn directly to the appropriate section of the text. All the best-known birding areas and larger centres can be found in this way. Otherwise, ascertain the general location of the commu-

nity in question. Northern Ontario is covered wholly in chapters 17 and 18, but for southern localities turn to the map of
southern Ontario showing the counties, and determine the ap-
proximate location of your destination. The table of contents
identifies the chapters covering the various counties (they're
also in the index). Each chapter covers one or more counties, in
a sequence that runs approximately west to east and south to
north.

At the beginning of each chapter is a map of the counties
covered, showing the main roads and localities mentioned in
the text. This should be adequate to enable you to select the
places closest to your chosen destination. This process is sim-
plified enormously if the reader has access to a reasonably up-
to-date provincial road map. The text maps are primarily to aid
in orientation, and should be used in conjunction with such a
map, rather than replacing it.

Each chapter begins with a summary of the subsections into
which it is divided. There follows a short general account of the
region, and then the discussion of the main birding areas. There
are a series of subheadings, with each section covering a specific location or route. More minor locations, such as isolated
sewage lagoons, are usually grouped together towards the end,
and the relevant chapters conclude with a brief summary of
areas within ready access of the main Trans-Canada and 400-
series highway routes. Communities are indicated by boldface
in the text, and discrete birding areas are shown in boldface
italic. Generally this format should enable users to find the section that interests them fairly readily. If you have difficulty,
select the nearest locality on the key map at the beginning of
the chapter, and look it up in the index.

If you are interested in a particular bird, start with the systematic list. This will give you a picture of the species' status,
and often will suggest locations where it can be found (note
that some of the larger species' groupings are preceded by general comments on the patterns of occurrence of the group as a
whole). Then check the index to see if there are further entries
for that species. Birds with a widespread distribution are simply listed in the introductory sections in chapter 2, but the more
local ones are often mentioned in the appropriate site descriptions. In general I have avoided pinpointing very specific sites

for breeding birds. Quite apart from any considerations of excessive disturbance, such sites tend to be evanescent: either the habitat changes subtly, or the birds die or move away. But if the habitat is suitable, there are often other birds in the general area, and a search will locate them.

Many of the finest Ontario locations are noteworthy mainly for their appeal during migration, when conditions change from day to day and year to year. Enumerating the rarities such sites have produced does little to guide the reader on what he or she may find on a given day. Yet it does add some spice to the heavy fare of directions and road numbers, and I have succumbed to mentioning more such occurrences than in the first edition.

The amount of detail given in the directions to birding spots varies. For provincial parks and Conservation Authority areas, which are usually well signposted on the access roads, few directions are provided. Areas of relatively minor interest also receive only brief mention, but for sewage lagoons and other places that can be hard to find, more detailed directions are provided, which should be adequate to locate them from the book alone.

If your time is limited, then the following suggestions may help you select a suitable area, and the Toronto section has suggestions for those whose available time precludes travel out of the city.

– In migration periods (which occupy much of the year) the shorelines of the lower Great Lakes (Erie and Ontario) are usually more productive than elsewhere. The major concentration points along these lakes are Point Pelee and Long Point on Lake Erie, and Presqu'ile and Prince Edward Point at the east end of Lake Ontario. Of these, Point Pelee, in spite of its crowds, continues to be the premier site, with Long Point as second choice.

– In the breeding season Rondeau and the Long Point area are probably the best locations to see southern nesting species, and Algonquin Park much the best for the mixed forest species. If time precludes visiting the latter, the woodlands of the Halton County Forest could be a good second choice.

– For hawks in the fall, Hawk Cliff and Holiday Beach are the best choices (although the entire length of the north shorelines can yield good hawk viewing). In spring, Beamer Point is the

only choice. The Niagara area is much the most productive location for gulls in later fall.
– Winter can be more variable. The west end of Lake Ontario is usually the best for waterfowl, and the Kingston and Ottawa areas the best for winter birds and owls concentrations, although these vary dramatically from year to year.

Some Thoughts on Birder Ethics

Around the time we were thinking about this second edition, Ontario experienced a flurry of serious trespassing problems from birders, and I was urged to include a section on this disturbing topic. The trouble is, most of the horror stories originate from a small but active group of slob birders – one was once apprehended walking from garden to garden in one of the more exclusive residential suburbs of Toronto, because he wanted to check along the otherwise inaccessible Lake Ontario shoreline there! The rest of us indulge in what a recent article describes as 'situational ethics.' Most birders have trespassed from time to time. We decide that it's okay in a given situation, perhaps because others do it, perhaps because we've always trespassed there and no-one seemed to object. And very often no one does object. Sometimes the person responsible would indeed 'Rather not know' (to quote the supervisor of a local sewage lagoon), or doesn't want to be bothered all the time by birders requesting access. But, of course, this doesn't remove the obligation to ask permission.

Bird-finding guides have a responsibility here, because they direct persons to these places. Unfortunately there's a limit to what a guide can do, beyond alerting readers to the problem. Such books serve the general birder – the slobs seem to find out where to go, guide or no guide. The approach used here is simply to try to avoid listing areas that are private property. In general, I have emphasized localities on public land. Sewage lagoons are an exception to this generalization: all lagoons are private property, even though owned by a public agency.

Unauthorized visits are more likely to be tolerated if the user is meticulous in other respects. If you insist on trespassing (or even where access is not a problem), don't block the gates, don't block the roads, don't break down the fences, don't damage the vegetation, close the gates and be as considerate and courteous as possible.

This consideration, of course, applies to the birds as well as to the local people. The problem with disturbance is one reason I have also avoided mentioning very specific nesting or roosting sites for such species as owls. The use of tapes is a perennial area of controversy: my own view is that limited, selective use is acceptable provided the context is carefully considered – how rare is the bird, is it subject to other tape disturbance, and so on? But this is a slippery slope!

The problem of disturbance is at its worst when an extreme rarity has the poor judgment to appear on private property, and the owners of the land have the poor judgment to tell someone about it. Local clubs have a role here that extends beyond the puritanical caveats that seem to be the main contribution of some at present. Clubs have arranged to have member birders present at such events to assist in crowd control and policing bad behaviour; others have arranged for regulated access to local 'hot-spots' in their areas. Such efforts have had considerable success, and I would urge others to follow suit.

The problem of trespassing is at its most ambiguous with sewage lagoons. In general these are at present posted against trespassing, although bird-watchers are often tolerated. The attitudes of the local ministry officials to this kind of use vary widely, from active encouragement to tossing birders out. But such attitudes are changing, mostly in the direction of greater tolerance. Be that as it may, this book tells where the lagoons are, not whether one can get into them or not. That must be assessed at the time of one's visit; seek the necessary permission if in doubt. Also be warned that hunting may be going on in these areas, legally or illegally. The ministry postings are made partly because of this activity, but mainly because of concern for liability. Whether bird-watchers continue to be tolerated depends increasingly on how everyone behaves, so do be responsible in visiting lagoons.

2 Ontario and Its Bird Life

The province of Ontario has an area of 1,068,587 square kilometres (412,582 square miles), or over four times that of the United Kingdom and a third more than the state of Texas. It is not only huge in area but in extent: it is over 1,600 kilometres from west to east, and also from north to south. In practical terms it is even more formidable: if you cross into the province from the Quebec boundary in the extreme southeast and drive to Manitoba you will cover well over 2,000 kilometres; cross from the United States at Windsor in the southwest and the distance is almost the same.

A region so enormous has a diversity of life forms to match. In the extreme south is the deciduous forest, which extends south to the Carolinas. In the far north is a tundra coastline at Cape Henrietta Maria. On the western boundary plants and animals more typical of prairies can be found. At last count 459 species of birds have occurred in the province, and at least 285 have nested.

For the travelling birder Ontario thus offers great opportunity, and for those who would cover it well great challenge. The greater part of the far north is inaccessible except by air and knowledge of its bird life is still fragmentary, although fieldwork during the preparation of the *Atlas of Breeding Birds* expanded that knowledge enormously. Even much of the south, away from the larger population centres and a few well-covered hot-spots, is not known in detail by birders.

Many birding visitors to the province, however, confine their visits to its extreme south, along the shores of Lakes Erie and Ontario. Their interest is less in the province's diversity than in its unique position astride the Great Lakes, with the concentrations of migrant birds these huge bodies of water create along their northern shorelines. The lakes act as both barriers and way stations: barriers to the north-south movement of landbird migrants, and way stations for waterbirds moving between the interior of the continent and the coasts. For such birders the fact that Point Pelee, for example, lies in the Deciduous Forest Region is incidental. Their interest is in the birds passing through, not in those that will nest there; and indeed on cold days in early May, Point Pelee sometimes seems to have little to offer beyond noisy flocks of grackles inspecting picnic tables. A finding guide can aid with the locations of these hot-spots, but defining what the observer will find there is more challenging. It varies from day to day and week to week, and no two years are quite the same. The section on seasonal changes at the end of this chapter is particularly important for the person who would cover the migration periods.

MAJOR HABITAT TYPES

Forestlands

Before settlement, most of the province was forested, and five major forest areas have been identified. The Deciduous Forest Region (J.S. Rowe, *Forest Regions of Canada*, 1972) occupies the southernmost peninsula, east to Grand Bend on the Lake Huron shore, through the city of London to Toronto on Lake Ontario, and then east in a narrow belt along the lake to the Kingston area. Here maples, beech, oaks, and basswood are the predominant trees.

North of this zone of hardwoods are the mixed forests of the Great Lakes–St Lawrence Forest Region. This is the characteristic forest cover over much of settled Ontario. Its northern limits extend to New Liskeard on the east and to Kenora on the west. It occupies the shoreline of Lake Huron apart from the narrow strip of deciduous forest at its south end, and the Lake Superior shore north through Lake Superior Provincial Park, and again around Thunder Bay and the Sibley Peninsula. It is a forest that consists of stands of sugar maple, beech, and other hardwoods in company with white pine, balsam fir, and hemlock.

To the north, forest composition changes again. The hardwoods are gradually replaced by birch and aspen, and the white and red pines by spruce. These trees are characteristic of the Boreal Forest, which is discussed in chapter 17 on northern Ontario. It extends almost to the shores of James and Hudson Bay, and is the predominant forest type over the largest area of the province. Northwards the trees gradually yield to the vast expanses of bog characteristic of the Hudson Bay Lowland, until on the north coast around Cape Henrietta Maria, the forest is wholly replaced by open tundra.

The title of Forest Region can be misleading: these categories reflect more than the kinds of trees that constitute the natural forest of an area. Closely associated with the dominant trees is the entire range of herbaceous flora, and to a lesser extent the fauna as well. Hence the regions are important even when, as is true of the Deciduous Forest, little natural forest remains.

The major forested areas remaining in the south are associated with the Precambrian Shield, and to a much lesser extent with the Niagara Escarpment. The characteristic countryside of the Shield is a rugged and scenic mixture of forest, rock, and small lakes. This occupies most of the land north of Lake Huron and extends south from there in a huge wedge – the Frontenac Axis – to Port Severn at the southeast end of Georgian Bay, and from there east roughly to Gananoque and Brockville. It then turns north almost to Arnprior, and parallels the Ottawa Valley before joining the river near Chalk River. This enormous area is covered predominantly in mixed forestland. The later chapters (12 through 18) all include Shield areas, but some of the richest forests are those of the Algonquin Highlands, covered in chapter 16.

The Niagara Escarpment is a limestone escarpment that runs in a huge arc, first following the north shore of Manitoulin Island and the east shoreline of the Bruce Peninsula. It continues close to the Georgian Bay shoreline almost to Collingwood and then runs south to Hamilton, after which it parallels the south shoreline of Lake Ontario to Niagara Falls. In places it becomes obscured, but associated with it are some of the largest and most continuous areas of woodland west of the Shield. In the southern sections deciduous forest predominates. Chapters 5, and 8 through 10 are those covering the major areas of the escarpment in the south.

Further tracts of woodland occur in the south on areas of infertile or poorly drained soil, often with extensive areas of reforestation, as described more fully below under farmland. Farming occurs in many places even in the north where suitable soils exist, and plants characteristic of one forest region can be found north or south of its limits where soils and topography combine to create the appropriate conditions. Many of the areas mentioned in this guide are of this kind: pockets of habitat different from their surroundings. Relatively few birds are uniformly distributed across a landscape of such diversity.

There follows a series of summaries of the more common species that are likely to be encountered by the birder in southern Ontario and the places they are most probably to be found in the breeding season. First, however, some cautions are in order. Distribution and habitat preferences differ from one species to another, and the habitat may even change geographically. For example, we have heard Connecticut Warblers singing and apparently inhabiting territory in four distinctly different types of habitat in different parts of the province. Furthermore, some species occur across several habitat types. Downy Woodpeckers and Black-capped Chickadees are more likely to be found in a woodlot than in a field, but shrubby fields often will yield both species. Finally, birds are much less selective about habitat during migration; to use another example, Yellow-rumped Warblers almost qualify as open country birds in fall, when they can be found masquerading as pipits on shorelines and feeding across weedy fields by the dozen.

Remember, then, in using the following listings of birds most likely to be encountered in various habitats, that they will not always be found there, and that they might be found elsewhere as well. In general these species will not be mentioned again except in the systematic lists.

Many birds occur in summer throughout the south's more accessible forestlands, in various stages of succession. These are:

Ruffed Grouse
American Woodcock
Eastern Screech-Owl
Great Horned Owl
Ruby-throated Hummingbird
Downy Woodpecker
Hairy Woodpecker
Northern Flicker
Pileated Woodpecker (local)
Eastern Wood-Pewee
Least Flycatcher
Great Crested Flycatcher
Blue Jay

Black-capped Chickadee
White-breasted Nuthatch
Veery (local)
Wood Thrush
American Robin
Red-eyed Vireo
American Redstart (local)
Ovenbird
Mourning Warbler (local)
Scarlet Tanager (local)
Rose-breasted Grosbeak
Chipping Sparrow

As a group, the diurnal woodland raptors are elusive and difficult to locate, and most are more conveniently looked for outside the nesting season. Most of the commoner species listed below under farmlands can also be found in the forested areas as well, occupying the edge habitats if not the woodland itself.

Farmlands

Discussion about the natural forest cover in the agricultural south of Ontario is academic. Even those areas that are forested have been manipulated extensively by man. In the southwest only isolated groves and woodlots remain in some parts, but elsewhere the south is a patchwork of fields and woodlands. Farther north, large areas of agricultural land occur around Sudbury, on Manitoulin Island, and north and east of Sault Ste Marie, and farther north again, in the clay belts around New Liskeard and Cochrane, near Thunder Bay, and in the extreme west around Rainy River. Rainy River is discussed separately in chapter 18.

The following breeding birds are commonly associated with farmlands and edge habitats, including the brush and scrub areas of field corners:

Red-tailed Hawk
American Kestrel
Killdeer

Rock Dove
Mourning Dove
Common Nighthawk

Chimney Swift (mainly urban)
Northern Flicker
Eastern Phoebe
Eastern Kingbird
Horned Lark
Tree Swallow
Bank Swallow
Cliff Swallow (local)
Barn Swallow
American Crow
American Robin
Gray Catbird
Cedar Waxwing
European Starling

Warbling Vireo
Yellow Warbler
Indigo Bunting
Chipping Sparrow
Savannah Sparrow
Song Sparrow
Bobolink
Red-winged Blackbird
Eastern Meadowlark
Common Grackle
Brown-headed Cowbird
Northern Oriole
American Goldfinch
House Sparrow

Several of these species, notably Mourning Dove, Chimney Swift, Eastern Phoebe, Bank Swallow, Gray Catbird, Warbling Vireo, Indigo Bunting, and Bobolink, become considerably more local northwards, and are increasingly hard to find there. References in the appropriate parts of the text to farmland species with more southern affinities usually imply that some of these species can be expected.

The text includes numerous references to poor or marginal farmland, or old fields and the like. Broadly, there are three kinds of environment that create such conditions. In the north, where the growing season is short and the returns from agriculture low, there is much pastureland that is reverting to or at least partly occupied by willow and alder scrub. Drainage is often poor, resulting frequently in areas occupied by sedges and, sometimes, open water. Farther south such conditions more typically reflect poor soils. They occur among the agricultural pockets on the Precambrian Shield, but more commonly on the thin soils of some of the limestone and moraine areas.

Limestones are most typical of Manitoulin Island and the Bruce Peninsula, the Carden plain east of Orillia, the Flamborough plain east of Cambridge (see Valens), much of Prince Edward County, and other parts of eastern Ontario. Typically the limestone bedrock is close to the surface and the rocky pastures contain shrub roses, hawthorns, and white cedars. Rail and stump fences are common and, again, extensive poorly drained areas may have heavy sedge growth.

The hilly, rolling country associated with glaciation occupies huge areas of the south, west of the Precambrian Shield. Soils are often pebbly with many large boulders, the hilltops are dry, and the hollows have small ponds and marshy areas. The landscape is not ideal for farming, and again there is dry pasture with scattered scrub, patches of marsh, and ponds, albeit in a very different landscape. The areas described under the Oak Ridges Moraine and around Peterborough are typical.

Reforestation is common in such country, usually with red pine, in extensive uniform stands. Often these stands seem avian deserts, but as they age a number of coniferous forest birds can appear, often far south of their usual ranges. These include:

Red-breasted Nuthatch
Golden-crowned Kinglet
Solitary Vireo
Magnolia Warbler
Yellow-rumped Warbler

Blackburnian Warbler
Black-throated Green
   Warbler
Dark-eyed Junco

In addition to coniferous forest species in the plantations and the typical farmland birds elsewhere, a group of rather local species can be found in these habitats. The most common are:

American Bittern
Northern Harrier
Upland Sandpiper
Common Snipe
Black-billed Cuckoo
Yellow-billed Cuckoo

Sedge Wren
Eastern Bluebird
Rufous-sided Towhee
Field Sparrow
Grasshopper Sparrow

To the north in the clay belts, with the exception of American bittern, Northern Harrier, and Common snipe, these species appear to be rare or wholly absent.

Wetlands

Ontario probably has more shoreline than any comparable area in the world. The Great Lakes shores alone amount to over 3,800 kilometres, and the seacoast along Hudson Bay and James Bay represents another 1,094 kilometres. The patchwork quilt of smaller lakes and connecting streams across the north and the Shield in the south is best appreciated from the air:

small wonder canoeing is a major recreational activity in the province!

The character of the Great Lakes shores varies: it is sandy, gravelly, or rocky depending on location. The beaches attract Spotted Sandpipers in summer, small flocks of shorebirds in migration, and patrolling gulls year-round where open water occurs. But the absence of significant tidal movement means that in most places large shoreline feeding concentrations of birds do not occur. Marshes, the mudflats associated with rivers, and areas of algal deposition are the places where birds gather. The last two develop frequently in autumn, when water levels drop and the green algae which have built up in the lakes over the summer are deposited in pungent masses.

The Great Lakes themselves are particularly noteworthy for wintering and migrant waterfowl, but the many offshore islands are nesting sites for herons, duck, gulls, and terns that feed along the shore and in the waterfront marshes. The colonies of these species completely cover many of the smaller islands, most of which are designated nature reserves or wildlife sanctuaries. Several of these islands are well known and most are regularly visited by Canadian Wildlife Service biologists or by teams from local nature clubs to band birds and assess the status of their populations. These places are not usually listed in this guide because the breeding colonies are vulnerable to disturbance and should be left undisturbed if possible. In any case, access tends to be difficult and all of the species can be readily seen along the shores.

Species nesting on the islands include:

Double-crested Cormorant	Ring-billed Gull
Black-crowned Night-Heron	Herring Gull
(local)	Caspian Tern (south only)
Red-breasted Merganser	Common Tern

The marshlands associated with the mouths of rivers along the Great Lakes, as in the marshes east of Toronto and at Kingston, and lakes and other waterbodies mainly south of the Shield, have a rich array of breeding species. In these wetlands extensive stands of cattail and open, shallow water areas are characteristic, although brushy areas with alder and willow and wet sedgy fields often occur. The most extensive marshlands include those on Lake St Clair and Walpole Island, at Rondeau, Long Point, Dundas Marsh, and Presqu'ile on the lower Great Lakes, and Luther, Tiny and Wye marshes farther north. Typical species that can be found there in summer are:

Pied-billed Grebe	Sora
Great Blue Heron	Common Moorhen
American Bittern	American Coot (local)
Black-crowned Night-Heron (local)	Spotted Sandpiper
	Black Tern (local)
Canada Goose	Belted Kingfisher
Mallard	Marsh Wren
Blue-winged Teal	Common Yellowthroat
Northern Harrier	Swamp Sparrow
Virginia Rail	Red-winged Blackbird

Swampy woodlands are often associated with the larger marshes, and there are some huge swamps in the south, such as Greenock Swamp and Minesing Bog. In addition to the landbirds these support, the following birds occur most commonly in wooded or partly wooded habitats:

Green Heron	American Woodcock
Wood Duck	Tree Swallow
Hooded Merganser	

The development of flood-control reservoirs and sewage lagoons has added important waterbird habitat. The lagoons in particular have become significant out of all proportion to their size; the fertile waters of these places can yield at different times marsh or mudflats for shorebirds, or open water for duck, or nothing at all, depending on their management. At Long Point, for example, it is possible to find the Port Rowan lagoons full of waterfowl when the huge marshes seem dead.

Lagoon management does vary, and these places can change in their productivity not only over the course of the year, but also over longer periods. Some have been consistently outstanding, but others have either lost their appeal or become more attractive to birds over the course of years. Most lagoons present wide expanses of open water, but often the edges have a growth of cattails, and sometimes one or more cells is heavily overgrown with marsh vegetation. In periods of draw-down, large areas of mud may be exposed. All the waterbirds listed above can occur, and in particular prairie species such as Ruddy Ducks and Wilson's Phalaropes are often associated with them. Other shorebirds can often be found along the shorelines even when no exposed mud exists.

Most of the species of ducks that occur in the province in migration must be added to the list of birds that can be found in marshes during the breeding season, even though there may be no evidence that they nest there commonly, or at all. Large numbers of waterfowl move through the region to breed farther west or north, and it is not unusual to find a few of these birds lingering in favoured localities such as sewage lagoons, and often nesting in small numbers. The more usual species are:

Green-winged Teal	Canvasback
American Black Duck	Redhead
Northern Pintail	Lesser Scaup
Northern Shoveler	Bufflehead
American Wigeon	Ruddy Duck

The lakes of the Shield and of northern Ontario tend to be unproductive of waterbird habitat. They are relatively infertile and have steep, rocky shorelines. More productive wetlands in these areas – and indeed in any of the forested country – often occurs in conjunction with beaver dams, where extensive flooding leads to the development of wet meadows and bogs. Breeding birds typical of this range of habitats include:

Common Loon	Osprey
American Bittern	Common Snipe
Great Blue Heron	Belted Kingfisher
American Black Duck	Olive-sided Flycatcher
Ring-necked Duck	Alder Flycatcher
Common Goldeneye	Tree Swallow
Hooded Merganser	Common Yellowthroat
Common Merganser	

Urban Habitats

Urban areas resemble a patchwork of open country and edge habitats, sometimes with more extensive wooded areas in parks and river valleys. Rock Dove, European Starling, and House Sparrow are the familiar city birds, but American Kestrels are regular, and in the more natural areas most of the common species listed under farmlands and forestlands can be found.

REGIONAL VARIATIONS

The Deciduous Forest Region

This part of Ontario includes some of the best-known birding localities in the province and most of the larger centres of population. Apart from the narrow strip along Lake Ontario east from Hamilton, it is usually referred to as the southwest, and is covered in chapters 3, 4, and 6 through 10. The entire region has relatively little natural forest left, although apart from the counties of Essex, Kent, and Lambton (chapters 3 and 4) farm woodlots and wooded river valleys are widespread. The natural forest cover, where it remains, is rich and diverse, with oaks and hickories joining the maples and beeches of the forests farther north, together with a scattering of more southern trees and shrubs, such as tulip-tree and sassafras, at their northern limits. Some of the best areas are at Rondeau and north of Long Point.

The three westernmost counties are heavily agricultural and there are flat plains with prairie vegetation in some sections that may never have been forested. The land along the Lake Erie shoreline continues generally flat, although more rolling country develops to the north, and between the Hamilton area and Niagara Falls the steep north-facing ridge of the Niagara Escarpment follows roughly the southern shoreline of Lake Ontario, with a narrow zone of orchard land between it and the lake. Some of Canada's richest farmland occurs in the region, although on the sandy soils of western Haldimand-Norfolk (chapter 7) extensive reforestation with pine occurs.

Southwestern Ontario's geographic position, both as the peninsular tip of the province and Canada's southernmost point, makes it one of the pre-eminent birding areas on the continent. The promontories along Lake Erie concentrate migrants moving to and from the north and east, and the relatively balmy winters allow species to survive that would succumb to the cold and ice elsewhere in the province. Springs arrive earlier and autumns last longer; here the average arrival dates for species can mislead, as there appears to be little difference in the long-term averages between areas across the south. But in a given year migrants at Pelee in early spring, for example, can be two or more weeks ahead of arrivals at Presqu'île at the eastern end of Lake Ontario.

The southwest is also of particular interest because it is the stronghold of southern species that occur only rarely elsewhere, and several species occur more commonly in this region in summer than in other parts of Ontario, although most are still rare and local. They are (asterisks indicate species present year-round):

Great Egret
Northern Bobwhite*
King Rail
Forster's Tern
Barn Owl*
Red-bellied Woodpecker*
Acadian Flycatcher
Tufted Titmouse*
Carolina Wren*

Blue-gray Gnatcatcher
Northern Mockingbird*
White-eyed Vireo
Prothonotary Warbler
Louisiana Waterthrush
Hooded Warbler
Yellow-breasted Chat
Orchard Oriole

Many more northern species are either very local or wholly absent from the southwest. Here and there are pockets of more northern vegetation, and along the northern edge of the region mixed forest communities begin to appear. It is in such places that the most widespread of these species, listed below, can sometimes be found. References in the chapters covering this region to wooded areas having northern affinities or species imply that some of these birds can be expected. Many are species that favour conifers, and appear wherever extensive stands of these trees, whether native or planted, occur. They are:

Yellow-bellied Sapsucker
Alder Flycatcher
Red-breasted Nuthatch
Brown Creeper
Winter Wren
Golden-crowned Kinglet
Nashville Warbler

Magnolia Warbler
Yellow-rumped Warbler
Black-throated Green Warbler
Blackburnian Warbler
Black-and-white Warbler
Northern Waterthrush
Canada Warbler

White-throated Sparrow   Pine Siskin (erratic)
Purple Finch

North and east from Hamilton, along Lake Ontario, the Deciduous Forest character becomes less pronounced, and intru-
sions of mixed forest more common. Typical southern species
become very rare or absent, and the bird life often more closely
resembles that of areas to the north.

The Lake Ontario sections of the region, however, are more
than thin echoes of areas farther west; they have a character of
their own. The Lake Ontario waterfront between Toronto and
Hamilton attracts large numbers of wintering waterfowl, and
the abandoned farmland around the urban areas attracts hawks
and owls in winter, while in the east the Kingston area attracts
even more noteworthy winter concentrations of raptors. The
Lake Ontario shoreline is also a rich area for birding in migration times. The Shield areas at the northeastern limits of the
Deciduous Forest region in the Rideau Lakes area are rugged
and heavily forested with oaks and hickories, and have a particularly rich breeding avifauna, while old field habitats also
abound in the flat limestone plains in the east, including much
of Prince Edward County (chapter 13).

THE GREAT LAKES–ST LAWRENCE MIXED FOREST

Although this region of southern Ontario is classified as mixed
forest, agriculture continues as the major land use both west
and east of the Precambrian Shield. However, unlike the areas
in the southwest, there are some considerable stands of woodland even here, particularly along the Niagara Escarpment and
in the Bruce Peninsula. Typically the forests consist of sugar
maple and beech, with basswood, red oak, yellow birch, red
maple, and ash. Red and white pines are the principal conifers,
with eastern hemlock and, in wetter areas, white cedar. Heavy
coniferous cover occurs only in the more poorly drained or
more northern sites, where spruce and other boreal species
also appear. On the Shield, and particularly across the
Algonquin Highlands, the landscape is dominated by mixed
forest.

There are several areas where poor soils have led to farm

abandonment and extensive reforestation. North of Toronto and the Lake Ontario lowlands, the Oak Ridges Moraine runs east from the Escarpment, creating a scenic and rolling countryside. Elsewhere extensive limestone plains occur. On these areas of limestone and on the moraine prosperous agriculture is interspersed with abandoned farms, providing the old field habitats described under farmland.

The region lacks migrant traps of the quality of those along Lakes Erie and Ontario. The shorelines of Lake Huron and Georgian Bay have the potential to concentrate migrants and to some extent they have not been fully explored. Certainly Manitoulin Island, the Bruce Peninsula, and areas around Nottawasaga Bay can yield good numbers and variety of both landbird and waterbird migrants. Farther inland Lake Simcoe, several reservoirs and three major wetlands – Luther, Wye, and Tiny marshes – are also excellent for viewing waterfowl passage.

In the areas west of the Shield the more southern species enumerated in the last section can sometimes be found as scattered individuals. The bush and woodlands of the escarpment and along the edges of the Shield itself provide strongholds for the following species, which are much less common or wholly absent northwards:

Turkey Vulture	Golden-winged Warbler
Yellow-throated Vireo	Cerulean Warbler
Blue-winged Warbler	

The main centres of abundance for several other more widely distributed species also lie south of the edge of the Shield, and they are at best thinly distributed north of it. These are:

Least Bittern	House Wren
Red-headed Woodpecker	Northern Cardinal
Willow Flycatcher	Rufous-sided Towhee
Purple Martin	Field Sparrow
Northern Rough-winged	Vesper Sparrow
Swallow	Grasshopper Sparrow

The easternmost parts of the region – the counties of far eastern Ontario – are also heavily agricultural, and the open flat plains south and east of Plantagenet attract hawks and other open-country species. There are extensive areas of poor and ill-drained pasture which are reflected in relatively high numbers of American Bitterns, Northern Harriers, Upland Sandpipers, and Common Snipe, and very high counts of Bobolinks and Red-winged Blackbirds.

The St Lawrence River forms the province's southern boundary between Kingston and the Quebec border, and it offers the birder a variety of waterfront habitats, ranging from marshes between Cornwall and Morrisburg to rocky islands in the Ivy Lea area. In autumn, low water levels on the river often produce extensive areas of mud shoreline, attractive to shorebirds.

The Frontenac Axis of the Shield separates the eastern counties from the rest of southern Ontario, and the heavy forest cover associated with it penetrates farther south here than elsewhere. The impact on the avifauna is dramatic; the boundary of the Shield with the agricultural lands to the east and west yields the richest assemblage of breeding birds in the province, with a wonderful blending of north and south, and an exciting variety of habitats. Some statistics tell the story; breeding bird surveys for Mount Julian in Peterborough County and Roblin in Lennox and Addington yield seventy to eighty species, while farther west good mixed habitat on the Streetsville and Palgrave routes have totals in the low sixties. Such surveys are essentially standardized samples over randomly selected routes, and as such are a good indication of the overall potential of an area.

This southern extension of the Shield is within relatively easy reach of the large population centres of the south, and much of it is cottage country, providing summer weekend retreats for these centres. Wooded it may be, but undisturbed it is not. There are areas of farmland along the Ottawa River, north of Sudbury, as well as in isolated pockets elsewhere.

The forests, particularly of the Algonquin Highlands between Highways 11 and 17, are diverse, and bird life is equally varied and rich. It is probably one of the best areas in Canada for breeding thrushes and warblers, and Algonquin Provincial Park (chapter 16) is the place to go not only to hear most of the thrushes and wood warblers on their nesting grounds, but also to become familiar with such species as Barred Owls, which can be rare and local farther south, and to see winter finches in season.

The following species – evidence of the strong northern component to the bird life – breed in the Shield forests but occur only occasionally, or in very limited areas, further south, although many also occur at the north end of the Bruce Peninsula (asterisks indicate species present year-round):

Merlin
Spruce Grouse*
Black-backed Woodpecker*
Olive-sided Flycatcher
Yellow-bellied Flycatcher
Gray Jay*
Common Raven*
Boreal Chickadee*
Ruby-crowned Kinglet
Swainson's Thrush
Hermit Thrush
Solitary Vireo
Philadelphia Vireo

Tennessee Warbler
Northern Parula
Cape May Warbler
Black-throated Blue Warbler
Bay-breasted Warbler
Wilson's Warbler
Lincoln's Sparrow
Dark-eyed Junco
Rusty Blackbird
White-winged Crossbill
  (erratic)
Evening Grosbeak

Some of these birds are relatively rare even in this region, particularly in the south. Four – the Evening Grosbeak and the Tennessee, Cape May, and Bay-breasted warblers – tend to increase enormously in numbers during periods when the larvae of the Spruce Budworm moth become exceptionally abundant. In times that are less favourable – for the species, not the forests – their ranges appear to contract northwards.

Many birds reach their northern limits across the southern Shield. They are sometimes much scarcer there than in areas farther south, but they are usually absent in the Boreal Forest Region. These species with southern affinities are:

Turkey Vulture
American Woodcock
Whip-poor-will
Chimney Swift
Ruby-throated Hummingbird
Eastern Wood-Pewee
Eastern Phoebe
Great Crested Flycatcher
White-breasted Nuthatch
Veery

Wood Thrush
Gray Catbird
Brown Thrasher
Warbling Vireo
Northern Parula
Pine Warbler
Scarlet Tanager
Indigo Bunting
Northern Oriole
Red Crossbill (erratic)

In winter eastern Ontario and the Shield have a more severe climate. Their proximity to large areas of coniferous forest result in winter birds such as Black-backed and Three-toed woodpeckers and finches appearing here sooner than in areas farther west, and in larger numbers. Owls in particular tend to be a feature of the winter scene.

On the Shield one encounters a problem which intensifies farther north. Good forest habitat abounds, and the selection of good birding locations is more a matter of watching for changes in the forest composition than of following directions in a book. At the same time, areas that are relatively commonplace in southern Ontario, such as marshes and open country, are often scarce and attract rarities. The abundance of water here is not paralleled by an abundance of waterbirds, as the Shield lakes are relatively infertile and in many places around Sudbury dead. There is little to attract either shorebirds or open-country species. Neither is it noted for migrant concentrations, but its forests, above all, are memorable.

SEASONAL CHANGES

The above picture of bird distribution is true for the breeding season, but is a very partial picture when the year as a whole is considered. In Ontario birds are on the move in every month of the year, and migration is heavy for some six months. Only for a brief period in June is bird distribution fairly static, when all the species enumerated above will be found occupied with the business of rearing families. But even then unmated and non-breeding birds can wander, often far from their established breeding grounds.

Winter

Winter is the time when birds are in the smallest numbers and it is a convenient departure point for a review of seasonal changes. There is much less variation in the onset of winter across the province than in its departure. Even in the south the first snow usually falls in late October, though it quickly vanishes. Not until late November or early December does the snow stay. By then freeze-up is well established in the north, where things will stay frozen for well over four months. Some areas never freeze, however, and in these patches of open water and sheltered land, duck and other species that normally move farther south can survive. (See chapter 17 for additional comments on the birds in northern Ontario in winter.)

In the south the characteristic pattern of alternating periods of colder and milder weather can result in substantial thaws and even in a total disappearance of snow on the ground for periods over the winter. The amount of snow is related less to temperature than to location; localities lying south and east of Georgian Bay, Lake Huron, and Lake Ontario (the 'snow belts') receive much more snow than do other areas, as the prevailing winds pick up moisture crossing the lakes.

Along the lower Great Lakes it is always rather a toss-up whether Christmas will be white or green, but by January snow and ice usually prevail. Daytime temperatures can drop well below -20°C but more often range between 0° and -10°C. Early March sees the return of warmer weather, but snow often lingers even here until late in the month, and early April blizzards are not infrequent, although rare enough to confuse road maintenance departments.

Bird distribution is far from static in winter. Even the species listed below as resident are often only questionably so. They are present year-round but also often migrate in numbers; who is to say that the starling at the feeder in December is the same one that nests in the garden in April? The following are resident year-round in the south:

Red-tailed Hawk	Pileated Woodpecker
Ruffed Grouse	Blue Jay
Rock Dove	Black-capped Chickadee
Eastern Screech-Owl	White-breasted Nuthatch
Great Horned Owl	European Starling
Downy Woodpecker	House Sparrow
Hairy Woodpecker	

The species that migrate annually to spend the winter in southern Ontario are relatively few. The common landbirds are Dark-eyed Junco and American Tree Sparrow. Several other species, however, appear almost every year in varying numbers; sometimes they are almost absent and in other years (often on a regular cycle) large invasions may occur. These erratic species are:

Rough-legged Hawk
Snowy Owl
Long-eared Owl
Short-eared Owl
Three-toed Woodpecker (rare)
Black-backed Woodpecker
Bohemian Waxwing (rare)
Northern Shrike

Snow Bunting
Pine Grosbeak
Purple Finch
White-winged Crossbill (rare)
Common Redpoll
Pine Siskin
Evening Grosbeak

In a similar class, but not really annual in occurrence and appearing only in small numbers, are Gyrfalcon, Northern Hawk-Owl, and Great Gray and Boreal Owls.

Waterbird numbers depend on the presence of open water, which varies greatly from year to year and during the winter itself. In severe winters even most of the Great Lakes freeze. Often the lakes are frozen too far out from shore to allow good viewing of the open water that remains. The west end of Lake Ontario usually remains open, however, and the typical winter waterfowl there are listed in the Toronto account.

The annual Christmas bird counts give a good picture of early winter bird numbers. In the north the number of species present on the censuses rarely exceeds thirty and is usually much smaller. Southern counts can exceed one hundred, although totals of twenty-five to thirty are more typical for inland localities. Even the largest counts include many species that are unlikely either to survive or to remain as the winter progresses, although in the south it is not unusual to find such species as crows present in substantial numbers throughout the season, gradually declining in abundance to the north and east. The following species (other than duck and gulls) are the principal ones that regularly linger over winter in varying numbers:

Great Blue Heron (rare)
American Kestrel
Mourning Dove
Belted Kingfisher
Red-headed Woodpecker (rare)

Northern Flicker
Horned Lark
American Crow
Red-breasted Nuthatch
Brown Creeper

Winter Wren
Golden-crowned Kinglet
Hermit Thrush
American Robin
Cedar Waxwing
Yellow-rumped Warbler
    (rare)
Rufous-sided Towhee
Field Sparrow

Song Sparrow
Swamp Sparrow
White-throated Sparrow
Red-winged Blackbird
Rusty Blackbird
Common Grackle
Brown-headed Cowbird
American Goldfinch

In addition, all three accipiters and Red-shouldered Hawk and Northern Harrier are usually present in small numbers, particularly in the south. Many other species can be found in favoured areas.

Winter birds tend to be concentrated in places where there is an abundance of food, and sheltered spots in mixed and evergreen woodlands are often the best natural areas in which to find birds at this time, especially if there is open water nearby. Man-made food sources are very important, and one should search newly manured fields (Horned Larks, meadowlarks, and Snow Buntings), feed-lots and corn cribs, especially in the southwest (blackbirds), dumps (crows and blackbirds in the south, ravens in the north), and, of course, feeding stations, which can yield almost anything. This is often the best time of year to see rarer resident species such as Red-bellied Woodpeckers and Tufted Titmice, which visit feeders more regularly in winter than at other times.

With regard to waterbirds, warm-water outfalls from power plants and the like can concentrate duck and gulls. The characteristic winter birds tend to be nomadic, even juncos and American Tree Sparrows moving freely, especially after storms.

Spring Migration

In the south, spring migration begins in February with the movement of small flocks of Horned Larks and Snow Buntings across the frozen fields, and of finches. Later in the month steady, high flights of crows scatter across the sky on mild days, and noisy flocks of immaculate Ring-billed Gulls appear along the lower Great Lakes, adding to the numbers of the rather scruffy wintering birds. In the north, the first movements can be a month or more later, and the entire migration is telescoped into a much shorter period, mainly from late April onwards. The chronology that follows is more applicable to southern Ontario, although even here there can be significant variations – sometimes a week to two weeks – in the overall status of migration between west and east. In general migration is earliest in the southwest and along the shores of Lake Erie, and is progressively later as one moves east and north.

March and early April bring heavy waterfowl movement, birds appearing in open leads as soon as the ice breaks up. Very heavy concentrations can occur at these points. There can be enormous gatherings of duck at this time (see Long Point, Lake St Clair, Presqu'ile). The weather in this period is stormy and unpredictable, and birds arrive in the pushes of warm air, often to move south again in prolonged wintry spells. Dramatic reverse migration can be watched along the lake shorelines at such times. Landbirds, especially blackbirds, move in numbers from late March on.

With April and May comes the major push of spring migration, slowly at first but with a flood of migrants in May, including virtually all the warblers. Much of the landbird movement is nocturnal, and on suitable nights the calls of migrants can be heard constantly overhead. Now the north catches up; there is not much more than a week's difference between the average May warbler arrival dates at Toronto and those along the north shore of Lake Superior. The movements are still closely associated with warm weather systems, and can be stalled completely in cooler periods.

Migrants are less selective than breeding birds in their choice of habitat. Nevertheless, it still makes sense to look for waterbirds in wet areas and forest birds in woodlots. Consider the weather: on cold, windy days sheltered sunny places closer to the ground are favoured. Look also for places that will concentrate migrants: the shoreline is one such place, and groves of trees, sheltered ravines, and pockets of vegetation along the shore are often more productive than similar areas inland. Concentrate on habitat edges, where woodlands and fields meet: a greater diversity of birds can be expected there. Large tracts of woodland or open country are often less productive than islands of habitat, where birds have less opportunity to disperse. In forested areas these islands are the open clearings. Along the shorelines, marshes and river mouths will yield dabbling duck, but also watch wet fields for these species and early shorebirds. Promontories into lakes are often especially productive, and Point Pelee, Long Point, Presqu'ile, and Prince Edward Point are among the finest migrant traps in North America.

The noteworthy widespread events in the spring migration include huge Canada Goose movements east of Oshawa and towards the west end of Lake Erie. These birds fly north, the main numbers in early April, when several thousand can be seen in a day in the Port Hope–Kingston areas. In late May, usually around May 24, there is a heavy Whimbrel movement along Lakes Erie and Ontario. About the same time Dunlin move in large flocks, with smaller numbers of Black-bellied Plover, Ruddy Turnstone, Red Knot, and Sanderling. Brant flights occur in late May and early June, and seem most regular in the Kingston area and north to Ottawa, although smaller numbers occur west to Toronto.

It is no accident that the shorelines of the lower Great Lakes – Erie and Ontario – are prominent in the above account. Point Pelee, Rondeau, and Long Point concentrate the migrants, but the entire shoreline from Kingston to Niagara and thence to Amherstburg can yield excellent birding. In spring other waterbirds that can be expected include loons (mainly Common, but some Red-throated), grebes (mainly Horned and Red-necked, but look for the rare Eared and the very rare Western), Double-crested Cormorants, Tundra Swans, all of the pond duck, and Redheads, Canvasback, Lesser Scaup, White-winged Scoter, and Red-breasted Merganser among the diving duck, in addition to the wintering species. Vagrant herons turn up, and shorebirds can often be found on wet fields back from the shoreline as well as along the shores themselves. Bonaparte's Gulls feature largely in heavy gull movements.

The section on Beamer Point deals with spring hawk flights. Farther north, see Manitoulin Island for movements of Oldsquaw, White-winged Scoter, and Whimbrel there.

By early June only a few landbirds are still moving in numbers. Blackpoll and Mourning are the last warblers to arrive with nighthawks, cuckoos, later flycatchers, and shorebirds. Usually by mid-June breeding populations are established and nesting is in full swing. Throughout the month, however, birds continue to move. Shorebirds in particular can be found roaming in the last two weeks – presumably either non-breeding birds or birds that have lost their nests or broods and started to move south immediately afterwards.

Ontario springs have very variable weather: on May 24 I have worn a parka in Toronto, but more often have felt too warm in shorts. The weather is changeable, so one can end up using both. Generally early May is quite cool everywhere, but by late May a light jacket often suffices even farther north.

The Nesting Season

The nesting season starts in February and March with owls and Gray Jays, and is well under way in April and May for resident and early migrant species. Even along the Hudson Bay coastline nesting activities are progressing well by the end of June. A few species, notably the crossbills, seem to breed when conditions suit them. Rock Doves can be found in breeding condition throughout the year, and Mourning Doves have been found nesting from at least March to October. In general, however, broods are out in early July and there is not much activity after mid-August.

Summer weather can be very warm – temperatures in the 30°C range are regular in southern Ontario – but less so in the north where there is usually overnight cooling (which you cannot depend on farther south!).

Fall Migration

If one defines summer as June, July, and August, then at least half this period is occupied by fall migration. The start of the fall shorebird migration usually seems to be under way by the beginning of July. Then such species as Lesser Yellowlegs and Least Sandpiper begin to appear in small numbers away from the breeding grounds. Momentum builds up during the month, with large swallow flights developing as well. Once again, the importance of the Great Lakes' shorelines emerges, particularly of the lower lakes. The swallow movements are most notable at

Long Point, at Point Pelee, in the Niagara area, and at the east end of Lake Ontario. Early fall is also a good time for southern herons to wander north, and they often end up in lakeshore marshes.

By August the main shorebird passage is under way, and flycatchers, thrushes, and warblers are also in good numbers by month end. August is still very warm, the vegetation is lush, and the birds are very quiet, so it does not seem like a big migration month, but in fact some of the heaviest movement of the year occurs then.

September is fall's answer to May; almost anything can turn up, and major hawk flights with the onset of brisk, cooler weather make mid-September a delight. Hawk flights develop along the north shorelines of the lower Great Lakes (see Holiday Beach, Hawk Cliff, and Prince Edward Point), but there are similar movements in the north around Marathon and north of Thunder Bay. Accipiters and falcons usually move singly and fairly low – often directly over the tree-tops – while buteos, Northern Harriers, and Turkey Vultures soar, often in high spiralling groups. The most spectacular movement is that of Broad-winged Hawks, which migrate in huge milling flocks, sometimes with a hundred or more birds in each. Blue Jays and Monarch Butterflies are other features of the lower Great Lakes at this time: the jays in long straggling flocks and the butterflies like huge dark snowflakes, all following the shore.

In September and October the west end of Lake Ontario and the south end of Lake Huron are noted for some pelagic species not normally expected away from the ocean. Jaegers (mainly Parasitic Jaeger, but with Pomarine Jaeger later), Sabine's Gull, Black-legged Kittiwake, and phalaropes are the species usually seen. They are sometimes visible from shore (see Sarnia, Kettle Point, and Hamilton) as well as on offshore boat trips that are sometimes arranged by local birders at Hamilton, Toronto, and Kingston.

By October the landbird passage is past its peak and the waterfowl hunting season has begun (usually about September 25). Away from favoured lakefront localities the countryside can seem very quiet and birds few. Yet this can be one of the most exciting months of the year, and in the south the autumn leaf colours reach their brilliant peak.

Late September and October can yield huge chickadee movements. Sparrows are still widespread, and less common species to be looked for include Sharp-tailed Sparrow in dense, short marsh vegetation – beggar's ticks beds are good – mostly in early October. Other species that are still moving in open country at this time include Horned Larks, American Pipits, Yellow-rumped Warbler and Palm Warblers, American Goldfinches, and small numbers of Lapland Longspurs. Hawks continue to move, principally Red-tailed and Rough-legged Hawks, and this is the best time to see Golden Eagles.

It is also the best time to see scoters, and waterfowl passage is heavy. Most of the duck listed for spring reappear, building up in large wintering flocks in November. Canada Geese move south over the same routes they used going north, but their movement is more prolonged so it tends to be less spectacular than in the spring. From the Bruce Peninsula south through London and Sarnia small flocks of Snow Geese may also be expected. Dunlins are the feature of the shorebird movements, but rarities such as godwits and phalaropes can often be found.

All movements described for October can continue into November, but the month's real interest comes in the flights – always unpredictable – of winter species such as Northern Shrikes and winter finches. Purple Sandpiper, Red Phalarope, and King Eider are other rarer species possible in later October and November. More predictable November migrants are American Tree Sparrows and Snow Buntings, and diving duck build up in huge numbers in areas where hunting does not disturb them (see Toronto, Prince Edward Point). The largest single concentration of waterbirds in this period is along the Niagara River. The gull flocks here can be one of the most outstanding birding spectacles in the province at any season. By early December elsewhere, apart from final hawk and waterbird movements, migration is over.

Autumn, like spring, has changeable weather. In September temperature ranges are similar to those in May, but by October and November it is usually cool, and often cold, raw, and windy. In autumn, cold triggers migration, warm weather stalls it. (This is easy to forget in October and November, when the most pleasant weather is often the product of warm fronts.) The northern shorelines of the Great Lakes are obstacles to southward movement: in prolonged periods of poor weather landbirds moving slowly south tend to concentrate in suitable habitats near the lake. The birder who waits for the sun will often be too late! By contrast, diurnal migrants move in good weather. For hawks, watch for cool, sunny days with moderate winds from the north and northwest.

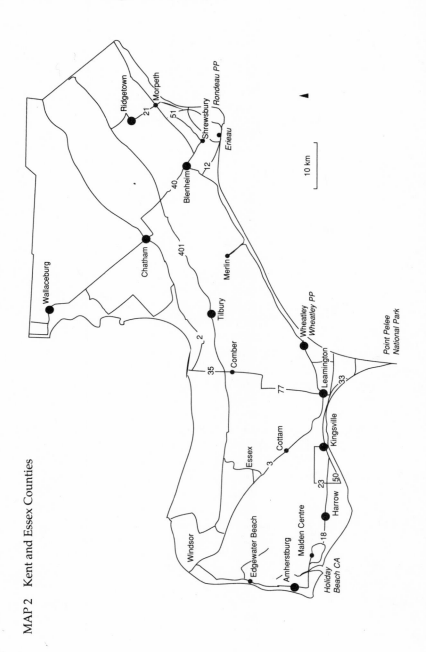

MAP 2   Kent and Essex Counties

3 Point Pelee and Area

Essex and Kent Counties

Point Pelee
Pelee Island
Rondeau and Erieau
East from Windsor
Holiday Beach
Around Kingsville
Stoney Point and the St Clair National Wildlife Area
Additional sewage lagoons in the Pelee area
Areas along Highway 401

For a birder a first drive through the flat arable farmland bordering Highway 401 in Essex and Kent counties seems to hold little birding promise. The sweeping vistas are little interrupted by woodlands or natural habitat, and the Carolinian forests that once must have covered much of this land seem hardly a memory. Yet these two counties offer some of Canada's most exciting birding. They are the stronghold of southern species that occur only rarely farther north, and their location as a peninsular tip to the rest of the province channels migrants and creates concentrations of species and rarities that have become internationally famous. In winter the area escapes the heavy snows that blanket much of the rest of the province, and huge flocks of crows roam the bare fields, while Horned Larks and Snow Buntings pick gravel along the roadsides. Springs are early – mid-March sees a major influx of migrants – and autumn drifts into winter sometime in early December. The summer heat, more oppressive than in areas farther east, but still moderate compared to conditions farther south, is made more bearable by the cooling breezes off Lake Erie.

The small (190,000+) city of **Windsor** on the river opposite Detroit is the main population centre. It is a major port of entry into Canada, and is served by a small airport and two road crossings into the United States. Highway 401, the main east-west controlled-access highway across the south of the province, starts here and provides ready access to all the areas described below.

Deservedly the best-known birding locality in Ontario, and probably in Canada, is Point Pelee. Its fame rests on the numbers of both birds and species that occur there during migration, and over the years more rarities have appeared there than in any other locality in the province.

Fifty kilometres east of Pelee lies the promontory of Rondeau which, while lacking the former's almost ideal blend of topography and location for concentrating landbird migrants, has a superb Carolinian forest and is a major migrant trap in itself. To the west, Holiday Beach Provincial Park near Amherstburg yields some of the continent's highest counts of migrating hawks in fall. In the north, along Lake St Clair, are extensive marshes which are particularly noteworthy for waterfowl concentrations in spring.

POINT PELEE

Point Pelee National Park, southeast of Leamington at the intersection of Highways 3 and 77, is a birding legend. In spring visitors from all over the world congregate on the point to view the restless tide of birds pouring north, to seek rare waifs from other parts of the continent, and to capture the excitement of watching migration actually in progress. On the second weekend in May it is usual for the loop road on the point to be closed by 8.00 a.m. because the large parking lot at the Interpretive Centre is full. Drive down in October, however, and at times you could be the only birder in the park.

While it is true that the peak spring warbler numbers occur usually around the second weekend in May, Pelee is a fascinating place in any season. In early May you can find the point cold, windswept, and almost empty of migrants. It is undoubtedly at its best when migration is at full flood, but there can be heavy movement from the first waterfowl in March through to the last stragglers in December. Late April to early May is the best time to observe southern rarities overshooting, and late May can be good both for shorebirds if suitable habitat exists – which usually means standing water on the onion fields – and for later landbird migrants such as cuckoos and Mourning and Connecticut Warblers (the park is one of the best places to see the latter). However, for general birding the earlier weeks of May are preferable because the trees are usually not yet in full leaf, and visibility is better. In July heavy swallow movement begins, which continues, with autumn shorebirds and the first warblers and flycatchers, into August. In September accipter passage is heavy, together with other hawks and landbirds. Hackberry fruits are attractive to many species in fall, and fruiting trees will often produce local concentrations of birds at that time. October and November yield waterfowl, including Tundra Swans.

The park is much less noteworthy for breeding birds than Rondeau, but many southerners have bred, including Chuck-wills-widow and, long ago, Bewick's Wren. It is one of the best places in Ontario to see Carolina Wren, Blue-gray Gnatcatcher, Yellow-breasted Chat, White-eyed Vireo, and Orchard Oriole in the breeding season.

In spring many of these species are easier to find, together with such species as Little Gull, Forster's Tern, Golden and Blue-winged Warblers, Northern Parula, Cerulean and Prairie Warblers, and Grasshopper Sparrow. The following birds are rarer but occur quite regularly in spring: Cattle Egret, Glossy Ibis, Red-bellied Woodpecker, Acadian Flycatcher, Northern Mockingbird, Prothonotary, Worm-eating, Kentucky, and Hooded Warblers, Louisiana Waterthrush, Summer Tanager, Blue Grosbeak and Dickcissel (both rare), Henslow's, LeConte's, and (rarely) Sharp-tailed Sparrows. Remember these are just the more likely species; at Pelee no rarity, no matter how improbable, should be dismissed. Rarities occur less frequently in autumn, but migrant numbers can be higher than in spring.

A feature of the migration in both seasons is the spectacle of birds leaving the tip. In spring this reverse migration occurs even in favourable weather, and large flocks of blackbirds and other species move rapidly south along the point, either to head off the tip, or to mill aimlessly above the bushes at the end. In autumn this movement is, of course, heavier and there is a greater sense of urgency as small passerines may try to fight their way out over the water into adverse winds. In winter there are often stragglers present, and rarities such as Mountain

Bluebird have turned up. At these times the red cedars in the old orchard areas and along the roads provide important shelter for landbirds, together with the low areas between the old beach ridges.

The park is a spit of land jutting out into Lake Erie south of Leamington, but the traditional Pelee birding area includes the entire area south of Highway 3 from Leamington, to Wheatley on the east (see Map 3). It includes the shoreline and Wheatley harbour, diked arable land, and the marshes along Hillman Creek as well as the point itself.

The park proper is roughly triangular in shape. Its narrow side joins the reclaimed farmland (the onion fields) to the north. Its east and west sides are long, gently curving sand and gravel beaches which finally meet in a slender sand spit. This tip – the southernmost part of Canada's mainland – alters from year to year, and the character of the entire park changes with the water level of the lake and under the impact of severe storms. In high-water years many areas can be flooded. A wooded dune ridge backs the West Beach, and the road runs down the east side of this ridge. The rest of the north end of the park is occupied by a large marsh, which narrows as the point itself narrows, and finally is replaced by deciduous woodlands. More open old field areas mark the sites of former farming and cottage developments. The road finally divides to form a loop which terminates at the Interpretive Centre. From here a free train service will take the visitor the remaining 2.3 km to the tip.

To reach Point Pelee take exit 48 from Highway 401 and proceed south on Highway 77 through **Leamington**, following the signs to the park. Before leaving town ensure you have adequate fuel: there are no service stations on the routes described below. Turn left (east) at the light at Seacliffe Drive (County Road 20), and bear diagonally right (southeast) on County Road 33. This passes a golf course and crosses a bridge over Sturgeon Creek, and then follows the shoreline to the park gates.

Obtain a park map and a bird checklist at the gate (note the scale of entry fees includes a four-day pass, currently $10, that is often the best for a short visit) and on arriving at the Interpretive Centre check with the staff for directions to any unusual birds.

Noteworthy areas within the park include the tip for the huge flocks of Red-breasted Mergansers in spring and autumn. Since the invasion of zebra mussels into the Great Lakes, these flocks have been augmented by large numbers of scaup and other mollusc-feeding diving duck. Other features of the tip are gulls and shorebirds on the sand spit itself, migrant landbirds in the bushes at the end, and views of birds flying off the point. (Birders should refrain from walking out far beyond the last line of bushes, as birds on the tip often do not return once they have been alarmed.) This area is usually best at dawn.

The road between the tip and the centre, the Post Woods nature trail that runs south from the centre, and the trail through Tilden's Woods northeast of the centre are all excellent for migrant landbirds (Tilden's is the best place for spring Prothonotary Warblers and Louisiana Waterthrushes). The Laurier trail near the start of the road loop has an excellent habitat mix with old field species such as chats, buttonbush thickets that can yield warblers, and swampy areas with rails, Green Herons, and Wood Ducks. The marsh boardwalk can be good for marsh birds generally. Old field areas near the tip can yield the elusive field sparrows such as LeConte's, Henslow's, Grasshopper, and Sharp-tailed Sparrow in season. Woodcock and Whip-poor-will are regular in the woods north of the group campground in spring. There really are no 'best' places for watching birds in the park – it is all superb. In addition to the regular trail network, the park staff mark out a series of seasonal birding trails for use in spring and fall. These can be as productive as the main trails themselves, and are an attempt by the park to provide birders with access to good areas which would otherwise be beyond reach. It is important for users to respect the trail system and not plough off into the vegetation after birds – a practice that formerly was rapidly destroying the ground cover.

The onion fields and Hillman (formerly Stein's) Marsh form important parts of the Pelee area, providing habitat for open field, marsh, and shorebirds less available within the park itself. Essex County Road 20 (which you will recall you turned off en route to the park to follow County Road 33) runs east to join the east beach of the point, winding along the south side of Hillman Marsh for its last 2 km or so. South of this road lies a grid of roads criss-crossing the low-lying fields, most of them bounded by deep drainage ditches, while the roads themselves follow the tops of the dike system. All these roads are worth covering, as the fields attract shorebirds, gulls, and open-country species. The ditches often yield heron and duck. Pools of standing water can be particularly productive.

One route is to turn east just outside the park gate on Mersea Township Road E. This road gives access to points overlooking the north side of the large Pelee marsh. The road ends in 3 km at Township Road 19. Turn north, and continue 2.1 km north to Township Road C. The ditches along this stretch can be particularly productive, as can the fields to the east, where gulls often gather in large numbers. Shorebirds can gather here, and in those rare periods when Buff-breasted Sandpipers are fairly regular in the province, this is the place to see them in early fall. Turn east on Township Road C, which goes past Marentette Beach (private) and then continues northwards along the beachline as the East Beach Road. Periodic views of the lake are possible, the trees along here can yield migrants, and the wires are particularly good for swallows.

Finally (some 2.4 km) the road curves west along the south shore of *Hillman Marsh*, now as County Road 20. Before turning left here first follow the dead-end cottage road which continues 0.5 km along the beach. The small parking area at the end yields good overlooks of the marsh. Then return to County Road 20 and follow the south shore of the marsh, stopping periodically where the road permits to view the wetland from the dikes. Continue 0.3 km past the junction with Township Road 19 and take the first right (County Road 37). Drive 1.5 km to the next intersection and turn right. Just before the bridge is the *Hillman Marsh Conservation Area* on the right, where there is an interpretive centre and access to a 4.5 km loop trail along the dikes and the south shore of the marsh. This is well worth while, and can yield waterfowl when the open waters of the marsh outside the dikes are empty.

Returning to the road, turn right to cross Hillman Creek and (0.3 km) turn right once more onto a road which now runs 2.5 km to the east shoreline. It follows the north side of Hillman Marsh and there are many points along it: the thickets and sedge areas around the boat ramps, and the marsh both west and east of the bridge crossing halfway down. Some 0.5 km from the bridge there is a path into the dike on the north side of the marsh. Other spots of interest include any wet areas behind the houses just past here to the south, and after passing Township Road 21, the woodlot to the south and the fields to the north, adjacent to the first house on the north of the road (now blue, but once painted purple, and hence still often referred to as the 'purple house'), and then the marshy areas on both sides of the road past here. Almost at the end is a small parking lot on the right. From here there are views of the shoreline and lake; depending on the lake levels and the state of erosion, it may be possible to walk south along the barrier beach. The rarities these areas have yielded over the years are legion. The woodlot and marsh by the purple house have been good for Prothonotary Warbler, the wet areas running to the marsh itself for King Rails, and one can usually be sure of all the more common marsh birds in season.

Just before the parking lot at the end a sideroad runs to the north through cottages. This road parallels the shore for some 3 km (it becomes Pulley Road) and turns left (Milo Road) to run along the south side of Wheatley harbour, where the gulls can be interesting. Access to the harbour here is via Kay Avenue about 0.5 along (just before the high wire fence). This ends at the harbour mouth in the tiny Getty's Beach. Milo Road itself ends at Township Road 4. Opposite is a small marsh, sometimes good for duck and Black-crowned Night-Herons. A right turn leads to the other side of the harbour or north to **Wheatley** itself (3 km), while a left turn ends up eventually in Leamington.

East 1.0 km of the main intersection in Wheatley is *Wheatley Provincial Park*, on the shore 2 km south of Highway 3. The hardwoods here are attractive, the lagoons along the shore and creek can yield waterbirds, and there may be duck and gulls on the lake. There is even a small but good sewage lagoon in the campground. (The whole place would probably rate much more highly as a birding spot if it were not so close to Pelee!) Township Road 4 is not a particularly interesting one for birds, as most of the best places are south of it. However, if one turns left on it (i.e., headed back to Leamington) the first 4 km can be worth while. It jogs left and then right, becoming County Road 3 in the process; a small creek crossing just west of the second jog may have waterbirds. Then it is usually better to take the first left to join County Road 37, which leads back to the roads around Hillman Marsh and the onion fields.

The route just described is merely one of many, and birders

without a car (or without the inclination to drive around dusty backroads) can spend days profitably without leaving the park itself. Going on about Pelee's quality is superfluous: suffice it to say that if you can visit only one place in Ontario, visit Pelee. For the tyro birder, however, one caution is in order. You may well leave more frustrated than when you arrived, and Pelee can seem a very lonely place! The sheer volume of birds on a good day can be bewildering and overwhelming.

There are several motels in Leamington, and private campgrounds there and off the road to the park itself (Sturgeon Woods Trailer Park), and at Wheatley Provincial Park. However, although accommodation in the area has increased in recent years, so has the demand, and it is still usually necessary to reserve months in advance for places in the peak periods. In busier times there is a small food concession in the national park, but otherwise the nearest restaurants are in Leamington, Wheatley, and along County Road 33. There are several good picnic areas in the park, and numerous washrooms (but none between the Interpretive Centre and tip terminal of the train).

PELEE ISLAND

Also south of Leamington, but this time over water, *Pelee Island* is located roughly 13.5 km south and east of the tip of Point Pelee (see map 3). In many ways the island shares many of the point's special features: it too has narrow promontories (at both ends!), concentrates migrants, and has Carolinian woodlands and an exceptional flora.

To reach it you must travel by ferry from either Leamington or **Kingsville**, a 22-km journey. There are usually about two sailings daily between mid-March and mid-December, and the current one-way rates are $10.50 for vehicle, $5.00 for passengers. Reservations are required both for the ferry and, once there, for accommodation on the island, which is very limited. Current ferry information can be obtained from Ontario Travel offices or by calling (519) 724-2115, which is also the number for reservations. These ferries arrive at Scudder. During the crossing watch the many gulls, terns, and other waterbirds en route, and as you come in look for Great Black-backed Gulls off Scudder Dock.

MAP 3 Point Pelee and Pelee Island

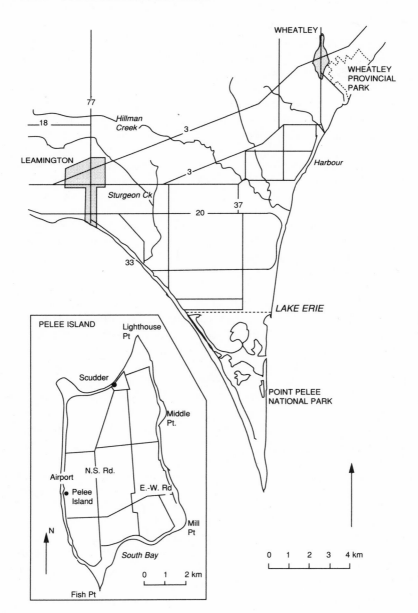

First head northeast from Scudder. After some 1.5 km *Light-house Provincial Nature Reserve* is passed to the north. A large colony of Double-crested Cormorants is the chief attraction here, in the dead trees standing in Lake Henry, and some Herring Gulls occasionally nest as well. Rafts of loons, grebes, and diving duck occasionally congregate offshore in Lake Erie. Lake Henry is a favoured foraging area for herons and Great Egrets.

Later in the season shorebirds and Caspian Terns congregate here, especially if there are mud flats, and Sharp-tailed Sparrows have been recorded along the south side of Lake Henry in September, when numerous raptors, especially accipiters, fly past the point. Upland areas of Lighthouse Point, particularly the fine oak-hickory, blue ash savannah, and shrub tangles, have Carolina Wren, Blue-gray Gnatcatcher, White-eyed Vireo, and Orchard Oriole in summer.

Continue southeast approximately 2.5 km from Lighthouse Point to *Browns Point*. This is a splendid privately owned bottomland woods with many oaks and hickories. Look for Carolinian species here.

The *airport*, a small grassed tract near the west centre of the island, is most easily reached via the North-South Road south from Scudder (some 4 km). Here Upland Sandpipers and Bobolinks (formerly Dickcissels) occur and Western Meadowlarks should be watched for. Farther south (about 7 km from Scudder) the *East-West Road*, a main road, which traverses the island from Vincent Barrie Park on the east to West Dock Town, passes through some excellent oak-hickory and red cedar savannah, deserving of more attention from birders. Whip-poor-wills and Chuck-will's-widow have occurred in summer, and in the scrub along the road a distinctive song type of Willow Flycatcher, sounding almost like an Acadian Flycatcher, occurs.

At the southeast end of this road, and of the island, are *Stone Road* and *Mill Point*, the latter directly accessible from South Bay on Lake Erie via Dick's Marina. This an extensive undisturbed tract of open savannah, with prairie elements, which usually has several pairs of Yellow-breasted Chats. Song and other sparrows, normally difficult to find on the island, occur here.

The southernmost extremity of the island, some 9 km from Scudder via the North-South Road, is *Fish Point Provincial*

Park Reserve including Fox Pond and Mosquito Bay. The swamp forests here are of outstanding maturity and were formerly the site of one of the largest heronries in Canada. Great and Cattle Egrets, Black-crowned and Yellow-crowned Night-Herons (the latter very rarely), King Rails, and Common Moorhens have all been recorded about the lagoon (Fox Pond). Great Horned Owls, Red-bellied Woodpeckers, Winter and Carolina Wrens, Blue-gray Gnatcatchers, and Prothonotary Warblers occur in the breeding season. Offshore and on the extreme southern spit, Double-crested Cormorants, Great Black-backed Gulls, and Caspian Terns occur regularly. Herring Gulls may breed here, and Piping Plovers formerly did so.

Wet meadows at the northwest base of Fish Point can have interesting shorebirds, and the low-lying fields farther north produce plovers and Northern Harriers. Waterfowl may mass off the point, and hawks and warblers funnel through it in migration. More upland areas have harboured Yellow-breasted Chats and Orchard Orioles during the breeding season.

Bald Eagles formerly nested at several sites on the island. Ring-necked Pheasants are probably more numerous than elsewhere in Ontario, but have greatly declined, and Yellow-billed Cuckoos seem more numerous than anywhere else in Canada. Barn Owls have been recorded and Eastern Screech-Owls are still fairly plentiful. Red-headed Woodpeckers, Carolina Wrens, and Eastern Bluebirds remain scattered but regular breeders, as do Orchard Orioles and Grasshopper Sparrows. Brewer's Blackbird has occurred. During migration the entire area provides marvellous birding and many rarities have been recorded.

Pelee Island is technically an archipelago which includes the provincial nature reserves of East Sister Island and Middle Islands however, these should not be visited during the breeding season without permission from the Ministry of Natural Resources.

RONDEAU AND ERIEAU

Some 50 km east of Leamington on Highway 3 is the town of **Blenheim**. To the south and east of the town lies another major promontory into the lake, this time Rondeau, a huge comma-shaped body of land enclosing an extensive yet shallow body of water known as Rondeau Bay. Along the north shore of the bay is the community of Shrewsbury, while at the southwest corner begins a narrow peninsula occupied by the fishing village of Erieau. A narrow channel joining Rondeau Bay with Lake Erie separates the eastern end of the Erieau peninsula and the southwestern tip of Rondeau. The combination of the extensive shoreline, rich southern hardwood forests, extensive marshes and swamps of Rondeau Provincial Park, together with waters of the bay and the lake, and the nearby Blenheim sewage lagoons makes this area one of the prime birding localities in Ontario.

The Blenheim *sewage lagoons* can be most productive. To enter them it is currently necessary to obtain permission in writing from the Town of Blenheim (the Clerk's Office, 35 Talbot Street West, Blenheim, N0P 1X0). The lagoons can be reached by driving west from the junction of Highways 40 and 3 in Blenheim, 2.9 km on Highway 3 to Harwich Concession 3 just outside town. Turn north and drive 1 km crossing the tracks, the lagoons are on the right. Depending on water levels they can be very productive, with Ruddy Duck and (occasionally) Wilson's Phalarope breeding, and a host of rarities recorded, including King Rail.

To reach the Erieau Road (County Road 12), return to Highway 3 and continue west for 1.4 km, and turn south. *Erieau Harbour* is approximately 12 km away at the end of the road. The black loamy fields as one approaches the village can yield migrant shorebirds. At 7.3 km, just outside the community, is a pond and marsh, *McGeachy Pond Conservation Area*, which is good for herons, duck, gulls, and, under the right conditions, shorebirds. Brewer's Blackbirds formerly bred nearby, and again a host of rarities have been recorded. There is a parking area 0.6 km beyond the start of the area and a viewing tower which gives good views of both the marsh and adjacent Lake Erie.

The pier area of Erieau (4.0 km from the pond) gives fine views of the lake and Rondeau Bay, as well as the western portion of the Rondeau Park beach. Bear right at the east end of the one-way road to reach the pier area. There are usually herons, duck, and gulls present. In early spring waterfowl concentrate on the waters of the bay. Occasionally a Bald Eagle may fly over, and shorebirds can be seen on the shoreline to the northeast or even on the pier itself. Autumn is one of the more productive times here, as Purple Sandpiper and Red Phalarope are sometimes seen on or near the pier or rocky breakwalls, and occasionally a Red-necked Grebe, King Eider, or Harlequin Duck may take refuge in the harbour from stormy weather. In autumn and winter, Snowy Owls are regularly seen on the gravel piles or on posts at the edge of the marsh. Rare gulls such as Laughing, Little and Lesser Black-backed show up regularly, and on one occasion a Black Skimmer blew in and stayed four days!

Rondeau Provincial Park is approximately 20 km southeast of Blenheim, east on Highway 3 and then south on Highway 51, which ends at the park gates. However, you can cut across country to Rondeau from the Erieau road, saving considerable time and distance, as follows. Heading north along County Road 12, approximately 3 km north of McGeachy Pond, turn right on the first gravel road heading east. Drive 3 km east to the road end at a T-intersection, and turn right on Concession 2 WCR. Follow this south some 2 km to the first street on the east, and turn left following the paved road. This road (Cathcart Street) follows the north side of **Shrewsbury**, and at a stop sign joins County Road 11. As a side trip, many of the roads on the right, running into Shrewsbury, will lead to or close to some of the small marsh remnants along the northwest shore of Rondeau Bay, and in some instances will provide access for viewing the bay itself. Some of these small marshy edges adjacent to wet, grassy fields are excellent locations to look for King Rail.

Returning to the main route, from the stop sign continue straight ahead on County Road 11 east for about 7.6 km to join Highway 51, and turn right (south) on the highway for 2.8 km to the park gate. Approximately 1 km before the park gate, the highway crosses the marshes at the north end of Rondeau Bay. These marshes can be productive of waterfowl and shorebirds in both spring and fall, and are another good location for rarities.

Another route to Rondeau is from the east, turning onto County Road 17 from Highway 3 at **Morpeth**. This county road goes straight to the lake, and then follows the shoreline closely before ending at Highway 51 just before the park. As you approach the lake south of Morpeth, there are cliffs along the shoreline from which it can be worthwhile scanning the water.

Large rafts of duck, especially scaup and mergansers, are often seen in spring and fall, as well as Oldsquaw, Common Golden-eye, and all three species of scoters. In September and October thousands of hawks, Blue Jays, and hummingbirds can also be seen, following the shoreline on their southbound migration.

As noted above, the peninsula occupied by Rondeau is shaped like a huge comma with the tail pointing north, and the park occupies some 3,254 hectares in all. On entering (entrance fee), obtain a map of the area, which shows the location of the trails.

On the bay side are extensive marshes which can be viewed from a walking trail leading across them (15 km return). It starts at the west side of the first picnic area you will come to, about 0.7 km south of the park entrance. The trail is partly wooded at first, before crossing the wide open sections of the marsh farther south. Landbirds are often visible from this first section, as are a few water and marsh birds. The latter increase in the open marsh areas farther along. The resident Bald Eagles are most often observed from this trail, and a host of rarities have been recorded; one spring a Sage Thrasher spent several days hopping about on the open path. In autumn, waterfowl hunting takes place on Monday, Wednesday, Friday, and Saturday, so it may be wise to avoid the marshes on these days.

The main area of the park is covered by probably the largest continuous stand of Carolinian forest in Canada. Tulip-tree, sassafras, spicebush, red mulberry, and black oak are some of the woody plant species present, with a host of herbaceous species as well. Unfortunately deer browsing is severe at present, and the only locations in which a good wildflower display can be seen is at one of the two deer enclosures, one just south of Bennett Avenue and other south of Gardiner Avenue. Watch for signs to these enclosures along each of these roads.

There are several woodland trails in the park, including Spicebush, Tulip-tree, Black Oak, and the South Point Trail. All of them can be excellent for observing the many spring and fall migrants. Southern species such as Red-bellied Woodpecker, Acadian Flycatcher, Carolina Wren, Cerulean Warbler, and Prothonotary Warbler all nest regularly.

Acadian Flycatchers are usually most abundant at the very end of May and in the first ten days of June. A few remain to nest, but because of the more open structure of the forest in the past decade, they are not as numerous as they once were. The north end of the South Point Trail and sections of Rondeau Road are the best locations for them, although they have been observed in a number of areas of the park where there are large, spreading trees, especially American beech.

Prothonotary Warblers are most often seen in or near the big sloughs at the south end of the South Point Trail, or along the Tuliptree Trail. Cerulean Warblers can be found most frequently amongst the tall oaks along the Harrison Trail just north of the group campground. Red-bellied Woodpeckers occur generally in the more mature sections of the forest, and Carolina Wrens are most frequent in open tangles of vegetation.

Less common southern nesting species include Tufted Tit-mouse, which occurs sporadically; White-eyed Vireo, sometimes found along scrubby forest edges and openings; Yellow-breasted Chat, found in dense raspberry tangles in the southern portions of the park; and Chuck-will's-widow. The last species made a minor invasion at Rondeau from about 1976 to 1986, when one or more were recorded throughout the breeding season from the Harrison Trail south of the Visitor Centre. In recent years, however, there have been only scattered records, and in some years they appeared to be absent.

Forest breeding birds regularly present at Rondeau but more typical of regions farther north include Pileated Woodpecker, Brown Creeper, Veery, Yellow-throated Vireo, and Mourning Warbler. Less common northerners found during the breeding season are Whip-poor-will, Winter Wren, Black-throated Green Warbler, Pine Warbler, and Canada Warbler.

Some of the beach areas have cottages and are quite disturbed, but movements of gulls, duck, and shorebirds can still be seen. One particularly good area is the south beach, reached by following the South Point Trail to the lake, and then heading west along the shore towards Erieau. After a short walk of about 0.5 km one arrives at the edge of the forest. From this point west to Erieau the beach becomes a narrow sand barrier separating the marsh and bay from Lake Erie. It is an excellent location to see many typical marsh species, shorebirds, gulls, and waterfowl. Spring waterfowl viewing can be especially spectacular, with ten thousand or more duck, geese, and swans present.

If time is limited, the most productive part of the park is the South Point Trail starting from the south end of Lakeshore Road, and then the side trip along the south beach. Virtually all of the regular species on the park checklist have been seen from this route, and most of the rarities have been seen from here – at least thirty species over the years. In migration the park can teem with birds, but they disperse widely in the tall woodlands. The widest part of the park is at the south end, so the birds are less concentrated than at Point Pelee. Still, a keen birder can discover virtually the same number of species at Rondeau, with the added appeal of a larger, very impressive forest and far fewer people.

There is a good interpretive program in season. Be sure to get a bird list from the Visitor Centre or Park Office, and ask the Visitor Centre staff for help in locating wanted species. The park campground has over 260 sites, and there are private campgrounds and bed and breakfast accommodations a short distance outside the park. The nearest motels are in Blenheim.

EAST FROM WINDSOR

If fall hawk watching is your objective, then head for Holiday Beach Conservation Area near the mouth of the Detroit River. There are two likely approaches to this location, from Windsor and Pelee respectively. Both have good birding en route. Highway 18 follows the river and the Lake Erie shoreline all the way from Windsor to Leamington, and provides an alternate (but slow) route to Pelee; Holiday Beach is on the way. However, the loop drive around Kingsville described below should satisfy anyone who simply wants a pleasant outing near Point Pelee.

From Windsor the route runs south along Ojibway Parkway (which becomes Highway 18), with views of the Detroit River along the Windsor waterfront. Waterfowl can be seen here in migration periods and over winter. At the southeast end of town is *Ojibway Park*, a city park that has produced interesting stragglers on occasion. This location is of more interest botanically, and the *Windsor Prairie Reserve* is just east of here along Matchette Road. This, believe it or not, is reputed to be the best remaining fragment of long-grass prairie in Canada.

Highway 18 then follows the Detroit River, and can be very

productive of waterbirds along its route. One noteworthy area is the mouth of the *Canard River* approximately 9 km north of Amherstburg. Here there are extensive marshes on both sides of the road and duck gather off the river mouth, especially large flocks of Canvasback in the fall. Depending on water levels, shorebirds can be numerous here in the autumn as well. The best viewing areas are on either side of the highway on the north of the bridge over the river (about 2 km south of the County 3 intersection).

South of Canard River is the small community of **Edgewater Beach**. The sewage lagoon drive here is on the left 2.8 km south of the bridge over the river, and almost opposite Waterfoam Street on the right.

HOLIDAY BEACH

Some 12 km southeast of Amherstburg Highway 18 crosses Big Creek. The marshes here usually have Great Egrets and other herons readily visible in the warmer weather. In a farther 3 km is the community of **Malden Centre**, and *Holiday Beach Conservation Area* itself is 2 km south of here via County Road 50. (Note that, by staying on Highway 18 you will arrive at Harrow and the areas described below.)

Holiday Beach is an outstanding observation point for fall hawk migration, and there is a good observation tower operated by the Holiday Beach Migration Observatory, which has conducted an organized count here since 1974. The observatory has published a booklet, *Hawks of Holiday Beach*, by Allen Chartier with Dave Stimac, available from Holiday Beach Migration Observatory, 1442 West River Park Drive, Inkster, Michigan 48141, USA for C$10.00 + $2.50 shipping.

Although the area is principally known for its migrant hawks, it borders the extensive Big Creek marshes and Lake Erie itself, and so can be a good place for waterbirds as well. Bald Eagles nest, and heavy westward landbird movements (notably of Blue Jays and hummingbirds) occur in the same period as the hawk movements, especially in the earlier morning. A baited waterfowl feeding pond is 1.2 km east of the area on County Road 50 with a small parking lot adjacent. There is fall waterfowl hunting in the park.

The hawk movements here in fall are larger than at any other

Ontario station, and are some of the largest in eastern North America. Migrants usually start to appear in numbers towards the end of the first week in September, but the main flights are from about mid-September on. In September Broad-winged and Sharp-shinned Hawks and American Kestrels in that order predominate. Broad-wingeds typically peak between September 12 and 18, and usually the first couple of days between these dates with optimum flying conditions will yield heavy flights. The numbers of this species drop off rapidly towards the end of the month, and an October Broad-winged is late. Sharp-shinneds, the next most abundant species, move in smaller numbers throughout September and October, with Red-taileds moving heavily through the second half of October. Good numbers of Turkey Vultures occur at this time as well. Outstanding numbers of Red-shouldered Hawks occur in late October and early November, and Golden Eagles are increasingly regular in the same period. The first half of November yields smaller numbers of migrants, principally Red-taileds, and limited movement can occur into December.

In September well over thirty thousand Broad-wingeds can be seen in a single day, and in all fifteen species of raptor occur regularly, although Ospreys, Northern Goshawks, eagles, Merlins, and Peregrine Falcons are usually only in small numbers. Often the soaring hawks are extremely high, and viewing can be better at Hawk Cliff, although on any day when there is heavy movement some birds are usually low enough to be seen easily. While the heaviest hawk movement is typically in late morning and around midday, birds can often be seen moving at lower levels before 10.00 a.m. and after 3.00 p.m.

The early buteo flights tend to be heaviest on sunny, cool days with moderate northwest winds and light cumulus clouds developing, and do not occur on rainy days or when the winds are southerly. If the winds are too strong the formation of the thermals needed for soaring is inhibited, and days without wind or with winds from another quarter do not concentrate the birds (which fly west) along the lake to the same extent. The same conditions are also ideal later in the year but occur much less often, and it is not unusual to see Red-taileds moving under heavy cloud and threatening skies. Accipiters and falcons depend less on soaring, and tend to move lower, in direct flight.

AROUND KINGSVILLE

Approaching Holiday Beach from Pelee, several areas around Kingsville can be worth a visit, and the loop drive below can be interesting even if you plan to go no farther west. A pair of Bald Eagles nests along the route, and the area can also often yield geese, great egrets, and shorebirds that may be absent around Point Pelee itself.

Kingsville itself is some 12 km west of Leamington on Highway 18. From the second light in town (Division Street) drive 1 km west to the intersection of Essex Road 50, which joins Highway 18 from the south a short distance past the creek bridge. Take a odometer reading here, turn south on County Road 50 and drive towards the shore. At about 2.5 km the road turns down along the shoreline. A few gulls may gather along here. Other points of interest are (distances from point to point):

3.4 km   (from Highway 18) a bridge over the small marsh along Wigle Creek.

0.9 km   McCain Sideroad stop street. Turn left.

0.5 km   Cedar Creek mouth. On the south is a parking area with washrooms. From here to the end of *Cedar Creek* marshes (about 1 km), there can be marsh viewing behind the houses on your right.

3.0 km   The lawns on the left along here sometimes have standing water, and hence shorebirds, in spring.

1.0 km   Turn north on County Road 23.

1.4 km   A view of an Bald eagle's nest over the fields on the right. Do not walk out into the fields.

0.7 km   Cedar Creek crossings. Herons and egrets are usual.

1.0 km   Another arm of Cedar Creek.

0.3 km   A small picnic area with washrooms on the left.

0.3 km   Highway 18. Cross this and continue north (note the next part of this route is the loop back into Kingsville; if you wish to continue west and eliminate this detour you should turn left here).

4.0 km   Turn right on Gosfield South Concession 3.

5.7 km   The feeding area of *Miner's Sanctuary* on the right. Scan the flocks of Canada Geese present in spring and fall for other species. Snow and White-fronteds are possible.

0.7 km   A pond on the right can have shorebirds and duck.

0.7 km   County Road 29. Turn right to return (3 km) to Kingsville main street (where a left turn takes you back to Leamington).

Turn right to continue west on Highway 18 to **Harrow** (some 15 km), where Yellow-headed Blackbirds have nested at the Harrow *sewage lagoons*. To reach these drive west on Highway 18 from Queen Street at the light in the centre of town 0.8 km to Roseborough Street on the right. Turn north, go 1.2 km to the end of the road at Concession 3. Turn left, and the lagoon drive is 1.5 km along on the south of this road. Return to Highway 18 and drive to **Malden Centre** (some 11.0 km), and then follow the directions above.

STONEY POINT AND THE ST CLAIR NATIONAL WILDLIFE AREA

North of Point Pelee, and forming the northern boundary of Essex County, is Lake St Clair. The east shoreline of the lake between Walpole Island and the mouth of the Thames River is a flat plain drained by an extensive network of ditches and dikes, and intensively farmed. There are few trees except groves of willows along the higher areas of the shores and dikes. These attract migrant landbirds, and there are extensive marshes along the lake itself. The open farmland attracts enormous flocks of blackbirds in late summer and fall, Horned Larks, Lapland Longspurs, and Snow Buntings in later fall, and waterfowl especially in early spring when huge numbers of Tundra Swans and Canada Geese gather on the corn stubble. The Lake St Clair area is reputed to be one of the most important staging areas for waterfowl south of James Bay. Shorebirds can be found on wet fields, and plover are regular in migration.

The main area lies west of Highway 40 between Chatham and Wallaceburg, roughly between the villages of Mitchell Bay and Prairie Siding (see map 4). To reach Lake St Clair from Leamington, drive north on Highway 77, crossing Highway 401 (when 77 becomes County Road 35) to the village of **Stoney Point**.

County Road 35 terminates at County Road 2, the main street

MAP 4   Eastern Lake St Clair

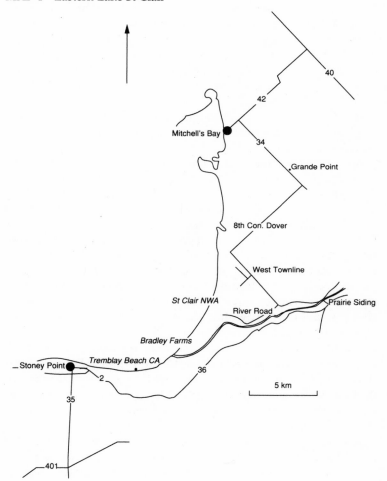

40

42

Mitchell's Bay

34

Grande Point

8th Con. Dover

West Townline

St Clair NWA

Prairie Siding

River Road

Bradley Farms

Tremblay Beach CA

Stoney Point

2

36

5 km

35

401

of Stoney Point. Continue straight ahead to the lake on Tilbury N Township 6-7 sideroad. At the lake turn right on St Clair Road. When water levels are high the lawns and fields along here may flood and attract shorebirds. Drive 2.4 km east to **Tremblay Beach Conservation Area**. This is an area of marsh, and at the gate a lane to the right leads south across the railroad tracks, to the *sewage lagoon*. Yellow-headed Blackbirds nest, King Rails have occurred, and all the usual marsh birds can be expected. In migration periods the trees along the shoreline of the conservation area should be searched for migrant warblers and other landbirds.

Return to the first road running south and drive to the next intersection (County Road 2) and turn left. This road runs some 12 km east to the Kent County boundary, when it becomes County Road 36. Continue eastwards 8.5 km through the village of **Prairie Siding** until the first bridge over the river at County Road 35. Turn left and cross here, bearing immediately left again (west) onto a road which soon becomes gravel, and curves up to run along the top of the Thames dike. This is the River Road, and it continues for 4 km, finally bearing sharp right and leaving the river to become the West Townline Road (but marked only 'Townline' here). In about 0.5 km it crosses an east-west road.

On the left hand (west) is the Dover River Road, and by turning left there one can drive to the **Bradley Farms** on the north bank of the Thames near its mouth. Formerly the marshes here were the premier birding locations in the area, but their quality has declined and currently access is uncertain. The future is also uncertain, and there is a possibility that some marsh restoration may occur. Access is always by permission, and a small fee is charged; however, at present attempts to visit may not be worth while. Bradley's is closed during certain times of the year.

If not visiting Bradley's, continue north on the West Townline road some 3.2 km to a bridge crossing the wide drainage canal on the west (left), and marked to the **St Clair National Wildlife Area**. The south side of the area, a large marsh, is managed for waterfowl and consists of extensive areas of cattails with open reaches and patches of shallow water. This road is poorly maintained and ends at 1.8 km, but it may be possible to drive along here and view the marsh. After driving this section, return to the bridge but do not cross it. Instead turn left (north) to drive up the west side of the canal, and at 1 km is a parking lot where one can walk along a dike (5 km return) which runs diagonally across the marsh to the west corner. There is also excellent marsh viewing on the left on the way up to the parking area.

These marshes are very productive: all the usual marshland species can be found in summer. All of the regularly occurring dabbling ducks and rails in the province have nested, and the area is one of the province's strongholds for Forster's Tern, with a good colony of Yellow-headed Blackbirds. It can be even more rewarding in early spring, when huge numbers of migrant waterfowl stage: swans, geese, and dabbling duck in the marshes and on the fields, and diving duck such as Canvasbacks on the lake. Later, if water levels are suitable, a good mix of shorebirds can occur, and this may be the marshes' main appeal during the later spring period.

After viewing this area, return to the bridge to rejoin the West Townline Road and continue north. After 1.4 km you pass the headquarters of the St Clair National Wildlife Area on the other side of the dike. Then the marshes continue, and for the last 1 km, to the point the road ends at Klein's Camp, there is marshland on both sides of the road. That on the east is particularly good for easy viewing of such marsh birds as gallinules and Pied-billed Grebes, as well as Yellow-headed Blackbirds; and rarities such as Little Blue Heron have occurred.

At this point you will have covered most of the most productive parts of the route. However, in early spring the waterfowl are as likely to be foraging on wetter areas of the neighbouring fields as in the marshes themselves, so finding the largest numbers is then largely a matter of driving the other backroads in the area and watching for the flocks (the backroads follow a rectangular grid pattern, so there is little danger of getting lost, but unmetalled roads at this time may be impassable). Another caution relates to the date of the spring concentrations. The peak Tundra Swan numbers are usually in the second half of March – my own records suggest March 15–26 – and many of the other waterfowl peak around the same time, but early spring in Ontario is notoriously unpredictable. An early season could see numbers thinning out rapidly towards the end of the month, while a cold, late year could delay movement by a week or more.

To continue the present route, turn east on the 8th Concession Dover and drive 7.6 km to County Road 34, also called the Winterline Road. Turn left (north), and continue for another 7 km, passing through the village of **Grande Pointe**, to County Road 42, the Mitchell's Bay Sideroad. Turn left here and drive 1 km west to the village of **Mitchell's Bay**. The waterfront here affords views of the lake, but the migrant concentrations of waterfowl are often too far from shore to be readily visible. East of town, 1.7 km, on the north of the County Road, is the village *sewage lagoon*.

From Mitchell's Bay you can retrace your route back. Alternatively, County Road 42 runs east to join Highway 40. From here it is some 9 km north to the town of **Wallaceburg** and the St Clair Parkway in Lambton County, and 18 km south to **Chatham** and Highway 401.

ADDITIONAL SEWAGE LAGOONS IN THE PELEE AREA

Comber – This village is noteworthy because most persons using Highway 401 to visit Pelee will drive through it, and its lagoons have been very productive (they have a large welcome notice at the gate erected by the Comber Chamber of Commerce!). Comber is the first community south of Highway 401 on Highway 77. To reach the lagoons, turn east at the south end of town onto County Road 46 from Highway 77. Drive 0.2 km to Windsor Avenue on the south and turn; the lagoon gates are 0.3 km ahead. Coming from Leamington, it is easier to turn onto Elizabeth Street, some 0.2 km south of the stop street at County Road 46. The lagoons are on the right where this street turns north.

Cottam – This village is north of Highway 3, about 7 km east of Essex (see below). The lagoon is east on County Road 27 from the intersection with Highway 3. Drive 0.2 km to the lagoon driveway on the right.

Essex – This town is on Highway 3, roughly halfway between Windsor and Leamington. There are two separate sets of sewage lagoons; however, on my last visit I was escorted out of one of them, so I would suggest asking permission prior to attempting to enter. The larger southwest complex is on the south of Highway 3 just west of the North Malden Road intersection, which is 2.2 km west of the intersection with Essex Road 23. The drive is 0.1 km south on the North Malden Road, on the right. For the northeast lagoons, turn north on Essex Road 23 and proceed 2.9 km to Essex Road 8. (To do so, cross Talbot Street on the stop light and bear right at a stop street immediately after.) Drive east 0.8 km and the lagoon drive is on the left.

Merlin – This village, 5.5 km north of Highway 3 between Wheatley and Blenheim, on County Road 7, has a sewage lagoon located on the north side of County Road 8. The driveway, leading over a large field, is 0.9 km east of the junction in the village of the two county roads.

Ridgetown – This town lies in the eastern part of Kent County, 7 km south of Highway 401 on Highway 21. This highway turns west in town, and then south again towards Morpeth. At the point it turns south, turn right on Erie Street. Drive north on Erie 1.4 km to Palmer Street, which is just before Erie Street crosses the tracks and turns right. Turn left on Palmer; the lagoons are 0.3 km along, both on the south and to the north across the railroad.

Tilbury – Tilbury lies south of Highway 401 between exits 56 and 63, but the lagoons are to the north, west of County Road 1. They are probably best viewed from the westbound lanes of Highway 401 between the two Tilbury interchanges (i.e., get on at No. 63 and leave at No. 56).

AREAS ALONG HIGHWAY 401

The Highway 401 route gives little hint of the area's ornithological interest, apart from the wintering species mentioned in the opening paragraphs. Yet it is never more than 25 km from the birding areas along the Lake Erie shoreline; however, an entire day or more can vanish if one is tempted to detour south. If you are really bent on getting somewhere but have a little time to spare, the lagoons at Comber or even Ridgetown might be worth a detour, and those at Tilbury are visible from the westbound lanes. The areas described under Stoney Point are also relatively close. The 401 picnic area in the westbound lanes east of Tilbury has a small sewage lagoon complex behind it.

MAP 5   Lambton County

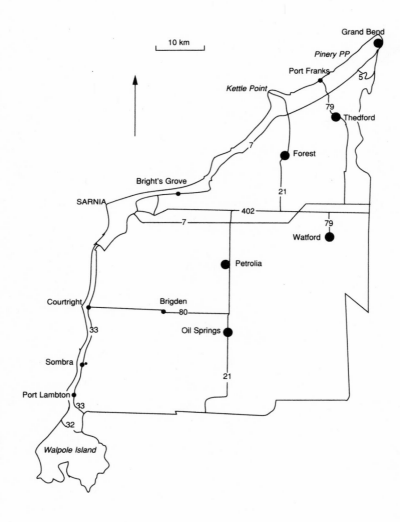

4 Sarnia and Area

Lambton County

Highway 402
Sarnia: Point Edward
        east along Lakeshore Road
        Sarnia Bay
The St Clair River
Walpole Island
Kettle Point
The Pinery
Additional sewage lagoons
    in Lambton County

Lambton County lies directly north of Kent County, with the St Clair River forming its western boundary, and Lake Huron to the north. These two features do much to define the area's attraction for a birder; fall waterbird migrants moving down the length of Lake Huron are gradually channelled westwards as the lake narrows until, at Sarnia, it ends completely. Birds must then follow the river, or embark on a long overland flight. In fact, it appears they do both. In winter, parts of the river remain open, so in this season it is also of significance for concentrations of wintering waterfowl. Inland from the lake can be of interest as well; Tundra Swans and other waterfowl can occur on wet fields in early spring, and again in small numbers in fall.

Lambton is noteworthy in other respects. With the two counties discussed in chapter 3, it forms Canada's 'deep south.' It too is mainly a flat plain dominated by agriculture, but there is more stock rearing, it is generally more forested, and to the northeast the country becomes more rolling; hence there is a greater diversity of habitats. Although it lacks recognized landbird concentration points of the quality of Point Pelee, or extensive tracts of readily accessible Carolinian woodland such as Rondeau, there are many opportunities for seeing both south-

ern species and landbird migrants. The Lake Huron shore channels spring migrants along it, and areas such as the Pinery
harbour southerners. Walpole Island, the Indian reserve that
forms a southern extension of the county at the mouth of the
St Clair River, is a fascinating and extensive area of forest, open
savannah, and marshland.

Like Essex and Kent counties to the south, winters are relatively mild and open, but the eastern parts of the county are
downwind of the prevailing winds across Lake Huron and can
receive considerable snow as a result. Springs are early and
autumns prolonged. Summers tend to be hot, and the county
does not receive the benefit of the cooling off-lake winds that
ameliorate heat waves to the south.

Sarnia is the main population centre (46,000+), and is a port
of entry from the United States (Port Huron) and has a small
airport. From here the controlled-access **Highway 402** runs east
to London. The areas described below under Sarnia are within
easy reach from it, particularly the Wawanosh Wetlands. But
on visits to Sarnia we usually find our time is better spent by
detouring to Strathroy lagoons in Middlesex County (exits 65
and 69). The areas around Komoka and Delaware in Middlesex
County are also readily accessible from exits 82 and 86.

SARNIA

The start of the St Clair River at Point Edward is probably the
best place in Ontario to see such pelagic birds as jaegers and
Sabine's Gulls close to the shore in season. These and large
numbers of other waterbirds move down Lake Huron in late
autumn, mainly during periods when the winds are northerly,
and they tend to appear around the mouth of the river at Sarnia,
or to move down it. The weather is critical; movements are
typically linked to strong cold fronts, generating raw, windy
days, often with snow flurries.

Point Edward is a section of Sarnia (see map 6); to reach it
take Highway 402 to exit 1 (Front Street). Then turn left (north)
on Front and drive 1.0 km to Victoria Avenue, then turn left
again. Drive to Fort Street (1.1 km) and turn right. Just before
the water treatment building a road (0.2 km) runs left. Follow

MAP 6   Sarnia Bay and Point Edward

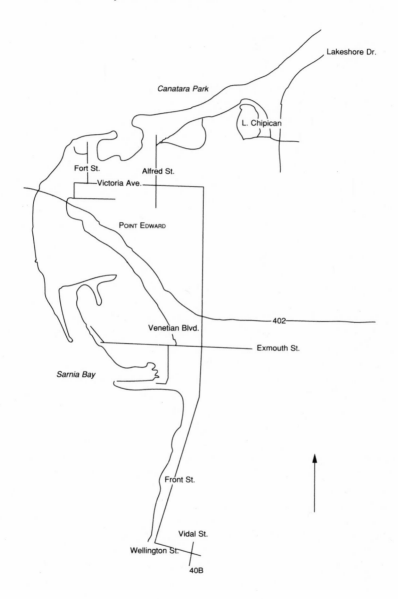

this around to a parking area overlooking the lake and river mouth. Walk east or west for additional viewing points, and there is further parking at the back of the treatment plant. Many landbirds, including hawks, move along the shoreline in fall and concentrate along the shore in spring migration. The area is also good in winter for duck, gulls, and possible Snowy Owls.

Jaeger and gull sightings start as early as the beginning of September and extend well into December; however, the best period seems to be late September through to mid-November. The dates of the flights and numbers of birds vary greatly from year to year, perhaps in part because suitable weather conditions do not always occur at the right times. Counts of the rarer species are never large, and the observer must be prepared for long periods when little happens. Typical season counts for Black-legged Kittiwakes range from ten to sixty (with as many as five a day, mainly young birds), Sabine's Gulls one to five, Parasitic Jaegers ten to thirty; and Pomarine Jaegers one to five. A variety of other species can be seen in the same movements, including other gulls and flocks of waterfowl such as scoters, later shorebirds, and Snow Buntings. While this is one of the most productive areas for viewing these birds at relatively close range, sightings are possible from elsewhere all along the shoreline, and particularly at Kettle Point. The large loon flights seen off Kettle Point, and flocks of Tundra Swans typically seem to cross inland before reaching the river mouth, and are best seen east of Point Edward. Do not become so preoccupied with watching for flying birds that you neglect the waters of the lake: many species land on the waters offshore.

If you wish to try some landbirding for a change, visit **Canatara Park** less than 1 km to the east. This park has more natural areas to the south, lake viewing to the north, a small lake, Lake Chipican, to the east, open water in winter, and the usual city park facilities including washrooms. There is a log cabin here where copies of the *Checklist of the Birds of Sarnia* can be obtained (they are also available at the information building at the Bluewater Bridge). Canatara Park is good for landbirds in spring, and Lake Chipican can yield migrant dabbling duck, and small rafts of such species as Redhead and Ruddy Duck, which may be absent on Lake Huron.

To reach Canatara, return to Victoria Avenue, turn left and

drive to Alfred Street (0.6 km), then turn left on Alfred. This road becomes Sandy Lane and at 0.4 km Lake Chipican Drive leads off to the right, continuing past treed and grassy areas to arrive at Lake Chipican after 1.3 km. The road then leaves the park, but runs along Lake Chipican for 0.5 km, to intersect finally with Christina Street North. A left here leads into Lakeshore Drive and thence out towards the locations described below. Just before the intersection with Christina a deadend road on the right leads along the south shore of Lake Chipican, and the parking here gives access to paths through the woodland.

Lakeshore Road eventually becomes County Road 7, leading to a number of good birding areas east of the city, and ultimately to Kettle Point. From Lake Chipican Road drive east some 7 km to the Blackwell Side Road and turn right. (All the side streets along Lakeshore tend to look alike, but Blackwell is signed to the Wawanosh Wetlands, and is at about 1800 Lakeshore. (Note: there is also a Blackwell Road, which runs east-west.) The *Wawanosh Wetlands Conservation Area* is on the west 2.9 km along this road. The wetlands are an area of flooded gravel pits that are good for waterfowl and herons, with shorebirds in spring and fall if water levels are suitable. There is a large Bobolink roost in August, and Dickcissels nested here on their last major invasion of the province. Birds move between here and the race track, below, and the concentrations can attract falcons to the area.

Hiawatha Race Track is a recently located area where flocks of geese and shorebirds sometimes congregate in fall migration. To reach it, continue south on Blackwell, crossing Highway 402 (no 402 access), to the stop at Highway 7. Turn right, and the entrance to the track is 0.4 km ahead on the right. Simply drive into the main parking lot and scan the fields to the north and west. The area is particularly attractive to plovers, and Buff-breasted Sandpiper has occurred.

Airport Road, about 1 km to the east, is the nearest Highway 402 exit to these locations, which can be reached by driving south to Highway 7 and then west. To the north Airport Road terminates in the airport grounds, but a sideroad to the east skirts the airfield perimeter and finally (as Tefler Road) runs north to end at County Road 7. The wide fields in this entire area are excellent for hawks and owls in winter (both Snowy and Short-eared occur), as well as Horned Larks, longspurs, and Snow Buntings both then and during migration periods. Later in spring shorebirds can appear, and flocks of American Pipits occur in fall. The area is also one of the better nesting locations for more local open country species, such as Upland Sandpipers and Grasshopper Sparrows; and Western Meadowlarks should be listened for in spring.

Bright's Grove is a small community farther east on Lakeshore Road. The sewage lagoons here have been consistently productive with a formidable list of rarity sightings; breeding waterfowl such as Green-winged Teal, American Wigeon, and Ruddy Duck occur in summer. Hence they are well worth visiting while in the Sarnia area. They are south off Lakeshore Road 1.2 km east of the Waterworks Side Road stoplight, itself 3.8 km east of Tefler. Driving from the east, this is 0.6 km past Errol Sideroad. (Highway 402 exit 15). The lagoons are not visible from the road; walk south down the lane to the line of trees. For persons continuing east, County Road 7 eventually joins Highway 21 near Kettle Point, and the Pinery is then farther east along Highway 21.

Sarnia Bay south of Point Edward is a productive area for waterbirds in migration and during winter (see map 6). From the intersection of Fort Street and Victoria Avenue described above under Point Edward, drive west (towards the river) on Victoria 0.1 km to its end at Livingston Street. Turn left and drive 0.1 km to Michigan Avenue. Turn right and follow this road (it loops into Alexandra Avenue) around 0.6 km to Venetian Boulevard, and turn right again. The ponds in this area attract large numbers of Canada Geese and Mallards, which in turn often attract other waterfowl. Follow Venetian to its end, driving past the Holiday Inn, to Exmouth Street (1.7 km). Turn right here: if you continue to the end of Exmouth you pass the grain elevators, where Peregrine Falcons have sometimes wintered, and there are more river views. Alternatively, a left turn 0.2 km from Venetian on to Harbour Road leads (0.3 km) to viewing over Sarnia Bay. Diving duck and gulls are the usual items of interest, again with the possibility of a Snowy Owl in winter. Glaucous Gulls are regular at this time, and other species are possible. Then return to Exmouth and drive east 0.3 km to Front Street and turn right. At Centennial Park there is a parking lot (0.9 km) where there are further views of the bay. This completes the coverage of the area. If you wish to continue down the St Clair River, drive south on Front 0.9 km to Wellington Street and then east 0.4 km to Vidal Street. This is Highway 40B, and a right turn leads to the areas described below.

THE ST CLAIR RIVER

The St Clair Parkway (County Road 33) follows the river south from the outskirts of Sarnia, just south of the intersection of Highways 40 and 40B, all the way to Walpole Island. It is an attractive drive, and can be a good one for birding, particularly from late autumn to early spring, when duck and gulls congregate on open water. Points of particular interest are *Willow Park* at the Lambton generating station just south of **Courtright** (usually a good place to view gulls, with waterfowl along the far shore in winter) and farther south 9 km at **Sombra**, where the river is often very good for waterfowl and gulls, particularly in winter. The best area is the 4 km or so between Lambton Road 2 north of the village and the bridge to the south of town.

Both Sombra and Port Lambton, some 6 km south, have sewage lagoons. For the one at Sombra continue south on the parkway 0.7 km from the street to the ferry to the United States. Sombra Road 11 is to your left. Turn here, and the *lagoon* gate is on the right just over the tracks, 0.3 km down this road. **Port Lambton** *lagoons* are at the back of a field off County Road 1, which joins the parkway just past the ferry dock entrance in Port Lambton. Drive 0.8 km east on County Road 1 to the track to the lagoon, which is on the right almost opposite the fire hall. Both of these lagoon complexes can be good; Little Gulls are often seen in spring and early summer, and in one year a White-winged Tern spent some time there. Just south of Port Lambton the road starts to follow the eastern side of Walpole Island, with extensive marshes along the shore.

WALPOLE ISLAND

Some 8 km south of Port Lambton, County Road 33 turns east, and County Road 32 goes west over a bridge to the *Walpole Island First Nation*. This is unsurrendered Indian Territory, with most of the habitation and the bulk of the 24,000 hectares lying south of Tecumseh Road, which runs west across to the far shore and the St Clair River. There are six islands in all, together with the surrounding waters of the delta complex, where the St Clair River empties into Lake St Clair. There is a confusing network of dirt roads, and much of the area is remote and relatively inaccessible.

The excellent and extensive marshes along the Lake St Clair shoreline make up one-third of the territory, known locally as Bkejwanong 'where the waters divide'. The remaining area is a mosaic of some of the best quality tall-grass prairie and oak savannah in North America, along with oak woodland, maple swamp, agricultural land, and residential areas.

There are about 230 species of birds recorded for the area, even though birding coverage has been very sporadic at best. Of these, 145 species and two hybrids have been recorded with at least some evidence of breeding. This is almost half of the species known to breed in Ontario; of these, twenty-five are considered rare in Canada, and thirty-seven rare in Ontario. One endangered species, Henslow's Sparrow, has nested in recent years.

Species occurring with at least some breeding evidence and characteristic of more southerly areas are Great Egret, Northern Bobwhite (probably the best location in Ontario to find this species), King Rail, Red-bellied Woodpecker, Acadian Flycatcher, Tufted Titmouse (more regular here than anywhere outside the Niagara Peninsula), Carolina Wren, Blue-gray Gnatcatcher, White-eyed Vireo, Blue-winged, Cerulean, and Prothonotary Warblers, Louisiana Waterthrush, Hooded Warbler, Yellow-breasted Chat, and Orchard Oriole.

Species occurring with at least some breeding evidence and characteristic of more westerly regions are Horned Grebe, Northern Shoveler, Gadwall, Canvasback, Redhead, Lesser Scaup, Ruddy Duck, Sandhill Crane, Marbled Godwit, Forster's Tern, and Yellow-headed Blackbird. Other significant wetland species include good populations of Least Bittern, American Coot, and Black Tern, a heronry of Black-crowned Night-Herons, and occasional nesting or sighting records of Little Gull.

As unsurrendered Indian Territory, Walpole should be considered private property. While the main road system is extensively used, persons wishing to bird should seek permission from the First Nation Chief and Council. Such visits require accompaniment by a band member, and indeed one of the best ways to see the marshes is to hire a boat; however, the cost of this can be considerable. Birding use of the island is relatively new, and the band's approach to handling it is still evolving. Arrangements should be made well in advance by phoning the Heritage Centre at (519) 627-1475, or writing to The Walpole Island Heritage Centre, RR 3, Wallaceburg, N8A 4K9. There may be a fee towards preservation of the area's environment.

KETTLE POINT

Kettle Point is also Indian Territory, and the village occupies a small promontory at the south end of Lake Huron. As such it is an excellent place for watching autumn waterfowl movements, which come closer to shore here than elsewhere on the lake. It also is a good location for migrant landbirds, and nesting birds include some more northern species.

Kettle Point is north of the point where County Road 7 ends (some 28 km east of the Errol Sideroad) at Highway 21, which continues east towards the Pinery. The highway westbound here curves inland towards Forest, and West Ipperwash Road turns north from County Road 7 immediately west of the Highway 21 intersection. Turn onto West Ipperwash Road, and then left 0.2 km ahead at a sign to Kettle Point Park (follow the sign for Kettle Point Concretions). This road runs west to the shore (2.5 km) and then curves to follow the shoreline north. At 4 km farther on are the concretions, with a historic site sign, and then the shoreroad turns sharp right 0.7 km ahead.

Interesting waterbirds can be seen all along here, but the best spots for watching migration are from the area of concretions up to the point the road turns. Here in autumn loons, duck, and gulls moving down Lake Huron are visible from the shore, particularly in periods of strong northwest winds. The species seen at the mouth of the St Clair River in Sarnia can be expected here too, and large flights of loons occur, including the occasional Red-throateds and (very rarely) a Pacific.

Migrant landbirds follow the shoreline in spring and autumn, and in spring considerable concentrations can occur. In the breeding season the extensive swampy woodlands can yield species rare in the southwest, such as Northern Harrier, Whip-poor-will, Sedge Wren, and Northern Waterthrush, as well as southern species such as Blue-gray Gnatcatcher and Golden-winged and Blue-winged Warblers.

THE PINERY

The *Pinery Provincial Park* (entrance fee) is an excellent birding park as well as being most important botanically. It is on Highway 21 some 15 km east of the Kettle Point turnoff, just past the village of **Port Franks**. The Pinery has an exceptional range of habitats. There are deciduous woodlands along the Ausable River, extensive oak-pine woodlands, and a fine dune system along the shore of Lake Huron. The deciduous woodlands have nesting Blue-gray Gnatcatchers, Cerulean Warblers, and other southern species including Prothonotary Warbler in the wet bottomlands. The pines attract Pine Warblers as well as more northern species such as Magnolia Warbler, and Prairie Warblers nest very locally at the rear of the primary dunes. In winter finches occur in the pines.

In spring migration Tundra Swans and other waterfowl can be found in the second half of March on the fields adjacent to the park, which runs an interpretive program to view them, and later the whole area can be particularly rich in spring landbirds. In autumn it shares some of the character of Kettle Point farther west as a vantage point for observing waterbird migration. Large loon movements occur.

There are several large camping areas, and this park has the most extended season of any in the province. There is a good interpretive program with a bird checklist, and usually at least one knowledgeable birder on staff.

The flocks of swans concentrate on the fields on the east side of Highway 21. The best place to see them is along the Greenway Road (County Road 5) 1.0 km east of the Pinery entrance, in the second half of March. The town of **Grand Bend** is 9 km northeast of the park on Highway 21, at the intersection with Highway 81. It has accessible *sewage lagoons* which can be reached by driving 1.1 km east on Highway 81 to Stephen Concession 22 on the right. Turn, and the lagoons (visible from the road) are 2.2 km along on the right. They can be very productive. (Note that Parkhill Reservoir, described in chapter 6, is 25 km south on Highway 81.)

ADDITIONAL SEWAGE LAGOONS IN LAMBTON COUNTY

Brigden – This village is west of Highway 21 along Highway 80. From the Moore-Brigden Road in the village drive west 2 km to Moore Road 9-10. Turn south and the lagoons are 0.5 km along on the left.

Forest – This town is on Highway 21 south of Kettle Point. For the lagoons, drive south on Highway 21 from the light in town where it turns south. Continue 2.4 km to Plympton Concession 12 on the right. Turn and drive west 2 km to a gravel (later clay) road on the right. The lagoon gate is 1.4 km north on the right.

Oil Springs – This hamlet is near the intersection of Highways 21 and 80. To reach the lagoon turn east on Main Street and drive 1 km to Frederick Street on the north; the lagoon gate is 0.2 km ahead.

Thedford – This town is on Highway 79 east of Kettle Point and west of Parkhill Reservoir in Middlesex County. The lagoons are on the right, driving west on Highway 79, just 0.5 km after the long curve to the left leaving the village.

Watford – This town is on Highway 79 south of Highway 402. The lagoons are down an extremely long drive. From the railroad bridge in town, drive 1.7 km south on Highway 79, and turn right on Brooke-Warwick Townline. The gate is 1 km along on the right, but one can hardly see the lagoons from there.

MAP 7   Huron and Southern Bruce Counties

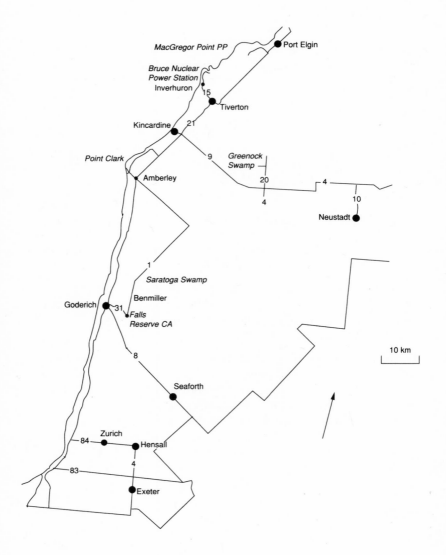

5 Eastern Lake Huron and the Bruce Peninsula

Huron, Bruce, and Grey Counties

The Huron shore north to Southampton
The Bruce Peninsula
Other sewage lagoons in the Lake Huron area

These three counties are isolated from the main communication networks of southern Ontario, lack major population centres – Owen Sound, with a population of some 20,000, is the largest town – and are also away from the prime birding destinations along the lower Great Lakes. Formerly they were rather neglected by birders, particularly those areas south of the Bruce Peninsula. The Bruce's reputation as a haven for some of the province's rarest and most attractive plants has drawn naturalists north to the peninsula, and it is now recognized for an outstanding array of breeding birds as well. The configuration of the area, with the sweep of the Huron shore, and the wide beaches and the numerous promontories on the peninsula itself, also combine to yield excellent birding in migration periods.

The two northern counties contrast sharply with the flat fertile arable farmlands to the south. Many expanses of flat countryside can be found, but drainage is often poor and pasture rather than cropland predominates. In fact, both the topography and the appearance of the landscape varies widely, with prosperous farmland in some areas, and abandoned pastures and wooded swamps in others. There are extensive areas of woodland, often in the swampy headwaters of creeks and rivers, and deeply incised river valleys bounded by woods and pasture.

As one drives north the countryside gradually changes; first the proportion of pastureland increases, then to be replaced by forest. Fields become rocky and uneven, the grass sparse and dotted with hawkweeds and mullein. Gradually, as one progresses north on the peninsula, the character of the forest itself changes until the tall mixed woodlands of the south end are replaced by conifers, and ancient cedars hang tenaciously in the crevices of the limestone outcrops. Open stretches of limestone pavement are interspersed with shallow fens, where pitcher plants and rare orchids grow. Ravens patrol the roads, and Hermit Thrushes and juncos sing from the bush alongside. While the sheer size of the region precludes quick coverage, few parts of the province can be so delightful.

Winters here tend to be long and snowfall heavy, although the climate on the peninsula itself is moderated somewhat by the surrounding water, enabling some southern species to survive north of their expected range. Winters also can yield vagrants that find themselves stranded at the ends of the many promontories.

Spring seems to creep up the peninsula, but warm days can bring the migrants flooding in, only to be blocked by expanses of lake to the north. Meanwhile waterfowl stage along the shorelines. Summer offers a wide range of species, from Yellowthroated Vireo and Cerulean Warbler in the deciduous woodlands of the south, to the occasional Blackpoll Warbler in the stunted black spruce on the islands at the northern tip. Old field habitats abound, and this is southern Ontario's stronghold for Brewer's Blackbird.

Fall arrives much earlier than along Lake Erie, and with it come falcons moving down the peninsula, and waterfowl again stage off the Huron shoreline, especially in periods of strong westerly winds. In both spring and fall the more extensive areas of open field can attract migrant shorebirds, and large flocks of pipits, Horned Larks, and Snow Buntings. There are several small sewage lagoons, with those at Exeter and Wiarton the most productive.

The principal access routes are Highway 21 from the southwest, following the Huron shoreline; Highway 10 from the Toronto area, and Highway 6 from Hamilton and Waterloo. Highway 6 is the only highway running north on the Bruce Peninsula itself, and at the north end it connects with the ferry to Manitoulin Island, offering a pleasant alternate route farther north. The main body of this account will review sites from south to north along the Huron shoreline, and then follow Georgian Bay south.

THE HURON SHORE NORTH TO SOUTHAMPTON

Highway 21, the 'Bluewater Highway,' runs parallel to the lakeshore for this entire distance of some 150 km, but it is out of sight of the water for most of its length. There is little of birding note between Grand Bend and Goderich, but a group of sewage lagoons lie inland at this point, including the consistently productive ones at Exeter and (considerably farther east) at Mitchell.

At **Goderich** there is access to the Maitland River mouth and Goderich harbour by driving north through town on Highway 21 to North Harbour Road and turning west. This road is just past the Old Jail, and immediately before the railway bridge on the highway as it curves right down the hill. Drive 1.7 km to the harbour, which can be good for gulls and duck. There is also access to the parkland along the river from this road.

The road to *Falls Reserve Conservation Area* is a little farther north along Highway 21: go to the bottom of the hill and turn right on County Road 31 just the other side of the Maitland River bridge. The area is 8 km east, at **Benmiller** (0.2 km west of the junction with County Road 1 northbound). This area has good woodland along the river and mixed habitats associated with the floodplain. There is a falls on the river, which curves round this area.

County Road 1 runs north from Benmiller some 10 km to **Nile** where it takes a jog. If you turn right here on West Wawanosh Concession 1 and drive east, in about 2.5 km you begin to pass the Conservation Authority lands associated with *Saratoga Swamp*, on the north of the sideroad. These wetlands continue for the next 3 km or so, and there are farther areas along Concession 2–3, the next sideroad to the north. The whole is heavily forested, including stands of white pine, and the mix of swamp, coniferous, and hardwood bush and rough pasture provides an excellent variety of bird habitats and of breeding birds.

Some 24 km north of Goderich at the village of **Amberley** the highway abandons any pretence of following the shoreline, curving inland. Some 4 km north is the *Point Clark* road (Huron Concession 2). This leads west about 4 km to the shore and then curves left. At 5 km from Highway 21 is Lighthouse Road, which leads (0.8 km) to the well-signposted historic Clark Point lighthouse on the shore. This point is the westernmost promontory along the Lake Huron shore between Cape Hurd and Kettle Point, and hence is an excellent place for viewing migration in both spring and autumn. It can be especially productive in late fall (November) for arctic gulls and later waterfowl movements. Loons, grebes, and duck all stage along this shoreline (Red-throated Loons are regular), and it is possible to continue north to Kincardine (some 13 km) along the shore road with good birding all the way.

At **Kincardine** there are two areas of interest in town. The town's main street is Queen, which is 1.5 km west of the highway, and parallels it. For the lagoons, go to Queen Street and turn left (south). Queen ends at a cemetery gate. Turn left here on Bruce Avenue and drive 0.8 km to the dump entrance on the right. The lagoons are behind and west of the dump. The town has erected a waterfowl-viewing structure here.

Returning to Queen Street, drive north 2 km to Lambton Street, and turn left at the light. The road leads down (0.5 km) to *MacPherson Park* on the shore, which provides views of the river mouth to the south and of the lake. Scan for duck and gulls: duck often hang around the river mouth when adjacent areas are frozen.

Some 15 km east of Kincardine is *Greenock Swamp*, the largest swamp in southwestern Ontario, along the Teeswater River. Highway 9 crosses the southern ends of this west of the Highway 4 intersection, but to visit a much richer area go to the junction of these two highways (25.6 km east of Highway 21) and turn north on Regional Road 20. Drive to the third sideroad (6.2 km) marked to Chepstow, and turn west. The most extensive areas of swamp are about 2 km ahead. There are trails here giving foot access both north and south. A good mix of typical woodland birds can be found, and Golden-winged and Cerulean Warblers have occurred.

Now continue north on Highway 21. The fields in this section of Grey County can yield huge flocks of Horned Larks, longspurs, and Snow Buntings in early spring and later fall, and in winter Rough-legged Hawks and Snowy Owls can be found. Western Meadowlarks should be listened for in the breeding season. **Tiverton** is the next community, and from here County Road 15 runs west to Inverhuron, with the *Bruce Nuclear Power Station* to the north. At the time of writing the future of this installation is in some doubt, but for the foreseeable future it will continue to discharge warm water into Lake Huron. These outflows concentrate birds in winter, with duck and gulls (including Glaucous and Great Black-backed), and small numbers of Bald Eagles. The best viewing is from Baie du Dore, just north of the plant.

MacGregor Point Provincial Park is an excellent birding area on the shoreline about 20 km north of Tiverton, and just south of Port Elgin. Offshore here large concentrations of loons, Horned and Red-necked Grebes, and other waterbirds occur in autumn migration. The park itself has the usual mixed woodland birds (120 species nest; if the woodcock don't keep you awake in the campgrounds, the Whip-poor-wills will!). Small lakes and wetlands, sections of sandy shoreline, and patches of open country provide other habitats. Least Bittern has occurred: so has American White Pelican, but I do not recommend spending much time searching for one. The sideroads which form the eastern and southern boundaries also pass through an excellent mix of habitats to the south of the park.

The waterfront at **Port Elgin** can be good for waterbirds and again it is worthwhile to follow the shore road north to Southampton, some 8 km north. This road hugs the shoreline, and after about 2.5 km curves around Miramichi Bay, then passes a promontory (McNab Point) before touching the shoreline of another small bay appropriately called *Horseshoe Bay*. This can be good for shorebirds in August and September.

At **Southampton** there is Chantry Island just offshore. This is a Canadian Wildlife Service sanctuary, with nesting cormorants, gulls, and Great Blue Herons, Black-crowned Night-Herons, and Great Egrets. Hundreds of duck gather here in summer.

THE BRUCE PENINSULA

At Southampton Highway 21 turns east, to cross the base of the Bruce Peninsula to Owen Sound. Persons driving north on Highways 6 and 10 (they run together at this point) reach the Bruce by passing through **Owen Sound**, unless they choose to bypass the town using County Road 18. As the main community serving this region it has many services that are hard to find on the thinly populated peninsula. It is not particularly noteworthy for birds, but there are two pleasant parks, one on the harbour, and one, Harrison Park, on the Sydenham River, and a couple of conservation areas adjacent on the escarpment.

From Owen Sound the easiest access to the Bruce is via Highway 70, which turns off Highway 6 some 5 km west of town, at the intersection of County Road 18. Highway 70 joins 6 about 15 km northwest, at **Hepworth**; from here you can turn north and head straight up to Tobermory, some 100 km distant. Many persons do, but those who do so often wonder what it is that is so exciting about the Bruce Peninsula! This account will follow the west shoreline north and return along Georgian Bay on the east. The route is very time-consuming even without birding. It follows gravel roads which are often quite rough and uneven, and it wanders around a great deal. Note also that service stations are scarce or absent along the way. It should be emphasized that good birding in this area is everywhere; specific sites are detailed below, but a great deal of the coverage is a matter of driving along slowly with one's eyes and ears open!

The Bruce Peninsula is a gently sloping limestone plateau, with many small lakes and a long indented shoreline. This is precipitous on the east (Georgian Bay) side and shelves slowly on the Lake Huron side, where a chain of offshore islands has breeding duck, gull and tern colonies, and a couple of heronries. The sheltered inner waters are attractive to waterfowl both breeding and in migration, when they are joined by Horned and Red-necked Grebes. Many of these birds will linger until the January freeze-up. When the lake levels are low – a cyclic phenomenon occurring over several years – fine shorebird habitat develops. The principal nesting species are Ring-billed and Herring Gulls and Caspian and Common Terns, along with most of the waterfowl listed for the breeding season in the south.

Inland drainage is poor, and open grassy fens and dense white cedar bogs are a feature particularly of the west shoreline, alternating with lines of sand dunes. Extensive summer

MAP 8   Grey County and the Bruce Peninsula

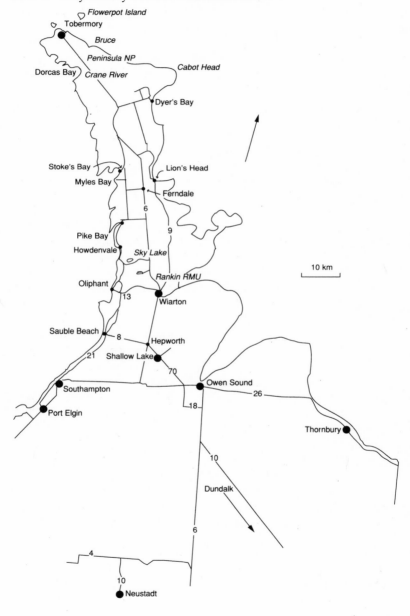

Flowerpot Island
Tobermory
Bruce
Peninsula NP
Dorcas Bay   Crane River
Cabot Head
Dyer's Bay
Stoke's Bay
Lion's Head
Myles Bay
Ferndale
6
9
Pike Bay
Howdenvale   Sky Lake
Oliphant   Rankin RMU
13   Wiarton
10 km
Sauble Beach   8
21   Hepworth
Shallow Lake
70
Owen Sound
Southampton   18   26
Port Elgin
Thornbury
10
Dundalk
6
4
10
Neustadt

cottage development is the other feature, and most of this shore-line is now lined with summer homes. The mix of heavy second-growth woodland, cedar bog, and marginal farmland on the peninsula yields a variety of habitats and an abundance of both forest and open country birds. Most of the species typical of old fields can be found, and hawks and Turkey Vultures are widespread.

County Road 21 turns left off Highway 21 just outside **Southampton** (immediately over the Saugeen River), and then parallels the shoreline northwards. It is not as good a birding road as it looks on the map, and it is best to head straight north to **Sauble Beach**. This is the most heavily used beach on the Bruce, and is usually approached from the east via County Road 8, which crosses the peninsula from the intersection of High-ways 6 and 70. The road servicing the beach parallels County Road 21 to the west, and has numerous parking areas along it. However, in the warmer weather it is best avoided, and gener-ally the beach is much too disturbed for many waterbirds to linger. In quieter periods the Sauble River outlet at the far north end should be checked over. Gulls and Caspian Terns loiter here.

Walker's Woods, a fine woodlot owned by the Nature Con-servancy, is on the west side of County Road 21, a short dis-tance north of the County Road 8 intersection; access points keep changing, but some can be reached by passing the woods on the left, and then taking the first left. Continue bearing left through the cottage development until the street turns west to head to the lake. At this point the woods are on the left. They are most noteworthy for their fine flora, but there is a good assortment of warblers, including Pine Warbler, and the Olive-sided Flycatchers seem to spend as much time around the adja-cent cottages as in the woods themselves.

Now continue north on County Road 21. The sideroad on the left at *Sauble Falls Provincial Park* leads to the north end of Sauble Beach and the mouth of the Saugeen. All the woods and open areas on both sides of the road can yield good birding. At **Oliphant** the county road turns right to head out to Wiarton. Turn left, and drive to the beach, where the road continues north and south along the shoreline. The waterfront here has been consistently productive of waterbirds. The shoreline shelves very slowly, and low water levels can expose huge areas of beach. In such periods Piping Plover has bred and large numbers of migrant shorebirds, particularly Red Knot, can occur, with Snow Geese in late autumn. The common warblers of the Bruce can be found along the shore roads behind the cottages.

The northbound road tends to be the best: it winds along for 2.7 km, passing shallow fens and woodland interspersed among the cottages on the right, and the shallow rocky shore on the left. At one point a boardwalk winds across one of the fens, and gives closer access to the woodlands at the back, which attract a good mix of breeding warblers. Finally the main road turns east to Red Bay and the shore road continues a further 1 km. Continue on this road, as the waters off this section of beach are less disturbed and often have loitering waterfowl. Common Snipe occur in the marshes.

Returning to the Red Bay road, turn east and continue east on the sideroad past the point where the Red Bay road turns north again (about 1.6 km; note this intersection, as you will return to it). The eastbound sideroad crosses a marsh at the north side of Spry Lake. Both Marsh Wren and Sedge Wrens occur in summer, with Sora and Virginia Rails, and Common Loons can be seen on the lake itself. This road joins County Road 13, leading to Wiarton, 1.9 km farther on. There is good birding all along this stretch.

At the county road, a right turn leads back to Oliphant, and the first section of road (just past the curve) is good after dark for woodcock. Barred Owls can sometimes be seen from the road here. A left on the county road leads to the *Rankin River* crossing, on the north 1.2 km farther on. There is parking here, and waterfowl can be seen, particularly Wood Ducks, as well as Green Herons, rails, Black Terns, and nesting Ospreys on Boat Lake to the south. This is one point of entry to the Rankin River canoe route.

Now return to the Red Bay road intersection described above and continue north. After about 2 km the road passes through rich wet woodlands, jogging right and then left again. The sideroads to Evergreen and Wildwood Lodges and to Little Red Bay ahead are both good for birding (the former should be walked only). Northern Saw-whet Owls have nested in the coniferous forests here, and all of the regular warblers –

redstart, and Nashville, Yellow-rumped, Black-throated Green, Blackburnian, Black-and-white, and Canada Warblers and Ovenbird are the most usual – are present, together with the other mixed forest species, including Olive-sided Flycatcher.

At some 2.5 km from the jog the surfaced Sky Lake road enters the Red Bay road from the right. The Sky Lake road goes east to Mar on Highway 6, running some 2.4 km east along the south side of *Sky Lake*. The marshes here are very disturbed, but at dawn can yield Pied-billed Grebes, duck, Black Terns, and Marsh Wrens. The bridge at the west end is another point of entry (southbound) to the Rankin River canoe route, which leads through Isaac and Boat lakes to terminate at Sauble Falls, 18 km to the south. The route passes through extensive marshland and the wooded swamps south of Boat Lake. It is excellent for breeding birds, and waterfowl concentrate on the lakes in spring and fall.

Two km north of the point at which the Sky Lake road joins the Red Bay road is Red Bay Lodge, set amid fine hardwoods, and a sideroad opposite leads to the beach. The woodlot north of this sideroad has a good mix of nesting birds, including Northern Parulas (walk the road to its end). The sideroad to Petrel Point is on the west 1.1 km farther north on the main road. The Federation of Ontario Naturalists has a reserve here (mainly for flora) on both sides of the road. Olive-sided Flycatchers have nested and snipe are common. Listen for Barred Owl at night.

After about 4.5 km from the Sky Lake intersection the Red Bay Road ends at a T-intersection. This is **Howdenvale**; turn left and follow the winding shore road along some 5 km to **Pike Bay**. The first section of this road, particularly around the *St Jean Point Conservation Area*, can be good for waterfowl.

At Pike Bay the main road turns east away from the shoreline, and ends at another T-intersection. Turn left here, and continue north. The road now passes through unimproved pasture interspersed with woodland and boggy areas. Watch for Eastern Bluebirds, Black-billed Cuckoos, and other edge and old field species. At approximately 9.5 km from the turn the Ferndale road crosses, with access east to Highway 6, and 1.5 km north of here a sideroad runs west to **Myles Bay** and *Black*

Creek Provincial Park Reserve. This is on the north shore of the bay; drive to a sand beach (roughly 2 km from the road) and park. A trail leads into the woodlands behind the beach, and a fine assortment of breeding birds can be found here, including the warblers mentioned above for the Little Red Bay area, together with Northern Parula.

The shallows behind the islands in the bay here, and in Stoke's Bay to the north, concentrate waterfowl during migration. Later fall brings large rafts of all three species of scoter. The south entrance to **Stoke's Bay** is a little over 2 km north of the Myles Bay turnoff, and the road meanders around the community, playing hide and seek with the water. Bear left on leaving the village, taking the north access road, to continue north.

About 2 km north of here the road loops around Ira Lake, giving some rather unsatisfactory views of the water. Black Terns nest, and other waterbirds can sometimes be seen. The gravel road continues then north another 5 km before entering Highway 6 south of **Miller Lake**.

The *Crane River picnic area* on Highway 6 about 6 km north of Miller Lake can be interesting; Pileated Woodpeckers and Mourning Warblers are usually present, and the blackflies are exceptionally vigorous. Farther north again (some 8 km) is the entrance to the *Cyprus Lake area of the Bruce Peninsula National Park* (there is an entrance fee), which lies well east of the highway. It is set amid heavy coniferous woodlands, and the bird life has a more northern character. Hermit and Swainson's Thrushes, Solitary Vireo, and Dark-eyed Junco are some of the species that occur more commonly in this north end of the peninsula.

A little farther north on the west of Highway 6 is the **Dorcas Bay** road, which runs southwest to the bay. The Federation of Ontario Naturalists has a reserve that occupies most of the land to the north of the road (its main interest is the fascinating flora), although there is a little township park at the northeast end of the bay. Again, the bird life is quite northern, and Cape May Warblers have been recorded in summer. Pine Warblers can be found in the pines of the township park and Olive-sided Flycatchers occur over the bogs. There is not usually much in the way of waterbirds, although snipe are very common and terns (Caspian and Common) usually loiter on the beach. Massassauga rattlesnakes are as numerous here as anywhere on the Bruce: listen for their buzzing, insect-like rattle.

The town of **Tobermory** is at the end of the highway about 11 km farther north, and is the southern terminal for the Tobermory-Manitoulin Island ferry. The small headlands around town concentrate migrant raptors and landbirds. There are no specific locations; you should drive to the ends of various roads east and west of the end of Highway 6, although the fields behind the township offices are a good place for hawk watching. In winter the town feeders collect out-of-range stragglers.

Flowerpot Island is part of Fathom Five National Marine Park, and lies some 4 km offshore from Tobermory. There are a couple of small excursion boats that will take visitors over to the island in good weather, and it is also possible to camp here. The island is uninhabited except for the lighthouse-keepers, and in character it is much like the mainland. However, there is a small bog along the west shoreline that seems to be a good place for lingering migrants. Blackpoll Warblers have summered here on occasion.

Now return on Highway 6 to the Dyer's Bay road. This is east off the highway about 4 km south of the Crane River picnic area, at the point the highway angles sharply right. The road is hardtopped for most of its 10 km or so, and is good for birding throughout its length. Watch the field areas for Eastern Bluebirds, and at some 7.5 km from the highway is an area of wet fields that, depending on water levels, can yield duck, rails, and shorebirds. Finally the road turns sharply right. The sideroad to the left at this point does not really go anywhere – simply north to the next sideroad, then west, and then south again, about 6 km in all. This block is worth the detour, however, particularly the northbound leg. It has recently been one of the most productive areas on the peninsula for Golden-winged Warblers, and Clay-colored and Grasshopper sparrows. Sandhill Cranes nest in the remote lakes of this area.

Continuing into **Dyer's Bay**, the crystal-clear waters offshore have small flocks of Common Loons in summer, but in migration periods (April/early May and October/November), hundreds of Red-necked Grebes gather, together with much larger numbers of loons, and numbers of Oldsquaws and scoters can be seen moving up the bay. North of the hamlet the shore road runs under the escarpment face at the very edge of the water for about 10 km to *Cabot Head lighthouse* and Wingfield Basin. This is an area of heavy woodlands, marsh, and open land that may well be the best area for migrants on the peninsula. Because of the configuration of the peninsula this represents its northeastern extremity, and hence acts as a trap for landbirds. Excellent spring hawk flights occur, with best viewing from the lighthouse, and from the fields east of the hamlet.

At this point the traveller has a choice: Those with little time should return to the highway, as the next areas are along it. Alternatively, about 4 km back along the Dyer's Bay road is a crossroads (Brinkman's Corners), where a left turn will lead south along gravel roads, mainly through heavy woodlands, to Cape Chin, and then via a winding road down into Whip-poor-will Bay, and thence to Lion's Head. Partly because it is not very busy, this is a good birding road throughout its over 20 km length, with swampy areas and old fields alternating with mixed forest.

Driving south on the highway two large prairie-like areas of flat open fields break the typical Bruce pattern of forest and rough pasture. The first is around the Clarke's (or Monument) Corners intersection, and the second, and much the largest, is around **Ferndale**. Using the backroad, they are respectively just southeast of Cape Chin, and through Lion's Head along the road out to the highway. The fields in both these areas should be covered. This country is good for Brewer's Blackbirds, possible Western Meadowlark, Upland Sandpipers, and other field species in summer. Eastern Bluebirds and Grasshopper Sparrows should be looked for in the old fields. Sandhill Cranes may be found feeding in areas back from the highway, and migrant shorebirds often loiter on the arable land, particularly on any wet areas.

At present the blackbirds tend to be along the sideroads north and (mainly) south of the **Lion's Head** road (County Road 9). The gravel concession roads both east and west of the highway should be covered, and the first north-south gravel roads on either side. Finding blackbirds in flat open fields might seem to be simplicity itself, but they are easy to miss. At any given time most of the birds in the colony may be absent, and the one or two remaining out of sight in the grass.

County Road 9 joins the main north-south sideroad from Lion's Head, and then turns south. It then continues all the way to Colpoy's Bay and is a delightful road throughout, passing tall mixed woodlands and increasingly prosperous farmland. It usually yields interesting birding, without having areas of exceptional note.

Continuing down Highway 6, the *Rankin Resources Management Unit* is a huge and diverse area including Sky and Isaac lakes. Albemarle Sideroad 25, 2 km south of Mar (the Sky Lake turnoff), runs east to Isaac Lake through the waterfowl management unit. Look for marshbirds as the road crosses the marsh at the bottom of the hill and waterfowl and shorebirds both inside and outside the feeding pens. Wilson's Phalaropes have occurred here, and one of the more reliable areas for Sedge Wrens (an oxymoron in itself) on the Bruce is in the brushy wetland at the foot of the hill. The lake (2.8 km) tends to be less productive but has breeding Pied-billed Grebes and Black Terns.

The attractive town of **Wiarton** bills itself as the gateway to the Bruce Peninsula. Turkey Vultures and ravens now nest on the cliffs north of town; for the latter, this approaches the southern limit of their range, which ten years ago was near Tobermorey. The *sewage lagoons* here are usually worth visiting. From the light at William Street in the centre of town drive south up the hill on the highway 0.9 km to Elm Street. Turn east and drive 0.6 km; the lagoon road is on the right just past the cemetery. Wiarton airport is farther east on Elm and might be worth checking for field species. Dickcissels (on their erratic forays into the province) have occurred here more frequently than elsewhere.

Shallow Lake is farther south again, halfway along Highway 70. *McNab Lake Conservation Area* is some 1.9 km along the sideroad running northeast from the centre of the village. There are wetlands along the road en route, and the entrance to the area is a poorly marked gravel road on the left. This leads down to the lake past some tall hardwoods where Yellow-throated Vireos and Cerulean Warblers occur (and likely nest). The wetland areas are good for Least Bittern and rails, and Sandhill Cranes occur.

OTHER SEWAGE LAGOONS IN THE LAKE HURON AREA

Exeter seems to have been the best of this group. Note that the communities of Exeter, Hensall, Zurich, and Seaforth, together with Mitchell in chapter 8, are all relatively close together, in the south of Huron County.

Dundalk – This village is off Highway 10 about halfway between Toronto and Owen Sound. The sewage lagoons are south on the first sideroad west of town. Turn west off Highway 10 on to County Road 9, drive 2.5 km to Proton Range SWT Sideroad 2, and turn south; the lagoons are 1.5 km on the left.

Exeter – Exeter is some 21 km east of the Huron shore just south of Highway 83, and northeast of the Pinery. The sewage lagoons are west of town south off Highway 83. From the intersection with Highway 4, drive 2 km west to Stephen Concession 2-3. The lagoons are on the left 0.8 km south on this road. They have been one of the more productive lagoons in this part of the region.

Hensall – This village is 6 km north of Exeter on Highway 4. The lagoons are west off Highway 4 south of town. From the junction of Highways 4 and 84 drive south 2 km to Hay Sideroad 15-16, and turn right. The lagoons are 0.7 km along on the right, just over the railway, and easily visible from both the tracks and the road.

Neustadt – Neustadt is relatively remote, some 10 km southeast of Walkerton and Hanover on county roads. For the lagoon, turn left as County Road 10 southbound jogs right. The lagoon is over a field on the left beside the railroad tracks at 0.5 km, with the driveway 0.3 km farther on.

Seaforth – This town is on Highway 8, northeast of Hensall. For the sewage lagoons drive north on Highway 8 from the main intersection in town with County Road 12. Go 2.5 km to Tuckersmith Sideroad 15. Turn left and drive 0.6 km past a cairn on the right, and turn right on a gravel road crossing the railroad tracks. The lagoons are just beyond on the left, and visible both from the tracks and the road.

Thornbury – This is the only town I know of with a lagoon along the Grey County shore of Georgian Bay. The sewage lagoon is 1 km east of the main intersection of Bruce Street and Highway 26. The short lane to the lagoon goes south off the highway opposite Grey Street.

Zurich – Zurich is some 10 km west of Hensall on Highway 84. The lagoons are at the back of the playing fields at the southeast end of town. Turn south on East Street.

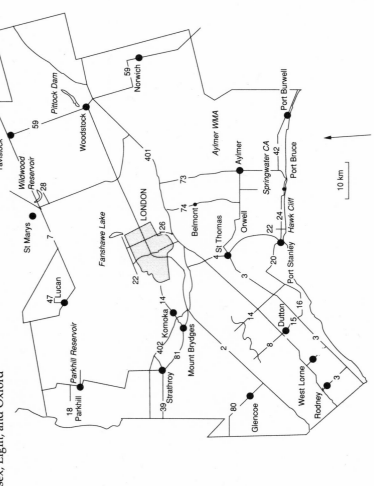

MAP 9   Middlesex, Elgin, and Oxford

6 London, Hawk Cliff, and Area

Middlesex, Elgin, and Oxford Counties

London
Hawk Cliff
Aylmer
Reservoirs in Middlesex and Oxford counties
Additional sewage lagoons in the London area
Areas along Highway 401

These counties are much more diverse than those to the west. Although heavily agricultural, the farming is more varied and areas of poor soils and of woodland more common. The countryside along the lake is mainly flat and becomes very sandy in the east, resembling the areas of the adjacent Haldimand-Norfolk Region. Elsewhere the landscape is rolling, yielding bucolic vistas of contented cattle and prosperous farms.

The city of London, with some 300,000 population, is the major centre for all of southwestern Ontario. Its airport is often the most convenient access point for the areas to the west: Pelee is roughly a two-hour drive away on Highway 401, which skirts the southern edge of the city. London is also an excellent birding city, but apart from Hawk Cliff, the counties lack birding destinations of the quality of those to the east and west. The winter visitor to the London area will be under no illusions about being in Canada. This is the snow belt, downwind from Lake Huron. The major storms usually hit southern Ontario with east to southeast winds, and London gets snow; when the storms are past the winds swing into the northwest and London gets more snow! Hence winter departs much more slowly than farther west, and we have driven through a London fall blizzard to visit a sunny and mild Sarnia.

LONDON

The city has a number of fine parks with walking trails, especially along the banks of the Thames River. These are good for migrants and the commoner resident landbirds. Springbank Park is north of Commissioners Road and Springbank Drive in the west of the city, and Gibbons Park is west of Richmond Street and north of Oxford Street in the north.

Fanshawe Lake, northeast of London, is a large Conservation Authority lake. This, with the Strathroy sewage lagoons to the west, are outstanding locations for migrant waterbirds. Waterfowl and gulls often gather in numbers on the waters here, and the area has produced many interesting records, from Forster's Terns in the early spring to Snow Goose flocks in the fall. From the intersection of Highbury Avenue northbound (the continuation of Highway 126; Highway 401, exit 189) and Highway 22, turn right on Fanshawe Park Road, which is County Road 31. Drive 2.4 km east to Clarke Road. Turn right for the dam area, which is in the grounds of the Conservation Area 2 km south, and which gives access to extensive parkland along the west shoreline. Alternatively, and preferably, turn north and drive 1.4 km to Concession 6, which dead-ends 1 km to the east. Park and walk straight ahead and to the left around the crest of the bank. There are excellent views of the lake, and landbirds along the fields and woods.

The *Westminster Ponds* are two groups of small lakes surrounded by woodland in the south of London. The Walker Ponds are northeast of the Wellington-Southdale roads intersection: The Pond Mills area is farther east near Highway 126. These sheltered ponds attract Pied-billed Grebes and pond duck, and the woodlands and old field areas landbirds, especially in migration. Collectively they form one of the better birding areas in London. One point of access to the Walker Ponds is from the back of the parking lot of the visitor centre 0.5 km north on Wellington Street (Highway 401 exit 186) from its intersection with Southdale Road East. There are other less accessible entry points along Southdale. For Pond Mills, follow Southdale Road east to the Pond Mills Road intersection. Bear left here, and the ponds themselves are on the right. This area is much smaller, and parking is quite limited.

Dorchester Swamp, east of London, is the large area of wet woodland around the intersection of Highways 73 and 401 (exit 203). It is privately owned and access is by permission of the local landowners. However, you can do some productive birding from the roads around the area themselves, and species with more northern affinities occur.

In season the Komoka area is one of the more interesting birding locales west of London. It is accessible via Commissioner's Road from London itself, or from Highway 402 exit 82. From the latter, head east 1.1 km on County Road 14 to the Townline of Lobo and Caradoc Townships. Turn left, and the *Komoka Swamp* lies 1.5 km north, starting just past the campgrounds, with a trail on the left 0.2 km farther on. The area is a wet woodland, with a good variety of woodland species; Blue-winged Warbler and chats have occurred.

Farther along (1.6 km) County Road 14 passes *flooded gravel pits* along both sides of the road. They extend through Komoka for some 2 km in all. These are excellent for migrant waterfowl, especially in early spring. Species to expect include Ring-necked Duck and Hooded Mergansers, as well as dabbling duck and the occasional Common Loon.

Parts of these areas are private property and although the public is tolerated in some areas, as usual, discretion should be used and permission sought if there is any question. Much is readily visible from the road itself.

County Road 14 westbound from Highway 402 exit 82, leads to Highway 81 at **Mount Brydges**, and by continuing westbound on it one arrives at **Strathroy** (402 exit 69; or 65 eastbound). The *sewage lagoons* here, which are west of town, have been the source of many noteworthy records. From the 402 exit 69, bear west towards Strathroy on County Road 39, which becomes Metcalfe Street in town. This street forms a main intersection in town at Highway 81 (Caradoc Street), and after crossing, curves right to become Albert Street. Drive west on Albert Street 2.7 km from the light at Caradoc to a sideroad on the left, with a small sign 'Waterfowl Viewing Area 1 km.' Go south 1 km and the lagoons are on the left. There is a parking lot.

Strathroy rarely disappoints in migration periods, perhaps because it is in a line with the Lake Huron shoreline and at least some birds seem to cross southwards at this point in fall. Scoters and Ruddy Ducks are regular among a wide variety of waterfowl; shorebirds, including phalaropes, are regular along the shorelines and abound in periods of drawdown; the ponds have had more than their share of Eared Grebes, and mixed gull flocks drift in and out. There are often hawks sitting along the treeline at the back, and bobwhites have been recorded.

HAWK CLIFF

Hawk Cliff is the best-known location in the province for viewing fall hawk migration and is a major hawk-banding site. It is also a good place to view other migrants (both landbirds and waterbirds) moving along the shore of Lake Erie.

The area is some 25 km south of London via Highway 4, which passes through the town of St Thomas and ends at Lake Erie in the fishing village of **Port Stanley**. To reach Hawk Cliff from here, at the point Highway 4 turns off Main Street in town to cross the river, turn east and drive diagonally up the hill on Joseph Street. This is County Road 23, and it turns left at the top of the hill to lead (1.6 km) to the intersection on the right with County Road 24. (Note that if you continue straight ahead you end up on Highway 4 again: coming south on the highway you can bypass town by turning at this point, but it is easy to miss.) Turn east on County Road 24 and drive 3 km, where the Hawk Cliff road is well marked on the south opposite the intersection of County Road 22 going north. The road dead-ends at the lake, and in hawk migration times is usually lined with parked cars. Outside the migration season the road may be barred (there is currently some uncertainty about future access here when the banding station is not manned: inquire locally).

The same hawk species occur as at Holiday Beach, although the totals seen are usually lower. The birds here are often easier to see, and as the area is closer to the large population centres in Ontario it has become known as the premier locale for watching fall hawk flights. There is usually someone available on weekends to assist with identification. There is limited accommodation in Port Stanley, but much in St Thomas, including camping at the Dalewood Conservation Area there. General information on the fall flights is given under Holiday Beach. Cooper's Hawks and Peregrine Falcons, both of which tend to move through Point Pelee, are often in better numbers at this station than at Holiday Beach, although the differences are not great. The totals of other species are sometimes much lower;

however, these differences may be between seven thousand and twenty thousand birds in a day, and even seven thousand Broad-wingeds are a spectacular sight!

Port Stanley has several other points of interest. If you drive to town on Highway 4 you can continue (crossing the river and bearing left) to the point where the highway turns right at the beach on the west of town. Drive straight ahead to the point the street ends. Cover the beach and the harbour from here. Large flocks of gulls loiter on the beach, and there is always the possibility of a rarity among the innumerable Ring-billeds. To reach the east side of the harbour return on Highway 4, crossing the river again, and turn right on Main Street, which ends 0.5 km ahead at a loading terminal. Turn left just before this and drive ahead to Little Beach, where you can view the lake east of the harbour.

For Port Stanley *sewage lagoons*, follow Highway 4 to the river bridge, drive west across it, and turn north on County Road 20. At 1.4 km is the intersection of County Road 21 on the right. Turn left here on a road winding up a hill and go 1.1 km to a gravel road on the right. Turn here again and the lagoons are 1.1 km on the left. They usually reward a visit with a good mixture of waterfowl, and rarities have been seen regularly.

If you plan to continue west along Lake Erie you can do so on good roads by returning to County Road 20 again and continuing 10.5 km north and west to the village of Fingal. Here a left turn on County Road 16 leads 3.1 km west to *Fingal Wildlife Management Area*. It is managed for bobwhites among other species, and is scarcely worth a special trip to visit, but County Road 16 eventually loops up to Highway 3 some 40 km east of Rondeau.

There are a couple of pleasant town parks in **St Thomas**, on the way down to Port Stanley. Pinafore Park can be reached by travelling on Highway 4 south from the junction of Talbot Street, continuing 2.6 km to a railroad crossing and turning left on Elm Street. Drive 0.6 km to the park on the right, which has a pond and natural woodlands. Waterworks Park and Dalewood Conservation Area is north of town. From the Highway 3 bypass take the First Avenue exit north 0.5 km to South Edgeware Road, and turn left. This road leads west 1.2 km down the hill into the park, which has a fair-sized water impoundment and natural woodlands. The Conservation Area is farther north on Dalewood Drive.

Note that County Road 24 continues east from Hawk Cliff and forms a pleasant route to Long Point. **Port Bruce** is the next community, with a small harbour, a beach and access to Aylmer via Highway 73. The lakeshore road then continues east as County Road 42, which passes through **Port Burwell,** where there is a stream and another small harbour, and finally crosses Highway 59 at the base of Long Point.

AYLMER

This town is some 15 km east of St Thomas on Highway 3, and 23 km south of Highway 401 exit 203 on Highway 73. There are three noteworthy areas around Aylmer. *Springwater Conservation Area* is to the west. From the intersection of Highways 73 and 3 drive west 4.2 km to **Orwell** and turn south. The area is 2.8 km down this road, and the fine Carolinian woodlot is just 0.5 km east on the sideroad there. This has been one of Ontario's more reliable stations for Hooded Warbler.

Another key Aylmer location is the *sewage lagoons.* Drive west from the town as above, but go 2.2 km to the first sideroad north. This is easy to miss. It is unmarked, just past Roger's Sideroad on the south (which is marked) and immediately on the other side of a green barn on the corner. The lagoons are on the left 1.1 km up this road. Controlled shooting occurs there, but at other times they have been most productive.

The *Aylmer Wildlife Management Area* is northeast of town, and has large feeding ponds. These are noteworthy for Tundra Swans (to fifteen thousand birds) and other waterfowl in the second half of March, and large numbers (more than ten thousand) of duck in fall. Shorebirds also can occur. To reach the area, drive north from town on Highway 73 to the first concession road on the east. This is County Road 32, signposted to the Ontario Police College. Go east one concession (2.2 km), turn north and drive 0.9 km to the entrance, which is just before the college (in fact, it appears to be part of the complex there). There are observation platforms overlooking the ponds.

RESERVOIRS IN MIDDLESEX AND OXFORD COUNTIES

Parkhill Reservoir is just northeast of the town of Parkhill, which is on Highway 81, 25 km south of Grand Bend and the Pinery. Good viewpoints of the water area start 2.2 km north of the junction of Highways 7 and 81. The entrance to the Conservation Area itself is to the east. Just before the first viewpoint, County Road 18 intersects from the west. If you turn here the woodlands of Parkhill Creek are just to your right at 0.5 km, and 1 km from the intersection the *sewage lagoon* gate is on the right. There usually a few ducks present on the lagoon. I have never found much on my infrequent visits to Parkhill, but it yields periodic rarity records. Waterfowl concentrations are to be expected in migration, and it certainly could be worth visiting on the way to Grand Bend.

There is less ambiguity about *Wildwood Reservoir*, which is mostly in Oxford County near the town of **St Marys**. It attracts large numbers of Mallards and American Black Duck in spring and particularly in later fall (over fifteen thousand in October–November), and other species should be looked for in these flocks. This reservoir is on Highway 7 some 14 km southwest of Stratford and just 2 km east of the junction with Highway 19 southbound. The west end (the widest and most interesting for waterfowl) is readily visible from the highway, which is the dam causeway, and sideroads to the east and south lead to other viewing points. East 1 km from the dam itself and opposite Perth Road 28 is the entrance to the Conservation Area, and 0.9 km along this road is the entrance to the *Dr R.S. Murray Forest*, a large area of mixed woodlands and pine plantations on the east shore of the lake. This tract can be good for landbirds.

The *Pittock Dam and Conservation Area* is east off Highway 59 just north of **Woodstock**, itself just north of Highway 401 exit 232. The Pittock Park Road is the second road on the east after crossing the bridge over the railroad. The park gate is 1.5 km ahead, and the north bank parkland provides excellent views of the large lake. Like the other reservoirs, it is heavily used for recreation, but waterfowl gather in spring and autumn, mainly Mallards, American Black Duck, and Common

Merganser. For some reason this lake seems less appealing to birds than does Wildwood.

ADDITIONAL SEWAGE LAGOONS IN THE LONDON AREA

Belmont – This village is on Highway 74 southeast of London, and some 8 km south of Highway 401 exit 195. The lagoon is 0.8 km south on Highway 74, from its intersection at the south end of town with County Road 34. Turn right on Yarmouth Concession 15 and drive 1 km west to the lagoon gates over the tracks.

Dutton – The town is west of London on County Road 15 just south of the Highway 401 exit 149. For the sewage lagoon, turn left on Shakleton just after crossing the tracks northbound on County Road 15 (County Road 13 eastbound is almost opposite Shakleton). Drive 0.4 km to the end of the street; the lagoon runs ahead beside the tracks.

Glencoe – Glencoe is in the west corner of Middlesex County, on Highway 80 north of Highway 2. The sewage lagoons are south on Highway 80; from the tracks across the road at the south side of town, drive 2.4 km to Ekfrid 2nd Range N road, and then turn left. The lagoons are 1 km along on the north.

Lucan – This town is east of Parkhill on Highway 4. To reach the lagoons, turn right on County Road 13, which is the first street on the right after crossing the tracks on Highway 4 westbound entering town. Drive 0.4 km, then turn left on County Road 47, the Fourth Concession. Continue 1.5 km to the point County Road 47 turns right, and turn left. The lagoons are on the left 1.1 km ahead.

Norwich – Norwich is south of Woodstock on Highway 59. The drive to the sewage lagoon is to the east of Highway 59 before the railroad tracks cross the highway, 1 km south of its intersection with Main Street.

Rodney – The town is just south of Highway 401 exit 129 on County Road 3. For the sewage lagoons, which have yielded some interesting reports (a Fulvous Whistling-Duck turned up one spring), drive south on County Road 3 1 km from the point it crosses the railroad in town, to County Road 2 (Back Street) on the left. Turn, and the lagoon gates are 0.7 km along on the north.

Tavistock – Tavistock is 29 km north of Woodstock on Highway 59. The sewage lagoons have yielded some good birds. They are at the back of the playing field, but perhaps an easier route to them is to drive north on Highway 59 to Hope Street East in the centre of town (this is County Road 24). Turn right on Hope Street and drive 0.4 km to Wellington Street. Right again, and the lagoons are clearly visible (and accessible) across the tracks ahead at the point this street (0.2 km) turns left.

West Lorne – This is another in the series of small towns just south of Highway 401, in this case off exit 137 on Highway 76. The sewage lagoons, which have been productive, are 2.7 km south on Highway 76 from its intersection with Elgin Road 2 in town. Turn west on Aldborough Concession 11 and drive 0.6 km; the lagoon drive is on the right.

AREAS ALONG HIGHWAY 401

(*Note that areas along Highway 402 are covered in the previous chapter.*)
In the west of the region the lagoons at Rodney, West Lorne, and Dutton are all readily accessible from the highway. One interesting spot on the highway itself is visible from the service centre eastbound between the West Lorne and Dutton interchanges. Just west of the picnic area are some ponds which occasionally have yielded a few ducks and shorebirds, and there is a small sewage lagoon over the fields to the south. The corresponding area westbound has its picnic area in a pleasant wooded area to the rear, and its small sewage lagoon is located just north of the westbound exit ramp. The woodlots along this stretch of road usually have hawks around them at all seasons; these will mainly be Red-taileds, but other species are possible in migration and in winter.

Northern Bobwhites have one of their centres of abundance in this southwestern section of the region. One favoured location is about 9 km north of the highway, in the area between Highway 2 on the north, the Thames River on the south, and

County Roads 8 (the Dutton exit 149) and 14 (the Iona exit 157; it becomes County Road 9 in Middlesex County). The roads closest to the Thames are best.

Farther east the Westminster ponds at London are fairly close to the highway, but immersed in the city traffic, and we have not usually found the detour to the Pittock reservoir worth the time lost. We have not seen much through Dorchester Swamp without leaving the highway; however, the crossroads both north and south of exit 203 might be worth a short detour during the song season.

The picnic site in the service area in the westbound lanes between Woodstock and Ingersoll is pleasant, but less productive of birds since it was extended westwards. The eastbound area lacks habitat: wait until the next service area near Cambridge, which is excellent.

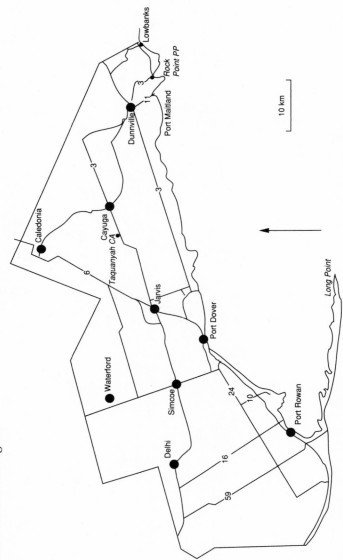

MAP 10   Haldimand-Norfolk Region

7 The Long Point Area

Haldimand-Norfolk Region

Long Point
Areas west of Long Point
The shoreline east of Long Point
Townsend sewage lagoons
The Grand River and Dunnville area
Other areas in the Haldimand-Norfolk Region

The Lake Erie shoreline east from Elgin County is bounded by a broad sandy plain which occupies the western half of Haldimand-Norfolk Regional Municipality. The agricultural lands here are subject to serious wind erosion, which has led over the years to extensive coniferous reforestation and the planting of windbreaks. Many of these plantings are now well grown and form some of the most extensive tracts of coniferous forest south of the Shield. The natural forests of the area are the deciduous woodlands common to the Erie shores; they exist today mainly as woodlots, some of which are quite extensive.

The countryside that has resulted is a patchwork of coniferous and deciduous forest, flat open fields devoted to orchards, tobacco, and soybeans, and deep stream valleys with tangles of sumac and wild grape. It attracts a rich assortment of breeding birds, and the following nesting species are possibly as readily or more easily found here in the appropriate habitats than anywhere in the province: Forster's Tern, Chuck-will's-widow, Red-bellied Woodpecker, Louisiana Waterthrush, Cerulean Warbler, and Hooded Warbler. Additionally, most of the species listed as Carolinian in chapter 2 occur at least in small numbers, as well as those with northern affinities. It is an excellent area for breeding raptors: Sharp-shinned, Cooper's, Red-shouldered, and Broad-winged Hawks all nest, as do Barred and Long-eared Owls. Gray Partridge and Wild Turkey are widespread but difficult to find.

Farther east the sand is replaced by clay and reforestation is no longer a major feature of the landscape. Flat agricultural land is the norm, although there has been heavy industrialization in the area as well; however, the region as a whole lacks larger population centres and, although it is served by good highways, it is away from the main transportation links. The main access routes are from Highway 401 eastbound via Highway 19, and Highway 6 from the Hamilton area to the east.

Tourist facilities in the Long Point area are limited. There is camping at Long Point and Turkey Point Provincial Parks and also at Backus Conservation Area. The towns of Simcoe and Port Dover have motels and hotels and there are many bed-and-breakfast establishments.

LONG POINT

The sand plain is terminated at Lake Erie by Long Point. On the map, this is the most impressive landform along the Lake Erie shoreline: it is an enormous sandspit that juts eastwards out into the lake. It is also one of the finest birding areas in the province. It is a migrant concentration point second only to Point Pelee and a major staging area for waterfowl – in terms of readily accessible, visible waterfowl numbers, the best in Ontario. Together with the diverse habitats to the north it has an extraordinarily rich breeding avifauna: more northern species in the coniferous plantations, southerners in the deciduous woodlands and shrubby edges, and marsh and waterbirds in the huge marshes. In winter this same combination of habitats yields some of the highest Christmas bird counts in Canada.

The marshes have a fine avifauna, including both the usual marsh species in the extensive areas of cattail (Least Bitterns can be seen as readily here as anywhere) and grass marsh species such as Common Snipe and Sedge Wren in the short grassy sections. Forster's Terns nest regularly and Little Gulls periodically, although the nesting areas are not readily accessible. However, the terns range widely, and this is one of the best areas to see this species during the nesting season. In recent years Sandhill Cranes have nested; they can be seen in the Big Creek marshes and flying over the campground at dawn. Woodcock occur in the wooded areas, which form islands of vegetation which concentrate landbird migrants. The mix of migrants seems to be similar to that described for Pelee, and its account will provide a reasonable guide to the rarities that can be expected.

Waterfowl concentrations towards the end of March and in early April are spectacular. Birds move in as soon as any open water can be found, and enormous numbers are usually present in the second half of March. Traditionally the point used to be noted as *the* place to see Tundra Swans at this time, but in recent years the birds tend to be more dispersed, the Lake St Clair area yielding much larger numbers of these beautiful birds. Swan identification at Long Point should be approached with care: Trumpeter Swans have been released in the area, and the occasional Tundra Swan is possible even after the huge flocks in March have departed. Mute Swans also occur. There is a controlled hunt on the point, but since the Big Creek Marsh and much of the area north of the provincial park is a sanctuary, waterfowl viewing opportunities still exist in hunting season.

The Long Point area is not easy to bird. Only the base of the 32 km sandspit is generally accessible (see map 11). Much of the area is private property, and even the beaches of the point beyond the provincial park are off limits and well policed. Accessible sites are rather dispersed, often requiring considerable time to cover, and in this vast expanse there are many places for migrants to vanish unseen. In early spring high water levels can create extensive flooding, and vulnerable areas like Hastings Drive can wash out. Even with these drawbacks, however, the area can yield some of the province's most exciting birding at any season. While it does not present the same opportunity for intensive coverage as Pelee, it does not – so far – have the same crowds!

One plus for the visiting birder is the presence of the continent's oldest bird observatory. Long Point Bird Observatory's (LPBO) influence extends far beyond the banding and research work that forms its core program. Of most interest to the visitor, it operates the Ontario rare bird 'hot line,' and publishes an excellent seasonal checklist and a birding guide. Although the account that follows draws on this guide (listed in chapter 19), the latter provides a more comprehensive account of birding sites in the area, and is well worth acquiring if it is proposed to spend time here. The Old Cut Field Station and Visitor Centre

MAP 11 Long Point and area

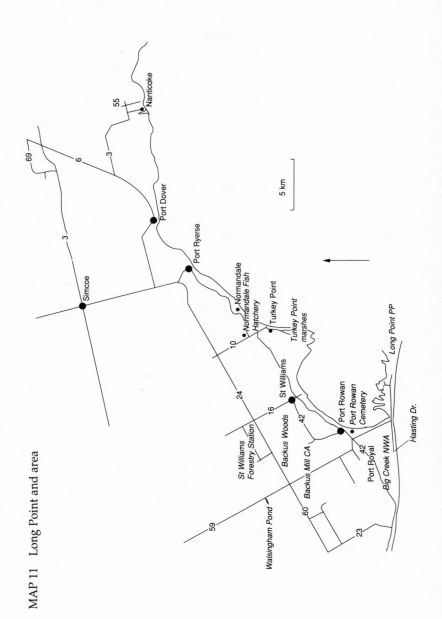

5 km

is the only LPBO station that is accessible to the general public (directions below; two others are farther east along the point). The centre and public viewing of the banding operation is open from 10:00 a.m. to 4:00 p.m. daily except Wednesdays and Thursdays. Here you can find what birds are around and get details on the LPBO program. Persons wishing to become involved in the observatory's program should contact the Migration Program Manager at LPBO, P.O. Box 160, Port Rowan, Ontario, Canada N0E 1M0.

Long Point extends eastwards out into Lake Erie from the village of **Port Rowan**. Highway 59 forms the causeway leading across to the main sandspit. Along the southerly, lake side of the point are long beaches backed by high sand dunes. On the north side, where the point creates a huge bay, extensive marshes have formed, and between the dunes and the marshes are varying amounts of woodland, much of it coniferous reforestation, interspersed with open grassy areas.

The Big Creek Marsh forms the base of the point; it is roughly triangular, with the causeway along the east side and the main dune ridge along the west. At the apex of the triangle the road joins the dune ridge to run along it, bordered by cottages and, on the bay side, shallow marshes. After some 8 km from the start of the causeway the road ends in Long Point Provincial Park, which terminates the publicly accessible section of the point.

Turning to a detailed review of the birding areas, the last intersection north of the point is with Regional Road 42. South (0.7 km) of here the Highway 59 causeway commences, and there is a small pull-off on the right from which the marsh can be viewed (traffic is often heavy on the causeway, and caution should be used at stops along it). By walking a short distance along the road the marshes on both sides can be scanned more easily; on the west exposed mud in late fall often attracts shorebirds, and gulls and terns loiter. The waters to the east are deeper, and attract a wider variety of duck, particularly in spring, when swans can be expected. Sandhill Cranes should be watched for as well from spring through fall. The road continues 0.7 km to Big Creek bridge where you can pull off again (duck and rails; open water in winter), and it then continues with the bay on the left and Big Creek Marsh and the National Wildlife Area on the right.

At 1.0 km from the bridge there is a signed parking lot on the right to the *Big Creek National Wildlife Area*, with a walking trail on the dikes leading to an observation tower. This walk is one of the best for marshbird viewing on the point. Everywhere Marsh Wrens and Swamp Sparrows bounce up and down, both species of bittern and rails can be heard and seen, and in the early morning flights of herons and waterfowl can be expected.

Continuing on the causeway, there is a viewing stand on the left at 0.9 km. In early spring the bay here can be filled with large flocks of waterfowl – mainly Redhead, Canvasback, American Wigeon, and coot, but with smaller numbers of scaup, Bufflehead, and Ruddy Duck. Later on, grebes and flocks of foraging Bonaparte's Gulls can be expected. About 300 metres farther along there is limited parking on the right of the road as the marsh opens up on the west. Here a different mix of early spring migrants, such as swans, and dabbling and Ring-necked Duck can be seen.

After crossing the Big Creek marshes the highway curves east to follow the line of the point itself. Turn right here on *Hastings Drive*, which runs in the opposite direction west along the shoreline with the Big Creek Marsh on the north. Flocks of Red-breasted Mergansers and loons can be seen on the lake off here in early spring and in fall, and there is more waterfowl viewing over the marsh, particularly from the parking area at the west end. Watch for Bald Eagle and other raptors. Migrant landbirds can be found all along the road, and it can also be good for wintering birds as well.

Return to the highway and continue east. This drive passes through the cottage community of Long Point, most of which is of no interest, but the eastern section of the cottage road that parallels the highway on the lake side can have a good variety of landbirds in migration (it is called Woodstock Drive; the best part is east from Norfolk Avenue). On the left, bay, side of the highway the bottom of *Teal Drive* at 1.1 km from the turn can have good views over the marshes and farther east the shallow marshes along the road itself can be good for herons and other marsh birds (there is a small parking area 0.4 km along on the left), and scrubby evergreens here attract migrant passerines.

At 2.3 km from Teal Drive is Old Cut Boulevard. Turn here, and the **LPBO Old Cut Field Station and Visitor Centre** is the fifth house on the right, with a sign on the lawn. Parking is available in the Old Cut parking lot opposite. Even when the observatory is not open birders are still welcome to bird the banding area; however, outside the times given above the staff is heavily engrossed in the operations of the observatory and generally unavailable to assist visitors. Go through the parking lot and follow a small path to the left of the buildings, leading to a clearing with a green boathouse. The main banding area is in the conifers on the right, and should be explored carefully; this tiny area is a major migrant trap and day counts of over one hundred species in spring are frequent. It is not unusual for two persons covering the area independently to have quite different – and outstanding – lists! Both Eastern Screech-Owls and Long-eared Owls have nested here, and Northern Saw-whets occur in fall. Please do not disturb the nets or any birds in them; they are serviced regularly. After covering the woods here walk down the road (Lighthouse Crescent) leading back to the highway, birding the conifers and shrubbery on the left.

Old Cut Boulevard continues into the main cottage area. The LPBO suggests that birders leave their vehicles parked in the Old Cut parking lot and walk this section. Continue to a Y-intersection where Roger's Avenue turns right. Both streets dead-end at the bay and both are of interest: by walking down Roger's Avenue one ends up at some boathouses with good views out over the bay and the outer sections of the marshes. Numbers of waterfowl, including scoters, occur in migration on the bay, and gulls and terns over the marshes. The left branch of the road leads to a productive marsh on the right and usually excellent land birding along the lawns and in the scattered trees of the cottages. Please be careful to respect the privacy and property of the cottagers both here and elsewhere on the point.

Continuing east from the Old Cut turnoff, Highway 59 soon terminates in **Long Point Provincial Park** (entrance fee), where the road forks past the gatehouse. The left leg leads to the campground, following the side of the marsh, with evergreen (mostly pine) reforestation plots on the right alternating with grassy and marshy sections, and areas of open dune. There is marsh viewing along here, and Sedge Wrens occur in the grassy tangles north of the road. The right leg of the entry road turns through one of the plantations into a long parking lot that runs between the lake side dunes and the evergreen plots.

On a good day in migration, passerines move steadily through the plantations of the entire park. Select the right clump of trees and it is possible to watch a continuous flow of migrants moving past, and every clump will yield a different mix of birds! Even on quiet days a search of the thickets will yield stragglers, and in late fall owls roost in the conifers to the right of the park entrance. The dune tops give good views of raptors moving down the point in fall.

Long Point is currently the only area in Canada where lyme disease has been found. Its vector is the deer tick, which is active throughout the warmer weather, and may be no larger than a pin head. While I know of no birders in the area contracting the disease, precautions are recommended.

AREAS WEST OF LONG POINT

To visit some of the areas on the adjacent mainland, return to County Road 42 and turn west (left). The route that follows describes a loop, but it is unlikely that a visitor would wish to cover all the places described at one time; all are readily accessible from Highways 59 or 24. County Road 42 leads to the village of **Port Royal** where noteworthy spots include the cemetery down a dirt road on the right at 2.5 km (distances are point to point), with views of Big Creek, and *Big Creek* itself at 0.3 km. Swallows and phoebes nest at the bridge and the willows here can attract migrants, while the ponds to the north attract geese and dabbling duck in spring. Farther along, *Port Royal Waterfowl Sanctuary* ('Lee Brown's') on the left at 1.4 km is no longer very productive but occasionally has interesting duck. The *Hahn Marsh*, with a small parking lot on the south at 1.9 km, provides more marsh access from the dike there. This area has consistently yielded rails in the winter, and at that time owls may roost in the pines along the creek to the west. Continue west another 1.9 km to a dirt road on the left. At the point where it turns left there is an overlook of the lake which has yielded views of jaegers and gulls in spring and fall during strong south or west winds, as well as cormorants and scoters.

The corn cribs along this route can attract large numbers of blackbirds in winter, and swans and other waterfowl may be seen in wet fields in early spring all the way to Port Burwell, and indeed along the entire Lake Erie shoreline. However, on this route drive east to Regional Road 23 (some 2.1 km) and turn north. Jog left at the intersection of Regional Road 22, continuing on 23, and proceed north three sideroads to Concession IV of South Walsingham (5.8 km from 42). From this point the Wilson Tract lies to the east. It is a premier area for breeding birds, and some one hundred species have been recorded. These include many of those listed in chapter 2 as having northern affinities, plus both cuckoos and a stellar group of warblers: Blue-winged, Golden-winged, Cerulean, and Hooded, as well as Louisiana Waterthrush. Wild Turkeys are regular, and Whip-poor-wills and possible Chuck-will's-Widow can be heard at night (about 1.0 km along Concession VI from the W. Quarter Line on the south side is reputed to be the best area), as well as three species of owl.

There are several access points to this large area of forest-land. The access roads form a large rectangle, with Concession IV on the south, Regional Road 23 on the west, Regional Road 60 (some 1.4 km ahead) on the north, and the W. Quarter Line of South Walsingham to the east. The forest itself lies on either side of Concession IV starting 1.7 km east from 23. At this point Concession IV becomes a sand road. It finally bends south and dead-ends at an old gate. This is the *Rowanwood Sanctuary* of the Norfolk Field Naturalists, and it can yield more woodland species. The trail ends in a small field which has bluebird boxes (and, one hopes, bluebirds).

Now proceed to Regional Road 60 and continue east to Highway 59. At this point the regional road ends and Highway 24 continues east, but before crossing, a detour 2.7 km north to *Walsingham Pond* may be worth while in spring. This is on the southwest corner of the highway and N. S. Walsingham Townline, and it can yield both dabbling duck and shorebirds. Return to Highway 24 and continue east. At 1.8 km from the intersection there is an entry to the woodlands on the south. This is *Backus Woods*, a fine Carolinian woodlot. The entry is an unpaved track leading into a small parking area, and thence a trail runs south through the woods to the next concession, a sand road of uncertain quality. The landbirds here are similar to those in the Wilson Tract. Pileated Woodpeckers are common and Prothonotary Warblers have nested in years when the pools are full. Louisiana Waterthrush and Barred Owl breed regularly.

By continuing east on Highway 24 some 4.5 km one comes to *St Williams Forestry Station* headquarters, with a pleasant picnic area on the south and a public fishing area and extensive woodlands on the north. The area of large evergreens here has created a huge island of habitat absent elsewhere in the region, and has attracted many species with more northern ranges and an exceptional abundance of raptors (Northern Saw-whet Owl has bred). It is a good place for Pine Warblers, and to see finches in the winter. The adjacent fishing pond sometimes attracts Hooded Merganser in early spring.

North again, and more readily accessible from the first east-west sideroad (Concession VI, another dirt road) 1.4 km north of the highway, is deciduous forest with typical Carolinian species. The same area can be reached by following a trail (of over 1.5 km) north from the east end of the fishing ponds. Several noteworthy breeding records have been established along here, including a couple of Ontario's few Lark Sparrow nestings in a clearing about 1.2 km west of Regional Road 16, which forms the eastern boundary of the area.

Just east of here Highway 24 crosses Regional Road 16. Turn south to the village of St Williams and then right in the centre of town onto Regional Road 42 (4.0 km), which runs west to Port Rowan. In spring wet fields to the north along here may yield a few duck and shorebirds. At the point the road curves south continue straight ahead on a gravel road and then turn right, following the signs to *Backus Mill Conservation Area* (entrance fee). This area has a small pond which can yield Hooded Merganser and the occasional shorebird, and Pileated Woodpeckers are regular. Then return to Regional Road 42, which leads into Port Rowan and eventually back to Highway 59.

Two sideroads on the west of Highway 59 may also be worth a visit. The first, north of the intersection of Regional Road 42 and the highway (1.1 km), is *Concession A* of South Walsingham.

West 1.8 km is a large swamp, which continues along the road for almost 1 km. By walking along the road here a good variety of marsh and landbirds can be heard and seen. Red-bellied Woodpecker, Carolina Wren, and Prothonotary Warbler occur. Do not leave the road: the entire area is posted and rigorously enforced. Along the next concession north (*Concession 1*) at 3.0 km, Big Creek crosses the road, and a short distance farther west is a wet field on the south that can be productive.

THE SHORELINE EAST OF LONG POINT

Regional Road 42 east of Highway 59 leads into Port Rowan. It first passes a gravel road on the right (0.4 km) which leads to *Port Rowan Cemetery*. The pond along the road can produce dabbling duck and the cemetery itself landbirds and, at far end, rails and other marsh birds. It is particularly productive in winter.

Return to the main road and drive 0.6 km to Mill Road on the north (the second road on the left). The *sewage lagoons* are 0.7 km along here on the right (it is best to park on the road: trucks use the drive regularly)), and are some of the most productive in the province. They can have waterfowl in plenty when the Long Point marshes seem to be empty, as well as shorebirds in season. There is hunting here in fall.

Continue into **Port Rowan**. At 0.8 km, where the regional road turns left in town, there is a parking lot on the right offering excellent views of the bay, and large numbers of waterbirds often can be seen. Duck and swans predominate in the spring, with loons and grebes in the fall, and lingering shorebirds later. Particularly large numbers of Little Gulls have been seen here in fall (266 on one day). Continue around the corner on to the main street, and take the first road to the right (Wolven Street, just past the tavern). This leads east along the shoreline and has a lake viewpoint at 0.7 km. It enters the St Williams road (Regional Road 16) immediately south of the Normandale sideroad to the east. The latter continues east along the shore as Lakeshore Road. At 4.1 km is the first glimpse of the large *Turkey Point marshes* ahead on the right, and at 0.9 km farther on, past the top of the hill, there is a good overview area. Much of this huge marsh is at the limits even of a telescope; the hillside itself is private property. Large numbers of duck and gulls can usually be seen in spring, and the spot is good for watching hawk migration as well.

Continuing east, at 2.1 km a sand road runs north through pine plantations that can attract nesting Pine Warblers and coniferous forest species, and formerly Prairie Warblers bred. In this kind of habitat this is a successional species, and eventually the trees become too large (similarly, the birds also once nested north of Highway 24 along the sideroad on the west of St Williams Forestry Station) so a systematic search here in areas with young trees could be more productive than visiting the former sites. At 0.9 km one arrives at the Turkey Point road (Regional Road 10). Here a left turn leads to the entrance to the fish hatchery, while a right leads down a hill to Turkey Point.

Turkey Point is of interest primarily in the winter when the swampy woods to the right at the bottom of the hill harbour an rich array of wintering species (Yellow-rumped Warblers are regular). The birds feed on poison sumac berries along the edge of the marsh, but to reach this area entails a 1.5 hour struggle westwards through the dense, wet bog. At this time of year there may also be wintering passerines in the community of Turkey Point itself, and good concentrations of waterfowl and gulls on any open water offshore. In migration periods the outer shoreline and the waters of the bay can be well worth covering, although they are frequently completely dead. Drive down the hill and turn right, and drive 1.3 km to Ferris Street. Turn left here; this ends at Ordnance Avenue, which (turn right) leads some 2 km along the shore to the pier and restaurant at the end with lake viewing all the way. Be sure to search any sandflats for shorebirds. Little Gulls are regular in late fall.

By turning north on Regional Road 10 from Lakeshore Road (i.e., away from Turkey Point) one comes to the *Turkey Point Provincial Park* entrance (0.3 km). It has a good diversity of breeding birds, including some more northern warblers. Then at 1.5 km is the entrance to the *Normandale Fish Hatchery*. There is a large pond here which almost always has a good assortment of duck in migration time, especially Ring-necked Duck and Hooded Merganser. There is a pleasant but rather long trail around it through the woods. This is not usually worth walking the whole way round, but the south side can be very productive and the wet areas at the beginning of the north side can have woodcock. The entry to this trail is on the right when driving into the parking lot. There is a dirt road with a bar across it at the beginning of the woods, and the south side trail runs along here. It should be walked as far as the dam. Be careful not to scare off the duck, as the path runs close to the water in places. The pines here and the area below the dam have a good assortment of nesting species, and the latter can be good in winter. In migration times the entire area can be productive.

The Normandale Road crosses the Turkey Point road and is interesting in itself. It drops down into **Normandale** and then twists up and down through a succession of other small communities: bear generally right to parallel the lakeshore. There is lake viewing from the *Van Norman Public Fishing Area* on the right entering Normandale and, continuing east, again at *Port Ryerse*. The narrow valleys these communities occupy, as well as Fisher's Glen, often attract landbirds in winter and in cold periods in migration. At Port Ryerse take Regional Road 57 out of town to Highway 24. A left here takes you back to Long Point and a right leads (via Highway 6) to Port Dover.

Highway 6 is **Port Dover's** main Street. At the bottom of the hill at the east end of town the highway turns north, towards the lift bridge over the river, but driving straight ahead leads to the harbour. Turn right at the water and drive out on the pier. There is parking here, and good views of the bay, and there are sometimes interesting gulls and waterbirds present. Return to the highway, turn right and cross the bridge over the river, and turn right again on John Street, signed to the Lakeshore Fish Market. This street soon turns right, then left (becoming in succession Brown, Dean, and Passmore; follow the fish market signs), and then leads down a hill to the Harbour Marina. Take the second left at the bottom of the hill and scan the bay from a parking lot on the right.

TOWNSEND SEWAGE LAGOONS

These large lagoons, situated between Simcoe and Jarvis, have become one of the major shorebird and waterfowl destinations in the region, with a host of rare migrants recorded and nesting Ruddy Duck. Gray Partridge occur in the neighbouring fields.

Drive east from Simcoe on Highway 3 some 14.2 km to Regional Road 69 on the north. Go north 1.4 km, take the first left after the railroad tracks (Nanticoke Concession 14 W 3) and the entrance to the lagoons is about 0.5 km ahead on the right. Park and walk in. (From Highway 6 the route is to drive west on Highway 3 some 3.0 km to Regional Road 69 and turn right, then as above.) A controlled hunt occurs here; in hunting season the area is open to the public on Tuesdays, Thursdays, and Sundays, and only one day a week after October (the Simcoe office of the Ministry of Natural Resources can provide more information).

THE GRAND RIVER AND DUNNVILLE AREA

In the east of the region, roads parallel both sides of the Grand River from Brantford almost continuously through to Dunnville. The major roads occupy the northeast bank, and Highway 54 in particular passes through excellent habitat – woods, riverside fields, and marshes – close to the river from north of **Caledonia** down to Cayuga. While probably not justifying a special trip, this area can be very productive of landbirds, particularly in winter, and in migration periods enormous concentrations of swallows can occur over the river in cool spells. West of **Cayuga** off Highway 3 is the *Taquanyah Conservation Area*, which has a mixture of good habitats, including a lake that can yield shorebirds, depending on water levels. The area is also good in winter, when the pine plantations can shelter owls. Drive about 5.5 km west on 3 to the third sideroad, turn right, and the area is some 1 km north.

The town of **Dunnville**, on Highway 3 near the mouth of the Grand River, has a number of interesting areas close by, the nearest being the extensive marshes west of town. These extend for some distance north from the Dunnville bridges across the Grand, and southwards almost to the river mouth. There are a variety of vantage points, from the bridges themselves and sideroads on both sides.

The road crossing the bridges is Regional Road 3, and the west bank of the river at **Port Maitland** is accessible from Regional Road 11, which turns south off Road 3 just after the second bridge. Drive 6 km south to a stop street and turn into the village. This road runs 1 km to the river mouth, the last half along the river. There are excellent views to the north, and of the piers and lake to the south. Straight ahead from the above stop street the road bears right as Lakeshore Road and parallels the shore for some 2 km. This is **Grant Point**. The shoreline here can yield shorebirds, gulls, and duck.

On Lake Erie east of the river mouth, **Rock Point Provincial Park** is 11 km southeast of town via Regional Road 3 (this forks south off Highway 3 just east of town). The park is noted for its shorebirds, which can occur in outstanding numbers and variety in the autumn, and which also can be numerous in spring. Its attractiveness depends on lake levels and the amount of algae built up along the shoreline.

Regional Road 3 continues east, eventually joining the shoreline of Lake Erie at Lowbanks. Another good vantage point exists at **Long Beach Conservation Area**, 2 km west along the shoreline. From Lowbanks east good opportunities for lake viewing exist along the shoreline roads almost continuously to Port Colborne. However, this route is a very slow one, and much of the year is unlikely to yield much that cannot be seen in other locations.

OTHER AREAS IN THE HALDIMAND-NORFOLK REGION

Jarvis – The sewage lagoons are south off Highway 3 about 1 km down a dirt road at the back of the lane into the car wash, opposite Walpole Street and 0.3 km east of the intersection of Highways 3 and 6. There are two separate sets of ponds here.

Nanticoke – Some 6 km north of Port Dover on Highway 6 is the intersection of Regional Road 3. Eastbound, this leads to Nanticoke and the industrial developments there. The regional road winds east and then south, and finally turns sharp left (the fields in this area have been reliable locations for Upland Sandpiper). At this point a road continues straight ahead to the village of Nanticoke. Continue straight ahead to the first road on the left (Rainham Road). Turn left here and drive into the village; and at 0.8 km turn right on Erie Street and drive to the shore, scanning the marshes along the creek on the right. The foot of the road gives views of the harbour. Returning, farther east again on Rainham Road (0.8 km; there is a light at the corner) is Regional Road 55 with lake viewing west of the power plant at its foot. The harbour here is particularly good in winter, as the warm-water effluent from the power plant keeps it open.

Delhi – This community is some 20 km west of Simcoe on Highway 3. One of the more reliable areas for Gray Partridge is north of town, and in the vicinity of La Salette. The fields in the block to the north and west of the hamlet (roughly bounded by a rectangle of some 4 X 5 km) are best.

Waterford – Waterford is north of Simcoe on the east of Highway 24. There has been extensive gravel extraction just east of the highway and many ponds have been created. Go north on Highway 24 1.3 km from County Road 9 and turn right towards Waterford on Mechanics Road. At 1.8 km along it is the *Waterford Conservation Area* on the south, and at 0.8 km parking for the *Waterford Ponds Wildlife Management Area* to the north. The ponds here have a fair amount of marshland along the edges, and some swampy areas with tamarack.

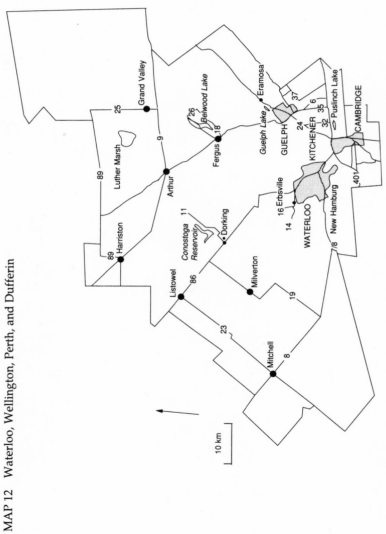

MAP 12 Waterloo, Wellington, Perth, and Dufferin

8 Kitchener-Waterloo, Cambridge, Guelph, and Area

The Counties of Wellington, Waterloo, Perth, and Dufferin

Cambridge
Kitchener-Waterloo
Guelph
Luther Marsh
Other reservoirs in the region
Sewage lagoons in the region
Along Highway 401

These counties lie almost entirely in the Great Lakes–St Lawrence Forest Region, although the northern edge of the deciduous forest reaches as far as Cambridge. Lying well inland from the Great Lakes and downwind of Lake Huron, they have more severe winters and heavier snow than areas to the south, and also lack areas of comparable birding quality. Nevertheless, the region is not without good birding spots; the mixture of forest types around Cambridge yields a fine diversity of natural communities in close proximity to one another, and Luther Marsh is a major wetland. There are a number of sewage lagoons, but only the ones at Mitchell have consistently yielded reports of interest.

The area is diverse. To the west the flat farmlands of Perth County are mainly devoted to stock rearing; they seem to have few areas of birding note, although the Ellice Swamp north of Stratford looks promising (the fifth sideroad on the east, north along Highway 19). Eastwards, the countryside becomes more rolling, with wooded hills and river valleys, and abandoned fields and reforestation appearing on areas of poorer soils. The line of the Niagara Escarpment parallels the easternmost edges of Dufferin County, and the region's northern tier of townships covers a high, flat plain of poorly drained countryside devoted to grain farming and stock rearing. This area lacks larger towns, and indeed the major communities of Kitchener-Waterloo, Cambridge, and Guelph are all clustered in the southeast, and all are served by the main artery of Highway 401.

CAMBRIDGE

This city of some 80,000 persons was formed by the amalgamation of the historic town of Galt with Preston and Hespeler. It lies along the Grand River south of Highway 401 exits 275, 278, and 282. The Grand River valley south of Cambridge supports fine mixed woodlands which attract both northern birds and southerners at the northerly limits of their ranges. The following loop (see map 13) will take you through some of the most productive habitat.

Starting from the intersection of Highway 24 and Regional Road 97 in Cambridge (Galt), drive west on 97, crossing the river. Just before the intersection with Regional Road 75 (formerly Highway 24A; about 0.5 km) turn left on West River Road. This runs south following the river and the scenic Galt ridge, and there is excellent birding along the entire route. Continue driving south until the road merges with the Glen Morris road (Regional Road 28), where a left leads back across the Grand River. Bear right, now driving west, for some 2.2 km to the first sideroad on the left. This runs towards a wooded ridge where (2 km) a small road barred with a green gate on the left runs down into the valley of the river. This area, together with the lands to the left, is *Spottiswood*, an area of deciduous woodland where southern species occur, including Acadian Flycatcher, gnatcatcher, and Cerulean Warbler. Most of the property, however, is private, but it is currently permissible to walk down the road.

Now continue south until a T-intersection. Turn right here and follow this road (it jogs first north and then west again) to Highway 24A. North on 24A is the entrance to the extensive *Pinehurst Lake Conservation Area*, where again southern species occur. Some 2 km farther on Highway 24 A the Brant County Line Road runs west (from the Despond Lake Trailer Park); the *Dickson Wilderness Area* is some 1.5 km along it. Yellow-throated Vireos and Cerulean Warblers occur here, and the feeders attract interesting wintering species, including Red-bellied

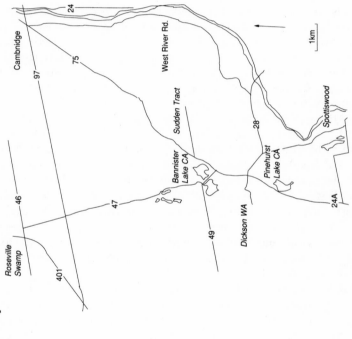

MAP 13   The Cambridge Loop

Woodpeckers. North again about 1 km, at the intersection of Highway 24A (which has now become Regional Road 75) and Regional Road 49, is **Bannister Lake Conservation Area**. There are extensive hiking trails among the rolling woodland around Bannister and Wrigley lakes, and an excellent mix of habitats, including marshland. Turn west on Regional Road 49 and there is parking at 0.1 km for access to these trails.

The first sideroad east of Regional Road 75 just north of this intersection (1 km; Dumfries Road 4) passes through another excellent area of woodland and wetland habitats, with walking trails on the north of the road. There is access from a small parking lot at 1.4 km. This is the **Sudden Tract**. Species present in summer can include Red-shouldered Hawk, Red-bellied Woodpecker, Willow and Acadian Flycatcher, Yellow-throated Vireo, and several warblers, including Golden-winged, Blue-winged, Cerulean, Mourning, and Northern Waterthrush. Louisiana Waterthrush has also occurred.

After covering the Sudden Tract return to Regional Road 49 and turn right. Just past the lake Regional Road 47 forks off to the right. Bear north here, and the road eventually crosses Regional Road 97 and after some 6.9 km ends at Regional Road 46. Turn left and drive west over Highway 401. Just ahead is the **Roseville Swamp** on both sides of the road, and continuing north and south. It has Northern Waterthrush and Mourning and Canada Warblers in summer, as well as small choruses of Winter Wrens and White-throated Sparrows. To complete the tour return to Regional Road 97, where a left returns to your starting point in Galt, and a right leads to Highway 401 exit 268.

Another good birding road southeast of Galt off Highway 8 is the historic **Cheese Factory Road** (Elgin Street south) which runs through rolling woodland and scrub, with small ponds. Willow Flycatcher, Eastern Bluebird, Pine Warbler, and (rarely) Yellow-breasted Chats have occurred. The road is the first concession west of the intersection of Regional Road 43 and Highway 8.

KITCHENER-WATERLOO

These twin cities – Kitchener is the southernmost – form the largest centre in the region, with over 220,000 population. They

are north from Highway 401 exit 278, and for the local visitor
there are several quite productive areas in the urban area itself.

The *Columbia* and *Laurel reservoirs* can be good for waterfowl and open country species in migration, and Pied-billed
Grebe, Canada Goose, Marsh Wren, and Swamp Sparrow nest.
The lakes are west from the Conestoga Parkway on University
Avenue to Albert Street; the Columbia reservoir is then north
on Albert to Columbia Street West, and west to the University
of Waterloo campus. The Laurel reservoir is along Conservation Drive, reached by continuing north on Albert Street to
Bearinger Road, and then west again.

Some city parks have natural woodlands. *Waterloo Park* is
west of King Street and south of University Avenue; the entrance is off Young Street West, which runs west from King,
one block north of Bridgeport. *Lakeside Park* has a small lake
that yields waterbirds. It can be reached from the Conestoga
Parkway via Homer Watson Boulevard north to Stirling Avenue, then west to Greenbrook Drive.

Homer Watson Park is south of the cities, at the corner of
Homer Watson Boulevard and Huron Road. It is the start of a
tract of natural land that runs southeast along Wilson Avenue
to the Blair bridge over the Grand River. This area includes
mixed forests, the Grand River itself, mill ponds and creeks,
and extensive trails. The Blair bridge has had nesting Cliff Swallows, and provides a good vantage point for seeing waterbirds.
The coniferous stands are good for winter species and owls,
and Pine Warblers nest.

Stanley Park Conservation Area is along Ottawa Street East
just east of the Conestoga Parkway, and is also accessible from
River Road farther east. There are trails here linking with the
peat bog in Idlewood Park to the southeast. There are good
mixed habitats and it can be especially productive in winter.

Schaefer's Woods is an extensive wooded tract of northern
character on both sides of Regional Road 14 west of **Erbsville**.
To reach this community drive west on Columbia Street to
Regional Road 16 and then north. Regional Road 14 jogs south
off 16 about 1 km west of the hamlet. Barred Owl and Long-
eared Owl, Winter Wren, Black-throated Green Warbler, and
Northern Waterthrush are among the species that have nested
here.

GUELPH

Guelph is northeast of Kitchener-Waterloo, and has a population of over 80,000. It is some 12 km north of Highway 401 via Highways 6 or 24, but most of the areas of interest are south of the city. Highway 6, the Hanlon Expressway, is the access route used here.

West of the Hanlon Expressway, starting from *Kortright Waterfowl Park* off Kortright Road (follow the signs), first check the heavily wooded banks of the Speed River to the west. These can yield good landbirding and the Speed itself sometimes has loitering duck, mostly semi-wild Mallards, although other species can occur. The waterfowl park itself (entrance fee) has a comprehensive collection of captive waterfowl.

Return east on Kortright Road 1 km to Downey Road (County Road 35), running south. Turn here and drive 4.3 km to the third sideroad west. Turn onto this gravel road; at 0.8 km it passes through Cranberry Bog, a heavily wooded area, and some 1.5 km farther it passes through another heavily wooded section, the *Little Tract* of Wellington County Forest on the south, and a privately owned bog forest on the north (access by permission). The trails of the Little Tract can yield an excellent cross-section of typical forest species.

The next sideroad north-south (4.2 km from your turn) is hardtopped County Road 32, on which you will head south; however, first turn right and cover the small lake 0.5 km north, *Neibauer's Marsh,* which can yield duck and other waterbirds. Then turn and drive south some 4 km, crossing Highway 401. Just over the bridge the *Puslinch Resource Management Area* is on the left and continues for 2 km along the north side of the first sideroad east. There are hardwoods, coniferous reforestation, and flooded gravel pits, and the whole area is managed mainly with an eye to small game production. Grasshopper Sparrows have bred here and there is a good mix of edge and woodland bird life. The area is also accessible from the service area on the eastbound lanes of Highway 401 between interchanges 282 and 295.

When County Road 32 turns west it runs along the north shore of *Puslinch Lake.* Most of the shoreline is private property, but the lake itself can be viewed for migrant waterfowl in early spring and late autumn from the end of a small sideroad south 1.5 km from the county road turn. West of here again Pinebush Road runs down the west of the lake. The south end is property owned by the Grand River Conservation Authority, giving access to the wooded southwest bay, with further viewing opportunities. Many rarer species of waterbirds have occurred on the lake.

To the **East Of the Hanlon Expressway**, the first road north of Kortright Drive is the Stone Road. Drive east 6.3 km, crossing Victoria Road (note that the University of Guelph Arboretum on the southwest corner of Victoria has good walking trails). The next cross-road is Watson Road: turn right here and go some 600 metres. A stile and a marked trail lead away to the left (east) at this point, which is about 150 metres north of the Eramosa River. This is the **Radial Line Trail**. It goes through wet cedar woodland along the river, open moraine country, pine plantation, mixed deciduous woodland, and open agricultural land. It is marked throughout, and returns to Watson Road about 600 metres south of the original starting point. The complete loop takes 1 to 1.5 hours of vigorous walking; bird-watching, it takes considerably longer!

The *Starkey Property* is south of the above. From the stile given as starting point, go south about 1.8 km to the village of **Arkell**, turn left (east) onto County Road 37 (known locally as the Arkell Road), go about 1.2 km to just past the old Starkey Farm on the south side (an old stone house with two rows of conifers in front), where a marked trail leads south uphill. It joins a loop on open upland moraine country and returns to the starting point. The open area has the usual species of such habitat, but also includes Grasshopper Sparrows (some years) and Hooded Merganser (breeds in some years on small ponds behind the hills). The southern end of the trail passes through open deciduous woodland.

Northeast of Guelph is the *Guelph Lake*, along the north side of Highway 24 immediately east of the intersection of County Road 40. This large lake is visible for some 2 km along Highway 24 east of here. Ospreys nest, and the area is good for waterfowl in early spring. Depending on the state of drawdown there may be mud flats in autumn, which can be very productive of shorebirds.

A little farther on the road crosses the lake on a causeway which gives good views on either side. About 0.8 km east of the eastern end, turn right (south) in the village of **Eramosa** onto a dirt road. After 1 km this road crosses a second causeway which gives another good overview of the lake, at this point shallower and more overgrown.

LUTHER MARSH

Roughly in the middle of the landmass of southern Ontario, northwest of Toronto and almost due north of Kitchener, the roadmap shows a blue patch marked Luther Lake. This isolated spot is one of the province's most significant wetlands. Luther Marsh is a huge area of some 6,500 hectares created by the impoundment of the Grand River. Lying between Highways 9 and 89, and west of 25, it is accessible only by gravel roads, but there are several good access points. The marsh has three main areas of interest: the actual lake and various islands and bogs therein, the northern woods, and Wylde Lake, which is an un-usual raised bog of a very boreal character southeast of the main lake.

The lake is noted as a waterfowl breeding area. Fifteen spe-cies of duck have been proved to nest, although not all do so annually. Very roughly in order of abundance, these are Mal-lard, Gadwall, American Wigeon, Blue-winged Teal, Lesser Scaup, Redhead, Ring-necked Duck, American Black Duck, Ruddy Duck, Green-winged Teal, Northern Pintail, Wood Duck, Hooded Merganser, Canvasback, and Northern Shoveler. Most of these species nest on the islands and around the north bog. The best areas are around Big Island, the north bog, and Wind-mill Island: examine secluded coves. All the typical marsh spe-cies also nest, as well as one or two pairs of Common Loons, Red-necked Grebes (rare), Wilson's Phalaropes, and three or four pairs of Ospreys. In fall there are large areas of mud and alga as the lake is drawn down, both around the edges and as semi-floating bogs scattered through the lake. These are very productive of shorebirds. The floating bogs are essentially bot-tomless and should not be walked upon.

The northern woods have typical woodland birds, including some more northern species, and Wylde Lake is noted for nest-

MAP 14   Luther Marsh

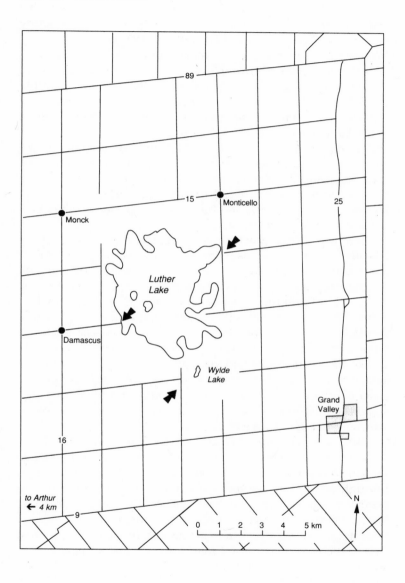

ing Lincoln's Sparrows. The sedge and grass areas surrounding the marsh have also yielded such species as Short-eared Owl and Sedge Wren, with occasional reports of mouth-watering goodies like Yellow Rail and LeConte's Sparrow.

To reach the east side of the marsh from the east, drive some 8.5 km north from Highway 9 on Highway 25 through **Grand Valley**, to East Luther Concession 6-7 on the west (see map 14). Turn here and drive west and then, as the road turns, north some 9 km in all to the well-marked entrance to the parking lot of the dam area on the left.

Coming from the west, drive 14.7 km east on Highway 9 from its intersection with Highway 6 at **Arthur**, to an unmarked road (it is some 2 km past a microwave tower) on the north. Go 8.2 km north, turn left (west) onto the unmarked gravel road which is Concession 6-7, and travel west and then north 6.9 km to the entrance as above.

There is a Purple Martin colony here, and overviews of the lake are possible from this point. There are specially good views from an observation tower located 1.5 km south of the dam, on an internal road (open to private vehicles) leading off from the parking lot. From the dam a second internal road, not open to vehicles, curves through the northern part of the area, roughly paralleling the shore, for 7 to 8 km. This road gives access to the large area of woodland on the north shore. Access to the other end of this road can be had via Concession 8-9 of West Luther Township. About 2.5 km from the dam a look-out tower gives a good overview of the lake. About 5.5 km from the dam a trail signposted 'Esker Trail' leads 1 km to another observation tower, which gives a good view over a willow swamp.

The dam is on Sideroad 20-21, and **Monticello** is located 2.2 km north of here. A road runs westwards from the village 7.5 km to **Monck**; west of Monticello 2.5 km this road passes through some good habitat. An open, wet, sedgy field on the northern side of the road has consistently yielded breeding Sedge Wrens for several years. At Monck turn south on Wellington County Road 16 to **Damascus**, for access to the west side of the lake. This county road runs north from Highway 9, some 13 km west of the Highway 25 intersection and 5.8 km east of Arthur. From 9, drive 8.2 km to Damascus General Store. Turn east, go 2.7 km, crossing one unmarked crossroad, to the lake. The road finally disappears into the lake, and is known locally as the Bootlegger's Road. It offers excellent views of the lake to the east and north.

Wylde Lake is also east of the Damascus road. Along Highway 9 the access road is 7.3 km from Highway 25 and 11.5 km from Arthur. It is the county line between Wellington and Dufferin counties – watch for the sign. Go 5.3 km north until the road takes a sharp left-hand turn. From here, walk eastwards through an area of scattered tamarack and wet sphagnum bog; the lake itself is a little less that 1.5 km in. The most interesting area is not the lake but the surroundings; Lincoln's Sparrows can usually be heard from the bend in the road itself. Note that on a dull day it is very easy to get lost in the Wylde Lake region, which is several square kilometres in extent. Take a compass.

Much the best way of seeing the lake and its birds is by canoe. Access is best from either the dam or the Bootlegger's Road (preferable in a west wind, because of shelter). A good route from the Bootlegger's Road is north, passing west of Big Island, then along the north bog to Esker Island, east to Windmill Island; if calm, go south to Prairie Island, back west to Heron Island, and back along the east shore of Big Island to the Bootlegger's. An important caution is that the lake can become rough very quickly in the event of a wind springing up. There have been two fatalities in recent years; do not be the third.

Up until 31 July each year a permit is required to put any boat, including a canoe, on the lake. These are issued at the superintendent's house at the dam; contact the Grand River Conservation Authority, 400 Clyde Road, Cambridge (519-621-2761) for details. Outboard motors are not allowed. Even with a permit, access to certain areas is prohibited during the breeding season. These include the vicinity of the heronry, several islands, including Windmill and Prairie islands, and areas around active Osprey nests. These restrictions are purely for the good of the birds, and responsible naturalists will abide by them meticulously; failure to do so will in any case result in prosecution under the Conservation Authorities Act.

In autumn (mid-September) the entire area is used intensively for hunting, and birding is not recommended in this period.

OTHER RESERVOIRS IN THE REGION

Dorking – This community is northwest of Kitchener-Waterloo on Highway 86, about halfway to Listowel. The *Conestoga Reservoir and Conservation Area* is 5 km northeast on County Road 11. The most accessible vistas of the waterbody are farther up this road. A half kilometre ahead is the dam itself, with gulls foraging at its base and excellent views of the large water area on the left. Another excellent vista is 1.5 km farther on again, where the widest part of the lake (which is roughly L-shaped) is visible beside the road. Other vistas are possible both from the county road and from sideroads around the lake to the north, south and west.

This area is heavily used for recreation, but waterfowl gather in spring and autumn; in addition to Mallards, black ducks, and Common Merganser, loons, geese, and other ducks occur, and shorebirds are possible depending on the state and date of the drawdown. The area has been good for herons. There are also old fields around the lake that can yield the interesting mix of species typical of such areas, and Short-eared Owls have bred here.

Fergus – Fergus is some 20 km north of Guelph on Highway 6. *Belwood Lake* is east on County Road 18 (Belsyde Ave) off Highway 6 at the south end of town. Belwood Conservation Area, 5 km on the left, provides good views of the dam and west end of the area, and farther east a section of the lake is visible at 1.6 km. Continue east on 18 to County Road 26 (4.5 km) and drive north some 3 km to the bridge, which provides views of the east end of the reservoir. There is further viewing possible from the cottage roads south of County Road 19, which runs west back to Fergus. The lake can be good for waterfowl in early spring and late autumn, Red-necked Grebes and herons in migration, and shorebirds in autumn.

SEWAGE LAGOONS IN THE REGION

Arthur – This is the town on Highway 9 southwest of Luther Marsh. The sewage lagoons are just north of the railroad tracks and east of County Road 14. From the intersection of Highways

6 and 9 drive north 0.8 km on 6 to the lights at Frederick Street. This is County Road 14. Turn right and then follow the road left as it turns on Eliza Street. The tracks are 1.2 km from the lights, and the lagoons can be seen behind the houses at this point.

Harriston – Harriston is at the intersection of Highways 9 and 89 in northwest Wellington County. For the sewage lagoon, drive west on Highway 89 from its intersection with Highway 9 in town. Turn right on John Street, drive two blocks to William, turn left there and cross the tracks; the lagoon road is on the right.

Listowel – This community is northwest of Kitchener-Waterloo on Highway 86. The sewage lagoons are 2.1 km south on Highway 23, from its intersection with Highway 86 northwest of town. Drive to Elma Concession 1-2 and turn right; the lagoons are 0.6 km along on the left.

Milverton – Milverton is south of Listowel, southwest from Highway 86 some 15 km on Highway 19. For the sewage lagoon, take Mill Street west in the centre of the village off Highway 19, drive 0.7 km, crossing the tracks; the lagoon drive itself crosses the tracks to the left.

Mitchell – The town is in Perth County, on Highway 8 northwest of Stratford. The lagoons here are extensive, and have consistently yielded interesting records, mainly of waterfowl. From the intersection of Highways 23 and 8 north of town, take 23 south 1 km to Frank Street. Turn left and drive 0.7 km to the turn on Wellington Street, where the lagoons are clearly visible on the right and the entrance is directly ahead. Wellington Street leads back to Highway 8 southbound.

New Hamburg – New Hamburg is west of Waterloo and north of Highways 7/8 halfway to Stratford. To reach the lagoons, drive west on Highway 7/8 to the Nith River bridge south of town. Turn south immediately over the bridge on Wilmot Township Road 12 and drive 1.4 km; the gate is on the left.

ALONG HIGHWAY 401

The stretch of Highway 401 across Waterloo and Wellington counties is both scenic and, given its character, quite productive. The first intersection eastbound is exit 268, which gives ready access to the loop described under Cambridge. The road then passes to the Doon Pinnacle hill on the left and crosses the Grand River. Occasionally a Pileated Woodpecker will fly over in this stretch, and the river at this point usually has a few Canada Geese and ducks, even in winter. Another spot for waterfowl is some 4 km further east, where the highway crosses the two channels and riparian woodlands of the Speed River.

Continuing east, Puslinch Lake is immediately south of the highway about 5 km east of exit 282, but entails a lengthy side trip; more interesting to the through traveller is the eastbound service area some 3 km further east. The picnic area here gives ready access to the Puslinch Wildlife Management area, described under Guelph above.

Highway 6 south at exit 299 gives ready access to both the Valens and Mountsberg Conservation Areas, as described in chapter 10. If you have time, an excellent diversion is to exit at 299 and go to Mountsberg, and then continue on to Campbellville at exit 312 (westbound travellers should reverse this; both routes are described below). The Campbellville exit also leads to Hilton Falls Conservation Area (also in chapter 10) with a return at exit 320, or vice versa.

MAP 15   Niagara Region

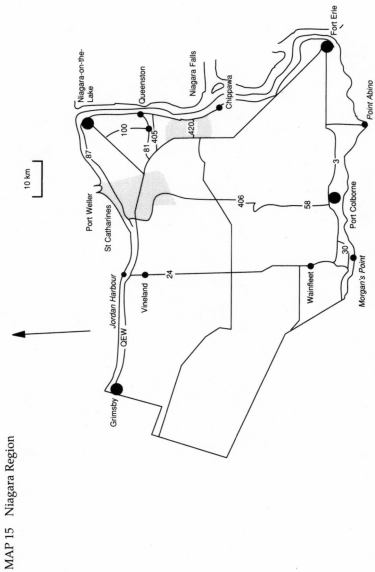

9 The Niagara River and Area

Niagara Regional Municipality

The Niagara River
St Davids
Port Colborne and area
West along Lake Ontario

Niagara Falls is one of Canada's major natural spectacles, and draws tourists from all over the world. The area is a major attraction for birders as well, but for different reasons: the Niagara River has become famous for the thousands of gulls that concentrate there in later fall and early winter. It is to see this sometimes rather uncertain spectacle, and the rarities the milling flocks contain, that most birders will travel to the area. Nevertheless, the Niagara Peninsula has more birding to offer than the river alone, particularly for a Canadian visitor.

The region presents an assortment of delights. Many of the Carolinian bird species that occur farther east along the Lake Erie shoreline occur here as well, and Tufted Titmice and Northern Mockingbirds can be found more readily here than elsewhere. The remnant bogs attract northern species – Lincoln's Sparrow has nested – and a few Barn Owls occur, but the tiny population is threatened and you are most unlikely to see them. House Finches, although no longer likely to spur special visits, first established themselves in this region of Ontario.

The river between Fort Erie and Niagara-on-the-Lake is most rewarding in late fall, but in the colder months the resident landbirds are of particular interest (mockingbird and Tufted Titmouse are the most noteworthy), and the area is still good for waterfowl at that time. The Niagara River is less noteworthy at other times, and some movements, such as the main fall hawk flights, bypass the peninsula completely. However, there are large movements of Common Nighthawks and Purple Martins in early autumn, and interesting waterfowl can turn up at any time. The escarpment channels hawk migrants in the spring, and gives Beamer Point (covered, together with Smithville sewage lagoons, in the next chapter) its claim to fame. Lake Ontario yields fall and winter waterfowl and Lake Erie shorebird migrants.

The region forms the peninsula between the west end of Lake Ontario on the north and Erie to the south. Bounding the north shore is a narrow, flat, and fertile plain where burgeoning urban growth threatens to smother the vineyards and orchards that make this one of Canada's premier fruit-growing areas. The plain lies below the sharp ridge of the Niagara Escarpment, southern Ontario's most imposing land form. To the east the scarp becomes hidden in a jumble of rolling hills before re-emerging in dramatic form along the Niagara gorge and at the falls themselves. South of the escarpment the land slopes gradually to Lake Erie; it is chiefly rolling farmland and orchards, but poor drainage creates areas of marsh and bog, and the pressures of creeping urbanization are here too.

This is a populous area. Niagara Falls has a population of over 70,000, but it is only one of a cluster of small cities, with St Catharines, at some 120,000 persons, the largest. The region's main artery is the controlled-access Queen Elizabeth Way (QEW) which parallels the Lake Ontario shoreline east from Hamilton, and then heads south to terminate at Fort Erie. This town is situated at the start of the Niagara River opposite Buffalo. The QEW has a spur leg (Highway 405) also linking with the United States north of Niagara Falls. For travellers from the west, Highway 403 through Brantford (Highway 401 exit 235) forms a tolerable access route. Specific birding locations along the QEW are not detailed – most people tend to head straight for the river – but some are given below under the section "West along Lake Ontario," and farther west, Beamer Point and 50 Point are covered in the next chapter.

Accommodation abounds in Niagara Falls and Niagara-on-the-Lake, but camping is extremely limited in the main birding periods (Niagara Falls KOA is open year round).

THE NIAGARA RIVER

The Niagara River and its vicinity are chiefly noted for their autumn and winter birds, particularly gulls and duck along the river itself. It is over 70 km from Fort Erie, where the river leaves Lake Erie, to the mouth at Niagara-on-the-Lake, and the Niagara Parkway runs beside or close to the river for almost the entire distance, and much of the route is through parkland. A full day or even more can be spent covering the area at peak periods, as enormous numbers of gulls and large flocks of duck can occur, particularly in late fall. Seventeen species of gulls have been recorded, most of them annually.

The peak periods are in late October through early December, when there are huge flocks of Bonaparte's Gulls, usually accompanied by scattered birds of rarer species: Franklin's, Little, and Common Black-headed Gulls and Black-legged Kittiwake are the most usual. Later most of these smaller gulls move out and Iceland, Glaucous, and a few Thayer's Gulls join the thousands of Ring-billed and Herring Gulls. There are small numbers of Great Black-backed Gulls through most of this period, and Lesser Black-backed Gulls are now regular.

Duck numbers build up in November. The principal species are Canvasback, scaup, Oldsquaw, Common Goldeneye, Bufflehead, and Common Merganser, but there are smaller numbers of American Black Duck, Mallard, Gadwall, and American Wigeon. The rarer species that can be expected include Harlequin Duck, all three scoters, and Barrow's Goldeneye, with scattered loons and grebes (Eared are rare but regular). Scattered shorebirds along the rocks around the falls regularly include Purple Sandpipers, which are then sometimes present well into winter.

In the route described below the most productive areas are around Niagara Falls itself, and to a lesser extent at Fort Erie and around Queenston, although there will be birds visible along the entire length of the river. Watch the ornamental plantings along the route for berry-bearing trees that can attract mockingbirds, waxwings, and other fruit eaters.

It is easier to cover the river from south to north, and you can omit the southern section altogether if time is limited. The account will start in **Fort Erie**, from the Lake Erie shoreline adjacent to Old Fort Erie. This point is some 3 km south along Lakeshore Road from the Peace Bridge (the bridge to the United States), which is also the end of the QEW and Highway 3. The kilometres that follow are from point to point. The route begins at Bardol Street, where Lakeshore Road begins, and assumes you will drive west and north following the shoreline and river bank. The name of the road changes; it is variously called Niagara Boulevard, Lake Shore Road, River Road, and perhaps other names I have never noticed. The main thing is to stick to the main road closest to the river.

0 km   Bardol Street. The rocks along this stretch of waterfront often have shorebirds, as do the lawns a little farther on. The waters in this section are good for scoters.

3.3 km   The Peace Bridge. Look for duck, gulls, possible phalarope. Several vantage points now follow in rapid sequence from the parking lots and drive-offs along the Fort Erie waterfront, and will not be listed separately.

2.6 km   Jarvis Street. This drive-off usually seems to conclude the most interesting sections around Fort Erie. From here to the control dam north of Chippawa (23 km) the duck and gulls gradually thin out, but interesting finds are still possible.

6.1 km   The marina waters concentrate duck when the neighbouring river is frozen.

1.4 km   A marshy area, good for pond duck (note hunting occurs in fall).

15.2 km   The control structures at the mouth of the Welland River at **Chippawa**. Gulls and terns loiter on them.

0.8 km   Keep right over the Chippawa bridge, and right again to continue along the parkway.

1.3 km   A large parking lot near the high gates and control dam on the river. A major stop for gulls, terns, and waterfowl generally. The control structure attracts Snowy Owls during incursion years. You are now entering **Niagara Falls**.

0.3 km   The road forks here into north- and south-bound lanes, and there is an entrance to a small parking area on the right. This is one of the best sites for viewing the rapids, and the gulls and duck below the dam.

0.3 km   Turn left into the entrance to a loop road around **Dufferin Islands**, with one-way traffic going north and parking at the bottom. Walk over to the river, which is often very productive here, because it is less disturbed than elsewhere. Gulls and duck loiter, and this is the place to see Purple Sandpipers. The woods of Dufferin Islands to the west of the road yield common landbirds. Pied-billed Grebe, herons, and puddle duck may be here prior to freeze-up.

0.3 km   From the end of the Dufferin Islands loop, the parking lot on the left for the greenhouses has heated washrooms open all year.

0.1 km   A small parking lot just north of the old power plant building on the right is perhaps the best single spot in the entire route. Gulls and duck are everywhere, possible shorebirds on the rocks, and a colony of Black-crowned Night-Herons in the willows on the small islands. If parking here is inaccessible, use the lot on the left just passed.

1.1 km   The main falls parking lot on the left is usually free from 1 December on. The low stone wall overlook here is a good place to view Table Rock and the other rocks and rapids above the **Horseshoe Falls**. Also look down into the gorge near the top of the falls.

0.4 km   If there is street parking available it starts here. Walk upstream to view the gorge if not covered at the last stop, and look downstream at the whole area, particularly about the power plant outlet in the gorge below the restaurant. The Victoria restaurant is open all year with a good snack bar and heated washrooms. Downstream from here is a belvedere (gazebo) at the edge of the gorge where a good view of the area is possible, particularly of the waterfowl upstream from the *Maid of the Mist* dock.

0.8 km   It is possible to walk or drive down to a boat ramp. Many rarities have been found in the gorge here, and it is one of the places King Eiders can turn up.

0.3 km   The **Rainbow Bridge** parking lots provide more views of the gorge. Highway 420 (QEW exit 30) terminates here, and it is the simplest access point for persons not wishing to cover the full route. Head south to the control structure at the entrance to Niagara Falls, and then follow the route as described.

6.4 km   Niagara Glen Nature Area, despite its name, has never yielded much in the bird line for us. Not worth stopping.

0.7 km   **Niagara School of Horticulture**. Park on the right and walk over to the grounds. There usually are active feeders: it is a good place for mockingbird and other landbirds.

1.4 km   A parking area on the right at the **Sir Adam Beck** generating station. Look down on the gulls here: good for white gulls.

1.2 km   The entrance to the bridge to the United States is on left.

0.7 km   Immediately past the entrance to Highway 405 the parkway turns right down the hill. To visit the hydro reservoir bounded by the wire fence and high embankments to the west, turn left here on Portage Road (It parallels Highway 405), and drive 3.4 km to Stanley Street. Bear left here over the bridge, and after 0.5 km turn left on the Fruitbelt Parkway, which dead-ends at the fence immediately ahead. There is a fisherman's access point here. Walk up the hill and scope the vast water area beyond. The reservoir's principal interest is the flocks of gulls that often gather there.

Returning to the Niagara Parkway, note that the berry-bearing trees and evergreens around the Brock Monument can attract landbirds. Now continue down the hill. At the bottom is an intersection with York Street: ahead is **Queenston**, and a left on York leads to St Davids (see below). To continue the present route, turn right and then bear left on Front Street.

0.4 km   A turn-off to the right opposite Dumfries Street leads down to parking areas where one can check gulls again (this area is particularly good for the smaller gulls) and walk upriver to cover the woodland for landbirds. One can also walk or drive down the hill to the dock and view the river from there. Continue north on Front, which finally turns onto Walnut, and right again on Queenston Street.

0.4 km   A small drive goes down to a park on the right, the other end of the narrow dirt road that goes north from the dock. There is more river access here. Queenston joins the parkway a little to the north. Continue on it. Usually there is not much new on the river along this stretch.

8.8 km   The road forks. Bear right, but first check the large oaks here and along John Street to the west for woodpeckers. This is called Paradise Grove.

1.2 km   One is now entering **Niagara-on-the-Lake**. Stop at Navy Hall for a view of the river. The well-grown gardens from here on are good for mockingbirds and wintering landbirds. One is now on Ricardo Street.

0.4 km   Collingwood Street, on the south of the marina, is good for the fly-past of Bonaparte's Gulls and allies in the hour before darkness. Some 50,000+ have been recorded here in late November and early December. The marina may have open leads with interesting duck in winter.

0.2 km   Turn right on Melville, then left at the Customs House, and check the river again. The road curves to join northbound Delater Street (good for mockingbird), and when it too curves, there is viewing of birds around the mouth of the river.

0.7 km   Turn right on Front Street. The streets to the left were Ontario's first breeding station for House Finches. They are still there, and a drive around looking at gardens and feeders may yield both these and other Niagara area regulars such as Tufted Titmouse or Carolina Wren. Front finally curves west at Simcoe Street.

1.0 km   Turn right on Queen Street and, 0.8 km along, check the river mouth and lake again.

This terminates the river drive. One is now at Lake Ontario, and can continue west along Niagara Boulevard, which curves around through well-grown gardens and, at 0.7 km, crosses a small creek that can be productive of landbirds. The road then turns south on *Shakespeare Avenue* and joins Lake Shore Road (Regional Road 87) after about 1 km. The lake end of Shakespeare is the preferred area for Tufted Titmouse and Red-bellied Woodpecker. At Lake Shore Road turn right, and at 0.7 km from the corner there are sewage lagoons on the right, some of which are visible from the road. Road 87 continues west some 10 km to Port Weller.

ST DAVIDS

This village is 3.9 km west on Regional Road 81 (York Road) from its intersection in Queenston with the Niagara Parkway. At St Davids there are some private *sewage lagoons* that can be visited with permission. Coming from Queenston, turn right (north) on Regional Road 100 (Creek Road). At 0.4 km there is a cannery on the right with a lagoon behind it. The other lagoons are 1.3 km farther north. Turn left here on a dead-end gravel road opposite a gas station. The lagoons are 0.7 km along on the right. To gain access to the ponds permission *must* be obtained from the manager at the cannery. Failure to do so could result in withdrawal of the privileges for everyone. The lagoons are closed on Sundays.

PORT COLBORNE AND AREA

Port Colborne is a useful starting point for some of the birding areas along the Lake Erie shoreline. The town itself lies at the entrance to the Welland Canal, and is served by Highway 58 from Welland to the north, and by Highway 3 paralleling the shoreline.

From the Highway 58 intersection, *Mud Lake* is east almost 1 km on Highway 3 to the light at Elm Street (Regional Road 80). Turn north here and drive 3.5 km to a small parking lot on the east side of the road. From this drive-off are two paths, one up to the top of the dike to connect with a trail along it and around the lake, and the other along the south side of the dike to connect with a boardwalk and trail running around the east side of the lake and into the cattail marsh. The lake is noteworthy for all the usual marsh species in summer and breeding records of several species of duck, including Ruddy. There is a controlled hunt here. On the other side of the road from the above parking lot is the local dump, which may yield interesting gulls.

The remaining sections of *Wainfleet Bog*, a massive peat bog now much reduced by drainage and development, can be reached from two points. Again taking the intersection of Highways 58 and 3 as a departure point, drive north on Highway 58 for 1.4 km to Barrick Road on the west. Turn and drive 1.3 km to the point the road dead-ends at a peat farm, currently called F.A.Y. Farm. Ask for permission at the office to go in and drive north across a small bridge about 1 km on a dirt-peat road, which leads to a small drive-off on the left side near some dense shrubs. A trail starts here and runs north, eventually into open untouched bog. Be sure to mark or otherwise note the point you enter the open bog, as it is easy to lose track of your position. Northern Harrier, Short-eared Owl, and Lincoln's Sparrow have all nested in this area.

To reach the second access point drive west on Highway 3 from the Highway 58 intersection 5.4 km to Wilson Road, which crosses the bog to the north. On the east side of Wilson there is a trail which runs through the poplar-willow woodland. After several hundred metres this comes out into mostly open bog, and eventually arrives at untouched areas of bog. This trail has to be watched for as it grows over. It runs east off Wilson near the only dirt road that comes in from the west. Whip-poor-wills breed adjacent to Wilson, and the species noted above also can be found here.

Just 0.8 km west of Wilson Road is the intersection of Highway 3 and Regional Road 30. To visit *Morgan's Point* turn south on 30 and drive 3.1 km (the road turns and runs west) to Morgan's Point Road on the south. Turn left and drive to the end (1.6 km), where the point attracts shorebirds and other waterfowl, and the pines to the west concentrate migrants.

Farther west along Highway 3, the flat farmland in the area west of the village of **Wainfleet** in Haldimand-Norfolk has sod farms that can attract numbers of plover and other shorebirds in the fall (mid-September is best). Specific locations vary; currently farms at Winger and Mount Carmel are the best. It is a matter of driving the roads in the area, most of which are laid out on a grid pattern, and watching for suitable fields. Continuing west on Highway 3 leads to the areas around Dunnville described in chapter 7.

East of Port Colborne (some 14 km east of the Highway 58 intersection) is the Point Abino road. This runs south some

6 km to *Point Abino*, a privately owned point with wooded hills that have some Carolinian species in summer (Acadian Flycatcher is regular in woods at Abino Hills west of the point, reached from Holloway Bay Road) and which concentrate migrants. Access to the point road is uncertain – permission may or may not be given at the gate – and parking is difficult.

WEST ALONG LAKE ONTARIO

The area around **St Catharines**, on the QEW west of Niagara Falls, is of interest for both the waterbirds along the Lake Ontario shoreline and for the woods and reservoirs on the Niagara Escarpment. **Port Weller**, the entry to the Welland Canal, is northeast of the city, and the canal piers are north of Regional Road 87 (QEW exit 44, and north on Niagara Street). On the west side of the bridge over the canal is Canal Road, leading to the beach at the west; and to the east is Broadway, which runs north to the other side. It is about 2 km to the open woods near the marina there. The whole area can be good for waterbirds.

Farther west, **Port Dalhousie** is at the mouth of Twelve Mile Creek. Continue west on Regional Road 87 (Lakeshore Road) about 5.5 km from the Port Weller bridge. Here Michigan Avenue on the right leads to the east side of the creek mouth. On the left is *Martindale Pond*, with an overview from Lock Street, to the right just ahead; and this leads to a large parking lot on the beach. Both the pond and the creek mouth can be good for waterbirds. Continuing west on Main Street, the road to Henley Island (1.7 km) and Regional Road 38 (a further 0.6 km) are both to the left (south) and provide views of the pond. Road 38 is Martindale Road, which leads (1.8 km) south to QEW exit 48. These are not exceptional areas, but may have good numbers of waterfowl during migration and in winter.

The areas around the Niagara Escarpment provide a pleasant drive through a variety of habitats, and yield good general birding rather than particularly noteworthy species. They can be reached from Highway 406 (QEW exit 49), the controlled-access road linking St Catharines and Thorold, and Welland to the south. The account below assumes a start at the intersection of this highway and Beaverdams Road (about 14.5 km from the QEW). If one turns east on Beaverdams Road one will cross

Gibson Lake, part of a power reservoir complex that extends east and west of here. At 1.9 km along is Decew Road, and a left turn here will lead 5.6 km west to Pelham Road. This route passes the reservoir complex to Decew Falls and the wooded areas on the public lands on both sides of the road.

If one turns west on Beaverdams Road from Highway 406 one comes almost immediately to the Merritville Road. Turn left here, and 2.6 km from 406 turn right (west) on Roland (or Holland) Road. This road leads to Hollow Road, 2.4 km on the left, and the *St Johns Conservation Area*, with fine Carolinian hardwoods. Continuing west it winds through beautiful rolling country to join the Effingham Road 3.4 km farther on, and you can drive south to Highway 20. Another good wooded area in this vicinity is the Hamilton Naturalists' *Short Hills* area. To reach it drive 3.8 km south on the Effingham Road to Mepler Road, and then 1.3 km west to Centre Street, where the reserve is on the northeast corner.

Vineland is farther west on the Queen Elizabeth Way. Exit 57 leads to Victoria Avenue (Regional Road 24). Turn north here towards the lake, and just past the service roads is the entrance, to the west, of the *Vineland Agricultural Research Station*. The grounds here are fine for migrant landbirds, and 0.9 km farther north where the road turns along the shore there is a vantage point for viewing the lake. Accipiters follow the shoreline in spring, and heavy flights of waterfowl (Common and Red-breasted Merganser, scaup, and, in spring, pintail) occur.

Jordan Harbour is east of here: return to the QEW and cross it to drive east on the South Service Road. The road turns south 1.5 km east, and views of the harbour can be obtained from the marina road directly ahead, and along the road to the south, especially at 0.7 km.

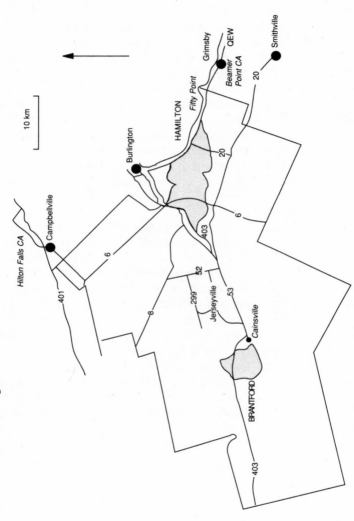

MAP 16   Hamilton-Wentworth Region

10 Hamilton and Area

Hamilton-Wentworth Region, Brant County, and Adjacent Areas

Hamilton – Dundas Marsh
– The north shore of Hamilton Harbour
– The east end of Hamilton Harbour
Ancaster
Beverly Swamp, Valens Conservation Area,
and the Puslinch wetland
Mountsberg Conservation Area
Halton Regional Forest and Hilton Conservation Area
Beamer Point and the Grimsby area
Brantford and area
Smithville

The city of Hamilton, sitting at the westernmost end of Lake Ontario, abounds with places of interest to a birder. Here the Niagara Escarpment curves along the lake, and below it the waters of Hamilton Harbour are cut off from Lake Ontario by the long sandbar of Burlington Beach. Both water and landbird migrants are concentrated here, and also farther inland. At the west end of the harbour Dundas Marsh provides the city with a major wetland, and there are wooded tracts along its shores, and inland along the line of the escarpment. This is still the Carolinian Forest Region, but it is here at its northerly limits and the mixed forests intrude along the region's northern boundaries, and with the varied exposures the escarpment creates.

This is an urbanizing area, with Hamilton's tentacles creeping inland towards Brantford and southeast along the lake. To the northeast even more extensive urban sprawl spreads along the lake from Toronto. This area, with the exception of the north shore of Hamilton Harbour, will be covered in the next chapter. In fact birders from both cities regularly cover the Lake Ontario shoreline there, but it is desirable to treat it as a unit. Three other locations lying outside the regional municipality are considered here, as they fall more logically into this chapter than elsewhere. These are the Halton County Forest, Beamer Point, and Smithville sewage lagoons.

The region is served by the Queen Elizabeth Way (QEW) from Toronto and Niagara, and access from Highway 401 is via either Highway 403 east from Woodstock and Brantford or Highway 6 (401 exits 236 and 299 respectively). Highway 403 bypasses the city to the northwest, while the QEW curves around the eastern perimeter. Hamilton airport is to the south on Highway 6, and provides an alternative access for air travellers not wishing to drive from Toronto. There is ample accommodation, including camping at Valens (year-round) and in Confederation Park east of Van Wagner's Beach.

The Hamilton area is milder than areas farther east: there can be as much as a week's difference in early spring blossom between Hamilton and Toronto. However, it is also downwind of the major storm winds sometimes deposit snow that areas farther east escape. The bonus for this exposure is that fall migrants on Lake Ontario often appear along the lakeshore here in easterly gales.

HAMILTON

Hamilton, with its associated communities a city of over 500,000, is a major industrial centre. Fortunately it is possible to cover most of the birding areas without entering the city itself, and Dundas Marsh is accessible with only minimal city driving. It is easy to get lost here, as the irregular configuration of the harbour distorts the grid pattern followed by most roads elsewhere in Ontario (see maps 17 and 18).

To cover the areas around Hamilton Harbour and Dundas Marsh (Cootes Paradise) take Highway 403 to the exit for Highway 6 north. At the first traffic light north of the interchange (about 0.5 km) turn right, following the signs for Highway 2 and Plains Road. This road runs south 0.8 km over Highway 403 again, and joins Highway 2 (Plains Road) at a T-intersection. Here a right turn will take you towards Dundas Marsh and a left turn to the north shore of Hamilton Bay. The Royal Botanical Gardens (RBG) administers most of the birding areas around Dundas Marsh. Its properties are extensive, and range from large formal gardens to the wild lands around the marsh itself. Until recently all of this was freely open to the public, but now a fee is charged for access to many of the areas, including some of those described below. The present situation seems rather ambiguous, but you can expect to be charged at least for entry to the RGB Arboretum, and perhaps other areas as well.

To cover **Dundas Marsh**, one of the premier birding locales along Lake Ontario and a very extensive area, the following loop is suggested. First turn right (south) on Plains Road and drive 1 km to the Guelph Road, which is past the Rock Garden and is signposted to the RGB Arboretum. Turn right on this road, drive down the hill, go 0.8 km to the *Arboretum* entrance on your left. It is a good idea to pick up a map of the RGB properties at the Interpretive Centre here if it is open (there is one posted outside if not). This shows all the areas described below. There is a circular parking area at the end of the road, and from here a network of trails leads down to the marsh. The trail to Bull's Point runs some 3 km along the wooded north shore. The area ahead and to the left of the parking lot as you drive in has fruit trees and shrubs that attract thrushes and waxwings in fall and winter.

Reaching the south shore and the west end is more complicated. Return to the Plains Road and turn right to continue south across the high-level bridge. This can be a good vantage point for watching hawk migration in autumn, although most of the parking is on the other side of the boulevard. At 1.9 km bear right on Dundurn Street and continue 0.6 km to King Street. Turn right here (west) and continue straight ahead on King Street at 0.9 km when the main flow of traffic angles left. The next light (0.2 km) is Longwood Road. Turn right here, and drive to its end. Bear left into a parking area which gives access to *Princess Point* at the southeastern end of Cootes Paradise. There are usually mudflats here and waterfowl. This is one end of the network of walking trails that lead along the south shore, which is also heavily wooded. The open waters off the point can have migrants such as Red-necked Grebe which will not be present in the shallower areas at the west end.

The west end of the marsh is accessible via Cootes Drive, which is a well-marked right turn off Main Street, west of the McMaster University complex. Returning south on Longwood,

Main Street is the first main artery south of King Street; turn right there and continue about 2 km to Cootes Drive and bear right. This leads to Dundas; the road crosses Spencer Creek 1.3 km from the turn, and there is limited parking along the road shoulder. This is the entrance to the *South Shore Trails* (it is signposted), which leads to vantage points for viewing the west end of the marsh.

The main trail follows the west bank (on the left as you stand with your back to the road) through tall willows, and finally opens up as the trail forks. To the right is a bridge across the creek, while the trail ahead will turn left and lead to an observation tower overlooking the ponds behind of the hydro station to the west.

The trail over the bridge leads east to a tower overlooking the main water areas and mudflats bounding the marsh. A spur track here continues on along the east bank of the creek until it too turns east to follow the bank of the old canal. Depending on water levels, it may be possible to continue along here to the mudflats. Cattail areas to the right of this track can yield Sharp-tailed Sparrows in later fall and the flats are very good for shorebirds throughout that season. The trail from the tower winds back into the woodland through dense tangles and across wet depressions back to the road: it is all wonderful habitat, and can teem with migrants on suitable days.

From the South Shore Trails continue 0.8 km on Cootes Drive to Olympic Drive, the first road on the right. Turn and drive past the hydro station to a sports complex on the right (0.9 km) and one can park at the back here and walk over to view the extreme west end of the marsh (the *Hydro Pond*). The allotment gardens here can be full of sparrows in fall.

Dundas Marsh has the usual assortment of breeding species, including a small colony of Black-crowned Night-Herons, but it is even more interesting in migration. Large numbers of duck and a few Tundra Swans are often present in March; in autumn, depending on water levels, the area can abound in shorebirds, including godwits and phalaropes. In fact, it can be good year-round.

Continue on Olympic Drive 1.9 km to Valley Road and the parking lot for *Borer's Falls Conservation Area* to the north. Valley Road itself leads 1.3 km to Rockchapel Road, where a

MAP 17 Hamilton West

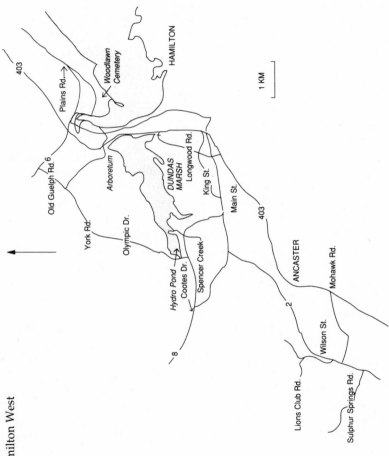

left turn leads to the Botanical Gardens' *Rock Chapel Sanctuary* (1.1 km). All these areas have the mixed woodlands and deep ravines characteristic of this section of the Niagara Escarpment, and where good vistas exist they can yield hawk viewing in the fall.

To return to the starting point, continue east on Olympic Drive (now York Road), which leads back to Highway 6 just 0.6 km north of the original turnoff to Plains Road.

It will be recalled that to cover the **North Shore of Hamilton Harbour** one should turn left on to Plains Road after leaving Highway 6. On the left at 0.8 km is a drive to parking for the Botanical Gardens' Rose Garden and the Cherry Hill Gate, and just past this entrance on the right of Plains Road is Botanical Drive, signposted to the Royal Botanical Gardens' headquarters and Woodlawn Cemetery. Bear right here and drive to Spring Garden Road, the first right. Turn again and *Woodlawn Cemetery*, which provides good views of the west end of Hamilton Bay, is on the left. Spring Garden Road itself leads down to the water and up the other side (as Valley Inn Road: this section is quite narrow, and there is a low bridge en route) to rejoin Plains Road. Just before the main road turns to cross the water there is a bridge directly ahead with a small parking area on the other side. A trail starts here and leads past marshes on the right where Black-crowned Night-Herons roost and duck and shorebirds congregate, mainly in fall. In addition to the waterbirds, fruit-eating species, attracted by the shrub plantings around the formal gardens, can be found in autumn and winter.

The back part of the *Holy Sepulchre Cemetery*, 0.8 km farther east on Plains Road from the Woodlawn Cemetery turnoff, also provides views of the harbour. The water below the cemeteries is often undisturbed and has duck and grebes close to shore, and the trees and grassy areas attract landbird migrants, particularly sparrows in fall.

From here continue another 2.1 km east to LaSalle Park Road (it is the first major intersection you encounter, just past a large shopping plaza), and turn right again. At 0.4 km is a stop street; continue straight ahead down the hill to the car park on an old loading dock. Here there are excellent views of Hamilton Harbour both east and west, and usually duck congregate off here in fall through spring where open water exists. Return to

MAP 18 Hamilton East

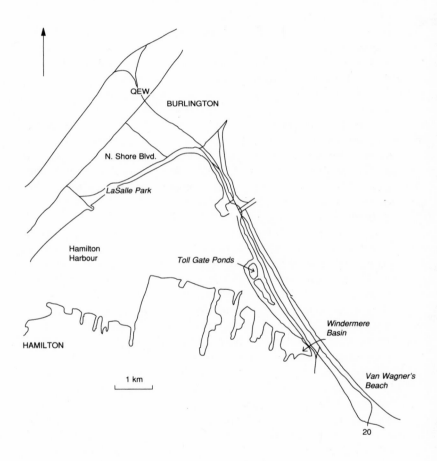

QEW

BURLINGTON

N. Shore Blvd.

LaSalle Park

Hamilton
Harbour

Toll Gate Ponds

Windermere
Basin

HAMILTON

1 km

Van Wagner's
Beach

20

the stop street and turn right onto Northshore Road to continue through *LaSalle Park* itself. The woodlands at the bottom end can yield landbirds. Continuing east on Northshore Road (later Northshore Boulevard) there are periodic views of the bay, especially at a small turnoff 1.5 km from the LaSalle Road intersection, and eventually one reaches the QEW exit 97.

Travellers coming from the northeast on the QEW should exit here to Northshore Boulevard to cover the areas just described, or to take the lakeshore back towards Toronto as outlined in the next chapter; however, if the objective is to cover the **East End of Hamilton Harbour**, then take the Eastport Drive from exit 97. This continues ahead paralleling the QEW. The harbour can be productive immediately after leaving the highway; to the west is a small island that often attracts loitering gulls and terns. For persons driving on Northshore Boulevard and wishing to cover Eastport Drive, turn left on to the QEW access ramp just before the QEW bridge, and then follow the signs to Eastport Drive. If you continue on under the QEW bridge you will come to Lakeshore Road in Burlington, and the lakefront route described in the next chapter.

This end of Hamilton Harbour is busy and very polluted. However, it concentrates waterfowl in autumn through early spring, when sizeable flocks of Canvasback and some scoters usually occur, as well as all the more usual wintering species described for the lakeshore. In winter any open leads or other water areas will usually yield duck; outstanding numbers of such species as Lesser Scaup, rare in winter elsewhere on Lake Ontario, can often be seen here. From late summer until freeze-up an enticing array of shorebirds can appear as well.

First, to get to the piers of the ship canal into Hamilton Harbour continue on Eastport Drive to the light at the Canada Centre for Inland Waters. Turn right here into the centre's grounds. Follow this road around (it curves left and then runs south to end at the ship canal). Turn left at the end of the road and drive into the area of waste ground adjacent to Eastport Drive and the canal. Park and walk out on the pier on the Burlington side and check it and the beach and scrub at its base, as well as the water areas. All can yield good birds. The Burlington-Hamilton Beach strip along here concentrates migrant landbird flocks moving along the lakeshore. (The waste ground on the lakeside of Eastport Drive just after crossing the lift bridge is also used for parking, but you must drive up over the high curb to reach it.)

From the Canada Centre for Inland Waters, continue on Eastport Drive, crossing the lift bridge. Now continue some 2 km, crossing under the QEW again (readers will be delighted to learn that none of this is as complicated as it sounds!), to some diked water impoundments on your right. These are the *Toll Gate Ponds*, and are one of Hamilton's birding hot-spots. Stopping is hazardous along here! Be careful. The trees at the back of the impoundments have nesting Double-crested Cormorants and a few Black-crowned Night-Herons (Snowy Egret has nested, the only nesting for the province), and the ponds are often full of duck, with shorebirds on any mudflat areas. The landfill area adjacent holds a gull and tern colony.

After covering the ponds carefully, continue on some 2 km past the landfill until the waters of the harbour open out on the right. This area, the *Windermere Basin*, is even less enchanting aesthetically than the ponds, but it can be great for duck, especially in winter when it has yielded a Tufted Duck with some regularity. This area is currently being filled and its final state is not clear at the time of writing; however, it is still very productive. Be especially careful stopping here as it is a 'no parking' area.

Just past the Windermere Basin, Eastport Drive ends at Woodward Avenue. Turn left on the lights here onto Beach Road, and drive under the QEW 0.3 km to the next light. There is access to the QEW here, but turn right on to Van Wagner's Beach Road. This has lake viewing on the left and some small (but often productive) patches of marsh on the right, between it and the QEW. There is a series of parking lots along the lakeside. (Note that if you do not turn on to Van Wagner's Beach Road you will be on Beach Boulevard, heading back towards the lift bridge and Burlington.)

Van Wagner's Beach is the extreme west end of Lake Ontario, directly downwind of the northeast to easterly gales that accompany fall storms, and it can provide a vantage point for seeing offshore waterbirds blown in close to shore. It is the lower Great Lakes' best place for seeing jaegers in fall (both Parasitic and Pomarine are regular), and Northern Gannets are rare but regular in bad weather, as well as rarer gulls and waterfowl. At other times the usual mix of migrant and wintering ducks and gulls occurs (see the description of the western lakeshore under Toronto), but there is not much to be expected in summer.

At 1.5 km the beach road curves to become Centennial Parkway southbound, which in turn becomes Highway 20 and leads to exit 88 of the QEW, giving access to 50 Point, Grimsby, and the rest of the Niagara Peninsula.

ANCASTER

Just west of Hamilton, near Ancaster, the deep, wooded valleys associated with the streams that feed Dundas Marsh provide a rich variety of habitats and good birding year-round. The Hamilton Region Conservation Authority has developed an extensive network of trails through this area, and there are a number of access points. To reach the area, exit Highway 403 at Mohawk Road and drive west (that is, towards Ancaster: Mohawk changes its name to Rousseaux) 1.7 km to Wilson Street (Highway 2). One access point is left on Wilson 0.7 km to Sulphur Springs Road. Turn right here and drive 1 km to a T-intersection where Sulphur Springs Road turns right. Continue right, driving down the hill 1.3 km to a parking lot for the Hermitage on the right. This lot gives access to the network of trails to the north. A second, more easterly, access point is right on Wilson from the light at Rousseaux and then drive 0.8 km to Montgomery Drive, the first left. Turn here, and continue 0.2 km to the Old Dundas Road. Turn right, and follow this road as it curves steeply down into the valley. The Old Dundas Road finally turns right on a stop street. Continue straight ahead here on Lions Club Road. The first right (Artaban Road), dead-ends at the Resource Management Centre, while the Lions Club Road itself leads about 1.0 km to the Merrick Field Centre. There is parking and access to the extensive trail system at both these points.

These areas are particularly good in winter for finches and wintering landbirds at the many feeders in the valley. There is an excellent mix of breeding birds including warblers (Blue-winged, Golden-winged, and Hooded have occurred) and the valley channels migrants.

BEVERLY SWAMP, VALENS CONSERVATION AREA, AND THE PUSLINCH WETLAND

Several areas of particular interest in the breeding season are northwest of Hamilton. They extend into Wellington County to the north and Halton to the east, but for convenience all are considered here together. This first group is between Highways 6 and 8 (in the vicinity of the African Lion Safari). They can be reached by driving north on Highway 6 from 403 (the exit used for the start of the Dundas Marsh loop) some 13.5 km to West Flamborough Concession 8 on the left (see map 19). The *Beverly Swamp* begins some 4 km west of here, but the most extensive area is farther west, past the Westover Road, in the 2.5 km stretch to the Valens Road. There are trails on both the north and south sides about halfway along the road here. The swamp is heavily wooded and excellent for warblers and other forest species. Many species with northern affinities breed, and Whip-poor-will, Acadian Flycatcher, and Yellow-throated Vireo also occur. Turkeys have been released in this area and man-made ponds attract waterbirds.

To the south Concession 7 also has an access area to the Beverly Swamp Reserve on the north 1 km east of Valens Road, and approximately 2 km east there is access to another extensive forest area on the south. This can be good for winter finches in season.

Continuing west on Concession 8 leads to the Valens Road. Turn right here, and at the next sideroad is a T-intersection, where a left turn leads to the entrance to the *Valens Conservation Area* (entrance fee). It consists of a large lake and marsh, which are attractive to waterbirds in migration, especially ducks in early spring. It is heavily used for recreation in summer, and there is controlled hunting in autumn. The internal road system of the conservation area gives access to the west side of the lake, and the marsh and wooded areas at the back. The Valens Road itself jogs east and then follows the eastern boundary of the area, with excellent views of the east side of the lake.

MAP 19   Valens and Mountsberg

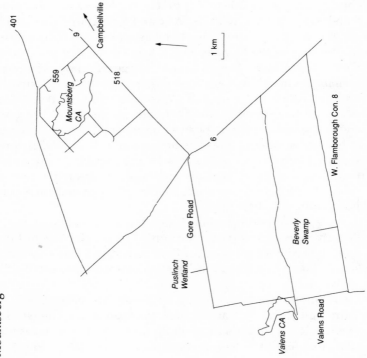

Continue north on the Valens Road some 3.3 km (it jogs right and then left again) to the Gore Road (Flamborough Township Line). Turn right here and continue 1.6 km to the next sideroad north. This road gives access to the *Puslinch Wetland*, an extensive area of bog and woodland where many northern species occur. A walk along the railroad can yield Virginia Rail and Sedge Wren, and the woodland trails typical forest species, while the bog itself yields such species as Nashville and Black-and-White Warbler, and White-throated Sparrow. Long-eared Owls have bred.

There are many old fields, Christmas tree farms, and reforestation in the rolling country of this area. The resultant mix has created conditions suitable for Grasshopper and Clay-colored Sparrow, as well as Upland Sandpipers. Given the successional nature of these habitats, identifying specific areas is probably not worth while, but a search in the breeding season for these species could be productive.

The Gore Road leads east to Highway 6. At this point Regional Road 518 lies opposite and leads to Regional Road 559, some 5 km ahead. This, highlighted in the account below, is the start of the route round Mountsberg Conservation area.

MOUNTSBERG CONSERVATION AREA

Highway 401 exit 312 in Halton County gives ready access to several areas of interest: to the north is the Halton County Forest, discussed below; and to the south is the attractive village of **Campbellville**. Some 4 km east of the community is *Mountsberg Conservation Area*. Mountsberg is particularly significant because it often contains waterbirds, especially shorebirds, at times of the year when other areas are unproductive. It is rewarding at other times too, however, with woodland birds along the trails and good numbers of waterfowl on the 200-hectare lake in early spring and later fall. Hooded Mergansers nest in boxes and often in Pileated Woodpecker holes, but are difficult to see. In autumn the lake is drawn down, exposing mudflats at various areas. The location of these varies from year to year, but at present the best areas are at the eastern side of the lake, on either side of the railway tracks. The mudflats are very good for shorebirds, and thirty-one species have been recorded.

To reach the area from Campbellville, turn right (west) before the railroad crossing on to Regional Road 9. Pass the Community Pond on the left; 1.6 km farther on is a cedar bog on the south side of the road, which is good for woodcock. Go a further 2.4 km to the town line, now **Regional Road 559**, and turn north. Continue along this road to the main entrance to Mountsberg (entrance fee). The Halton Region Conservation Authority conducts a vigorous outdoor education program here, involving numerous aspects of nature interpretation. A bird-banding program has also been carried out for several years; public demonstrations are given on a regular basis.

From the parking lots at the centre trails run south to an observation blind, and north across the railroad tracks, leading to a wooded pond and looping over to follow the shoreline of the main lake northwards to an observation tower.

North on the townline road some 500 metres, at the top of a small rise in the road, tracks lead off to both the left and right (there are gates at the entrance of each). Trails are marked, and the right-hand track leads through a good variety of woodland. Walking along the left track takes you through several hundred metres of wet and dry woodland and terminates at a lookout tower on the lake. Good trails then lead in both directions; the left leg is the continuation of the trail described above running north from the centre. Continuing on the townline road; it curves west and then curves again down a hill to enter a long causeway crossing an area of open water and marshland. There is a viewing tower here at the east end, and the entire causeway gives excellent views of the extensive area of wetlands to the south.

After covering this area carefully, continue west and take the first sideroad south. Follow this road around to the next intersection on the east. Turn left and drive to the end of the road at the water, where there is a parking area and another viewing tower to the southeast, all giving further views of this extensive man-made lake. Return to the intersection and turn south (left), then left again just past the railroad tracks. This road leads directly back to the Campbellville road again, now called Regional Road 518.

A left turn here returns to Campbellville. A right leads to

Highway 6, and then north to Highway 401 exit 299, or to Valens Reservoir and the areas described in the previous section.

HALTON REGIONAL FOREST AND HILTON FALLS CONSERVATION AREA

Northeast of Campbellville lie the extensive woodlands of Halton Regional Forest. This is the largest publicly accessible area of escarpment woodland close to Toronto. The area is divided into a number of tracts, of which the Turner Tract is best known. The forest's character is changing owing to both natural processes as it matures and to the Ministry of Natural Resources' management practices. It is of prime interest for its exceptional wealth of breeding birds. At least 111 species have been reported as breeding, including 14 species of warblers.

The terrain is heavily wooded over much of the area, with almost pure deciduous stands, many mixed stands, and six large plantations of conifers. Many beaver dams are present, and as a result there are extensive flooded areas containing dead trees and marsh vegetation. On the eastern side of the area the Niagara Escarpment runs due north from Highway 401 to **Speyside**. As a result of this diversity, most of the landbird species listed as occurring in summer in the region can be expected here. Other breeders include Northern Goshawk, Blue-gray Gnatcatcher, Yellow-throated Vireo, Blue-winged, Golden-winged (and hybrids), Nashville, Chestnut-sided, and Cerulean Warblers, and Purple Finch. The area can also be good for winter finches in late autumn through early spring.

There are several access points (see map 20). What follows assumes a start at the Campbellville 401 exit 312, but from the east an exit at the Milton (320) interchange is more direct. Distances are point to point. Going north from the **Campbellville** interchange on Regional Road 1, the first point is the entrance to the small Currie tract opposite the racetrack at about 1 km. Next, turn right on Sideroad 10 (1.1 km) and drive 1.3 km to the point the road turns north. There is entry here to the Turner and Mahon tracts, and 0.5 km farther north, another entry leading to the Robertson tract. Continue north (now on the 4th Line) to Sideroad 15 (about 3 km) and turn right again. At

MAP 20   Halton Regional Forest

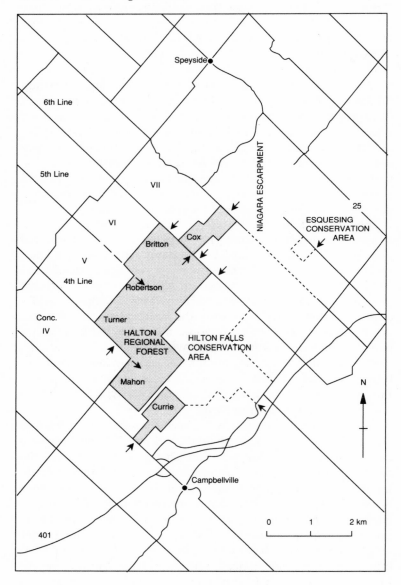

1.4 km the 5th Line runs south to dead-end in 1.4 km; walk south from here into the Robertson tract (parking is rather unsatisfactory). The 6th Line, another 1.4 km east, has many good access points. The first, 2.0 km south, is west of the road, leading into the Britton tract, then 0.3 km farther east to the Cox tract, another to the Britton tract west at 0.3 km, and then 0.5 km west again for pedestrian entry to the northeast end of Hilton Falls Conservation Area. Here you are 2.9 km north of Sideroad 5, for return to Campbellville or Milton.

Farther east on Sideroad 10 (the east-west road you were on prior to turning on to the 6th Line), the next sideroad on the south is the Milton Townline Road. It runs 2.4 km south to an entry to the east side of the Cox tract. The road itself dead-ends farther on.

From the corner of the 6th Line and Sideroad 5 (which is also Regional Road 9, and is so called farther east and west) you can turn west and drive 1.6 km to the main entrance to *Hilton Falls Conservation Area*, which has a small Interpretive Centre, parking, and washrooms, extensive and well-marked hiking trails, and an entrance fee. You can get a map of the trail system here, which leads through similar habitats to those in the rest of the forest, and view the lake above the dam (usually rather unproductive). The area is 4.5 km east of Campbellville, and Regional Road 9 leads back there.

BEAMER POINT AND THE GRIMSBY AREA

Grimsby is east of Hamilton along the QEW to Niagara. It is best known for Beamer Point, a major observation point for spring hawk migration. Leave the QEW on Christie Street south (exit 71), which continues south up the escarpment as Mountain Street. At the top turn right opposite the church on Regional Road 79. Follow this road around west 1.7 km to the entrance to the *Beamer Point Conservation Area*, north along Quarry Road. Turn right and drive down to the entrance of the area on the right. The best observing is from the parking lot itself, although the woods and fields adjacent can have interesting passerines at the time the hawks are moving.

Unlike autumn hawk migration, the spring movement tends to be associated with the movement of warm air into the province. The principal species observed are Sharp-shinned Hawks (April and early May), Red-tailed Hawks (March and April), and Broad-winged Hawks (late April to early May). Substantial numbers of Turkey Vultures also occur, and in March Red-shouldered Hawks are common. This is one of the best places in Ontario to see the latter species, although all the movements are closely related to weather. In all some fifteen species are regular, but Ospreys, Northern Goshawks, eagles, Merlins, and Peregrine Falcons are never seen in any numbers. The count totals do not equal those recorded at the autumn hawk stations, and an entire season's totals may only equal the thousands of Broad-winged Hawks alone that can occur on big days in fall at Hawk Cliff or Amherstburg. Nevertheless, the movement can be very exciting and the birds are often agreeably low, in many cases moving over at treetop height.

Farther west, towards Hamilton, QEW exit 78 joins 50 Road, which leads to *Fifty Point*. This is primarily a lake-viewing location, and is perhaps second only to Van Wagner's Beach in this regard. But it also turns up birds that do not appear at Van Wagner's. It is most productive in fall.

BRANTFORD AND AREA

This city, some 40 km west of Hamilton via Highways 403, and 2 and 53, is not noted for outstanding birding areas. However, there are a couple of areas near town that might be of interest to someone in the area. At *Cainsville*, on the eastern outskirts of the city, the sewage lagoons are on the east side of Shaver Street, which is on the south of Highway 2 just 0.9 km east of the major intersection of Highways 2, 53, 54, and 403. Four kilometres west of this intersection, in Brantford itself, is *Mohawk Park*. This is at the foot of Lynnwood Drive and 0.3 km south of Colborne Street, the name of Highway 2 at this point. The park is a large city park with mixed woodlands, and a lake that can be productive in migration times.

Gray Partridge are relatively widespread on the escarpment south of Hamilton. Finding them is another matter. There have been a variety of places over the years that have been identified as 'sure-fire' for these birds, which are often easiest to find in winter. The current area is north of Highways 2 and 53, and west of Highway 52. Go north on the latter to the first intersection, the Jerseyville Road, and drive the north-south roads in this area, north to Regional Road 299 and west as far as Jerseyville itself, searching the field edges for the birds.

SMITHVILLE

This town, on Highway 20 about halfway between Hamilton and Thorold, is in the Niagara Region; however, the sewage lagoons seem to be covered mostly by Hamilton birders. The lagoons are on the east side of town, and have been very productive. From the railroad bridge crossing Highway 20 drive east 0.8 km to Regional Road 614 on the right. Turn and drive 0.3 km, crossing the stream. The long drive into the lagoons is on the left. Park on the road past the bridge and (preferably) crawl under the fence at the ditch. Above all, do not climb the fences of the adjacent fields.

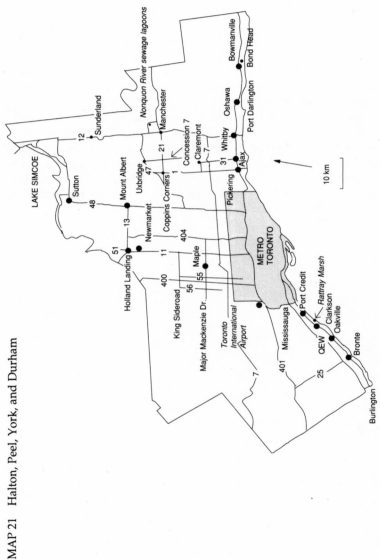

MAP 21   Halton, Peel, York, and Durham

11 Toronto and Area

Metropolitan Toronto and the Regions of Halton, Peel, York, and Durham

Metropolitan Toronto
Lake Ontario west of Toronto
Toronto Islands
Tommy Thompson Park (the Leslie Street Spit)
The Lakeshore east of Metropolitan Toronto
The Oak Ridges Moraine and the Nonquon lagoons
Southern Lake Simcoe
Other sewage lagoons north of Toronto
Areas along Highway 401 and the Queen Elizabeth Way
Areas along Highway 400

Metropolitan Toronto is a city of over two million persons, with all the urban sprawl that implies. Like all large cities, its shadow extends far beyond its formal boundaries, and the southern parts of the regions of Halton, Peel, York, and Durham are all heavily urbanized, giving the entire conurbation a population of three million or more. In spite of its size, however, it has many excellent birding locales, most of them associated with the Lake Ontario shoreline.

Toronto is the entry point to Ontario for overseas visitors, and indeed for most persons arriving by air; and the major provincial road network radiates outward from the city, with Highway 400 to the north and Highway 401 and the Queen Elizabeth Way (QEW) serving the west and east. Most of this area is covered in detail in my *A Birdfinding Guide to the Toronto Region* (available from the author at 1 Queen Street, Suite 401, Cobourg, Ontario K9A 1M8), and for this reason only the major sites are covered below, and then in far less detail than in the local book. The easternmost areas from Whitby onward are in Durham Region, and are also covered very thoroughly in Tozer and Richards' *Birds of the Oshawa–Lake Scugog Region*.

The Niagara Escarpment towers over the flat countryside in the west of Peel County. Its woodlands resemble the adjacent areas to the west, and for this reason the *Halton County Forest* is considered in chapter 10. This tract of escarpment woodland north of Highway 401 and west of **Milton** is the closest extensive area of this kind to Toronto.

The relatively flat agricultural country that is vanishing under the urban growth is bounded on the north by the Oak Ridges Moraine, a belt of rolling hills with a scenic mixture of farmland, abandoned fields, cedar bog, and forest. There is much reforestation in conifers, and increasing amounts of estate housing for the affluent. The result is often a rich mixture of habitats that can be very rewarding in the breeding season. Northeast again are the lowlands bounding Lake Simcoe, with a shoreline dominated by the summer cottages of the city dwellers to the south. It is particularly productive in later fall, when the cottagers have gone into hibernation.

To the south is Lake Ontario itself. Its shoreline runs northeast, and the northerly component is an important one, as winter lasts noticeably longer to the east, in Oshawa for example, than in Oakville. A series of small rivers and creeks runs south from the moraine, often forming deep valleys or ravines. These watercourses usually have narrow flood plains bounded by steep wooded banks, with mixed hardwoods and some conifers. In some cases the flood plain itself is still wooded, with patches of swamp and marsh, but in the more heavily used parks this lower land is typically mown grass with picnic tables and other facilities. The narrow, cool, wooded ravines sometimes have pockets of plants with northern affinities, but in warmer areas on sandy soils some Carolinian floral elements occur near their northeasterly limits. In the built-up areas these valleys are often the only remaining pockets of natural habitat.

In general the resident bird life in even the most extensive urban natural areas lacks the richness of similar habitats outside of the city. In migration periods, however, these islands of natural vegetation in the sea of buildings become migrant traps, and provide excellent birding on the right day. Along the lake this quality is even more pronounced, and the region's major birding areas lie along lakeshore.

METROPOLITAN TORONTO

The Municipality of Metropolitan Toronto (usually referred to simply as Metro) covers 624 sq. km, most of them urbanized (see map 22). Formerly Metro was an aggregation of the City of Toronto and suburban boroughs. Most of these boroughs have now decided that they're cities too, but the visitor simply sees one sprawling metropolis, albeit with many neighbourhoods. In this avian wasteland anything green becomes a refuge, and Toronto's river valleys – the Humber, Don, Highland Creek, and the Rouge are the principal ones – fill the role admirably. The Metro Parks Department, as opposed to those of the individual cities, administers much valley land, as well as Toronto Islands, and its 'passive recreation' mandate allows for the retention of much natural habitat. The best of its most accessible parks are discussed below, but *Highland Creek* and *Morningside* are others in the east end, and there are numerous smaller areas. The following assumes the visitor will have access to a city road map: the directions start from the major thoroughfares in each case.

The city cemeteries are also islands of green, and *Mount Pleasant Cemetery* in particular (off Mount Pleasant Road north of St Clair Avenue) can be very productive, especially in late fall. The waterfront and its associated parks, however, are Toronto's best birding areas. For convenience these are discussed later, under the headings of Lake Ontario east and west.

Pearson International Airport is often the visitor's first view of Ontario. It is northwest of the city, and is also one of the better places for wintering raptors such as Rough-legged Hawks and Snowy Owls (the Red-tailed Hawks there are probably residents); we've rarely landed at Pearson in winter without seeing buteos.

Once in the city, access to birding may depend on whether the visitor has a car or not. With a car, an available day, and a willingness to handle the heavy traffic, the eastern lakeshore could be the place to go; in summer, spend more time in the areas on the northeast moraine. The Islands are an excellent full-day alternative in migration periods, with or without a vehicle. With less time, consider Humber Bay Park and High Park,

MAP 22   Metropolitan Toronto

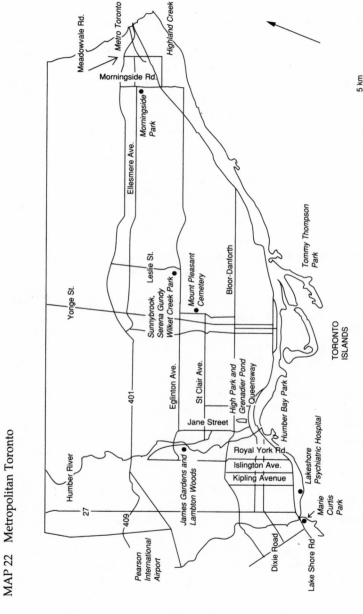

unless you are in one of the Don Mills area hotels, where the Wilket Creek complex is close at hand. Tommy Thompson Park is a remarkable area, but it is only open on weekends, and rather hard to get to.

Both High Park and James Gardens are in the west end of the city. To reach *James Gardens and Lambton Woods* go south from Eglinton Avenue on Scarlett Road (the first intersection west of the Humber River) 0.3 km to Edenbridge Drive. Turn right, drive 1.1 km and the James Gardens parking lot is on the left, just before the road turns to go up the hill (there is a smaller parking lot a little farther east). Using public transportation, take either the Royal York or Anglesey bus to Edenbridge Drive and walk east. From the parking lots there is a paved footpath running along the river down to and through the woods, and a trail paralleling it inside the woodlot itself, with several side trails. All should be explored.

This park occupies the Humber River flood plain and the slopes to the west. It is one of the richest areas of mixed woodland in Toronto. A Great Horned Owl is regular, the conifers and wet areas – which often remain open throughout the winter – attract winter birds, and there are summer records of a number of rarer species. Fall is probably the most productive period, when the profusion of fruiting shrubs induces migrants to linger. James Gardens – the formal gardens on the west of the parking area – can be excellent for migrants, and the river itself can yield an assortment of waterbirds, especially in migration. The outfall of the creek through the golf course opposite is often the best area, and Black-crowned Night-Herons roost in the trees here.

High Park and *Grenadier Pond* are very accessible. The park is situated south of Bloor Street and west of Keele Street, which becomes Parkside Drive below Bloor. All the wooded areas can be productive; however, the best are along Grenadier Pond on the west side, and the wooded valley running north on the east parallel to Parkside Drive. High Park is very busy even by Toronto standards, and the access and parking arrangements are under review at the time of writing. I have tried to anticipate the probable arrangements below, but there may be changes.

The main road through the park is Colborne Lodge Drive.

Enter from the north off Bloor Street at the light 0.4 km west of Keele. The road almost immediately divides into two one-way roads. The southbound leg bears west (as West Road) and follows the high land above Grenadier Pond. Continue on to the Grenadier Restaurant (about 1 km; the parking lot is good for hawk watching in fall) where you join Colborne Lodge Drive again. Turn sharp left here (don't go down the hill) and drive about 0.2 km to park south of the swimming pool. This point gives easy access to the allotment gardens and wooded valley on the east side. This whole area can yield excellent birding, particularly in migration. The park as a whole has been the source of a number of unusual breeding records, including Eastern Bluebird near the allotments, and Orchard Oriole near the boathouse on Grenadier.

Coverage of the west side is from outside the park proper. From Keele drive 1 km to Ellis Park Road, which is just past the park, and turn south. At the bottom of the hill (0.3 km) you can turn left into Wendigo Way, which is located in a small ravine which can be very productive, and from here you can cover the wooded bank at the northwest end of the park. Public transportation access is from the High Park subway stop. Cross Bloor Street and walk west, watching for the staircase that leads down to Wendigo Way, just east of the corner of Ellis Park Road.

From Wendigo Way return to Ellis Park Road, and go a further 0.2-0.3 km south, parking at some point along the lower end of the hill. From here you can bird the small marsh at the north end of Grenadier Pond, which you'll discover is a fair-sized lake. This marsh area can be particularly good in winter because the water remains open. Grenadier Pond should be covered early in the day if possible, as it is heavily used year-round. In spite of this there can be interesting birds in the shallower areas even when the walk is crowded and the lake is full of pleasure boats. Northern Shoveler are in good numbers every fall and often well into the winter.

From here you can drive up the hill and turn left at the top on to Ellis Avenue, which runs down to the Queensway and Sunnyside, and just before the Queensway traffic lights you can view the lower end of Grenadier Pond on the left. There is a resident Mallard flock, and the wide water area here often has interesting duck or gulls, especially in late fall, early spring, and winter. There may be wintering blackbirds or sparrows in the cattails. You cannot park in the southbound lane of Ellis Avenue; however, there is parking on the east side of the road a little north of the lights. Public transportation access to this point is by taking the Queen Street car to Ellis Avenue, where Grenadier Pond can be covered as part of a trip to the Lakeshore.

The major natural park area in the north-central area of the city is the *Sunnybrook, Serena Gundy,* and *Wilket Creek Park* complex. The main vehicle entrance is on the west side of Leslie Street, just north of Eglinton Avenue and opposite the Inn on the Park. From here the park road descends the hill and then forks, with the right fork curving round, following the river, and then curving back over the playing fields of Sunnybrook Park to a woodlot overlooking the Wilket Creek. By public transportation the Leslie Street or Lawrence East buses are the best way of reaching these parks.

These parks have extensive grassed areas with picnic tables and are heavily used – on hot weekends in summer it is often necessary to close them to automobile entry – but they also have excellent habitat for landbirds and can be quite productive, especially in the early mornings. Over the years they have produced Three-toed and Black-backed Woodpeckers as regularly as anywhere around Toronto, and at least one pair of Pileated Woodpeckers is resident. They're also good for winter finches, and large flocks of robins and waxwings may overwinter.

The more productive areas include the Wilket Creek valley extending north from the park road at the bottom of the hill as you enter, and just past this the wooded areas around the large parking lot on the left between the road and the river. Farther along the road turns to pass the horse stables and police station, and the only washrooms open year-round. Park here to cover the feeders and barn areas for wintering species, and walk back down the road towards the river and cross the bridge. Ahead and on your right the conifers can yield winter finches and migrants, and the dirt path to the right leads through less manicured areas towards York University. If the road past the horse stables is open as far as the woodlot at the end this is also often good for migrants.

The *Royal Ontario Museum* is at the southwest corner of Bloor Street and Avenue Road in midtown Toronto (100 Queen's

Park, Toronto M5S 2C6). It has a major collection of bird skins, nests, and eggs, and is the official repository for bird records for the province. It also operates the Ontario Nest Record Scheme, to which birders are encouraged to contribute.

LAKE ONTARIO WEST OF TORONTO

Western Lake Ontario has some of the province's largest concentrations of wintering waterfowl; depending on ice conditions elsewhere, between a third and a half of all the birds in the province winter here. Over the years some thirty-five different species have occurred, with up to 30,000 individuals annually. The principal species are Canada Goose, American Black Duck, and Mallard (all feral), Greater Scaup, Common Goldeneye, Bufflehead, Oldsquaw, and Common Merganser, with smaller numbers of Mute Swan, Gadwall, American Wigeon, and Redhead. All the waterfowl that occur in the province can turn up, and Snow Goose, Harlequin Duck, and Barrow's Goldeneye have been rare but regular. The common gull at this time is Herring, with smaller numbers of Ring-billed and Great Black-backed. Iceland and Glaucous are regular.

Since the appearance in the 1990s of zebra mussels in the Great Lakes, the traditional patterns of wintering waterfowl distribution have changed dramatically. The flocks in many previous areas of concentration – for example, west of the Humber River mouth – have largely disappeared, and enormous concentrations have appeared farther west. These flocks have been augmented in late winter by thousands of White-winged Scoters, particularly off Burlington, together with a few eiders. Whether these spectacular numbers will continue in future years remains to be seen.

The lakeshore as a whole can also be of great interest in migration periods with Common Loon, Horned and Red-necked Grebe, White-winged Scoter, and Red-breasted Merganser appearing, as well as the shoreline movements of shorebirds and landbirds characteristic of the north shores of the lower Great Lakes. In late autumn this has been one of the better areas in the province for King Eider, Purple Sandpiper, and Red Phalarope.

The lake can be productive from September through May, with shorebirds in early June, in later July, and in August (depending on water levels). It is less interesting in summer, and it can be very disturbed in warmer weather. Even then, however, birds often can be found in secluded areas. It is best of all from late fall (mid-October) to early spring (March), when the large numbers of wintering waterfowl are present, and it becomes particularly exciting when a sudden sharp cold spell overtakes a period of warm weather in spring, stimulating reverse migration. At these times movement along the waterfront can be spectacular. Lake viewing can be *very* cold even if it seems mild inland: be forewarned!

The lakeshore is of interest all the way to Hamilton, and because coverage is easier going from west to east the account that follows starts at Highway 2 east of the QEW at **Burlington**. The shoreline here runs in a north-easterly direction, but for practical purposes the account that follows assumes you are travelling east. Highway 2 parallels the lake, running fairly close to it all the way to Toronto. For most of the route it is called Lakeshore Road. It runs through a virtually continuous belt of housing, although the communities are given below to satisfy the curious. Lake viewing is confined mainly to the short streets that dead-end at the lake, and almost any street can yield sightings. Persons wishing a more detailed coverage should refer to the *Toronto Birdfinding Guide*, as the following lists the main vantage points only. At each stop carefully scan both the water surface and the sky for waterfowl and gulls.

Take QEW exit 97 (North Shore Boulevard) to follow Highway 2. Pass the hospital on your right and proceed through the traffic lights. Then turn right immediately into the parking lot of the Tourist Information Centre in *Spenser Smith Park*. There are washrooms here, and excellent views of the lake. Take an odometer reading here; and the figures that follow are kilometres from point to point, and the QEW exit numbers are given as appropriate for roads having access to the highway. This westernmost section of the lake is the most productive of jaegers (September-October), Red-necked Grebes in spring and fall, and White-winged Scoters.

2.4 km   Guelph Line, Burlington (QEW 102).
0.8 km   *Sioux Lookout Park*, Burlington. There is a parking lot here.

1.3 km   Walker's Line (QEW 105).

4.1 km   Burloak Road and the Pig and Whistle Inn (QEW 109).

0.8 km   *Shell Parkette*. Scan the Shell pier immediately to the west carefully for gulls, as a number of uncommon species have summered here, and watch for jaegers in the fall. The heavy shrubbery both here and on the north side of the road in the *Shell Park* (its auto entrance is 0.4 km farther east) attracts migrant land birds. In this park is a small creek with some small wooded areas, and there are public washrooms in the sports centre, but these may be closed in winter.

1.8 km   Bronte Road (QEW 111). You are now in **Bronte**. The stretch of parkland beside the Bronte Creek mouth, called *Fisherman's Wharf*, gives an excellent view over Bronte Harbour and the adjacent lake. The tame duck flock here sometimes has some interesting stragglers in winter. The road next turns east into Ontario Street, with views of the lake to the south and east. Return to Lakeshore Road via Nelson Street.

1.1 km   Third Line (km from the corner of Nelson Street).

0.9 km   Coronation Park Boat Ramp.

2.9 km   Holyrood Avenue. The tiny Holyrood Park at the foot gives lake access, and there is good landbird habitat adjacent. You are entering the town of **Oakville**.

0.8 km   Kerr Street. (QEW 117). The public is allowed into the grounds of the Water Treatment Plant at the foot of this road, for views of the wintering duck which can be expected west of Oakville Harbour.

0.6 km   Navy Street. Drive south to the last street east (Front), turn, and proceed to its end at Dunn Avenue (0.3 km) where *Dingle Park* gives views of the lake. Then return to Lakeshore Road via Dunn Avenue. Note that the next road east, Trafalgar Road, is the last good access to the QEW(118) prior to the junction of Highway 403, bypassing downtown Toronto.

0.8 km   (from Dunn Avenue) Park Avenue. This road turns at its base east along the lake on the Esplanade, which in turn merges into northbound Howard Avenue. From Howard you can go east via Carson Lane to Chartwell Road and cover it as well. All these roads can yield excellent waterfowl viewing.

1.1 km   (from Chartwell) *Gairloch Gardens*. These gardens are sometimes good for landbirds. If you walk through to the lake a large flock of duck is usually present.

0.4 km   Arkendo Drive. There is lake access from the turning circle at the end of this road, and also views of the shrubby tangles along the creek to the east. This sheltered area can be good for landbirds in winter, and there is also access to it on the other side of the creek from the foot of Winston Churchill Boulevard (QEW 124) 0.2 km farther east.

1.1 km   *Lakeside Park*. Park in the small lot here and walk south to cover the bay formed by the St Lawrence Cement Company pier and the oil refinery pier to the east. There are usually good numbers of dabbling duck, particularly Gadwall and American Wigeon, feeding on the algae along the shore here in winter. This is **Clarkson**, although the communities from here east to the Metro boundary are all now amalgamated into an amorphous blob called **Mississauga**.

At Southdown Road (0.5 km) the road turns north. By continuing north you can reach the QEW (126), but otherwise at 1.2 km turn right onto Orr Road, and proceed 1.5 km to Meadowwood Road, checking the woods en route. Turn right on Meadowwood and go to its end (0.6 km) in Country Club Crescent, then right again and follow this road until it merges with Watersedge Road, just before both roads end in *Watersedge Park* (0.6 km). The beach in front of the refinery can be very productive. Now return the way you came, north on Meadowwood, but passing Orr Road. At 0.3 km past Orr is Greenglade, with a footpath near the corner leading into Rattray's Marsh. Another entry to the marsh footpaths is from Meadowood itself at 0.3 km. Lakeshore Road, now going east again, is 0.6 km farther. Turn right onto Lakeshore Road and continue east.

The most direct access to *Rattray Marsh* is from the foot of Bexhill Road (0.8 km); however, the best by car is 1.6 km east of Meadowwood Road, just west of the Lorne Park Road traffic light, where there is an entrance to *Jack Darling Memorial Park*. (At the time of writing this entrance is closed for park remodelling; it is assumed this is temporary, but if not the foot of Bexhill would be the preferred access.) Drive south to the lake and turn right, checking the trees and shrubs en route for migrants, the beach for shorebirds, and the lake for waterfowl. The lake to the west of here is one of the most reliable locations for Red-necked Grebes, particularly in fall. Drive west to the parking lot, and from there walk west about 0.5 km to the marsh, which is the only one of any size along this route.

At the marsh you can continue west along the shingle barrier beach, which provides the best, and for some parts the only, views of the marsh. If there are mudflats shorebirds may be present, and duck and herons are usually visible in season, especially in the section to the north-west, where Black-crowned Night-Herons roost in the trees. Be sure to cross the shingle bar as far as the outlet for the best viewing. Returning to the east side, you can now follow the path that curves around the east side of the marsh. The wooded bank here can be excellent for migrant landbirds. Shortly the path joins another leading up the hill to Bexhill Road, and at this point you will find a map of the area. The woodlot on the knoll to the south can concentrate migrants, and the path you are on continues west to cross the north end of the marsh. North of this path is an extensive area of wooded bottomland. Paths run through this area also, and the whole can yield excellent birding year-round.

From Rattray's, return to Lakeshore Road and continue east. The highway now runs farther from the lake as it enters **Port Credit**, where the harbour area (Stavebank Road S., the first light over the river bridge, gives the best access) can yield duck. From Stavebank onwards Lakeshore becomes even busier, and although shoreline viewing continues from the streets to the south, it is usually better to continue directly on past Highway 10 (QEW exit 132) and Dixie Road (QEW exit 136). You pass an area of industry on your right, and the tall chimneys of the Lakeshore Generating Station.

Shortly past the Dixie light and before crossing the creek (0.4 km) turn right into the west side of *Marie Curtis Park*. This is one of the more productive areas in this section, although some of the best habitat is the woodlot and small stream valley in the industrial area immediately northwest of the park itself. Drive south, scanning Etobicoke Creek to the east for waterbirds.

Towards the mouth you will usually find a resident duck flock. The lake can be good for loons and grebes in migration, and to the north is the woodlot and valley. Some of this can viewed from outside the fence, including a wooded pool towards the east side, which may have Green Herons or Black-crowned Night-Herons. To cover the rest, however, you must cross the fence. This area is private property, but most of the time the huge gaps in the fence testify to its regular use by the public. The woodlot is excellent for migrant landbirds, the old field behind has sparrows and other edge species, the dense pines at the north end attract wintering owls, and the marshy lower reaches of the creek occasionally yield herons and duck. The future of access, such as it is, is uncertain.

Even more ambiguity surrounds the area west of the park. The creek forms the western boundary, and if you cross it at its outlet and walk around the fence you can follow along the shore south of the sewage treatment plant fence. The grassy mounds in the grounds (viewed through the fence) may have loitering gulls and shorebirds, and further west is a headland of landfill south of the generating station. On this landfill is a large pool that has developed some marshy areas and is very attractive to waterbirds in migration and during the summer. It often yields species not usually present on the lake itself, particularly when the lake is rough. Just who owns this area is unclear, as is its future, although there is talk of a cycle path along here.

Return to Lakeshore Road, cross the creek and (0.4 km) take the first right onto 42nd Street and drive down to Lake Promenade. You are now in Metropolitan Toronto. Lake Promenade winds eastwards with lake viewing on the right; street names change from time to time, but follow the direction that keeps you closest to the water. There has not usually been outstanding birding along here, but a Harlequin Duck has wintered for some years and other good sightings occur periodically, and in the current state of flux anything is possible. You can return to Lakeshore along any of the north-south streets, and must do so at 23rd Street. Obstructing easterly progress is the old *Lakeshore Psychiatric Hospital*, which is no longer active and undergoing massive transformations.

From 23rd Street continue east on Lakeshore for 0.7 km, passing Kipling Avenue (QEW 141), to turn into the grounds of the hospital. These can yield excellent land birding, and a landfill that is still under development is pushing far out into the lake. It has already attracted a wide assortment of birds (even a Rock Wren!) and it should be of even greater interest when it is complete. Waterfowl concentrate around the sheltered headlands. Access will change as development proceeds. East of the hospital the side streets resume their game of tag with the lake (Lakeshore Drive is the cross street); there are usually duck all along here if you have time available. The cross street returns you to Lakeshore Road (now Boulevard) along 1st Street, some 0.8 km west of the light at Royal York Road.

East of Royal York 2.3 km (just past a very large new condominium complex) is *Humber Bay Park*. This is a landfill park which has become a premier lakeshore birding area in the west end of Toronto, second only to Tommy Thompson Park in its productiveness. There are two entrances: Humber Bay Park West is dominated by marinas, but is still worth visiting.

Turn right on to the park road then take the first turn left, into a large parking lot (there are washrooms here), and view the waters of Mimico Creek to the east and a shallow embayment to the north. This is one of the few places along the route where shorebirds occur regularly, and an assortment of duck is usually present. Next, return to the main access road, turn left and drive to its end. On your right are marinas and to your left is a long lead from the creek, and then the lake itself. Turn into any of the small parking lots and view the water areas and the headlands for waterbirds, shorebirds, and open country species, and examine coniferous and shrub plantings for landbird migrants and, in winter, owls. Walk north along the west shoreline to view the long lead of water between the mainland and the marinas. Rarer species such as Red-throated Loon have appeared here when there is not too much boating disturbance.

Now return to Lakeshore Boulevard and continue east, crossing the creek to turn right at the next light (Park Lawn Road, QEW 144; but see below) into Humber Bay Park East, much the best of the two sections. Here the road leads directly to a large parking lot, with a series of artificial pools to the south, and a long lead from the lake to the north. Follow the same routine as on the west side: the entire area can be most productive, especially on foggy days in spring migration, when all the thickets can teem with migrants.

Although Humber Bay Park is not much to look at, it is very popular and often very crowded in good weather. Get there early! In summer it is generally too busy to be very interesting. Motorists coming from the east on the QEW *cannot exit* at Park Lawn Road: you must cross the Humber River on the Gardiner Expressway (the continuation of the QEW across downtown Toronto) and take the right-hand lane to Lakeshore Boulevard, then proceed west to the Park Lawn Road intersection (0.5 km), which is the first major intersection you will encounter. If you decide to use Lakeshore Boulevard instead you will find it merges with the right-hand lanes of the Gardiner just east of the Humber River, and you then should follow the same route.

Continuing east from Humber Bay Park Lakeshore Boulevard crosses the Humber River. Birding along this stretch is by a series of right-hand turns into the parking lots servicing the parkland here. The route is not as productive as Humber Bay Park, and is best in late fall, winter, and early spring; however, maintenance of the parking areas in winter is irregular. Enter each parking lot, and scan the shoreline, the waters both inside and outside of the breakwall, and the wall itself for gulls and duck. Point to point distances are given from the exit of one parking lot to the entrance of the next.

This route cannot be covered from east to west by automobile. Persons coming from the east should use the *left-hand* lane of Lakeshore Boulevard approaching the QEW intersection (just past Windermere Avenue). Just before the road veers right under an overpass to join the Gardiner Expressway, and west of Windermere, this lane permits a U-turn.

The lakeshore east of the Humber mouth is known as *Sunnyside*, and the first parking lot entry is immediately east (0.5 km) of the Humber River. On leaving here you may wish to check the foot of Grenadier Pond by turning left at the first traffic light onto Ellis Avenue (see High Park above). Otherwise continue east 0.2 km through the light to the next parking lot, and then a short way farther on (0.2 km) to a small parking lot servicing a food concession just west of Sunnyside swimming pool (a large concrete structure). The next stop (0.3 km) is a lot just east of the pool, followed (0.1 km) by a boat-launching ramp just west of a footbridge crossing the Boulevard.

East of the footbridge the divided highway ends, and the areas could be covered, I suppose (if your nerves are good) from the west-bound lanes! The next areas are not open during the Canadian National Exhibition in the last two weeks of August. Continue east past the Boulevard Club to the top of the hill, and enter (0.8 km) a parking lot servicing the Toronto Sailing and Canoe Club and *Argonaut Rowing Club*. This is a good spot from which to survey the bay. Finally, continuing east 0.1 km, you pass under another footbridge and can turn immediately into Marilyn Bell Park (this area is noteworthy mainly for gulls on the breakwall, but check the grassy areas as well as the water).

On re-entering Lakeshore Boulevard you are driving south of the Canadian National Exhibition grounds, and the road ahead leads to downtown Toronto past the Toronto Island ferry docks. Birding is possible all along the waterfront and around the harbour as far as Leslie Street, which is the entrance to Tommy Thompson Park. It is all described in the Toronto guide, but the route is quite complicated, busy, and perhaps more appropriate to a resident birder than a visitor.

TORONTO ISLANDS

The Toronto Islands consist of a hook-shaped strip of land enclosing Toronto Harbour, and are islands by virtue of the two shipping channels, one at the east end just west of Cherry Street (Eastern Gap) and the other at the foot of Bathurst Street (Western Gap). The area adjoining the Eastern Gap is called Ward's Island and is largely occupied by housing. The outer shoreline runs roughly southwest for some 3 km, gradually curving to Gibraltar Point at the Islands' west end, where it hooks north to terminate after another 2 km at the Western Gap. The Islands just south of this gap are at their widest and this area is occupied by a small airport.

The Islands are accessible only by ferry, with the terminal at the foot of Bay Street. Public transportation links are from the Bay bus (No. 6); parking is on the northwest side of the Bay–

Queen's Quay intersection, with entry a little west on Queen's Quay. You should phone the Ferry Docks (367-8193, listed under Metro Parks) for the ferry times before setting off, and be sure to pick up a schedule at the dock *before* embarking; there are none available on the other side. In the warmer weather ferries serve Ward's Island (the residential area), Centre Island, and Hanlan's Point to the west.

A small train service runs periodically on the Island from Centre Island to Hanlan's Point, and bicycles can be rented. There are a few food concessions, two small restaurants on Centre Island, and frequent public toilets. In winter, however, the ferries are few, everything is closed, and there is negligible shelter. Winter trips are primarily productive of waterfowl, while wintering landbirds occur at feeders, especially near the Island school. The conifers sometimes yield owls during this period. The Islands are an outstanding migrant trap, and from early fall to late spring they offer some of the best birding areas in the region, and have yielded a number of extreme rarities. In summer they are very crowded and birds are few.

The best parts are from Centre Island westwards, although the trees, lawns and waterfront throughout can be productive on a good day. Grassy lawns, planted beds of shrubs, and trees (mostly large old willows and cottonwoods) form the cover over most of the area, but natural vegetation backs the beaches and there are several wholly natural areas consisting of open cottonwood woodlands with an understorey of dense shrubbery. A few areas of marsh and wet meadows also occur along the lagoons.

Ideally an Island trip starts with an early ferry to Hanlan's Point. Points of particular interest include the trees and shrubbery around the ferry dock (these are often alive with migrants), the grassy areas of the airport (waterfowl and shorebirds in season), the western beaches and lake, especially the airport beach to the north, and all tangles of dogwood. Watch for hawks in fall, especially accipiters, which often congregate in numbers in September towards the southwest tip, when other features are milling flocks of Blue Jays and hosts of Monarch Butterflies.

The woods near the Island school are often productive, as are the feeders there. The wilderness area lies behind the water purification plant, and can be entered through the gate at the north end of the fence along the east side. Access is limited, but sometimes one can walk in: the area can be good for Northern Saw-whet Owls in October, and migrant passerines in spring and fall.

TOMMY THOMPSON PARK (THE LESLIE STREET SPIT)

Leslie Street is at the east end of the industrial port area of downtown. The Gardiner Expressway ends here, making the street easily accessible. At its foot is a 5 km-long spit of land extending out into Lake Ontario in a southwest by west direction. It usually called the Leslie Street Spit or the Eastern Headland, but its formal name is Tommy Thompson Park. It is constructed of landfill and does not look much like a park. At present it is largely undeveloped, except for a paved road along the centre, a lighthouse at the far end, a few temporary buildings, and some portable toilets near the gate and at the tip. Future development plans are very indefinite at this time, and landfilling continues. A useful *Checklist of the Birds of the Leslie Street Spit* is available from Friends of the Spit, P.O. Box 467, Station J, Toronto M4J 4Z2.

The area is open to pedestrians or cyclists on weekends and holidays between 9.00 a.m. and 6.00 p.m. year-round. A free bus runs during part of this time. At present the service is from June 6 to September 7. It leaves the entrance on the hour, returns from the tip on the half-hour, and stops at designated spots. There is car parking just inside the first gate at the foot of Leslie. During the nesting period the areas of the gull and tern colonies are off-limits. Call the Metropolitan Toronto Region Conservation Authority ([416] 661-6600) for the latest information. Quite apart from its quality as a birding area, a walk on the headland is an unforgettable experience. It is, of course, very exposed and can be cold even on a warm day.

The lakeside of the headland is armoured and formed into a series of small bays, with shingle beaches falling off rapidly into very deep water. Active areas of filling lack much birding appeal except loitering gulls, but on the north side of the centre road are four large bays where sandy beaches have been formed, divided by low fill ridges. These areas are growing over with dense thickets of cottonwoods and willows and have been colonized by a huge gull and tern colony. In 1992 over 42,000 pairs of Ring-billed Gulls nested, together with 100 pairs of Herring Gulls and 300 pairs of Common Terns. The trees supported over 800 pairs of Black-crowned Night-Herons and a small group of cormorants. Wilson's Phalaropes and several species of waterfowl have also nested on the headland.

It is even more exciting in spring and fall. Not only do open country species such as Horned Larks, American Pipits, and Snow Buntings occur in large flocks in migration, but numbers of other passerines occur as well, as do Snowy and Short-eared Owls. Hawks follow the headland west in fall. The lagoons are very attractive to waterbirds, and shorebirds are possible on any mudflats or more open areas.

Up to 1978 30 to 50 per cent of all the exceptional rarities reported in the region were on the headland. It has been less productive recently, perhaps owning to the difficulty of finding birds in the heavy vegetation that now covers the more established sections; but it is still one of the premier birding locales in Toronto. Its sheer size and the constant changes that are occurring make it impractical to identify specific areas of coverage.

THE LAKESHORE EAST OF METROPOLITAN TORONTO

The area immediately east of Metro along the shores of Lake Ontario lacks the continuous string of urbanization that dominates the shoreline to the west. While urban development is occurring very rapidly, much of the shore is publicly owned, and the woodlots, marshes, and abandoned farmland in the area provide an outstanding mix of habitats, with the lakeshore forming a major flyline for migrants. Heavy hawk flights can develop, and waterfowl and shorebird movement can be watched offshore. If water levels are low, extensive areas of mudflat attract shorebirds, the best shorebird habitat in the region. The area is of less interest in midsummer and in winter, but can be productive at any season. The best places are between Pickering on the west and Oshawa on the east (Highway 401 interchanges 394 and 419), and the area can be covered from either direction, although this account goes from west to east (see maps 23 and 24).

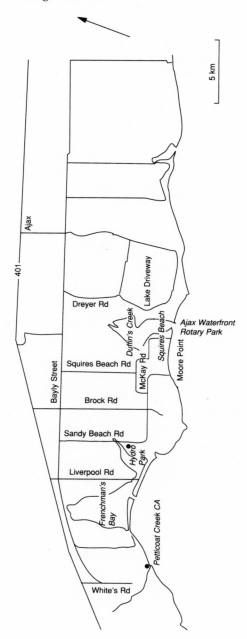

MAP 23 Ajax and Pickering

Drive east on Highway 401 to White's Road (exit 394). Turn south and drive to *Petticoat Creek Conservation Area*. Park just outside, and walk straight down the track (not the road) into a wooded valley which ends at the lake. Keep to the east side and work up and around, returning to the park entrance (excellent for migrant landbirds).

Return on White's Road to Bayly Street (Regional Road 22), on the right just before the 401 intersection. This runs due east to Whitby, where it becomes Victoria Street West. The areas of interest are all south of this road. From this point *Frenchman's Bay* lies to the southeast; it is good from autumn to spring for waterbirds if it is not frozen over. Turn right on Bayly and proceed some 1.3 km past housing development to a drive on the right leading down to *West Shore Community Centre*. Here it is normally possible to drive in and park, and then follow a small path that runs southeast into the longer grass. After a few yards this emerges through the shrubs to a vantage point overlooking the marshland, open water, and mudflats at the north end of the bay. This can be one of the most productive locations on the route you will be following, and often will have a wide variety of water and shorebirds present. Use caution when emerging from the shrub screen, as birds are often quite close and a sudden disturbance may cause everything present to panic. In winter and early spring large gull flocks, including white gulls, loiter on the ice of Frenchman's Bay. They are visible from here or from the easternmost streets in the housing development.

After viewing the birds here continue east crossing on the light at Liverpool Road (lake views and a small marsh at its end) and proceed 0.8 km farther to Sandy Beach Road. Turn south, cross a stream (there may be waterbirds here on both sides of the road), and over the bridge turn right into the parking lot of *Hydro Park*. Cover the woods north of the parking lot for landbird migrants and follow the edge of the water around towards the lake. The high ground west of the parking area gives excellent views over the marsh. In fall Black-crowned Night-Herons roost in the alders on the far side of the marsh to the south, and the high mound can also be a good spot for watching fall hawk movement – accipiters and falcons are the most regular migrants, but buteos can occur in good numbers as well.

Sandy Beach Road runs south to the nuclear power plant, and then east as Montgomery Park Road. Continue through the light at Brock Road (Regional Road 1; 401 exit 399) and 0.3 km farther the road turns north, now as McKay Road. First, however, continue 0.8 km, straight ahead and then right, to the end of the road at **Moore Point** on the lake. This yields excellent lake viewing, with loons, grebes, and mergansers on the waters to the east (Red-necked Grebes formerly staged here and are still regular) and movements of waterfowl and gulls (this location is not in the *Toronto Guide*).

Now return to McKay Road, which loops around the northern perimeter of the water treatment plant, crossing Squires Beach Road. Finally it curves south and at 1.9 km crosses Montgomery Park Road again. Turn left here, and in 0.2 km this road also turns south to run down to the Lake as Frisco Road. At the corner is a small parking lot and there is a marsh to the northeast. This is the **Corner Marsh**, although the name tends to be given indiscriminately to the entire area, more accurately called **Squires Beach**. Continue south for additional lake views, and walk over to cover the mouth of **Duffin's Creek**, where almost anything can turn up in migration periods. At the Corner Marsh itself there is also a good woodlot and further marshes to the north (walk along the edge of field), and the large overgrown hedgerows are productive. In migration periods this entire area can teem with migrants, and if the marsh water levels are low good numbers of shorebirds can be found. This area has been one of the better places in the Toronto region for godwits.

From Squire's Beach return to the first north-south road (Squire's Beach Road) and proceed north to Bayly Street and continue east some 3.2 km to an intersection, with Dreyer Road to the south and Westney Road on the north. Turn right here and drive south to Lake Driveway West at 1.2 km. Turn right, and continue 1.5 km to **Ajax Waterfront Rotary Park**. This park occupies the east side of Duffin's Creek and from it you can view the creek mouth and the marshes opposite and to the north. Note that the latter is not visible from the Corner Marsh side of the creek, so this park is worth visiting even if you have covered the west side thoroughly.

The next outstanding area on this route is through **Ajax**, and just past the north-south road that marks the Whitby boundary. Now Bayly Street becomes Victoria Street West, and at 0.5 km past this is a small sideroad, Hall's Road, running south to *Cranberry Marsh*. The marsh lies to the east and there are access points at 1.4 km, where a grove of trees joins the road, and again at 0.3 km near the end of the road. There are viewing platforms overlooking the marsh at both locations, and the lake should also be checked again: this is a good place for loons, and Red-throated has occurred fairly often. Cranberry is the finest marsh in the Toronto region, with a rich marsh flora and equally rich bird life. Summering waterfowl have included Lesser Scaup and Ruddy Duck; American Coot and Little Gull have bred, and in fall migration it is one of the more reliable locations for Snow Geese. There has been a host of rarities recorded in this marsh, and because its water levels are less prone to fluctuate than those in the other waterfront marshes it often contains a different mix of waterbirds. The lake offshore from here is also a good location in summer for species which normally move north, and the access road is an excellent vantage point for watching hawk migration.

Return to the main road and continue east 0.6 km to *Lynde Shores Conservation Area* on the south side of the road. Here are a small marsh, an old woodlot, and heavy thickets worth investigating for landbirds. The woods have trails through them and bird feeders. There are public toilets and a picnic area here too (the only toilets along this route apart from those at gas stations!). A short distance east the Lynde Creek (Baseline) Marsh borders both sides of the road. Although disturbed, it usually has some waterbirds present, and Least Bitterns have occurred.

The access road to *Whitby Hospital*, Gordon Street, is 1.6 km farther east. Drive to the bottom, watching trees and lawns for birds, and at the end check the lake and shoreline. A dirt road branches off east just before the main road curves right. The former goes to Whitby Yacht Club, passing through cottonwoods and scrub on the way and allowing a closer view of the shoreline to the east. The main road curves around the shore, and just as it turns up the west side of the hospital grounds a short sideroad goes off to the left (west) leading past a small water treatment plant to a rough parking lot near the lake. Park, and walk west along the gravel bar across the mouth of

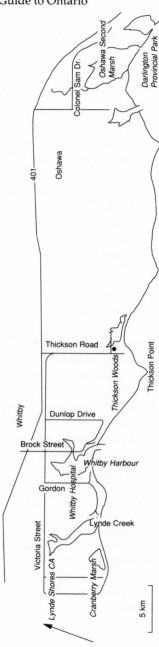

MAP 24   Whitby and Oshawa

Lynde Creek. Check the marshes, the end of the bar, and the willows. Then retrace your tracks to Victoria Street West.

Brock Street (Highway 401 exit 410) is 0.8 km farther east, and gives access both to the town of Whitby to the north, and to the east side of *Whitby Harbour*. Turn south on Brock at the light and drive 0.6 km to a bridge crossing a stream, Pringle Creek. This spot has marsh on both sides of the road, and the scrubby trees to the southeast have roosting Black-crowned Night-Herons. There are often mudflats here, which attract shorebirds, and the tame duck flock attracts wild birds: even if you see nothing else you should get a few Canada Geese! From here continue south, following the shore to a gravel road running between fuel tanks and the harbour. Check the harbour and the far shore at this point, and proceed along to the harbour mouth. Scan the piers, the shoreline to the east, and the lake. Then rejoin the main road, which is now called Water Street and is heading east. Turn north when the road ends in Dunlop Drive and continue until this road ends in Victoria Street East.

Turn east and follow the road around to the Thickson Road (Highway 401 exit 412). At the south end of Thickson Road the vantage point is high, and gives good views of the lake; loons, grebes and diving duck are often present in migration. To the east at this point is the privately owned Thickson Point, where the houses bordering the road back onto a woodlot with old pines. The road edges and the adjacent gardens should be carefully checked for migrants. A private road to the Corbett Creek water treatment plant goes east from Thickson Road 0.3 km from its end, running down the north side of the woods to Corbett Creek and the marsh. Birders are tolerated on this road, and both the marsh and the trails through the adjacent *Thickson Woods* can be most productive, especially during migration. A wide assortment of rarities have been recorded.

Now return to Highway 401 and drive east through **Oshawa** to the Harmony Road exit (419), which leads to Farewell Street. Drive south on Farewell 0.8 km from the light at Bloor Street, to Colonel Sam Drive. One of the finest cattail marshes in the region, *Oshawa Second Marsh*, now lies to the southeast. There are two means of access: the first is to continue south a farther 0.3 km, past the pollution control plant. There is parking here, and you can walk east on the south side of the fence along the plant boundary, and then south along the creek into the marsh. However, the detail of the access here is likely to change in the future. The other location is currently better. Turn east on Colonel Sam and drive 2.8 km to the GM offices, where trails lead to the east side, with viewing towers. There is visitor parking opposite the building, and trails originate from the rear of the employee parking lots to both east and west. The westerly one is the best (and in any case the trails link up), and the rear of the parking lot here is often empty.

The marsh is an exceptional staging ground for waterfowl and gulls, and was the site of the continent's first Little Gull nesting (but they're long gone!). Shorebirds are numerous in periods of low water levels. The cedars south of Colonel Sam Drive can yield owls in the fall, and at the point the stream crosses under the road (0.6 km from Farewell) there is viewing of the small section of marsh to the north. Stop here with care, however, as this can be a busy road. Further east *Darlington Provincial Park* (entrance fee; 401 exit 425), can be of interest outside the hunting season. The beach can have shorebirds and gulls, the marshy edges Sharp-tailed Sparrows in migration, and the ravines other passerine migrants. The north end of the marsh here is also visible from the trails behind the GM offices described above.

There are additional wetland areas farther east, but they do not seem to be very productive. At **Bowmanville** there are several marshes along the lake. From Liberty Street (401 exit 432), turning east on the Base Line and then south on Bert Street. Drive 0.3 km and turn sharply left just past the railroad tracks. This road leads to the east side of the river at Port Darlington (1.7 km), but a turn west on West Beach Road at 1 km makes it possible to cover the extensive marsh from here to the beach (1.5 km).

Farther west a second marsh can be visited by returning to the Base Line and heading west, or leaving 401 at Waverly Street (exit 431). Either way, turn south on County Road 57 and drive 1.4 km south to the shore. A large marsh lies over a field to the east, and more marsh is along the cottage road that runs east at the shore. Where the southbound road reaches the shore, view the lake and piers of the St Mary Cement plant to the west for waterfowl and gulls.

Farther east again, from Highway 401 exit 440 at **Bond Head**, there is a small harbour and limited marshes along the creek. Take the road south to the lake (about 3 km). This leads to the east side; the west is accessible by turning west on a sideroad immediately past the railroad bridge.

THE OAK RIDGES MORAINE AND THE NONQUON LAGOONS

Some of the more interesting parts of the Oak Ridges Moraine are northeast of Toronto near the town of **Uxbridge**. They include extensive stands of pine plantation of varying ages, and oak-pine woodland communities. Many of the woodland roads of this forest are open to the public for hiking and skiing. This area is of interest for breeding birds, and is also good in winter in 'finch' years.

Uxbridge is on Highway 47, and the pine zone is on Concession 7 due south of town, and along Regional Road 21, which is some 6 km south, and runs east from Goodwood. One of the better areas starts some 2 km south of the junction of Concession 7 and Regional Road 21. Here there are tall pines, succeeded by an open area near a communications tower on the east. The good habitat continues for about 4 km. The pine woods are interspersed with open bushy areas (Brown Thrasher, Rufous-sided Towhee, and Field Sparrow) and small pines (possible Clay-colored Sparrows), and the mature trees can yield finches such as crossbills. Red-breasted Nuthatch, Hermit Thrush, Solitary Vireo, and Pine Warbler all have nested, as has Henslow's Sparrow in the past.

The *Nonquon River (Port Perry) sewage lagoons* are relatively close to this area. Return to Regional Road 21, turn right (east), and drive to the intersection with Highway 12. From this intersection in **Manchester** drive north to the third road to the east. This is Scugog Line 8 (not Durham Road 8, which is the second road), and is an excellent birding road all the way to the lagoons, 3.1 km along on the right. The five lagoons are among the most productive in the region, and often have a good mix of shorebirds still present in early June. Wilson's Phalarope have summered here. Note this area is easy to reach from the eastern lakeshore, and the route passes another good birding site. Brock

Road, servicing the nuclear plant east of Frenchman's Bay, is Regional Road 1 (401 exit 399) and it runs north, crossing Highway 7, and then crossing Regional Road 21 at the hamlet of **Coppins Corners**. From here Concession 7 is two sideroads east.

Claremont Conservation Area is east of Regional Road 1 on Regional Road 31, about 2.0 km north of the intersection with Highway 7. There is a nature trail here through mixed woodlands, and coniferous stands that attract winter birds. The extensive multiflora rose hedges along Sideline 12, the western boundary, are often productive in winter if they have fruited well. This is one of the few places in the Toronto area where Bohemian Waxwings have appeared with some regularity. To reach it go west from the park entrance about 0.8 km and turn right (north). This road ends at Concession 8. If you then return to Regional Road 31 you can continue north on Regional Road 1.

At the hamlet of Coppins Corners some 12 km farther north the road crosses Regional Road 21. Turn right, and Concession 7 (described above) is the second sideroad to the east.

SOUTHERN LAKE SIMCOE

Although it is much smaller than the Great Lakes, Lake Simcoe is still a huge body of water and it attracts waterbirds in migration. It is neglected by birders in favour of Lake Ontario, but it has its own distinctive quality, and can be very productive from early April (the ice break-up) to Christmas (freeze-up). The best times are April and May, and September to December. Fruitful observation points are in the lake's southeast sector, and flocks of scoters and other diving duck, gulls, and numbers of loons and grebes can be seen there. Bonaparte's Gulls are often very numerous, Little Gulls are regular, and occasionally a Common Black-headed Gull can be found. Jaegers have been recorded as well, and more systematic coverage would likely turn up other less common species.

The main access routes to this part of Lake Simcoe are Highway 48 (401 exit 383) and 12 (401 exit 410), with the two highways joining to parallel the east shoreline. Unfortunately the shore of the lake south of Beaverton is almost wholly devoted to cottage development, and although it is paralleled by a road, most of the way lake access is difficult.

MAP 25   Southeastern Lake Simcoe

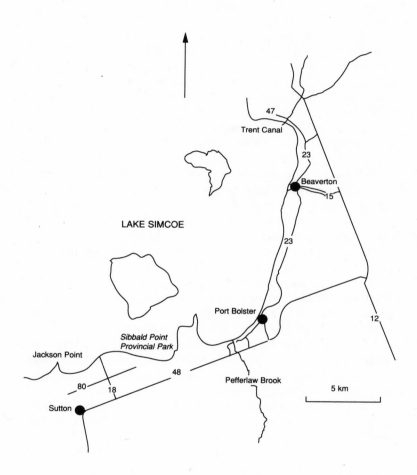

This account will start at **Beaverton** (see map 25), which lies west of the Highway 12 on Durham Road 15. To reach the *pier* there, drive west on Durham Road 15 to the intersection in town of Durham Road 23 northbound (at the bridge over the river). Continue west, bearing right at the fork, on Simcoe Street. At 0.8 km from the bridge the road ends in a large one-way loop: bear right down Harbour Park Crescent, and there is parking on the lower level from which it is possible to scan the small harbour. The pier is just west of here, and there are good vistas over the lake from it, as well as possible ducks and geese in the small bay to the south.

The town also has a large and very productive *sewage lagoon* complex. To reach the entry to this, return on Main about 1 km to Durham Road 23 south (Osborne Street). Turn south and drive 1.3 km, then turn right on the 5th Line of Thorah Township (marked Cedar Beach), and the east lagoon gates are 0.5 km ahead on the right. The western cells are just on the other side of the railroad tracks which cross the road 0.2 km ahead, and it is possible to cross the tracks between the two sets of lagoons. These are especially attractive to Bonaparte's and other small gulls, but the full range of waterbirds may turn up.

To cover areas north of Beaverton, follow Durham Road 23 north from the bridge in town described above. Continue north about 3.2 km to a Y-intersection, and bear left there, now on Simcoe Road 47. This soon starts to parallel the lake, and after 1.7 km crosses the Talbot River. The best vantage point is 0.6 farther, at the bridge over the *Trent Canal*. There is small parking lot on the northwest side, with a picnic area, and the piers here provide an excellent view over this part of the lake.

Going south from the Beaverton lagoons on Durham Road 23, a string of cottages parallel the shoreline to the west all the way to **Port Bolster**. There is limited lake viewing until, at some 8 km, the regional road bears left and Thorah Concession 1 continues straight ahead. This merges almost at once into Thorah Park Boulevard, and there is a small shoreline park which finally provides a fair vantage point.

The cottage problem intensifies westwards towards the mouth of *Pefferlaw Brook*, one of the best locations on the route. Continue on Thorah Park Boulevard, which curves round to rejoin Durham Road 23. Immediately past this intersection turn right on Clovelly Cove Road. This road soon begins to parallel the shoreline, where there is limited viewing at 0.7 km. Continue, bearing right on Irving Drive to keep close to the shoreline, until the road finally curves left (0.6 km from the start of Irving), and a small dead-end cottage road continues on ahead. Drive ahead 0.6 km to a vacant wooded cottage lot with a well-used track to the shore.

This is much the best point for viewing the flocks of birds gathered on the flats at the mouth of the creek. A telescope is still useful, and if this vantage point is inaccessible the only vista is a small parkette 0.5 km back along the road, but then a 'scope is essential! Now return to the main road and turn right. This road (Riverview Beach Boulevard) leads out to Highway 48. Turn right on 48, and drive 1.5 km to Holmes Point Road. Turn right again, and drive 0.9 km to the shore, where *Holmes Point Conservation Area* gives views of the lake. Bear right, and drive a farther 0.6 km to the parking lot of the Peninsula Restaurant, which allows further views of Pefferlaw Brook mouth and rock jetty.

This completes the southeast sector of the lake, but there is more lake viewing to the west. Continuing west on Highway 48 to York Road 18 leads to *Sibbald Point Provincial Park* (entrance fee). There is good lake access here.

Returning to York Road 18, a left-hand turn from the park exit leads south to the first cross-street, Black River Road (York Road 80). Turn right (west) and drive 2.1 km, where the *Sutton sewage lagoon* road is on the south. It has occasionally yielded something of interest. A right turn on York Road 18 leads to the lake, where the road curves left and follows shoreline. About 1 km farther west it crosses the mouth of the *Black River*, and this area can also be very productive. West again is Jackson Point, and continuous cottage development, but the road runs close to the beach periodically. It offers additional opportunities for lake viewing all the way to Cook's Bay.

OTHER SEWAGE LAGOONS NORTH OF TORONTO

Holland Landing – This village is east of Highway 11 at the point the main highway turns west, north of **Newmarket**. To reach the lagoons, drive north through the village on Regional

Road 51, and from its intersection in town with Thompson Road (just south of the post office) continue 1.8 km to Cedar Street on the east. The lagoon gates are 0.6 km along, at the end of this street.

Mount Albert – Mount Albert is just north of County Road 13 running east from Holland Landing. To reach the lagoons turn north on to Centre Street (the main street) and drive 2 km to Doane Road on the right. The lane to the lagoons is 0.7 km along this road on the north.

Sunderland – Anyone following Highway 12 north from Whitby passes through this village. The small lagoons are to the north; from the intersection of County Road 10 in town drive north to the next sideroad east. Turn, and the lagoons are on the south beside the railway, a little over 0.5 km along.

AREAS ALONG HIGHWAY 401 AND THE QEW

The volume of traffic on Highway 401 as one approaches Toronto is very heavy, and this continues for roughly 90 km, with the road gradually widening to sixteen or so lanes across the core area. The QEW and the Gardiner Expressway are even busier. The peak traffic periods are roughly between 7.00 a.m. and 9.00 a.m., and 4.00 p.m. and 6.00 p.m., when all three highways sometimes look like extended parking lots, but the roads are busy day and night. Hence birding along the highways themselves can be hazardous, even when there are birds to seen, and the comments below must be read with this in mind.

The land bordering the QEW is built up throughout most of its length. Hawks sometimes can be seen in the more open areas, but in general birding opportunities are few. *Bronte Creek Provincial Park* (entrance fee) is north of the highway between exits 109 and 111, with access via Burloak Drive (exit 109), and has fine mixed woodlands along the river.

This entire route is rarely more than 2–3 km from the lakeshore, and the exit numbers of the main access roads are given throughout the lakeshore west account. Ironically, perhaps the area which can be reached most quickly is at the eastern end of the QEW, where the exit lanes enter Lakeshore Boulevard directly: Humber Bay Park, Sunnyside, and High Park are all nearby, and the access details for these are given above.

The western section of Highway 401 in Halton County is still atop the escarpment, and northbound from the **Campbellville** exit (312) leads to County Road 9. East along here is the *Hilton Falls Conservation Area* and other parts of the Halton County Forest, described in Chapter 10. Return to 401 by continuing east to Highway 25 (401 exit 320), and then south. If you stay on 401 the highway soon drops down from the escarpment, with the imposing dolomite cliffs of Mount Nemo to the south, as well as the waters of Kelso Conservation Area. The latter also continues on the north of the road as an arm of wetland. This area is not particularly productive, but Turkey Vultures are regular along the scarp edge, and sometimes waterbirds can be seen.

You are now on the Peel Plain, and the farmland here is attractive to hawks, especially in winter. This is particularly true of the abandoned fields that become increasingly common closer to the city, and on the prairie-like expanses of *Toronto International Airport* on the north of the highway between exits 346 and 352.

None of the better Toronto birding areas are very close to 401 until the eastern side of the city. *Morningside Park* is on the southwest corner of Morningside and Ellesmere, the first major intersection south of exit 387. The next exit (Meadowvale Road, exit 389) leads north to *Metro Toronto Zoo*, which encloses much natural habitat in the Rouge Valley. Note that the eastern section of 401 has very heavy traffic eastbound on Friday evenings and westbound on Sunday afternoons. At Meadowvale the areas along the eastern lakeshore are now near at hand, and all are readily accessible from the highway. Our own favourite spots for a quick stop are at Brock Road (exit 399) for *Moore Point*, and Brock Street (exit 410) for *Whitby Harbour*.

One small but quite productive area of marsh is visible only from the westbound lanes of the highway. This is 2.4 km west of Brock Street (exit 410), and just past an area of tall sound screen fencing along the road. This fragment of wetland is associated with Lynde Creek and can be full of waterfowl, especially in spring, although stopping here can be hazardous.

AREAS ALONG HIGHWAY 400

Unlike the major east-west arteries, Highway 400 starts close to the northern suburbs of Toronto and quickly runs out of town. Heavy traffic is to be expected from Highway 7 south, and the highway as a whole has very heavy traffic northbound on Friday evenings and southbound on Sunday afternoons.

The first area of interest northbound is at Major Mackenzie Drive (exit 35). The fields in the next few kilometres can be good for hawks, and construction pools can yield shorebirds in season. To reach a small but well-known shorebird spot drive west 1.0 km on Major Mackenzie Drive to Weston Road (Regional Road 56). Turn south here, and 0.3 km on the west is a wet field where horses and donkeys are pastured. The ponds here, colloquially the *Donkey Ponds*, do not look promising, but they can be very productive in spring and fall with shorebirds and open country species, and hawks attracted to all the activity. The days of these ponds are numbered, but they were in 1979 for the first edition of the Toronto guide, and they're still there!

Between Major Mackenzie Drive and the next exit north, the King Sideroad (Exit 43), lie the two *Highway 400 service centres*. The one on the northbound side of the highway has some small sewage lagoons on the south side of the centre. The first can be viewed from the access road to the centre, but to see the second you will have to walk down the path to the ponds. The lagoons serving the centre on the southbound lanes are on the road in to the picnic area, which itself is adjacent to some woodlands where Red-shouldered Hawks have nested in the past. These lagoons are below the access road, and fully visible from it. The lagoons have a few nesting waterfowl and occasionally attract migrants.

East from Highway 400 on Major Mackenzie Drive is the village of **Maple**, the present site of the Toronto sanitary landfill. This is the largest and most active of the dumps currently in use around Metro, and it attracts huge numbers of gulls year-round. On weekday mornings when the dump is active thousands of Ring-billed and (during the winter) Herring Gulls gather here to feed, and later in the day loiter on adjacent fields. Careful examination of the flocks will usually yield less common species, particularly Iceland and Glaucous Gulls in winter, but at other seasons as well. Access to the dump is difficult, and the visiting birder might do better in the early afternoon looking over the fields where the gulls loiter. One of the most productive spots at present is the *Shur Gain farm* on the northeast corner of Major Mackenzie and Jane Street (Regional Road 55 the first major intersection east of 400). View from about 200 metres north on Jane.

By the King Sideroad (exit 43) the highway is climbing into the moraine; the height of land is ahead and then the road drops down to the flat vegetable farms of Holland Marsh. The moraine is good birding country and a slower, but more interesting and attractive route is to detour west to Regional Road 56 again from exit 43, and drive north on 56 to Highway 9 (exit 55). This 12 km stretch traverses an excellent mixture of habitats, including some small lakes.

MAP 26   Peterborough, Victoria, and
Northumberland Counties

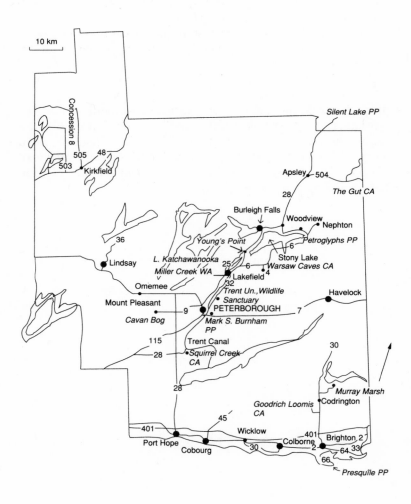

12 Peterborough, Presqu'île, and Area

Victoria, Peterborough, and Northumberland Counties

Peterborough
Highway 28 north of Peterborough
South and west of Peterborough
Other sewage lagoons in the Peterborough area
The Carden Plain
Presqu'île Provincial Park
Inland from Brighton
East along Lake Ontario and Highway 401

East of the sprawling mass of Toronto and its satellite communities the rolling, scenic countryside of the Oak Ridges Moraine approaches the lake. Beyond it to the north drumlin fields and further moraine land continue up to the Precambrian Shield. The Shield itself gradually probes south as the lakeshore angles gently north: Shield occupies the northern edge of Victoria County and maybe a third of Peterborough County. To the south, along the lake, the narrow agricultural plain continues east through Northumberland County to Trenton. It all adds up to a diverse and picturesque region with prosperous agriculture and orchards alternating with reforestation, cedar bogs, and rocky fields. Some of the long valleys between the hills are occupied by narrow lakes: Scugog, Rice Lake, and the Kawarthas, with patches of marsh along their shorelines, but subject to heavy recreational use. North again is the edge of the Shield: wild and beautiful country dotted with lakes that are a canoeist's dream. In the extreme northwest of Victoria is a flat limestone plain, the Carden Plain, where the shallow soils provide further old field habitats.

Highway 401, following the lakeshore eastwards, is the main

communication artery across the region, with Highway 7 roughly paralleling it some 40 km to the north. The other main highways angle up through the hills, but populations grow thinner to the north, and northeast of Peterborough towns are few. This is cottage country, and access roads that are pleasantly uncluttered during the colder months become busy in summer and jammed with urban refugees on the weekends.

The region is rich in birding potential. While the southern specialties are scarce, a few are scattered along the lake; and along the Shield boundary northerners such as raven and Gray Jay appear, close to the open-country birds of the old fields. To the south the lake continues its role as both barrier and pathway, with Presqu'île hooking out to concentrate the flow of migrants. Winters grow longer and more severe as one moves east and north, but the compensation for the later springs is that flights of winter finches and other northerners may occur here without penetrating farther west.

PETERBOROUGH

This attractive city of over 60,000 population abounds in good places for birding. It lies along Highway 7, with Highway 115 forming the main communication link to Highway 401 and the west. Peterborough County birds are well covered in an excellent book, *Our Heritage of Birds: Peterborough County and the Kawarthas*, by Doug Sadler. It is essential reading for anyone planning to do much birding in this area.

To visit some areas in Peterborough itself, on approaching the city from the southwest along Highways 115 or 28, exit the controlled access highway at the Parkway (this is the point the two highways intersect with Highway 7). Continue north about 1.8 km to the major intersection at Lansdowne Street. From this point *Jackson Park*, in the northwest of town, lies ahead. The Parkway soon merges into Clonsilla Avenue, which in turn joins Charlotte heading east. Turn left at the first main intersection on Charlotte onto Monaghan Street, and drive north on this road until it ends at Parkhill Road. The park entrance is opposite. It is a large, well-wooded area with mature pines, excellent for viewing migrant landbirds. It is possible to follow the deep stream valley for several kilometres by walking with care along the railroad track.

Mark S. Burnham Provincial Park is roughly 6 km east on Lansdowne, which becomes Highway 7 outside town. The entrance is 0.6 km past the lights at the intersection of Peterborough County Road 30 (Keene Road). It also is a fine area of old woodland. Both these parks have the customary breeding birds (Blackburnian Warbler has nested in Jackson) and are rewarding during migration.

The Otonabee River and the locks of the Trent Canal are also east along Lansdowne; continue until the road crosses the river, and turn left at the second light, onto Ashburnham Drive. At the next light north (Marsdale Drive) the entrance to *Beavermead Park* lies on the left. It borders Little Lake, an enlargement of the river that is used as a staging area by waterfowl.

To reach the *Trent University Wildlife Sanctuary*, continue north on Ashburnham to the next intersection at Maria Street (0.5 km). Turn left here and cross the bridge, and then right immediately on to Armour Road. Now continue some 6 km to the stop street at Nassau Mills Road. Turn right here, crossing the bridge, then right again (0.6 km) onto University Road. Watch for the entrance to the parking lot 0.6 km on the left. There is a network of walking trails here in an excellent mixture of habitats, including cedar bush, bottomland woodland, and old fields.

HIGHWAY 28 NORTH OF PETERBOROUGH

The Otonabee River is a flyway, and has patches of open water in winter, often the only open water in the area. Rarer waterfowl occur from time to time. River Road provides a beautiful and rewarding drive north from Peterborough along the east bank of the Otonabee and the Trent Canal. From the area described above, return to Nassau Mills Road and turn right. Now follow this road around as it runs close to the river (it becomes River Road, County Road 32). Watch under the bridges for Cliff Swallows, and the river and patches of wetland for waterbirds. As the road curves into **Lakefield** County Road 33 intersects from the right. Turn, and drive 0.5 km to the *sewage lagoons* on the right (do not block the lagoon gate). Many rarities have occurred here over the years, including the province's second Spotted Redshank in 1980.

Return to County Road 32 (Water Street in Lakefield) and

drive north to Highway 28. Turn left, crossing the river. To the north this widens to form *Lake Katchawanooka*, and there is an extensive marsh at the south end. This is accessible from Lakefield Municipal Park (turn right at the first light over the bridge, Clement Street, and drive to the end), and has Least Bittern and Marsh Wren. Now continue on Highway 28 as it curves south just outside Lakefield. Some 1.4 km from this point turn right on the first sideroad (the 7th Line of Smith Township) and drive 5.8 km to *Miller Creek Wildlife Area*. There is a small parking area on the left here that gives access to an old railroad track which passes through a swamp. The area is good for general birding at any time of year.

Return to Highway 28 and turn north (left) on it, returning to Lakefield. About 4 km north of town there is a Y-intersection with County Road 6 (Stoney Point Road) veering off to the east. This leads east some 9 km to County Road 4 on the right. About 3 km south is *Warsaw Caves Conservation Area* (entrance fee), where there is a good trail system as well as the caves. Olive-sided Flycatcher has bred here. County Road 6 continues north and east, and after about 18 km passes the Northey's Bay Road, providing a pleasant alternate route to the Petroglyphs, described below.

Highway 28 continues to **Young's Point**, where a fine stand of White Pine on South Beach Road (on the right just before the highway crosses the bridge) can yield northern species, including Northern Parula and Yellow-rumped Warbler. County Road 25 runs west off the highway just across the bridge, and it curves south to follow the west bank of Lake Katchawanooka. Osprey nests are visible along here, and the lake can yield early migrant and overwintering waterfowl.

North of Young's Point, Highway 28 is also the access highway to some outstanding wilderness canoe trips in the Shield country between **Burleigh Falls** and **Apsley**. Anyone planning such trips needs detailed topographic maps, so they are beyond the scope of this book (a number are outlined briefly in Doug Sadler's book above). These trips will yield the typical Shield thrushes and warblers, and nesting Turkey Vultures. Along Long Lake there is a population of Prairie Warblers which sometimes can be seen along the north shore close to the boat ramp. The access road to this is on the west of the highway 20.2 km north of Burleigh Falls.

Petroglyphs Provincial Park is an outstanding area near **Nephton**. This Shield park protects some of the finest Indian rock carvings on the continent, but it also has a fine mixed forest including stands of large pines, and several areas of marsh and bog. This variety attracts an assortment of more northern bird species, including Gray Jay at its southern limits. The access route to the Petroglyphs is east off Highway 28 at the north end of **Woodview** (0.8 km past the General Store, itself 8 km north of Burleigh Falls). Here the Northey's Bay Road follows the shore of Stony Lake; the park entrance is well signposted some 12 km off the highway. There is no camping in the park; the only facilities are a loop road of some 6 km (leading to the Visitor Centre and the glyphs site), a couple of picnic areas, and some excellent, but rugged, hiking trails. The area is gated in winter, necessitating the use of skis or snowshoes.

The entire area offers a rich array of breeding birds, with typical forest species closely adjacent to the birds of open agricultural areas. The breeding season brings some sixteen species of warbler, including Black-throated Blue and Pine, with Yellow-throated Vireos and both species of kinglet, together with occasional Olive-sided and Yellow-bellied Flycatchers. In addition to Gray Jay, Black-backed Woodpeckers occur, and ravens, Turkey Vultures, and Bald Eagles can be seen in summer.

The area is perhaps even better known for its winter birds. At that time the pines along the park entrance road have proved a good place for Red Crossbills and other finches, and Black-backed and Three-toed Woodpeckers can sometimes be found there. The particular interest in winter, however, is the presence of numbers of both Bald and Golden Eagles, attracted by deer kills. The area is part of the Peterborough Crown Game Preserve, with a large population of white-tailed deer. Typically the eagles are seen overhead, and they often follow foraging ravens. With luck and caution they can be located at a kill; the best locations within the park itself are around the Petroglyphs enclosure at the far end of the loop road, and nearby at the small lake visible on the east of the road at the point the two legs of the loop run together. It should be emphasized that, particularly in winter, this is a remote area and it is very easy to get lost in the bush.

One nearby location for seeing eagles in winter is the dump at Nephton. Drive east from the park entrance to the stop street at County Road 6 and turn left (this is the same county road mentioned under Warsaw Caves, above). Continue past the Blue Mountain Inn 1.2 km to West Kosh Road, the first sideroad on the right. The dump is 2.3 km along here; to reach it cross the tracks and bear left at the Y-intersection, and it is on the right 0.6 km past the fork.

Another scenic location for northern species is a deep gorge of the Crowe River, the *Gut Conservation Area*. Drive north on Highway 28 to Apsley, and take Highway 504 some 11 km east to Lasswade. Then continue east on a gravel road about 7 km, watching for the conservation authority sign (it is before the Crowe River crossing). Further north again on Highway 28 (about 15 km from Apsley, and actually just inside Haliburton) is *Silent Lake Provincial Park*, with a lake encircled by a trail. Hooded Merganser breed, and again northerners occur.

SOUTH AND WEST OF PETERBOROUGH

Two areas of interest south and west of Peterborough are Cavan Bog and the Squirrel Creek Conservation Area. For *Cavan Bog*, take County Road 9 (Sherbrooke Street in the city) west, crossing Highway 7, which at this point runs north. Soon the road drops down to run through the swampy woods, which continue west to the village of **Mount Pleasant**. Most of the property is privately owned, but much can be seen from this road and the sideroad immediately to the south. There is a good range of habitat types here.

The Otonabee River runs south from Peterborough to Rice Lake. *Squirrel Creek Conservation Area* is east of Highway 28 some 2 km south of the city, on County Road 28 east of **Millbrook**. There are good wetlands along the river here and along the sideroad to the south, which runs east to Bensfort Bridge, with river viewing.

OTHER SEWAGE LAGOONS IN THE PETERBOROUGH AREA

All these sewage lagoons are connected with communities along, or close to, Highway 7. Travellers along 7 should note this string of lagoons continues to the east: see Marmora, Madoc, and

Tweed in the next chapter. Most of them have yielded interesting reports from time to time.

Havelock – For the sewage lagoons turn off Highway 7 on to Highway 30, drive 1 km to the Old Norwood Road on the east, and turn. The lagoons are down a narrow lane 0.8 km along on the right (south).

Lindsay – The sewage lagoon complex is off Highway 36 north. From the intersection of Highways 36 and 36B (Queen Street) drive north 2.8 km to the point the highway curves right. Turn left at the curve on Ops Concession 6 and immediately (0.2 km) left again on a road that runs down past the landfill site to the lagoons and river.

Omemee – The sewage lagoons are quite small but easy to cover. Turn north on Regional Road 7 (poorly marked, but it is opposite the post office in the centre of town, and is signposted to Bobcaygeon), drive 1.5 km and turn left (west). Drive 0.4 km, and the lagoons are on the right.

THE CARDEN PLAIN

The flat limestone plain north of Kirkfield has a mix of marginal farmland and woodland. Most of the area is devoted to cattle rearing, and most of the birds of old field habitats are present, including species now rare elsewhere. Upland Sandpiper, Red-headed Woodpecker, Cliff Swallow, Sedge Wren, Eastern Bluebird, Loggerhead Shrike, Golden-winged Warbler, and Field and Grasshopper Sparrow are among the species that can be found on a tour of the backroads here. A very useful and detailed guide is Ron Pittaway's 'A Birder's Guide to the Carden Plain,' *Ontario Birds* 9.3 (December 1991) and the directions that follow are based on this, with my thanks to the author. The area is thinly populated, and the gravel roads are narrow and sometimes in poor condition; please use discretion in stopping to avoid blocking them. Viewing should be confined to the road, as the plain is mainly private property.

The area is east of Orillia and Highway 12, and a useful starting point is from the village of **Kirkfield**, 16.9 km east of Highway 12 on Highway 48. From Kirkfield head north on

Highway 503 to the lift lock of the Trent-Severn waterway
(3.2 km). There are toilets and a picnic area here. Then continue
north to the point 503 curves west. Halfway around the curve,
at 2.4 km, a gravel road turns off to the east. Turn right here
and then almost immediately (0.2 km) left to continue northwards. This is Concession 8, and is excellent birding throughout its 9.5 km length. Stop on the corner, and frequently as you
drive north. At 2.9 km is a bridge crossing an extensive sedge
marsh which can yield American Bittern, rails, snipe, and Sedge
Wrens.

The road continues north through scrub woodland and overgrown meadows to a T-intersection. Turn left here and drive
through coniferous woodland (Hermit Thrush and Yellow-
rumped Warbler occur; at night Whip-poor-wills and Common
Nighthawks sit on the road) for 4.9 km to the Dalrymple Road.
Another left here leads down the east shore of Dalrymple Lake
back to Highway 503 (4.2 km). Turn left again on 503 and drive
1.6 km to the first sideroad on the right, following it 1.7 km to a
point where the road forks. This area has been good for Loggerhead Shrikes. Now take the left fork and follow the road until it
turns sharp right, then almost immediately (3.4 km from the
fork) turn left on a narrow road that passes Cranberry Lake to
the east. At 1.6 km the road runs close to the lake and it is
possible to view it at a distance: Least Bitterns, Black Terns, and
Marsh Wrens nest.

In another 1.5 km you arrive at an intersection. Both the first
1.5 km of the road ahead, and the road to the right 1.0 km to the
next corner, have been good for Loggerhead Shrikes. To complete the present route turn left, and follow this road 6.3 km to
its end in a T-intersection. Bear right here to cross Canal Lake
on a causeway, where an Osprey nest occupies one of the hydro poles, and Common Loons and Common and Caspian Terns
can be seen. The road joins Highway 48 5.6 km west of Kirkfield.

East of Kirkfield (12.1 km) Highway 505 runs north to join
Highway 503. This 18.7 km stretch can yield many of the same
species as the route just described.

PRESQU'ÎLE PROVINCIAL PARK

Brighton [401 exit 509] is the nearest community to *Presqu'île
Provincial Park*, one of the premier bird-watching locations in

the province. The park is 4 km south on Northumberland County Road 66, which runs south off Highway 2 at the west end of town. The county road runs south to the lake and then curves west to cross the north end of a marsh. From this point *Brighton sewage lagoons* are easy to reach. At the point the road curves, a sideroad (Harbour Street) continues south, then turns east to follow the shoreline. This road winds around for 2.2 km before ending at Prince Edward Street. The water leads along here can yield waterbirds, especially terns; and the sideroads to the south, especially Baldwin Avenue, give excellent views of the north shore of Presqu'île Bay. Turn right at Prince Edward Street; the lagoons are 0.4 km along on the north.

Returning to County Road 66, continue west to the bridge over the marsh, and pull off the road to view the wetlands on both sides. Pied-billed Grebe and Common Moorhen are often visible, and the spot is a good one for American Bittern. Duck loiter on any exposed flats to the north, and in early spring a fine array of waterfowl can be expected.

Past the marshes the road turns south again on the base of the sandspit that forms the point, and the park gate is just ahead (entrance fee), with the main office on the right. A feeder here often attracts landbirds in the colder months. Presqu'île is of interest year-round. The park has a good bird checklist, and Steve LaForest's *Birds of Presqu'île Park* (available at the park bookshop) is an invaluable reference for anyone planning to spend time here. Hunting occurs on Mondays, Wednesdays, Fridays, and Saturdays in autumn from late September, which limits both access to some areas and the number of birds that can be seen.

The park occupies a hook-shaped peninsula. The base of the point runs south from the park gate and has wide sandy beaches on its west (Popham Bay) side and extensive marshland bordering the sheltered waters of Presqu'île Bay to the east. The road itself crosses an area of open, low-lying sandy pannes between the dunes on each side, covered with scattered small cedar, pine and poplar. Much of this is flooded in spring and some is wet year-round. It is a fascinating area botanically, but not so good for birds. Snipe are common and small numbers of other shorebirds and puddle ducks feed in the wet areas. Migrants fly over and follow the line of cottonwoods along the beach to the west or the heavier woodland that has developed to the east. East of the dunes is a series of narrow finger-like spits (the 'Fingers') which are densely forested, mainly with white cedar, but some areas of tall pine occur. These are separated by marshy areas, but marsh viewing is easier elsewhere; however, the woods can be good for migrants, particularly on windy days, and in winter.

Driving south across the pannes the visitor passes sideroads leading to the beaches on the west (numbered 1 to 4, although Beaches 1, 2 and 3 are usually closed except in summer), and one to the marsh boardwalk on the east. When open, Beach 1 gives access to the less productive north end of Popham Beach; however, it can be good for loitering gulls and occasional shorebirds. Beach 4 is the usual birder access point, and from here one can view the sweep of open beach to the north, and the section to the south. This is left in its natural state, and leads to Owen Point, the southwestern tip of the park. The character of the beach along this stretch varies greatly, even from day to day. At one extreme, sometimes in spring the lake will be lapping at the roots of the line of scrubby willows; at the other, often in fall a wide area of open beach will be exposed, covered in an odiferous carpet of green algae. This can be teeming with shorebirds, and dabbling duck and gulls forage in the shallows. The line of dense willows is hard to bird, but migrant passerines occur, and sparrows will forage on the ground at the very edge of the willow screen. These are usually Savannah or Song Sparrows, but other species occur regularly, and it is one place where Sharp-taileds have occasionally been found in September.

Popham Beach – the manicured, northern stretch should be carefully scrutinized as well – is one of the most reliable locations in the province for shorebird migrants. Numbers may not be great, but an excellent variety occurs. In fall Sanderlings, Semipalmated and Least Sandpipers predominate, with Semipalmated Plovers, followed later by Dunlin. These are joined by a few Red Knots and White-rumped and Baird's Sandpipers, and small numbers of yellowlegs, dowitchers, and Black-bellied Plover. In spring the small peeps are joined by Red Knot and flocks of Whimbrel. Rarer species occurring regularly include godwits and phalaropes, with Purple Sandpipers in later fall. Almost anything can turn up; the province's first Mongolian Plover was here.

To the southwest are two offshore islands, Gull Island and High Bluff Island. These are off-limits during the breeding season, and support a huge Ring-billed Gull and Double-crested Cormorant colony, and a small heronry of Black-crowned Night-Herons. Herring gulls, Caspian and Common Terns, and many waterfowl either nest here, or summer in the offshore waters (American Black Duck, Mallard, Northern Pintail, Blue and Green-winged Teal, Northern Shoveler, Gadwall, American Wigeon, Common Goldeneye, and Common and Red-breasted Merganser). Great Black-backed Gulls have also nested.

Owen Point is a concentration area for landbird migrants, including hawks; hunting Merlins constantly harass the fall shorebirds, and in fall accipiters fly west off the point. The loop of shoreline along Popham Bay to the north can also have loitering gull flocks along its length. In later May and again in fall Brant flocks can be expected, and in October the waters along the lake are one of the best places in southern Ontario for seeing all three species of scoter.

The other sideroad along the pannes leads to the marsh boardwalk. This loops southeast through the marshes, curving back to the inner shoreline, and a return walk leads through the dense cedars bordering the marsh. There is a viewing platform at the start and a viewing tower overlooking the pools at the south end. The marsh teems with Marsh Wrens, Common Yellowthroats, and Swamp Sparrows; and Pied-billed Grebe, both bitterns, Common Moorhen, Sora and Virginia Rail all nest, with a varied assortment of duck. Black Tern numbers are declining, but Caspian Terns from the lakeside forage constantly over the water. Sometimes Northern Harrier and Sedge Wrens are present. The walk is heavily used, and best at dawn and dusk.

At the point the road curves left, just past the entrance to Beach 4, is the parking lot for the park store on the right. This provides access to the mixture of open habitat back from Owen Point to the south. Along here thickets of juniper, cedar, and hardwoods, with open wet and grassy areas, attract landbird migrants, and woodcock breed. At the base of Owen Point itself is an overgrown area of marsh which can sometimes be of interest.

Past Owen Point the shoreline turns eastwards and becomes rocky. Returning to the road, this now also curves east onto the low limestone plateau which is the île part of Presqu'île. To the north is the main marsh, with excellent marsh viewing along the road. To the right the road to the campgrounds and the rest of the park soon branches off. There is an observation platform on the left just past this turn (opposite the campground parking lot), and Least Bitterns can sometimes be seen here at dawn.

The main road follows the south shore of Presqu'île Bay to the private cottage area; usually it is better to turn right and go into the park itself, but in late March and early April the cottage road can give the best views of the thousands of ducks (mainly scaup, Ring-necked Duck, Canvasback, and Redhead) that congregate along the edge of the ice. The right fork into the main body of the park first passes the large campground parking lot. Here there is the bird sightings board, a record book for more noteworthy sightings, and a feeder which is maintained and productive in the winter. The campgrounds occupy roughly the first half of the south shoreline. There are interior roads to the camping areas. The one running west along the shore passes the Pines campground, with Pine Warblers and Red-headed Woodpeckers, followed by a small swamp and marsh; the one running east (often closed, but it can be walked) passes through mixed woodlands and conifer plantations. They are both worth covering.

The main park road itself continues east and soon divides to form a large loop. A turn right leads to the day-use and picnic area, which is good for viewing migrant waterfowl offshore (loons and diving duck concentrate), and a few field birds and migrant hawks, although most buteos tend to bypass the point. A left turn at the intersection leads through extensive mixed woodlands, where the main nature trail, Jobe's Woods, is sometimes worth covering. The woods around the beginning of this have recently been the most reliable location for Black-backed and Three-toed Woodpeckers in late fall and winter. The road then passes through more woodland and reforestation, and emerges to cross an old field, the Calf Pasture, where a sideroad leads north to a boat launch. This area is one of the better birding spots: there are good views of the bay to the north, the marshy area in the small bay can have unexpected waterbirds (Pied-billed Grebes are usually present), and the little point and shoreline willow and cedar groves attract migrant landbirds. It is especially productive on stormy days when the winds are from some quarter of the south. The adjacent open fields are good for open-country species and watching hawk movement.

The main road continues through scrubby cedar woodlands bordering the cottage area (the best area for gnatcatchers) and links up with the other leg of the loop just outside the parking area for Lighthouse Point or Presqu'île Point proper, site of the Interpretive Centre, which usually closed except in summer. The heavy shrubby growth both on the point itself and along the roads into the parking lot can be good for migrant landbirds.

Presqu'île is not a concentration point of the quality of Pelee or even of Prince Edward Point. But it does concentrate migrants – for landbirds, Owen Point, the Calf Pasture, and Lighthouse Point are best – and has a unequalled mix of habitats in a relatively small area. If you own a bicycle, this is the perfect place for it. There are also many walking trails through the woods, and on cold days in spring and fall these can be more productive than the points themselves. In summer the park is heavily used, but shorebird passage can be seen through much of the period. In winter the point is very exposed and the surrounding lake often covered in shifting masses of ice. The campgrounds and loop road are usually closed, but the shore road to the lighthouse may be open. At these times finches may be seen in the conifers, waterfowl, mainly Oldsquaws, Common Goldeneye and Bufflehead, can be found in open water leads on the lake, and landbirds can be found at feeders at the campground parking lot, outside the main park office, and on the cottage road. Snowy Owls and white gulls are regular along the shore, and Great Gray Owls have occurred.

Brighton has two motels, and there is a restaurant just outside the park gate. The park campgrounds are, of course, ideally situated, especially High Bluff, which is immediately adjacent to Owen Point.

INLAND FROM BRIGHTON

There are two areas north of Brighton along Highway 30 that are of note, primarily in the breeding season. About 6.5 km north of the Brighton interchange on Highway 401 (exit 509) is the sideroad on the west leading 3 km to *Goodrich Loomis*

Conservation Area. This an area of mixed habitats – cedar bush, deciduous woodland, and old fields – with a network of walking trails.

Farther north again, some 12.5 km from 401 (1.9 km north of the crossroad in **Codrington**) is Brighton 8th Line or Goodfellow Road. This runs east and then north into the *Murray Marsh*, a vast swamp which is otherwise rather inaccessible. The road passes Cameron Road on the south at 2.4 km, and then angles backwards and forwards before turning north for the last time at 4.8 km from the highway, entering the formally designated wetland area and continuing 2.1 km to dead-end at a parking area. This latter section is subject to flooding. The accessible wetland consists of an extensive cedar-alder swamp, with open cattails to the east among dead cedar snags, and smaller areas of tall poplar and other hardwood, as well as cedar-tamarack. More of the swamp appears on the east of Cameron Road, which runs south to Brighton through a variety of habitats. There is little open water visible anywhere. Both these areas have a good assortment of breeding species.

EAST ALONG LAKE ONTARIO AND HIGHWAY 401

For the birder travelling east from Durham the route along 401 is scenic but not especially interesting, although there is much good habitat along the highway. Lake Ontario here is both less accessible and less productive than farther west, but it still can yield good birds. Access to this section of lake is from Highway 2, and the route to Presqu'île is actually shorter following this highway east from Port Hope. However, as the road passes through a series of small communities it is usually slower, even without birding!

To go to **Port Hope**, exit Highway 401 on Ontario Street south (Highway 28, exit 464), and follow it into town, keeping right as the highway bears left on to Mill Street. Ontario Street ends at the light at Walton Street. Turn left here and then take the first right on Queen Street [0.1 km]. Drive south on Queen; the road parallels the Ganaraska River, crossing Robertson Street, and then bears right as Hayward Street. The harbour, which is separate from the river, is on the left 0.1 km ahead. It can yield waterfowl and gulls.

Now return to the first cross-street (Robertson) and turn right, crossing the river, and continue straight ahead from the stop sign at Mill Street. You are now on Peter Street (Highway 2 east), and at the top of the hill (0.5 km) there is a light at Hope Street. Turn right and follow this road past a small sewage pond to the lake at the mouth of *Gage's Creek*. There is lake viewing along here (loons, grebes, and mergansers in migration) and the marshes, thickets, and willows along the creek can be good for migrants.

Cobourg is some 10 km farther east (use 401 exit 474). The harbour here can yield duck, gulls, and occasional shorebirds. There are two access points: the west side at the foot of Hibernia Street (the light on Highway 2 with the police station on the southeast corner), and the east, and easiest side, at the foot of Division Street south from the junction of Highways 2 and 45 in the centre of town. Neither Cobourg nor Port Hope harbours attract large numbers of waterfowl, but it is not unusual to find birds there that are absent at Presqu'île, and Cobourg can be good for gulls. The industrial mall at the east end of Cobourg at Normar Road, just before the bridge over the railway, is attractive to hawks, Snowy Owl, and Northern Shrike during the colder months.

At **Wicklow**, some 15 km east of Cobourg on Highway 2 (from 401, leave the highway at **Grafton**, exit 487, and then drive east about 3 km), *Wicklow Beach Road* goes due south to the lake from the centre of the hamlet. It then curves east along the lakeshore, and the lake at this point is good for loons and grebes in migration. The wet woodlands of *Haldimand Conservation Area* are on the left, with a pond to the east that can yield duck and herons, especially in spring. From Highway 2 to the pond is 8.5 km.

This road now runs east to connect with Highway 2 again at **Colborne** [401 exit 497], becoming County Road 30 in the process, and often has good birding en route. After passing through the hamlet of Lakeport, the road turns sharp left and crosses the railroad, then right again into Colborne. Instead of turning right, continue straight ahead on the gravel road (Ontario Street), and down the hill to the creek. Just before the bridge the *sewage lagoon* gate is on the left, and the lagoon itself is down a long drive. Highway 2 is directly ahead.

Some 4 km east of Colborne the highway passes through **Salem**. Watch for the cemetery on the right; 2.2 km from this point is Barnes Road and, 1.3 km farther again, Hunt Road. Barnes runs south through wet woodland and Hunt through a diversity of habitats; both are good for birds, and both end at Lakeshore Road, running east. Immediately past Hunt Road this passes a good marshy section, and then runs through a cottage area where the wet fields on the north of the road can be good for dabbling duck and shorebirds in spring. Eventually, some 3.7 km from the marshy area, the road jogs right and joins the *Presqu'île Park* road as the latter curves left just north of the park gate. To go to **Brighton** (401 exit 509) or to cover the marshes on the way into the park as described above, turn left; to head into the park itself, turn right.

At Brighton both Highways 2 and 401 swing away from the lakeshore as this curves south to Prince Edward County; however, Highway 30 in Brighton continues south of Highway 2 as County Road 64 (Prince Edward Street), which eventually joins Highway 33 at Carrying Place. This is the access highway for the west side of Prince Edward County, and it intersects with Highway 401 outside Trenton (exit 525). About 2 km south of Highway 2 in Brighton, County Road 64 curves east to skirt the shoreline marshes. Brighton *sewage lagoons* are on the north at this point (directions to them from Presqu'île are given above).

County Road 64 then continues east to the Murray Canal. To cover more of the shoreline, which is interesting mainly in early spring, immediately after crossing the canal bear right on the sideroad to *Barcoven Beach*. The first sideroad on the right along here ends at Presqu'île Bay, and has views across to the park. It can be a useful vantage point for observing waterfowl that are a little too far from the park side to see clearly, but hardly warrants a special trip unless something especially intriguing has been seen. The Barcoven Beach sideroad also joins the shore farther east, and then turns north to return to the county road. At the point it turns there are excellent views of the entrance to *Wellers Bay* in Prince Edward County. In early spring this area of water opens up first, and can be full of duck.

There are two sets of rest areas on the stretch of Highway 401 across Northumberland County. One is between Newcastle and Port Hope, and the second between Brighton and Trenton. The picnic areas are pleasant but not exceptional. The wooded area of the Trenton one eastbound and the mixed cover of the Newcastle one westbound are probably the best, and there is a small sewage lagoon associated with the latter along the re-entry lane to the highway.

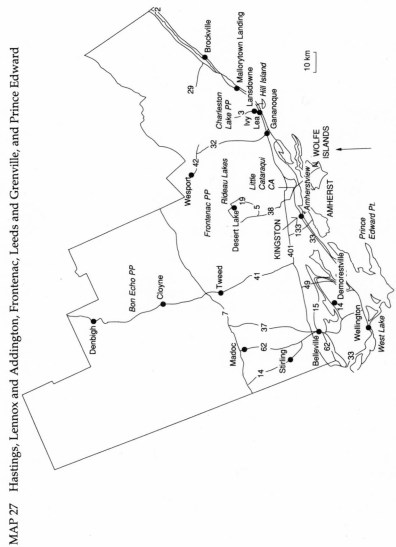

MAP 27   Hastings, Lennox and Addington, Frontenac, Leeds and Grenville, and Prince Edward

13 The Kingston Area and Prince Edward Point

The Counties of Hastings, Lennox and Addington, Frontenac, Leeds and Grenville, and Prince Edward

Kingston
Amherst and Wolfe Islands
The Rideau Lakes
Prince Edward County
Highway 401 east
Other locations and sewage lagoons in the Kingston area

Southwestern Ontario is the glamour spot, but for superb birding year-round, the Kingston area is hard to beat. These counties embrace the southernmost extension of the Precambrian Shield – the Frontenac Axis – and the diverse forests here attract a rich assortment of breeding birds, offering a fascinating mix of northern and southern species at the limits of their respective ranges. Much of the Shield is bounded by limestone plains with shallow soils and marginal agriculture, yielding the characteristic birds of old field habitats, while the extensive marshes in the many sheltered bays and along the Cataraqui River are ideal for waterbirds. All these things combine to yield the richest nesting avifauna in Ontario.

In migration time Prince Edward comes into its own, but there are many other places where migrants gather along the shorelines of the lake and the St Lawrence River. Winters are long and cold, with much snow; but they bring wandering owls and hawks to Wolfe and Amherst Islands, and flights of finches and other northerners that may never appear farther west. Ron Weir's account of Kingston area birds (see chapter 19) is a valuable reference for persons proposing to do much birding in the region.

The main arterial link across the area is Highway 401, and Kingston has its own airport. North of 401, however, the highway network is sparse and population centres are scattered, and most of Prince Edward County is also off the beaten track.

KINGSTON

Kingston, an attractive city of some 60,000 persons, has the Shield country of the Rideau Lakes to the north and is itself located on the Napanee limestone plain with the offshore islands of Amherst and Wolfe to add to its diversity. There are several excellent birding spots around the city itself. The first of these, the *Cataraqui Cemetery*, is on the east side of Sydenham Road 1.4 km south of its interchange with Highway 401 (exit 613), and immediately north of the junction with Highway 2 (Princess Street). There is parking just north of the cemetery itself. The area is small, but the back part especially can be most productive during migration.

Little Cataraqui Creek joins Lake Ontario just west of the city, and the marshes along its lower reaches can yield a rich array of marsh birds in summer, and migrant duck and (depending on water levels) shorebirds in migration. A railroad track along the creek's east bank between the Bath Road and King Street West and about 1 km west of Portsmouth Avenue can be used to gain access to the area, which also contains some hardwood bush that can be productive in migration. Parking is possible both on the south side of Bath Road and the north side of King Street W. The Rideau Trail also follows the creek's east bank.

The *Little Cataraqui Conservation Area* is about 1 km north of Highway 401 on Division Street (exit 617). It is well marked on the west of the road, and has a large waterbody (good for duck) and associated mixed woodlands.

Going west from the city on Highway 33, the *Amherstview sewage lagoons*, just beyond the village of Elmwood, have been some of the most productive in the province. Watch for Maple Ridge Drive on your right; 0.3 km ahead are the stoplights at Coronation Boulevard, and the sign for Lennox-Addington County. Turn right here and drive 1 km, crossing the railroad, and turn west on a road marked to the golf course. At 1.9 km this road turns right into the golf course, and a rough track continues on beside the railroad, eventually leading to the lagoons.

AMHERST AND WOLFE ISLANDS

About 10 km farther west on Highway 33, and 0.3 km west of its junction with Highway 133 (Highway 401 exit 593), is the Amherst Island ferry (40 cars; fee). The ferries start at 6.20 a.m., leaving the mainland hourly on the half hour, and on the hour from Stella (Amherst Island). The pattern of birding is similar on both Amherst and Wolfe islands. Both have a network of gravel roads and on both the flat farmland is interspersed with woodlots and areas of marsh. The land is private, but most birding can be done from the roads. A typical day's trip is devoted to following these roads around and covering adjacent fields, wetlands, and waterfront from them. The quality of some of the sideroads varies considerably, and at times they may be in very poor condition, especially in early spring.

The islands have gained international fame as a haven for hawks and owls in winter. Ontario's largest numbers of Snowy Owls and Rough-legged Hawks have occurred on Wolfe Island, and Amherst played host in early 1979 to an amazing concentration of ten owl species, including an estimated, unprecedented 34 Great Gray Owls. Both islands experience huge build-ups in the numbers of voles and mice, and these in turn attract raptors year-round, but particularly in winter. The outbreaks are periodic, and vary from one island to the other, so do not expect to drive down to Amherst next January and see ten species of owl! However, there are usually fair numbers of the commoner species reported in any year, with the later winter (February) generally being the best time.

Please note: Virtually all of the land on Amherst Island is privately owned. If entry on to private property is desired, permission must be sought and any limitations scrupulously observed. Above all, birders should ensure that neither they nor their vehicles block the narrow roads at any time. Being an hour late for work because you missed the ferry due to

a slob birder blocking the road is likely to infuri-
ate anyone. Recent failures to observe such simple
courtesy on Amherst have poisoned the atmo-
sphere towards birders. This bad behaviour has
extended to harassment of the birds themselves.

On Amherst the best approach is to follow the road along the
north shore eastwards (see map 28). At about 3 km a small
sideroad runs south. This road has yielded Henslow's and
Grasshopper Sparrows in the breeding season, but is best known
for a small woodlot which has been publicized as a location for
owls in the winter. However, the property here is owned by
several individuals, some of whom will not tolerate trespass on
their lands. The local birders sometimes bring organized groups
here, having made appropriate arrangements in advance, but
casual visitors **should not visit this area**. Owls are possible all
along the route, especially in vole years, and in any case Short-
eared and Snowy Owls and Rough-legged Hawks favour the
more open fields.

In migration times the gravel beaches and bar at the east end
of the island (where the Kingston Field Naturalists have a reserve) can yield shorebirds, waterfowl, and herons. Scan the
water along the road periodically and then continue south as
the road bends. At the southeast corner it is possible to park
and walk east to the bar. Scan the marshy areas and the beach
on the way. At least an hour is required. The KFN would ap-
preciate receiving the species tally and numbers from visitors
to their property (P.O. Box 831, Kingston, Ontario K7L 4X6).
Continuing west, the swamps and marshes along the southwest shoreline are rewarding during migration, and the latter
have nesting Soras and Virginia Rails. Waterfowl raft offshore
and should be looked for at any of the many vantage points.
Both islands are excellent for field and open-country birds, and
large flocks of Brant occur in late May.

Wolfe Island is divided into two by Bayfield Bay (see map
29), with the largest land mass to the west and a long, narrow
extension east. It is the western section that is most productive.
Winter birding entails covering the many sideroads, and watching for Rough-legged Hawks, Snowy Owls (usually present here
even when absent elsewhere), and Snow Buntings, as well as
occasional Lapland Longspurs.

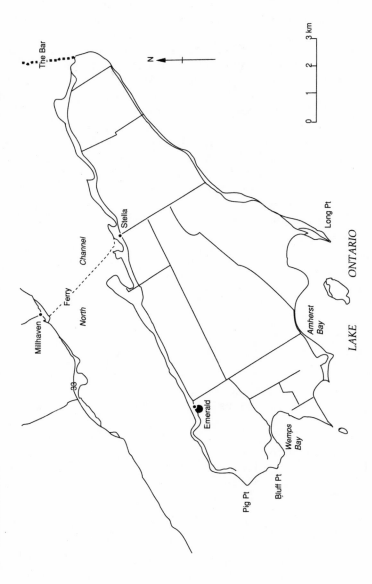

MAP 28   Amherst Island

Highway 95 is one of the better routes: it runs south from Marysville and then turns east to a ferry terminal (from Cape Vincent in New York State); and the last, easterly section of the highway is one of the best places at all seasons, as are the roads around Reeds Bay. There are many secluded bays in this area, with sand and gravel beaches and bars. Duck, shorebirds, and gulls congregate and the waterfowl (mainly scaup) raft offshore. In early spring Canada Geese and dabbling duck feed on the fields adjacent to the lake along the marshy southwest shore. Gray Partridge can turn up anywhere along the route.

The ferry for Wolfe Island (fee; space for 55 cars) leaves from Kingston at the foot of Barrack Street south of Ontario Street and one block east of Princess Street, which is directly accessible from Highway 401 exits 613 and 617. A partial ferry schedule at present is:

Leave Kingston		Leave Wolfe Island	
	6:15 a.m.		1:15 p.m.
	7:15 a.m.		2:30 p.m.
	8:30 a.m.		3:30 p.m.
	9:30 a.m.		4:30 p.m.
	11:00 a.m.		5:30 p.m.
	12:30 p.m.		

THE RIDEAU LAKES

The Rideau Lakes area north of Kingston is heavily forested Shield country with an excellent assortment of breeding birds. There are several interesting and scenic drives through it, although the roads are narrow and winding, and it is easy to get lost. This is beautiful country, particularly in autumn. Just do not expect to be able to cover it in a hurry! One good route is to drive north from the city on Highway 38 some 20 km to **Harrowsmith** and turn east, on Frontenac County Road 5. Drive to **Sydenham** and turn north at the flashing light onto County Road 19. If one sticks to 19 the route is fairly straightforward. It initially bears generally northeast, but then winds around back to Highway 38 again, and is gravelled for much of its more that 30-km length.

Starting with an odometer reading at the corner of County Roads 5 and 19: at 12.3 km a road to the right leads to *Frontenac Provincial Park*, a large wild area with backpacking trails, ca-

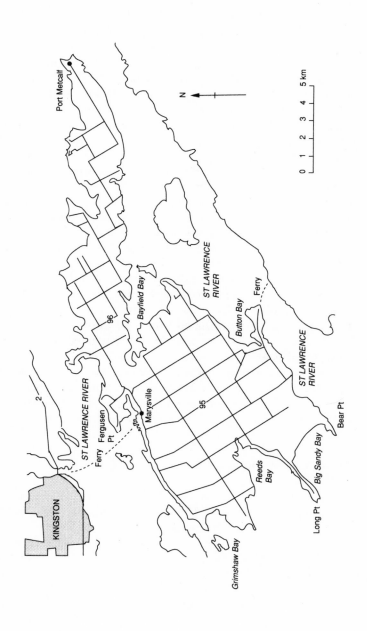

MAP 29   Wolfe Island

noeing, and interior camping. At 14.1 km the road passes through the *Otter Lake Sanctuary* of the Kingston Field Naturalists. At 17.1 km the County Road bears left and down the hill into the small community of **Desert Lake**. If you go straight ahead instead of turning left, the road passes through country east of Desert and Canoe lakes. Canoe Lake has Prairie Warblers along the west shoreline (only accessible by canoe). However, it is easy to get lost in the maze of unmarked sideroads winding through this area (even County Road 19 is unmarked for most of its length) and a topographic map is needed to explore them. Continuing on 19, after Desert Lake there are more sideroads, but all fairly obviously secondary to the county road. One on the left just after leaving Desert Lake leads to Holleford and back to County Road 5, but the caution above applies here also. County Road 19 eventually joins Highway 38, where a left turn takes you back to Kingston.

These roads are warbler country, and the woodlands of this southerly extension of the Shield attract southern warblers as well as more northern ones. Nashville and Canada Warbler are recorded in boggy coniferous areas, but Otter Lake has Golden-winged Warbler and Cerulean Warbler. The area is a stronghold for both Yellow-throated Vireo and Cerulean Warbler, and is currently the eastern limit for Blue-winged Warbler. The Rideau Lakes area have a host of intriguing breeding and summering records: both Louisiana Waterthrush and Three-toed Woodpecker have nested, southern and northern species in remarkable proximity; northerners such as Yellow-bellied Flycatcher and Philadelphia Vireo nest in small numbers; and even Golden Eagle has been reported in summer.

PRINCE EDWARD COUNTY

The southern part of Prince Edward County has several outstanding birding areas. Thin pasture and old field habitats abound on the limestone soils to the south of Highway 33, the main road crossing the county. These attract such species as Northern Harrier, Upland Sandpiper, cuckoos, Brown Thrasher, and Grasshopper Sparrow, together with a few remnant Loggerhead Shrikes and, until recently, Henslow's Sparrows. Golden and Blue-winged Warblers and Clay-colored Sparrows can be found in more brushy areas, and Northern Mockingbirds occur. Terry Sprague, who has birded the county for many years, has written (with Ron Weir) an annotated checklist (mentioned in chapter 19) and also a useful 'Birding Site Guide to Prince Edward County' (*Ontario Birds* 5:1 [April 1987]).

Prince Edward Point, one of the premier migrant concentration points in the province, is located at the southeastern tip of the county. The route to the point differs depending on whether one is coming from east or west. From the east, take the Adolphustown-Glenora Ferry (at present free, every 15 minutes). This is about 35 km from Kingston via Highway 33, and the point is some 40 km by road from the ferry. Leaving the dock at **Glenora**, first check gasoline. There are no service stations on the roads you are about to follow (see map 30). If you need gas, go straight ahead to Picton and get some. Otherwise turn left at the top of the hill onto County Road 7, which then passes **Lake-on-the-Mountain Provincial Park**. Continue to County Road 25 (2.4 km from the park, marked to Waupoos); turn right, and then at 1.8 km bear right on County Road 13 (to Milford), and follow this road around to Black River. Drive through the hamlet and then follow the directions in the second paragraph after next.

Coming from the west, turn south in Picton on to County Road 8 to Waupoos; this is right at the Y-intersection just past the light at the corner of Highways 33 and 49. (Note the caution above about gasoline.) Just outside Picton you will pass the *Macauley Mountain Conservation Area* on the right, with a world-champion array of bird-houses! There is a low escarpment here with walking trails through a variety of habitats, and in the breeding season these can yield a mix of the usual edge species, together with woodland birds such as Pileated Woodpecker, Eastern Wood-Pewee and Winter Wren; and Clay-colored Sparrows occur on the plateau above. In migration periods one's time is usually better spent covering the areas that follow. One can now follow County Road 8 to the right-hand turn on to County Road 13 described above; or alternatively bear right off 8 on to County Road 17 at about 2.5 km, and drive to the point 17 turns right. Turn left here and drive east on County Road 16, which joins Road 13 just outside the hamlet of Black River. Turn right and follow 13 south.

MAP 30   Picton and Southern Prince Edward County

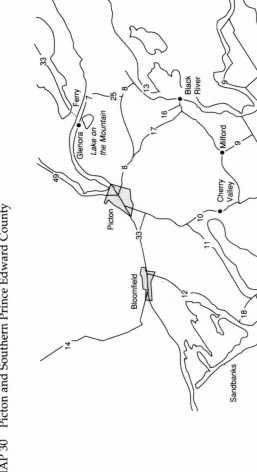

At Black River east and west routes join. Continue straight on at the junction with County Road 9 on the right, which goes to Milford, and which is also the road to Point Petre. Milford has the nearest gas station to the point, so note the intersection: it is not signposted at present, but is opposite the Mariner's Memorial Park and Lighthouse. County Road 13 ends at this intersection, by the way; at the next road sign you will find you are on County Road 9! Rose's Lane, 3.6 km farther on, is the next important intersection.

At Rose's Lane one can take an alternative route to the point by turning right on a gravel road. Dealing with this route first, drive 1.7 km and turn left, checking the creek en route for bitterns and duck. The low cedars to the northeast of the creek have had Clay-colored Sparrows in summer. Around the corner, the old fields to the right are good for hawks. Yellow Rails have occurred in migration in some of the weedy wet areas (about 0.5 km along) and Sharp-tailed Grouse are present but rarely seen. If the fields are being grazed over the grass may be short enough for plover and other open-country species on migration. A sideroad to the south at 3.2 km, which leads to the shore, is sometimes passable. Otherwise continue east to rejoin the main road at 7.1 km from your turn-off.

Proceeding on the main road past Rose's turn-off, a farther 2 km will lead to Smuggler's Cove, the nearest campground to the point. *Little Bluff Conservation Area* is next (2.2 km) and has a small marsh to the left on the way in. A stop street 4 km from here marks the entry from the right of the alternative route from Rose's Lane. Follow the main road left.

From this point on the bushes and weeds along the road can be alive with migrants. Hawks are often moving down the point in fall, and the open water to the left, although usually not very productive, can yield small flocks of scoter and other duck, as well as loons and grebes. Just at the point where the paved road ends (1.1 km) a track to the right which passes a marsh on the south shore may be passable. Next, a pond by the road (2.6 km, at present just past a mailbox marked 'Wannamaker') can be surprisingly productive of shorebirds and other species. Ontario's first Chestnut-collared Longspur and the area's first Say's Phoebe were observed here, and Cliff Swallows have nested on the adjacent barn.

At 2.3 km you enter *Prince Edward Point National Wildlife Area*, and the most productive parts of the point, best birded on foot. First, the road runs through Traverse Woods, which are excellent for landbird migrants. Past here it curves at Point Traverse. Watch for hawks, duck on the pond to the right and on the lake, and landbird migrants everywhere. About 1 km farther on, the road turns right through the fishing village (no facilities) of Long Point Harbour and enters another woodlot. Here the road deteriorates rapidly: it curves around the harbour and about 1 km from the harbour dock arrives at the lighthouse entrance. This is on Prince Edward Point itself. The observatory here is run by Kingston Field Naturalists, and has an active banding program.

The best areas here are off the point and along the south shoreline to the west for gulls and diving duck. Huge rafts of scaup and merganser occur in autumn and gull movements occur in migration times. The water between Point Traverse and Prince Edward Point often have scoter and Oldsquaw and the shoreline rocks may have shorebirds. The swampy woodland at the harbour, although small, can be most productive, and all the old fields can be alive with sparrows and other migrants. Hawks and other diurnal migrants tend to drift down to the point from Point Traverse and then mill around over the fields to the west. Northern Saw-whet Owls are regular in October, but hard to find during the day. The energetic work of the Kingston club has yielded a host of interesting breeding records from Prince Edward Point. Blue-gray Gnatcatchers nest, Orchard Oriole and Yellow-breasted Chat have occurred in summer, and there is a good variety of the more usual summer birds.

Point Petre is at the other end of the county, and it also concentrates migrants. To reach it from Prince Edward return to the County Road 9 junction noted above, turn left, and drive 1.5 km to the curve in the road where Royal Street goes off to the left. Turn onto this gravel road, which runs virtually due west for 7.5 km before curving to join County Road 24. Turn left on to this road and drive 3 km to *Point Petre Recreational Area*. Watch for Eastern Bluebirds on the wires along this stretch of road. The main road continues 1.7 km to the lighthouse station. Any of the small roads down to the shore on the west can be interesting, and on the west just at the start of the recreational area is a picnic area in a woodlot. This overlooks Soup Harbour and gives excellent lake viewing for waterfowl. A gravel road 0.3 km on the east past here leads back to Prince Edward. Its condition, and more particularly that of sideroads running south from it, can be uncertain, and you should have a topographic map if you plan to explore. Petre badly needs more coverage. Although it is nowhere near as productive as Prince Edward, the mix of birds tends to be different and the opportunities for lake viewing are better. Whenever we have visited Petre we have always seen something we had missed earlier at Prince Edward.

To get to Petre without visiting Prince Edward drive southwest on the Cherry Valley Road (County Road 10) from the west end of Picton and turn left in Cherry Valley, continuing on 10 to the junction, at about 2 km, of County Road 24 on the right. Turn here; this road leads directly to the point.

There are some other good locations on this side of the county. Some 14 km from Point Petre via County Roads 24 and 10 (along the route just described) is the junction on the west of County Road 11, which runs along the north side of East Lake. **Beaver Meadow Conservation Area** is on the right 0.8 km along County Road 11. This area has a trail leading through swampy woodland, ending at a viewing tower which overlooks a shallow lake with many dead trees. Species such as Wood Duck, which may be hard to find elsewhere, occur here; and there is a Great Blue heronry to the left of the trail end. Tree Swallows and other hole-nesters abound, including Red-headed Woodpecker. There is hunting here in fall.

Continuing west on County Road 11 leads to **Sandbanks Provincial Park**. At 7.6 km you come to a T-intersection; turn left here on County Road 18. The **Outlet Beach** section of the park is 0.7 km ahead, and incorporates the heavy cedar cover along the barrier beach fronting East Lake. This can be good for finches, and the East Lake outlet attracts Green Herons, but the Lake Ontario shoreline here in fall is the main point of interest. Shorebirds can gather at the mouth of the outlet, and gull flocks feed offshore and loiter along the beach. Watch for Little and

Common Black-headed Gulls among the large numbers of Bonaparte's; both have occurred.

To reach the *West Lake* sector of Sandbanks, turn off County Road 18 on to County Road 12 just before the Outlet Beach park area. This road leads along the shore (lake viewing) 3 km to a stop street, with the park gate immediately opposite. A left turn here leads down a dead-end road 1 km to some stone entry gates. This is *West Point*, and there is a small parking area just before the gates. From the shoreline here there are views of the Sandbanks beach to the north and the waters offshore. Loons, diving duck, and shorebirds are possible in migration, with more gulls, and landbirds move along the shoreline.

Returning to the West Lake sector of Sandbanks and entering the park, the road soon ends behind the beach. This sector has a relatively small (but productive) area of coniferous plantation and mixed woodland, magnificent sand dunes, a long sandy beach, and many small sedge-margined pools backing the first line of dunes and along the entry road. These pools can be good for shorebirds, and Mallard, Blue-winged Teal, and snipe nest.

Leaving the park gate, turn left to continue to County Road 12 and a return to Highway 33. At 1.4 km the road turns sharply right, and on the left is a parking area. This gives access to a walking trail which backs the dune ridge, and it leads to an open area where duck and shorebirds can be found in migration. Leaving this parking lot, the road now passes a campground (Sandbanks Beach Resort) on the left, on its way into West Lake and (at 2.7 km from the parking area) a sideroad on the left which leads 1 km across a causeway to Sheba Island. This short stretch, signed to Edgewater Park, provides excellent views of an area of cattail marsh to the east. County Road 12 now continues east some 8 km to Highway 33 at **Bloomfield**, where a right turn leads back to Picton.

Turn left here, and continue left on 33 at the Highway 62 intersection. Now watch (0.4 km from 62) for a small cemetery on the right, and turn diagonally left here on to Church Street immediately opposite. This is signed to Wesley Acres Church camp, and coming from Wellington it is 0.4 km past the Bloomfield sign at the entry to town. This road dead-ends after 4.2 km at the camp, and its last 2.2 km is dirt. It crosses some marsh at 1.3 km, and runs beside an extensive area of cattail for its last 1.6 km. The first 0.5 km of this section provides the best marsh viewing.

Continuing east on 33, the village of **Wellington** is the next community. Here (2.8 km from Church Street in Bloomfield) there is viewing of the north corner of West Lake on the left, at the foot of Belleville Street (the LCBO building). Better views are possible by continuing 0.3 km to turn left on Beach Street, and following this road 0.7 km along the beach to parking at the West Lake outlet. The beach can yield shorebirds and gulls, and the outlet area other waterfowl, especially in early spring. Over the outlet is the north end of the 8 km-long Sandbanks beach. Coming from the north, Beach Street is 0.3 km past the post office and churches.

Although there are huge areas of marsh in the many bays and inlets of Prince Edward County, relatively little is readily accessible by road, and much of that is dominated by solid stands of cattail. Two good areas are mentioned above, and further sections along the Bay of Quinte are accessible between Highway 62 south of Belleville and Highway 49 north of Picton.

Demorestville, accessible via County Road 14 from the west, County Road 15 from the east, and County Road 5 from Picton, gives access to the large *Big Island marsh*. Drive north 1.8 km from the village on County Road 5 to the intersection of County Road 21, and continue north on this road, which leads about 1 km across the marshes on a causeway. This marsh is heavily overgrown with cattails, and is more interesting in spring before they have grown up, but there is also good canoe access along the road.

Another area is farther west on the *Huff's Island* sideroad. This is east off Highway 62 some 6 km south of the **Belleville** bridge and 18.5 km north of Bloomfield. The areas of marsh are along this road itself, 1.7 km from the highway (the best section is 2 km from this point) and north along the first sideroad on the left. The marshes here start 0.5 km along the road, which is currently closed at this point, but it can be walked. Extensive cattail marshes with open pools and brushy areas are present at these locations. Both here and the Big Island marsh have yielded an array of rarer species, as well as an excellent assortment of the common marsh birds. Bitterns, Sora and Virginia Rails, Black Terns, and Marsh Wrens all nest, and King Rail has occurred.

HIGHWAY 401 EAST

The Kingston section of 401 is one of the most scenic parts of the entire highway, particularly east of Kingston. There are two sets of rest areas; one west of Kingston and the second east of Mallorytown. The Kingston ones, both set in woodlands off the highway, are the most pleasant.

At **Belleville** (exits 525 and 526) the marshes along the Bay of Quinte are as accessible as anywhere. The Huff's Island section described above is east off Highway 62 some 8 km south of the Belleville bridge.

At **Gananoque** the *sewage lagoons* are east off Highway 32 immediately north of Highway 401 exit 645. The lagoon road is on the right 0.2 km north of the 401 westbound exit, and there is about 1 km of narrow road to the gate. The Gananoque waterfront itself is good for migrant waterfowl, which concentrate in the river here in early spring, and the Thousand Islands Parkway (401 exit 647) between town and Ivy Lea, some 15 km east, has views of the fine marshes along the St Lawrence. Duck congregate here, too. This parkway is very scenic, but much slower than 401.

At **Ivy Lea** (exit 659) the St Lawrence River is usually open in winter and both winter and early spring migrant waterfowl can be seen. Canvasback, Redhead, scaup, Oldsquaw, and Common Goldeneye are the usual species, and the occasional Bald Eagle winters.

The islands along the *International Bridge* (exit 661) east of the community have an introduced (but long established) population of Wild Turkeys. These birds occur on *Hill Island* and I have heard a variety of directions to them over the years; what it all boils down to is that they are easiest to find in winter, when they are coming to feeding stations provided by residents on the island. As is the way with feeder owners, their enthusiasm seems to wax and wane and I suppose the birds move around to wherever the pastures are greenest – or corn is thickest, in the present case! They are also more prone to visit feeders when the snow cover is heavier, so snow conditions are also a factor. Probably the best approach is to cross to the island – it is at the end of the first span of bridge, and there is a $2.00 toll – and inquire. The most recent directions I have seen locate the birds southwest of the highway.

Many of the islands in the river east and west of Ivy Lea form the St Lawrence Islands National Park. The headquarters are at **Mallorytown Landing** (exit 675) east on the parkway, and there is primitive camping and good birding on the islands.

Some 5 km north of the Ivy Lea exit on Leeds and Grenville County Road 3 is the village of *Lansdowne*. To find the sewage lagoon here, drive north on County Road 3 into town and up the hill to the point where the road jogs right. At the jog keep right on King Street and drive 0.3 km to the end of the street; the lagoon gate is next to the tracks ahead.

Charleston Lake Provincial Park is about 14 km north of Lansdowne on County Road 3. It is set in Shield country among a network of lakes. There is a diversity of habitats with good birding along the extensive canoe and hiking trails.

North of Brockville (401 exit 696) there is an excellent wetland and large woods between Highway 29 and Leeds County Road 6 (North Augusta Road; 401 exit 698) to the east. It lies north of Centennial Drive, which is itself 4 km north of Highway 401. At the east end is an extensive area of woods and wet bush crossed by County Road 6 starting about 1 km north of Centennial Road. On this road the small *Broome-Runciman Dam Conservation Area*, 1.3 km west from North Augusta Road, affords excellent views of the east end of the large lake. To reach the north side go one sideroad north on Highway 29 from Centennial Road (this intersection is marked Airport Road to the west). Turn east and drive 2.2 km to the entrance of *Buell's Creek Conservation Area* (entrance fee) on the south. Linking the two east-west sideroads, and east of Highway 29, is McLarry Road, a rough dirt road which, however, has views of the west end of the lake and trails leading to it.

To the west of Brockville and well out of town on Highway 2, Brockville Cemetery and the adjacent creek and the St Lawrence River can provide good birding. The portion of the cemetery south of the road is best, but there is no parking there.

OTHER LOCATIONS AND SEWAGE LAGOONS IN THE KINGSTON AREA

Cloyne – This is the nearest community to *Bon Echo Provincial Park* and is on Highway 41. This road traverses wild and rugged country, particularly farther north near Denbigh. It has a mixture of northern and southern species, and the park is a good base for exploring the area. Bon Echo is 10 km north of Cloyne, and it and Frontenac are the largest parks in eastern Ontario. In addition to the spectacular Mazinaw Rock, Indian pictographs, and a memorial to Walt Whitman (of all things) it provides 6,644 hectares of wilderness camping, hiking, and canoeing. This is Shield country and closely resembles the areas described in chapter 15. Prairie Warblers have bred along the shoreline of Mazinaw Lake, outside the park.

Madoc – Madoc is on Highway 62 north of Belleville and immediately south of Highway 7. The sewage lagoons are on the west of Highway 62 beyond the south end of town (0.6 km past the playing field at Seymour Street). They are visible from the highway.

Stirling – Stirling is at the junction of Highways 14 and 33 between Trenton and Marmora. For the sewage lagoons, drive to the end of 33 in town, and just before the junction of Highway 14 turn right (south) by the bank onto Henry Street. Drive 1.2 km and the lagoon drive is on the right.

Tweed – Tweed is on Highway 37 north of Belleville and some 10 km south of Highway 7; for the sewage lagoons go 0.3 km north of the river bridge at the north end of town. Turn right on Hastings County Road 9 (or 39 – both signs appear). Drive 1.6 km and turn south on a narrow dirt road. The lagoons are beside and visible from this road, 0.8 km along on the right.

Westport – A couple of areas are of interest in Westport, quite apart from the village itself (which must rate as one of Ontario's most beautiful) and the marshy areas surrounding it. The *sewage lagoons* are on the west of Highway 42 down a farm lane 0.2 km south of the intersection of the highway and County Road 10. By turning onto this county road one can drive up the hill at the northeast side of town and turn into the *Foley Mountain Conservation Area* on the right at the top. There are excellent mixed woodlands here, including tall red cedars, and the ridge forms a flyline for migrant landbirds. Continuing on towards Perth, County Road 10 runs through some farming country. Watch the wires for Eastern Bluebirds. South of town the County Road runs through typical Rideau Lakes countryside en route to Kingston.

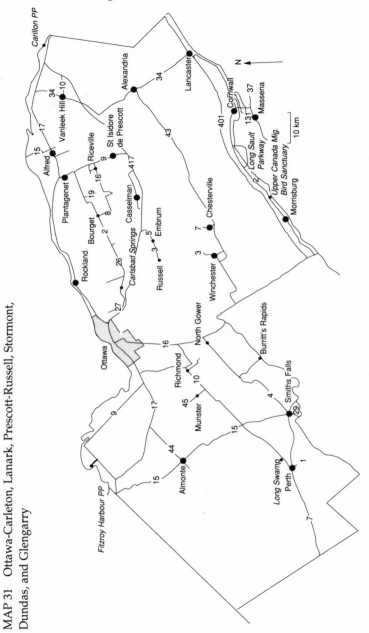

MAP 31   Ottawa-Carleton, Lanark, Prescott-Russell, Stormont, Dundas, and Glengarry

14 Ottawa and Eastern Ontario

The Regional Municipality of Ottawa-Carleton, and the Counties of Lanark, Prescott and Russell, and Stormont, Dundas and Glengarry

Ottawa
Areas west of Ottawa
Highways 417 and 17 westbound
Highways 401 and 2 east
Other sewage lagoons in the east

The far eastern counties of Ontario are dominated by Ottawa, a city of over 300,000 inhabitants. As the nation's capital, it has a good airport and is well served by Highways 417/17 from the east and west. Since the region's southern boundary, along the St Lawrence River, is traversed by Highway 401 (with Highways 15, 16, and 31 linking it to Ottawa itself), the region is well served by major highways.

Since the first edition of this guide, much fieldwork has been done in eastern Ontario as a whole by members of the Ottawa Field-Naturalists. New localities have been identified and some old ones have lost their appeal. Bruce DiLabio has been particularly active in this work, and I am indebted to him (and Laurie DiLabio) for key input to this revision.

With the exception of the Shield areas in western Lanark County, which physiographically have more in common with the Kingston chapter, this is an agricultural region. Much of it is flat, and there are some extensive forested areas of poor drainage, which provide havens for more northern species such as Lincoln's Sparrow and Dark-eyed Junco, as well as more typical wetland birds such as American Bittern and Northern Harrier. Many of the small towns have sewage lagoons, and these have added a dimension of fertile open water which has been very attractive to waterfowl. The lagoons of eastern Ontario have yielded many new regional breeding records, and a number of provincial firsts. The region is also one of the strongholds of Gray Partridge in Ontario, but the birds are hard to find.

Farming is mainly devoted to milk and stock production, often on rather poor soils. Such soils are particularly prevalent on the limestone plain of Lanark County east of the Shield, and in the areas bordering the Ottawa River. The species that favour such areas – Upland Sandpiper, Eastern Bluebird, Loggerhead Shrike, and Clay-colored and Grasshopper Sparrow – have been in relatively good numbers here, although the shrike is now absent from most of its former range. The country between Smith's Falls and Almonte is typical, and shrikes linger on in the area between Smith's Falls, North Gower, and Burritt's Rapids. In winter the region's rather more severe climate and its proximity to large forest areas seem to result in frequent movements of winter birds such as Three-toed and Black-backed Woodpeckers and finches. Owls in particular tend to be a feature of the winter scene.

OTTAWA

Ottawa, with its green belt and its abundance of parks, has many areas of interest to the birder in the city itself. It attracts a rather different mix of migrant waterbirds from that in areas farther west. Most noteworthy is the regular occurrence of small numbers of Arctic Tern on the Ottawa River in late May or early June. Conceivably the river offers a flyway between James Bay and the St Lawrence, bypassing the land masses farther east. Ottawa also attracts a rich variety of winter birds. Good numbers of finches and Three-toed and Black-backed woodpeckers occur periodically, and the city has played host to numbers of Gyrfalcons, Great Gray Owls, and Bohemian Waxwings more frequently than have other places in the south. Winter is also a good time for Gray Partridge, which are particularly common around Ottawa. The Ottawa Field-Naturalists' Club maintains a number of public feeders in winter which can repay visits (specific locations vary; contact the club at [613] 722-3050).

Parkways follow the river between Britannia on the west and Rockcliffe Park on the east, and the wooded areas and ravines of Rockcliffe Park itself can be rewarding. *Britannia*, however, is probably the most productive area (see map 32). It lies north-west of the intersection of Highway 17B (Richmond Road) and Highway 17 (Carling Avenue). Britannia Road (off Carling just west of the above intersection) leads north to Cassels Street, where a right turn leads to the Britannia Filtration Plant. It is possible to park both outside and inside the plant grounds, and cover the river and rapids, the beaver pond to the south, and the wooded areas. Access to the pinewoods east of Britannia Road can be gained from the cross-streets. There is a good cross-section of the common breeding birds of the region here, and the whole area is a migrant trap. Hawks move across the river at this point, and duck can be seen on the pond. It attracts dabbling duck including Wood Duck, Gadwall and American Wigeon, as well as Hooded Merganser.

Most diving duck occur on the river. In winter the Deschênes Rapids remain open throughout, and Common Goldeneye and Common Merganser can be found (watch for Barrow's Golden-eye: a few may overwinter). Rarer gulls and terns such as Franklin's and Little Gulls occur in migration, and in late May and early June migrant Arctic Terns should be watched for here. During spring and fall, if water levels are low and rocks are exposed, watch also for Lesser Black-backed Gulls.

To the west of Britannia lies Andrew Hayden Park, which provides limited access to birding along the river, including shorebirds in season on the mudflats. This strip of parkland is west on Carling from Brittania, at the foot of Pinecrest and Acres roads.

A good location farther downtown is the area of the *Arboretum*. Take the Rochester Street exit from Highway 417 (the Queensway). Drive south to Carling Avenue, then west one block to Preston, then south again to join Highway 16 (the Driveway). Turn right on Highway 16 and continue to the traffic circle, where 16 continues south, the Driveway turns west into the experimental farm, and a road to the east enters the Arboretum. This again is a migrant trap; in winter the pines attract finches and the large number of fruit trees attract overwintering American Robins, Bohemian Waxwings, and Pine Grosbeaks, with Gray Partridge near manure piles on the farm.

The *National Museum of Natural Sciences*, at Metcalfe and

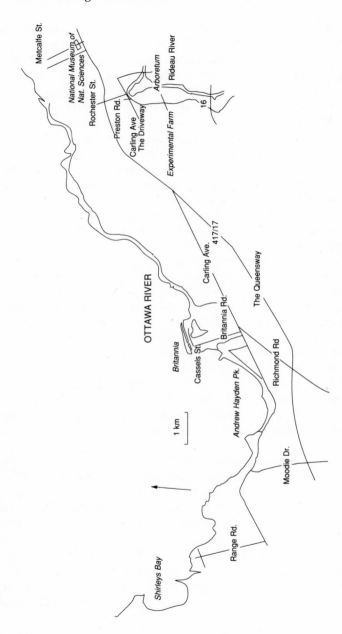

MAP 32   Ottawa along the Ottawa River

McLeod streets, has a permanent exhibit hall on the birds of Canada, and is the centre for bird information and records for Canada as a whole.

To the west of the city along the river is *Shirleys Bay*. Here a long dike leads out into the Ottawa River, and this is the site of some of the most outstanding waterbird finds, especially shore-birds, in the region. However, access to it is on the basis of an agreement between the Department of National Defence and the Ottawa Field-Naturalists' Club, as it is across DND prop-erty. Entry is prohibited when the adjacent pistol firing range is in use; access is forbidden if a red flag is flying. To find if you can enter, the club suggests you phone the training coordinator (991-5740), or when not available, the range warden (991-5741).

To reach Shirleys Bay follow Carling Avenue west from Brit-annia and through Crystal Beach (the road is the old Highway 17, and scan the river for waterfowl en route). Watch for the well-marked Moodie Drive stoplight, just before the Bell North-ern Research Laboratories, on the left. Continue 2.4 km farther along Carling and watch for Range Road on the right. Turn here, and follow the road to the river. When the road veers left, continue straight ahead to the parking area. Shirleys Bay is to the left. Walk down the track and out onto the dike. Access is allowed only on the causeway and the two islands at the end. The enclosed waters attract dabbling duck and shorebirds, while the open river here can yield loons, grebes, and diving duck.

Southeast of the city is *Mer Bleue*, a large peat-tamarack bog that occupies an area between Blackburn and Carlsbad Springs. It has yielded some remarkable breeding records, including Northern Hawk Owl and Palm Warbler. Lincoln's Sparrows are common nesting birds, and recently Sandhill Crane has bred. Drive east on Highway 417 to the Anderson Road exit (104) and proceed north on Anderson (Regional Road 27). Some 2 km north is the Ramsayville Marsh, a productive cattail marsh, and farther north again two sideroads on the right (Ridge Road and Dolman Ridge Road) dead-end in the marsh. There are many walking trails and a wide variety of habitats.

In early spring (late March to early April) migrant waterfowl concentrate on fields in this area. From Anderson Road and Highway 417 drive north about 1 km to Russell Road (Regional Road 26) Turn right and go east some 3 km through *Carlsbad*

Springs to Regional Road 31 and turn left. Drive about 2 km north, and in high water-level years waterfowl can be seen on the flooded fields to right. Species include Canada Goose, Snow Goose, and Northern Pintail. Watch for Tundra Swan and Greater White-fronted Goose, and raptors such as Northern Harrier, Red-tailed and Rough-legged Hawk, and Snowy Owl. Drive a farther 1 km to Perrault Road, turn right, and then continue east to the next sideroad south (Concession 8). Turn right and return to Regional Road 26, scanning for waterfowl all along the road.

AREAS WEST OF OTTAWA

Moodie Drive, noted above under Shirleys Bay, is Ottawa-Carleton Regional Road 10, and this leads some 20 km southwest to the village of **Richmond**, which has two areas of note. Approaching Richmond from the Ottawa side, watch for the intersection of Regional Road 8, signposted to Manotick, on the left. Turn onto this road and drive 0.8 km to *Richmond Conservation Area* (the sewage lagoon) on the right, which can be rewarding.

Then return to Regional Road 10 and continue 1.8 km into Richmond, where Regional Road 5 enters, signposted to North Gower and also on the left. To reach *Richmond Fen*, turn here and drive 1.8 km to the railroad crossing. Park and walk about 5 km down the railroad tracks on the southwest side (on the right leaving Richmond) until the swamp opens out on the left. Yellow Rails have occurred consistently, and the area is also good for Sedge Wrens, Least Bittern, and other species. The open country around Richmond is productive of open-country birds, and Gray Partridge occur.

Munster is north on Regional Road 45, some 10 km west of the intersection of Regional Roads 10 and 8 (above, east of Richmond), and it also has a productive sewage lagoon. Turn right off Regional Road 45 at the flashing light in the village, drive 1.3 km to the first intersection, Copeland Road, and the lagoons are on the left.

Farther west, **Almonte** is at the intersection of Highways 15 and 44. The sewage lagoons here have been some of the more productive in the area, and the town is on the northwest edge of the Smiths Falls limestone plain. The sideroad running north-west from town just east of the railway passes through some habitats typical of the shallow soils of the area, with marginal farmland and scrub; this has yielded species typical of such areas, such as Eastern Bluebird. To reach the *sewage lagoons*, follow Highway 44 southwest through town (past the pleasant Metcalfe Conservation Area) to the highway's end at Highway 15. Cross 15 onto Regional Road 16 and drive 0.7 km, where the lagoons are on the right. Wood Ducks are regular, with other waterfowl.

Perth is considerably farther south and west in Lanark County. Here *Stewart Park*, behind the town hall, can be good for landbird migrants. Entering Perth on Highway 43 from the northeast, the highway turns left in town and then right again onto the main street (Gore Street W.); the town hall is 0.3 km south on the right. If you continue south on Gore Street 2 km (it becomes Lanark County Road 1) you can visit *Perth Wildlife Reserve*, 2.2 km down a sideroad to the east. Halfway down you pass the Perth sewage lagoons. The reserve itself has a baited pond and a 3-km nature trail with views of the Tay Canal and adjacent marshland. East of town 2 km on County Road 10 is the southern part of the extensive *Long Swamp*, north of the road. It is good in summer for warblers and in winter for finches and waxwings. The same area is on the south along Highway 7 east of Perth, while on the north is the even larger area of Blueberry Marsh.

HIGHWAYS 417 AND 17 WESTBOUND

Highways 417 and 17 are the main east-west routes in the Ottawa area, and they also pass close to some of the best birding areas to the east of Ottawa. Highway 417 is the access route most travellers would use between Ottawa and the provinces to the east. At the first exit from the highway (exit 5) west of the Quebec border is *Carillon Provincial Park*, located on the south shore of the Ottawa River just above the Carillon Dam. It provides excellent vistas of the wide river at this point, and has shoreline marshes, second-growth forest, and a beaver pond.

Vankleek Hill (exits 17 or 27) has a productive *sewage lagoon*. To reach it coming from exit 27, turn east from Highway

34 on to Main Street (County Road 10), drive 1.1 km, crossing the railroad, and turn right on a gravel road. The lagoon is 1.3 km along on the left. (Using exit 17, County Road 10 is the road into town.)

The *sewage lagoons* at **St Isidore de Prescott** (exit 51 and north on County Road 9) are down a farm lane off County Road 3 at the north end of town. Take County Road 3 west (marked to Embrun), and drive 1.3 km to a paved road on the right, which becomes a farm lane after 0.5 km. The lagoons are to the north-west, and occasionally Ruddy Duck and Wilson's Phalarope have nested there.

County Road 9 continues north from St Isidore to **Plantagenet**, just south of Highway 17. The *South Nation River* between Plantagenet and St Isidore floods the countryside in early spring (late March to early April) and attracts enormous con-centrations of waterfowl at this time – a possibility that was suggested speculatively in the first edition of this guide! The principal species are Canada Geese and Northern Pintails, with much smaller numbers of Snow Geese and other dabbling duck, but anything could turn up.

To cover this area, drive north on County Road 9 towards Plantagenet to the point at which the road crosses the South Nation River. Immediately before the bridge turn left onto a sideroad which runs west alongside the river and follow this, bearing right at the T-intersection. This is one of the better areas for concentrations. This road eventually dead-ends, so return to County Road 9 and drive south to the next crossroads (County Road 16). Turn right here and drive west some 9 km, watching for flocks on the right, through **Riceville** to County Road 19, and then turn right. Drive north through Pendleton, again watch-ing for birds, especially where the road runs along the river. When this road crosses County Road 2 turn left towards Bourget. The road soon jogs south, and then west again, crossing Cobb Lake Creek. There can be excellent viewing from this point.

If you return east on County Road 2 you will eventually arrive back at County Road 9 south of Plantagenet; alternatively you may wish to continue west through **Bourget** some 25 km, to the outskirts of Ottawa and the smaller waterfowl concentra-tions described there under Carlsbad Springs. Be warned that the flooding in this area can make some or all the roads described above impassable; be particularly cautious about proceeding on roads that appear soft and muddy.

The productive *sewage lagoons* at **Casselman** (exit 66) can be reached by leaving Highway 417 and driving north 1.2 km into town. Watch for Laurier Street on the right just by the Banque Nationale and before the church (and past the flashing light at the St Isidore sideroad). Turn, drive 2 km to Concession 5, and turn right; the lagoon path is immediately around the corner. Nesting species include Common Moorhen, American Coot, and occasionally Ruddy Duck and Wilson's Phalarope.

The next set of lagoons are at **Embrun**, which is southbound from exit 79 on County Road 5. Drive 2.4 km to County Road 3. Turn right here and continue 3.2 km into the village, to St Joseph Street. Turn south (left), drive 1.2 km to the next intersection, and turn left again. The lagoons are about 0.5 km along here on the left. Wilson's Phalarope has bred, and an excellent assortment of shorebirds and waterfowl have occurred.

West of Embrun on County Road 3 is the village of **Russell**, with another *sewage lagoon*. From the centre of town, drive east 0.8 km on 3 and turn right (this corner is some 5.7 km west from Embrun). Drive south almost 1 km to the lagoon road on the left; the lagoons are well back in the field. Note also the directions in the Ottawa account above to Carlsbad Springs via exit 104.

To the west of the city there are fewer places of note along Highway 17, and most are well off the road. Almonte, covered above, is some 16 km west of the highway. Farther west, along the river near Arnprior is *Fitzroy Harbour Provincial Park*, with vistas of the widening river above one of the dams. Downriver from there Regional Road 9 passes Constance Creek to its east. There is an interesting variety of habitats on the sandy soils in this area.

HIGHWAYS 401 AND 2 EAST

Highway 401 east of Iroquois is pleasant but unexceptional, passing through countryside where farms alternate with areas of bush and small areas of wetland. There are two rest areas westbound and one eastbound; none are particularly attractive to birds.

On the other hand, some of the most interesting parts of the St Lawrence River are between Morrisburg and Cornwall along Highway 2 to the south, which closely parallels the controlled-access highway. The *Upper Canada Migratory Bird Sanctuary* includes Upper Canada Village, but its main entrance is well marked approximately 14 km east of **Morrisburg** (401 exit 750). The feeding ponds and viewing tower are 2.6 km south, and there are some 6 km of well-laid-out nature trails passing through old pasture, swamp, maple woodlot, and cedar woods, with several viewing blinds. During migration the whole place can be alive with birds, especially Canada Geese. Drive 0.5 km farther to the causeway and view the water areas on each side for duck and shorebirds, and the trees on Nairn Island (the park area to the south) for migrant landbirds.

Some 6.5 km east of here is the start of *Long Sault Parkway* (401 exit 770) a scenic toll road linking a number of islands which are entirely devoted to parkland. The area acts as a migrant trap to some extent, and offers excellent views of the St Lawrence. Watch for Bald Eagles in summer. There is hunting here, so in autumn the area is less productive than the sanctuary for waterbirds. The parkway rejoins the main highway 7 km farther east (401 exit 778). Even if you do not cover the Long Sault Parkway, Highway 2 itself can be most interesting because of the many areas of marsh, open water, and mudflats between Morrisburg and Cornwall, 5 km to the east.

At the west end of **Cornwall** the Saunders Dam and Power Station dominates the waterfront. Coming from Cornwall itself (401 exit 789) you follow 2nd Street W, which leads to the grounds of the power station. The large parking lot overlooking the water is at present open during the summer, but access can be obtained at other times by phoning for permission, and access to the observation deck may also be granted.

Access from the American side is both easier and the viewing is better, as the sun is behind the observer. Prior to crossing the border, however, it is advisable to check the times of access to the dam there, by phoning [315] 764-0226. To reach the American side, drive into Cornwall and follow the signs for the bridge to the United States. The road crosses the two bridges and passes through customs. Finally it arrives at a traffic circle, where Route

37 west (a divided highway) leads to Massena. Follow 37 west some 9 km to the Route 131 intersection, opposite a large shopping mall. Turn onto Route 131, which crosses a bridge and then enters Robert Moses State Park, becoming Powerdam Road. This goes under the Eisenhower lock, passes an information centre, and then (9.3 km from Route 37) ends at the gatehouse.

Below the dam exceptional numbers of Common Merganser and Great Black-backed Gulls congregate in winter, with other waterfowl including Glaucous and Iceland Gulls. It is probably the best place in the east of the province for seeing the rarer gull species in later fall. There are large gull numbers at other times as well, although the duck disperse once the St Lawrence Seaway opens (usually in March).

Back on the Canadian side, one can get to the head pond from the dam by turning left outside the plant gates onto Saunders Drive. Make two more left turns: first onto Power Dam Drive and next onto Highway 2 (the banks of the dam are on the left throughout this drive). Continue west on Highway 2 to the western limit of Cornwall, and immediately before a railroad track crosses the road turn left into *Guindon Park*. The boat-launch area offers excellent views of the head pond. Look over the gulls and waterfowl: the best time here is in early spring and in fall (mid-October to freeze-up). Species to be looked for include Common Loons, Red-necked and Horned Grebes, Brant and scoters. Red-throated Loons are occasional, and the less-common fall gulls include Iceland, Lesser Black-backed, and Glaucous. A Marbled Murrelet even turned up on the head pond recently!

Now follow the internal park road (Trillium Drive) east, either as far as it will go or out on to Highway 2 again. This gravel road passes through old field and second-growth woodland habitats, and is good for migrant landbirds, particularly in autumn. Watch for Gray Partridge.

Lancaster is only 14 km west of the Quebec border, at the point Highways 401 and 2 merge (exit 814). To reach the *sewage lagoons* here, drive north on Highway 34, cross the railroad, and turn east at once on John Street. Drive 0.2 km to the point the street turns; the lagoon road continues east alongside the tracks.

OTHER SEWAGE LAGOONS IN THE EAST

Alexandria – Alexandria, Chesterville, and Winchester are all adjacent to Highway 43, which is roughly equidistant between Highways 401 and 417, and parallels them both. Drive into town on Highway 34 and watch for St Paul Street on the east (just next to the Ottawa Hotel). Turn and drive 2.1 km past the cathedral; the lagoon complex is down a long dirt road to the right after the main road has curved northwards.

Alfred – Alfred and Rockland below are both along the old Highway 17, paralleling the Ottawa River. The sewage lagoons are at the southeast end of town in an area of flat, poorly drained farmland, site of the Alfred bog. It is attractive to open-country species, Northern Harriers, and Common Snipe. The bog itself (mainly in private ownership) is some 8 km southeast. To reach the area, drive to the intersection of Highway 17 and County Road 15 North (15 South is at the other end of town). Turn south opposite the county road and drive 1.6 km, the last section being gravelled. The lagoons are on the left, and have proven to be some of the most productive ones in the region, attracting a range of breeding species including Northern Shoveler, Gadwall, American Wigeon, Ruddy Duck, Common Moorhen, American Coot, and Wilson's Phalarope. A good assortment of migrant species has also been recorded.

Chesterville – From the south end of town follow County Road 7 (Main Street) north to the river. Cross the bridge and turn immediately on Water Street (right). Drive 0.2 km and turn on a gravelled road that passes the dam and runs along the river. The lagoons are 0.5 km along on the left.

Rockland – Rockland lies off Highway 17 south of the highway. The sewage lagoon is on the north side of the highway roughly halfway between the main business exit to town and the Laurier Street exit to the east.

Winchester – Follow County Road 3 (Main Street) as it runs east through town, and continue on it as it turns north (now Ottawa Street). Watch for the lagoons on the right, and park at the gate. These lagoons have attracted a range of breeding species, including Northern Shoveler, Gadwall, American Wigeon, Ruddy Duck, Common Moorhen, American Coot, and Wilson's Phalarope.

MAP 33   Muskoka, Parry Sound, Manitoulin, and Southern Sudbury

15 Eastern Georgian Bay and the Sudbury Area

Simcoe County, the Districts of Muskoka and Parry Sound, Manitoulin and the Southern Part of Sudbury District

Simcoe County
Highways 400 and 69 north
Highway 11 north
Sudbury Regional Municipality
Manitoulin Island

This chapter will cover four rather distinct areas: Simcoe County; the northward routes of Highways 11 and 69 through the districts of Muskoka and Parry Sound; Sudbury and its environs, including the Regional Municipality and the District of Sudbury south of and including Highway 17; and finally, Manitoulin Island.

SIMCOE COUNTY

The northwest of Simcoe County is dominated by the Niagara Escarpment, and to the northeast are the ancient rocks of the Precambrian Shield. In between is a diverse landscape much modified by glaciation, with gravelly ridges, picturesque gorges, extensive bogs and wetlands, together with some areas of prosperous farmland. In the north lie the shores of Georgian Bay and to the east Lake Simcoe. Ott Devitt, in his classic book on the birds of the county, said that 'few counties in Ontario are as well provided with such a diversity of habitats to the support of a varied birdlife.' The region is a major location for summer cottages serving the urban areas to the south, and much of the emphasis in birding the county has been on the breeding birds; but the presence of the lakes and major land forms can channel bird movements and yield good birding in migration periods as well. Winters are cold and snowy, but they often offer the birder influxes of finches and other northerners that may move no farther south.

Barrie (50,000 population) and Orillia (24,000) are the major communities, and Highway 400 is the main access route to the county. The main birding destinations are associated with three major wetlands and the shorelines of the two major waterbodies. The following account runs roughly from south to north (see map 34).

The **Southern End of Lake Simcoe** has been one of the few easily accessible places where birders could hope to find Yellow Rails. Typically the rails prefer 'grassy' marshes with shorter vegetation, and quite shallow water levels. Unfortunately this kind of marsh is readily drained for agriculture, and this has been the fate of most of the suitable ones around Lake Simcoe. The birds have been found erratically in such habitat north of Bradford, and there are other marshes of more general interest in the same area.

From the intersection of Highways 88 and 11 in **Bradford** (where 11 turns north; this is some 6 km east of Highway 400 exit 64) drive 8.5 km north to the 13th Line of West Gwillimbury Township. Turn east and drive to the extreme end of the 13th Line, where you can gain access to the dike system along the Holland River. The marsh to the north was formerly productive, but not recently. By walking south along the dike here for 1 to 2 km, other areas where rails have occurred may be visited. Their presence in any event depends on water levels, and sometimes all these areas can be dried out and unsuitable for them.

For other excellent marsh areas (but not Yellow Rails) return to the first sideroad southbound, crossing the railroad tracks, and drive south. This road jogs left briefly at the end of the 12th Line, and then ends at the 11th Line. Roughly halfway between the two watch for a short sideroad on the left leading to a parking area. This gives access to a tower looking over a 500-acre cattail marsh to the east, and also to the extensive dike system around this marsh, which is managed for waterfowl production. The area around the tower is good for Sora and Virginia Rail, and the marsh has all the usual marsh birds, including American Bittern, Ring-necked Duck, Hooded Merganser, and Black Tern.

A second access point to this same area is from the foot of the 10th Line (it is necessary to return to the highway and drive south one sideroad). This ends at a pump house, and the southeast corner of the dike system is on the north here.

West of Bradford, and of Highway 400 exit 64, are some sod farms and a couple of sewage lagoons that can yield shorebird migrants in season. **Beeton** is on County Road 1, which runs west from Highway 27 north 1.4 km from the Highway 88 intersection (Highway 27 is itself some 4 km west of 401 on 88). The *sewage lagoon* is off the first street north entering town from the east (Patterson Street), which is 1.1 km from the railroad crossing at the west end of town. Turn north, drive 1.5 km to Lily Street, and turn east; the lagoon gate is 0.6 km along on the left.

County Road 10, which runs north to Highway 89 one sideroad west of Beeton (and then, after a jog right, north again to Angus and the Minesing area) passes a series of *sod farms* in the flat country along the Nottawasaga River. These farms are both along the county road itself and along the grid of sideroads to the east and west. They can attract shorebirds in migration, mainly in late spring and early autumn. Specific locations depend on the character of the fields from year to year, the amount of standing water, and the state of migration.

Tottenham is on County Road 10 southwest of Beeton. The *sewage lagoon* is just past the Conservation Area to the west of town. On County Road 10 go to the light on Mill Street, turn west, and drive 0.8 km; the lagoon is on the right.

West from Barrie along Highway 90 (400 exit 96) is the *Minesing Swamp*, an exceptional area for both birds and botany. Here some southern species occur close to more northern ones, as hackberry forest and black spruce bog exist almost side by side. The swamp has several access points. Drive east on Highway 90 to the intersection with Simcoe County Road 28. Go north on 28 for 7.5 km; the next half kilometre or so crosses the eastern (Willow Creek) part of the swamp. Golden-winged Warblers have occurred in the bushy areas at the beginning of this section, near the railway track.

MAP 34   Simcoe County

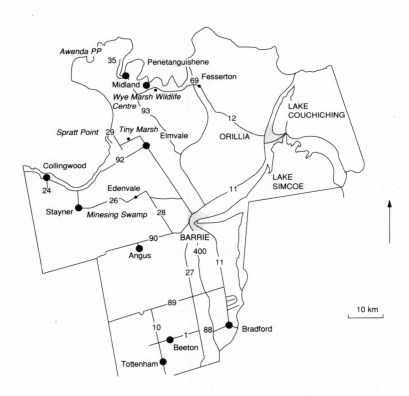

Farther along Highway 90, Concession Roads 11 and 12 of Vespa (the first west of County Road 28) lead north into a black spruce section of the swamp, with an abundance of warblers. Farther west again, and on the eastern edge of the village of **Angus**, Sunnidale Concession 21-22 leads north into the swamp, this time to end at Iron Bridge. There is canoe access here to the Nottawasaga River north into the area, and the levees have southern plants such as hackberry, with Blue-gray Gnatcatchers and Yellow-throated Vireos occurring. In spring the flooded fields west of the lower stretch of this sideroad teem with waterfowl, with thousands of Canada Geese, Northern Pintail, and other duck. Canoe access from the north is at the Nottawasaga River crossing at **Edenvale** on Highway 26. The swamp is upstream from here, and many noteworthy features – a large heronry of Great Blues, and Cerulean Warblers and Yellow-throated Vireos nesting near the junction of the Nottawasaga and Willow Creek – are accessible only by canoe.

The **Georgian Bay Shoreline** has been identified as a flightline for both waterbirds, and hawks and other landbirds. In the northwest of the county, along Highway 26, the **Collingwood** waterfront is well situated for viewing such movements. From the main intersection of Highways 24 north and 26, turn east and drive 0.3 km, and turn left after the highway crosses the first set of tracks. This road leads to the elevator, and provides views of the harbour on the west and a small bay to the east. Look for gulls and duck, and shorebirds and open country species along the bay.

Returning to the highway, continue east 0.7 km to the point the highway turns right. Huron Street turns left here, and leads to Sunset Point Park on the beach. The road runs a short way both east and west. The park itself is manicured, but the adjacent cedars and trees south of the road can concentrate landbirds, and there are excellent views out over the water, which should be particularly interesting in autumn when there are storms from the north.

Stayner, some 5 km south of Collingwood on Highway 26, has a sewage lagoon. Drive east on Highway 26 from the junction of Highway 91, and at 1.3 km turn north on Mowat Street. The lagoon is down a farm lane 1.1 km on the left.

Farther east from Collingwood the shoreline becomes lined

with cottages, but there is one vantage point on the **East Side of Nottawasaga Bay** that has proved to be a good spot for watching migrant loons, duck, and gulls. This is Spratt Point, and it is very close to an even more exciting birding area, Tiny Marsh. To reach them both drive northwest from Barrie on Highway 27 to Elmvale. (Highway 400 access to all the areas that follow would be from exit 121.) There are sewage lagoons at **Elmvale**, on the way to our main destinations. Proceed north 1.5 km on Highway 27 from its intersection with Highway 92 in town, and then turn east on Flos Concession 10. The lagoon gate is 0.7 km along on the north, but drive a little farther and view them readily from the road itself.

From the lagoons continue north on Highway 27 to the point at which it takes a long curve east. Turn west here on the Tiny-Flos Townline, and drive 200 metres to northbound County Road 6. One access point to the east side of *Tiny Marsh* is 1.5 km up this road, where a westbound sideroad dead-ends at the marsh. The main access route, however, is by continuing west along the Townline another 3.6 km to the causeway, Interpretive Centre (there is a bird checklist), and observation tower north of the road. This 567-hectare marsh is managed by the Ontario Ministry of Natural Resources and Ducks Unlimited primarily for waterfowl production, but it is an excellent place for shorebirds and other species. A Snow Bunting even spent one summer along the north-south causeway.

Other access points to the area are from County Road 29, 2.5 km farther west. North on this road at 1.5 km is a sideroad to the east which dead-ends in the marsh, and 1.5 km farther again the eastbound sideroad will take you to the north end of the causeway. And from this corner you are only about 1 km from the road to Spratt Point.

Continue north on County Road 29 from Tiny Marsh to Concession Road 4 (it is 4.1 km from the Tiny-Flos Townline that leads to the Tiny Marsh Interpretive Centre). Turn west, and bear left on the hardtop road 1.4 km from the turn. At Edmore Beach, 1.1 km farther, turn right on Balmoral Avenue. This gravelled road parallels the shore and has water access at several points, particularly 0.5 km along, which is *Spratt Point*. Immediately past here it rejoins the main road and one can return to County Road 29.

Continuing north on Highway 27 towards **Midland** leads to Wye Marsh, yet another extensive wetland. Highway 27 bears right to join Highway 93 going north, and in some 11 km Highway 12 intersects from the east. Turn right on 12 and follow the signs to *Wye Marsh Wildlife Centre*. This is a non-profit organization, committed to promoting an understanding of wetlands. The main entrance is some 5 km east of Midland, and opposite the Martyrs Shrine. The centre is formally open from 10.00 a.m. to 6.00 p.m. (4.00 p.m. from Labour Day to Victoria Day), and the entrance fee is currently $5.00. Wye Marsh has excellent interpretive facilities, with well-maintained walking trails, canoe channels, floating boardwalks, and strategically located observation blinds. All this makes the entire thousand hectares of the preserve readily accessible to the keen birder. In addition to the marsh itself, there is a variety of habitats, including hardwoods and old farmland. There is a checklist based on twenty years' observations, and all the species usual to such habitats can be found on the network of trails. Least Bittern, Sedge Wren, Yellow-throated Vireo, and Grasshopper Sparrow all occur. The marsh is also a site for the reintroduction of Trumpeter Swans, which in 1993 nested here in the wild.

Continuing north on Highway 93 leads to **Penetanguishene**, and north again via Simcoe County Road 35 is *Awenda Provincial Park* (entrance fee), which occupies an extensive and heavily wooded section at the north end of the Huronia peninsula. The cover is mainly a fine stand of the typical mixed hardwoods of this region, with all the associated woodland birds of the region. Trails and interpretive facilities are available.

HIGHWAYS 400 AND 69 NORTH

Highway 400 traverses Simcoe County through good habitat most of the way, and the appropriate exits to the locations covered in the county are given in the accounts above. The highway itself has few specific areas of birding interest, and the service areas lack appeal. Indeed, the traveller should be aware that north of Barrie there are no rest areas on 400 and few on 69. The latter is a rather narrow, busy road with negligible shoulder most of the way north to Parry Sound (it is currently being upgraded, but these comments still seem valid). There are many areas where one is tempted to stop, but few where one can do so safely. Indeed, this entire route can be a major bottleneck on summer weekends.

Where 400 ends near **Fesserton**, the first section of Highway 69, north to the area of Port Severn, is less inhospitable, and there are views of the extensive marshes along Matchedash Bay. These are relatively little covered, but there is a huge blackbird roost here and there have been interesting waterbird reports from time to time. The network of sideroads from the main highway gives ready access.

North of **Honey Harbour** the highway starts its long, scenic journey across the Precambrian Shield. Granite outcrops alternate with small lakes and forest dominated by hardwoods and majestic white pines. Common Ravens patrol the highway, and Broad-winged Hawks replace the Red-taileds of the more open country as the common raptor. Any stops along the highway are likely to yield a good cross-section of the commoner birds of the mixed woodlands. Species such as Yellow-bellied Sapsucker and Dark-eyed Junco are now more regular, but the true northerners such as Gray Jay and Boreal Chickadee are still either very rare or absent. Wetlands tend to be less productive than in areas south of the Shield; typically Common Loons and Common and Hooded Mergansers may be present, and Ospreys on larger water areas.

Highway 69 by-passes **Parry Sound**, but the town has a number of interesting areas nearby. Mill Lake, on both sides of the highway itself, can be productive of waterfowl in winter, but Powerhouse Falls on the Seguin River are usually better. These are 0.9 km north on River Street from its intersection with Bowes Street. Bowes is the southernmost exit to Parry Sound off Highway 69, and the River Street intersection is 1.8 km from the highway. Bowes Street also passes the extensive coniferous plantations on Tower Hill to the south, which are good for winter landbirds. The feeders and mountain ash trees on Belvedere Hill (off Waubeek Street) attract Bohemian Waxwings and landbird stragglers at this time, and the dump off McDougall Road, east off the highway 1-2 km north of Bowes, has gulls and ravens.

Both Highways 518 and 124, running northeast from Parry Sound, are good birding roads, and the sideroads off both highways can be very productive. The areas around **Waubamik**, **Dunchurch**, and Ahmic Lake on Highway 124, and around **Orrville** on 518, have been reported as excellent, and old field habitats here have yielded Eastern Bluebird and Golden-winged Warbler.

The wild coastline south of Parry Sound is the site of probably the largest concentration of Prairie Warblers in Canada. The birds frequent open rocky areas with scrubby white pine, oak, and juniper cover, where they are locally abundant. At present there is no ready road access to this area, but by boat or canoe the birds occur around Spider Bay, Spider and Cowper lakes, and the west end of Conger Lake, along the east shore of Blackstone Harbour, and along the shorelines of Moon Island. Farther south again they occur on some of the islands of *Georgian Bay Islands National Park*, along the Gibson River near its outlet to Go Home Lake, and along Twelve Mile Bay, which is accessible via District Road 12 off Highway 69. The Atlas showed that the main population was between Honey Harbour and Parry Sound, with birds north to Pointe au Baril.

Killbear Provincial Park, northwest of Parry Sound, is on a peninsula which looks as though it should concentrate migrants. The forest is hemlock and maple, and a good mixture of warbler species can be found, and Barred and Northern Saw-whet Owls have occurred. North of Parry Sound areas of extensive rock outcropping appear along the highway, alternating with rather impoverished pine forest and interspersed with small wetlands and bogs. Some 12 km north of Britt is *Grundy Lake Provincial Park*, an excellent Shield park which contains a Great Blue heronry. Northern Saw-whet Owl, Whip-poor-will, Black-backed Woodpecker, Warbling Vireo, and Pine Warbler (approaching their northern limits), and Golden-winged Warbler have all been recorded.

At French River the highway crosses into Sudbury Regional Municipality, and 27 km north again, is the intersection of Highway 637, the road to **Killarney**. This community is near nowhere: it is 67 km from Highway 17, and *Killarney Provincial Park* is situated astride Highway 637 just northeast of it. This is a large wilderness park; its main focus is on canoeing, and it offers some of Ontario's most beautiful scenery. Unlike Quetico and Algonquin, its birding potential is relatively little explored.

It has yielded records of species as diverse as Connecticut Warbler and Warbling Vireo in summer; but the townsite is also of interest in migration periods, when bird concentrations can occur in the open areas around the community. It is also possible to hike along the shoreline, and the twin *sewage lagoons* are just east the village on the south side of Ontario Street (opposite the landing strip).

HIGHWAY 11 NORTH

The Highway 11 route northeast from Barrie is more hospitable to the driver than Highway 69, but less interesting to the birder. Just outside **Orillia** Highway 12 joins 11, and some 7 km east of this intersection on 12 is the crossing between Lakes Simcoe and Couchiching. The water areas here will yield the usual Caspian and Common Terns in the warmer weather, and Bonaparte's Gulls in late summer. There are also extensive cattail marshes which are accessible by boat. Here you are very close to the Carden Plain, described in chapter 12.

From Orillia northwards the countryside becomes progressively more forested as the marginal farmland is gradually replaced by trees. As described in the corresponding section along Highway 69, the mixed forests here are rich in breeding birds, and northern species such as ravens appear, while the open-country birds and southerners thin out. The woodland is typically well back from the highway, which is dual-lane most of the way to North Bay, and busy. There are all the usual enticements to the outdoor recreationist in this area, one of the most popular destinations in the province. It is to be avoided above all on summer weekends!

The first really noteworthy site is at **Bracebridge**, where there is an extensive and productive *sewage lagoon* complex. It can be reached from Highway 11 by exiting on the interchange south of town (marked Highway 118). This is Muskoka District Road 4; turn towards Bracebridge and drive 4.7 km to Beaumont Drive (Muskoka Road 16) on the left, which follows the river. Turn and drive 0.8 km to James W. Kerr Park, also on the left. Drive in and walk up the hill at the back to reach the lagoons. From Bracebridge itself drive south through town to the river bridge and then turn right on to Beaumont Drive as above. The lagoon area is excellent for landbirds in migration as well as duck and shorebirds.

North of **Huntsville** Highway 60 runs east, and it is about 30 km to the west gate of Algonquin Park (see chapter 16). Farther north, *Arrowhead Provincial Park* is a pleasant birding park with a good nature trail along the river. Farther again, and currently accessible from Highway 592 at **Novar**, Highway 518 runs northeast to Kearney and Sand Lake. This road passes through marsh and spruce swamp habitats, as well as cleared land. It has yielded an excellent mix of old field and forest birds. At **Powassan**, near the boundary of Nipissing District, the *sewage lagoon* can be viewed from the southbound lanes of Highway 11. The gate is 0.7 km north of the intersection of Highway 534, the main access road into town.

SUDBURY REGIONAL MUNICIPALITY

The forests in the immediate area of Sudbury and Copper Cliff are impoverished as a result of pollution from heavy metal deposits. Scrub birch and aspen, with large expanses of bare rock, make the area unappealing to the eye and unrewarding as a birding locale, although there has been some recovery in recent years. The noteworthy locations listed below are sewage lagoons or wetlands enriched by waste run-off. Several of these were exceptionally productive at one time, but have been much less so recently.

Sudbury itself (population some 90,000) is unlikely to make anyone's list of the birding spots one most wants to visit, but *Kelley Lake*, west of the city and just south of Highway 17, can be productive, with shorebirds and duck on migration. Wilson's Phalaropes are among the species recorded in summer. The east end is the best, and it is easiest to approach the lake from the south, along Southview Drive. From the city drive west on Highway 17 to Kelley Lake Road and turn south, or south on Regent Street to Bouchard Street and turn west. Both these streets lead to Southview, and you then drive west with lake viewing all along the road on your right. This road finally enters the southwest bypass, linking Highways 69 northbound and 17 westbound, and the bypass itself runs along the shoreline of the west end of the Lake. The traveller using the bypass should watch for Southview Drive on the east – it is some 4 km north-west of the lights at Long Lake Road.

Some 19 km east of Sudbury is **Wahnapitae**, and the sewage lagoon complex here has been productive. Travelling east on Highway 17, cross the bridge over the Wahnapitei river, and turn immediately right on Highway 537 (Hill Street). Drive 0.6 km and turn right onto LaMothe Street. The lagoons are at the end 0.8 km along. Further east small communities on Highway 17 with sewage lagoons are Verner and Warren; these are covered in chapter 16, but there are other lagoons in the towns north of the city. The nearest to Sudbury is at **Garson**, northeast of the city on Regional Road 86. The sewage lagoons here are 1.5 km west of Regional Road 86 on O'Neil Street West, which is 0.5 km south of the light at Margaret Street. Cross the tracks on O'Neil and turn right immediately on Heino Street. The lagoon gate is 0.2 km along on the right. If coming from Sudbury, a faster route is to drive 5 km from the intersection of Highways 17 and 86 in town to Donnelly Street (signposted as the Kirkwood Mine Road). Turn left and proceed to O'Neil, turning right there and left on Heino, just before crossing the tracks.

To reach the sewage lagoon in **Capreol**, the northernmost community in the Sudbury Regional Municipality, continue on from the end of Regional Road 84 (Dennie Street) to the flashing light at Hanna Avenue. Turn left and go 0.3 km, following the street as it curves right (now as Young Street) and crosses the tracks. Turn left and bear immediately left again on a gravel road. Drive 0.7 km and cross a bridge to the right; the lagoon is straight ahead.

To reach the sewage lagoons at **Chelmsford**, in the northwest of the municipality, drive north on Highway 144 to the stoplight at Regional Road 14 (Errington Street). Turn right, and continue 1.6 km to a four-way stop at Main Street. Turn left, cross the bridge, and turn right (0.3 km) on Montpellier Street. This road turns (0.4 km) to cross the railway, and the lagoons are on the left 0.6 km farther on.

MANITOULIN ISLAND

Manitoulin Island is in marked contrast to the Shield areas. It resembles the northern parts of the Bruce Peninsula, and like it is a tilted limestone plateau with shelving beaches on the south, much marginal farmland, poor drainage, and thin soils. The entire island is a well-known place for birds, but like the Bruce Peninsula it is difficult to pinpoint specific localities. The poor pastures are excellent for Upland Sandpipers – possibly one of the largest populations of this species in Ontario – and like the Bruce are good for Eastern Bluebirds. Few Loggerhead Shrikes remain from a previously large population. Common Ravens are significantly more common than on the Bruce, and Turkey Vultures less so. Highway 6 is the land link with the mainland to the north (see map 35), and it is worth driving for the views alone. Driving south the white quartzite ridges and rugged forested country of the Killarney area first dominate, until the road finally drops down to the flat limestone plateau of Great Cloche Island.

Little Current is the first town encountered on Manitoulin Island itself. Here *Low Island* can be interesting at times during migration, particularly for open-country species. Southbound, turn right (north) at the intersection of Highways 6 and 540. This road leads down to the business section. Bear left at the bottom of the hill, and follow the main street west up the hill (Robinson Street) 0.8 km to Hayward Street on the left. On the right is a gravel road which leads down to the town park on Low Island. The *sewage lagoons* are off Highway 540 west of town. Go west 0.5 km past the highway maintenance yard, which is just before the corner at the end of town. The lagoons are 0.6 km down a track on the left.

Highway 6 is the major route south across the island, and the only part that the traveller using the ferry to the Bruce Peninsula will see. The one area of possible note is the sewage lagoons at **Manitowaning**, which are to the east of the highway approaching the village; however, to date they have been rather unproductive. The Highway 6 route is roughly 60 km across the east end of the island, but it is over 120 km to the west end, with good birding through much of the way. Highway 540 westbound is the main route west from Little Current, and in the south Highway 542 runs west from Tehkummah to link with 540 at Gore Bay.

South Baymouth is the ferry terminal at the south end of Highway 6. The town is a good place for migrant concentra-

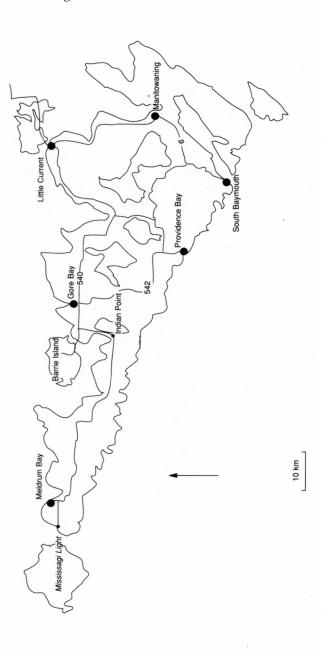

MAP 35   Manitoulin Island

tions at times, when the trees and shrubs around the cottages and motels near the ferry docks can be alive with birds. A short distance up Highway 6 (about 1 km) is a park area on the west which can be productive. Manitoulin's south shore is a good place to see large flights of Oldsquaw, White-winged Scoter and Whimbrel in May, and waterbirds generally. There are few easily accessible locations, but South Baymouth itself gives some views, and **Providence Bay** farther west also has a good sand beach.

The Tobermory–Little Current ferry (the Chi-Cheemaun) is a large car ferry that crosses four times daily from mid-June to the beginning of September and outside those times twice daily (three on Fridays) from late April to mid-October. The crossing costs $23.00 for automobiles and $10.50 for passengers, and takes 1 3/4 hours. Reservations and current fee schedules are available from Owen Sound Transportation Company, Box 336, Owen Sound, Ontario, N4K 5P5 1-800-265-3163. There is rarely much to be seen from the Chi-Cheemaun; all we have seen are gulls and hummingbirds (however, most crossings are not in migration periods).

Gore Bay is the administrative centre for Manitoulin Island, and to reach it you will pass through some typical Manitoulin countryside along Highway 540, running across the north of the island and now paved for all but its last 9 km or so. It links some of the best birding areas: Mississagi Light near Meldrum Bay to the west, the Gore Bay area, and Little Current on the east. At Gore Bay, the *sewage lagoons* are on the west side of the western leg of Highway 540B, which loops into town and out again, and 1.4 km from the main highway.

Continuing west on 540 from this intersection, at 5.4 km the main highway turns left and the road to the airport continues straight ahead. After some 4 km this road crosses a causeway to *Barrie Island*, where there is wetland associated with the waterfront. American Bittern, duck, snipe, and other waterfowl occur. Both the airport and the fields of Barrie Island have at different times been dancing grounds for a flock of Sharp-tailed Grouse. The presence of these birds was confirmed during the Atlas work, and additional sites were recorded near Mindemoya, along Highway 542. The Manitoulin birds were once a mixed population of Sharp-taileds and Greater Prairie-Chicken. This was the only occurrence of the latter in Ontario in recent years, but none has been seen since 1969 and the birds are apparently now Sharp-taileds only.

Return from here to the main highway and turn right to drive south 8.3 km, crossing the causeway between Wolsey Lake and Bayfield Sound. At the south end of this is *Indian Point*, site of a highway picnic area. It does not look like a migration concentration point, but it can be a good one. When you have birded this area and the adjoining waters, continue on Highway 540 to Mississagi Light or return to Little Current.

At the end of Highway 540 just outside **Meldrum Bay** is a small road running some 10 km westwards to *Mississagi Light*. The area around the lighthouse here is a migrant trap of note, as birds following the south shore of the island westwards end up here, and it is also a good spot for watching waterfowl movements. Loons both fly south down the straits and concentrate here, and Red-necked Grebes gather nearby. Significant hawk flights can develop. Unfortunately access has been uncertain; the road serves a gravel pit adjacent to the lighthouse, and then continues to the lighthouse area (which is also a campground). If the latter is closed (from mid-September to mid-May) the gate to the last 1 km or so of road may be locked, necessitating a walk in. Parking at the gate is limited; please do not block it or the road. Please remember also that the area is private property, and that future access, even as limited as it is now, could be denied.

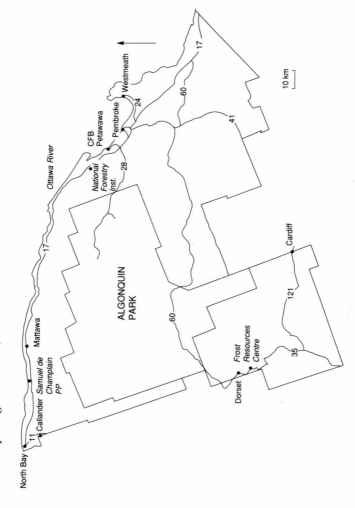

MAP 36   Southern Nipissing, Haliburton, and Renfrew

16 Algonquin Park, Pembroke, and North Bay

Renfrew and Haliburton Counties, and the District of Nipissing South of Highway 17

Algonquin Park
Haliburton County
The Pembroke area
The North Bay area

This chapter includes some of the agricultural lands along the Ottawa valley north from Arnprior, but the area is mostly Shield, heavily forested, and very picturesque. The main Trans-Canada Highway (Highway 17) traverses the northeast boundary of the region, and the two larger communities, the cities of Pembroke and North Bay, are associated with it. Otherwise population centres are relatively few, and they and the limited road network primarily service the recreational activities that abound. In spite of its relative remoteness, the southwest of the region is only some 200 km from Toronto, and Ottawa is even closer to the east. Hence air access is probably easiest through one of these two larger centres.

The forests here are diverse, particularly those of the Algonquin Highlands between Highways 11 and 17, with hardwoods mixing with spruces and other boreal species. White pine, eastern hemlock, and balsam fir are their major constituents. Bird life is equally varied and rich. It is probably one of the best areas in Canada for breeding thrushes and warblers, and there is a strong northern component to the bird life as well. Many southern species reach their northern limits through the region, and are much scarcer – or become scarcer – than in areas farther south. There is an abundance of water in small lakes and areas of bog, but this is not paralleled by an abundance of waterbirds, as the Shield lakes are relatively infertile. There is little to attract either shorebirds or open-country species, and habitats that are relatively commonplace in the rest of southern Ontario – marshes and open country – often attract rarities for the region. For forest birds the birder encounters a problem which intensifies farther north. Good habitat abounds, and the selection of good birding locations is more a matter of watching for changes in the forest composition than of following directions in a book.

Algonquin Provincial Park is noted as one of the best places for persons living farther south to see winter finches in season. The region as a whole, however, is above all noteworthy for its wealth of woodland breeding birds. This is the place to go to hear most of the thrushes and wood warblers on their nesting grounds, and also to become familiar with such species as Barred Owls and Gray Jays, which are rare or absent farther south.

ALGONQUIN PARK

Algonquin Provincial Park (entrance fee) is both the oldest provincial park and, with an area of over 7,600 square kilometres, one of the biggest. Highway 60 between Dwight and Whitney crosses the southwest corner of the park, and is the main public road through it. The nearest larger town here is **Huntsville**, to the southwest in the District of Muskoka. The interior of the park is accessible by canoe, and there are over 1,600 km of canoe routes. Specific routes will not be identified here because to my knowledge none offers significantly different birding to that available elsewhere in the region; however, the canoe routes and backpacking trails are undoubtedly the best way to see the park.

Algonquin occupies an area of rolling highlands, and the forest presents a mix of southern and northern species. The mixture in Algonquin is particularly rich, including as it does a more northern element as well, because of its higher elevation. Much of the variety is accessible in the relatively short distance along Highway 60. There is an excellent visitor centre with a skilled and knowledgeable interpretive staff, which can be of great help in giving directions to locating particular species. Several fine nature trails as well as a couple of major backpacking trails are accessible along the highway. Algonquin Park is noted for its wildlife-viewing opportunities, for both mammals and birds. In spring and early summer, black bears, moose, beaver, and white-tailed deer are frequently seen at close range. The park has become famous as a place to hear timber wolves in late summer and early autumn.

Birders are primarily drawn to Algonquin for its northern specialties, and warblers on their breeding grounds. Boreal forest species such as Olive-sided Flycatcher, Gray Jay, Common Raven, and Boreal Chickadee occur regularly along Highway 60 in the park. In addition, careful searching in favoured locations can yield Spruce Grouse, Black-backed Woodpecker, Yellow-bellied Flycatcher, Lincoln's Sparrow, and Rusty Blackbird. Remember, however, that Algonquin's continuous forest cover can make these birds very difficult to find.

The park has an excellent variety of breeding warblers. The commoner species are Nashville, Chestnut-sided, Magnolia, Black-throated Blue, Yellow-rumped, Black-throated Green, Blackburnian, Pine, Black-and-white, Mourning and Canada Warblers, with Ovenbird, Northern Waterthrush, Common Yellowthroat, and American Redstart; however, at least five other species have bred as well. Common Loons nest on most of the larger lakes, but duck are scarce. The commonly observed raptor along Highway 60 is the Broad-winged Hawk (frequently perched along the utility lines), and Ospreys are occasionally noted over lakes near the road. At night one should listen for Barred and Northern Saw-whet Owls, the former year-round, the latter from March to May. Both are common.

Outside the breeding season, the park is worth a visit in late autumn through early spring to see winter finches and resident species. Both eagles occur rarely during this period as well, feeding on wolf-killed deer. Some of the park's most-wanted birds are best sought outside the breeding season. Spruce Grouse are easiest to locate in the spring (April and early May) when the birds are displaying, and in fall (September-October) when they may sometimes respond to taped calls. Gray Jays are also far more easy to see outside the warmer months of summer.

Much birding can done from the highway, but it is busy and if you plan to do this get out at dawn ahead of the traffic. Stop regularly, selecting variations in the habitat along the road, and drive with the windows open. Most of your 'watching' will be done initially by ear! In addition to the marked nature trails, there are many sideroads (some disused) and old trails along the road than can be explored on foot. It is emphasized again that naturalists at the visitor centre can provide detailed information on particular species at the time of your visit. Be sure to stop in.

Some specific locations of interest follow, but no attempt has been made to be exhaustive. The distances given are from the West Gate: the distances along the highway within the park are marked in this manner also.

0 km   The West Gate.

3 km   The Oxtongue River picnic grounds and start of the Western Uplands Backpacking Trail. Gray Jay and Boreal Chickadee are frequent in the heavy spruce to the east.

7.2 km   The Whiskey Rapids Trail. This is an excellent nature trail, and in my experience one of the more productive spots for Boreal Chickadees.

15.4 km   The Arowhon Road, and Mizzy Lake trailhead. This is an 11 km loop trail, with one of the best locations for Spruce Grouse at the far end. In spring through fall the long hike can be avoided by driving up the Arowhon Road to an old railbed. Turn right here and continue to a locked gate. Park (not blocking the gate) and walk about 1 km to a point where the railbed joins the Mizzy Lake Trail at a pond (Wolf Howl Pond). Search the forest on both sides of the pond for the grouse, and for Olive-sided Flycatcher in the more open areas.

16.7 km   The Hardwood Hill picnic grounds. Black-throated Blue Warbler and other deciduous woodland species occur here.

22.3 km   An abandoned railroad bed here offers a good walk in either direction.

30.6 km   The road to the airfield. A very productive spot for field birds and rarities (an island of open country); also waterbirds on Lake of Two Rivers.

42.5 km   The Spruce Boardwalk Trail. Olive-sided Flycatchers occur infrequently, and there is a good chance of spotting Spruce Grouse near the trail. This is the most accessible location for these birds in the park.

43.0 km   The Park visitor centre. Magnificent dioramas depict the park's major habitats.

45.2 km   The Beaver Pond Trail. A varied and productive nature trail through wetlands and coniferous habitats.

46.3 km   The Opeongo Lake Road. At the south end of Opeongo Lake are some of the best marshy areas accessible from the highway.

53.0 km   There is a gravel pit here on the north side, and a small bog adjacent to it. Spruce Grouse are possible.

55.8 km   The East Gate.

Algonquin Park has produced a series of publications on the park's flora and fauna. Birders would be particularly interested in the booklets on birds: *Birds of Algonquin Park* ($2.95), covering the more common summer birds, and *Checklist and Seasonal Status of the Birds of Algonquin Park* ($1.25). In addition, illustrated trail guide booklets, each with a different natural or human history theme, are available for each of the trails along Highway 60. General information and a publication price list are available from the Ministry of Natural Resources, Box 219, Whitney, Ontario, K0J 2M0. Current bird-finding information can always be obtained at the visitor centre [km 43], or by phone ([613] 637-2828).

The only other section of the park accessible by public road is from the east side, north of **Pembroke**. Here the *Sand Lake Gate* access is from the Sand Lake Road (County Road 28). To reach this, from the intersection of Highways 17 and 41 outside Pembroke, drive 13.4 km northwest on Highway 17 to the County Road 26 intersection. Turn left, and then right at 0.4 km onto the Achray Road. This is County Road 28, and it runs (paved for a few kilometres and then gravelled) west for 32 km to the Sand Lake Gate on the eastern boundary of Algonquin. Proceed into the park on Sand Lake Road through young forests of birch and poplar, and extensive stands of both red and white pine, which are dramatically different from Algonquin's Highway 60 hardwoods. Common birds of the pine forest include Olive-sided Flycatcher, Pine Warbler, and Dark-eyed Junco.

Some 10.5 km in from the Sand Lake Gate is the Barron Canyon Trail. This trail, about 1.5 km long, leads to and along the edge of the spectacular Barron River Canyon with 100-metre vertical granite walls, before looping back to the parking lot. Common birds in the gorge include Yellow-bellied Flycatcher, Hermit Thrush, Northern Waterthrush, and Dark-eyed Junco, all of which should be heard from the top of the Canyon. Close to the water's edge far below, Barn Swallows and Eastern Phoebes build their nests on the vertical rock walls – a contrast to their usual sites on man-made structures.

Another 8.5 km along Sand Lake Road brings you to the turn-off on the left to Achray on Grand Lake. Here there is a campground on the lake, with a good beach.

Upon returning to the Sand Lake Road, there is a choice of returning to Pembroke (turn right), or taking a left turn and driving some 35 km farther on to Lake Travers. An extensive area near Lake Travers was clear-cut to salvage the jack pine forest killed by budworm in the past, and this section may produce American Kestrels, Eastern Bluebirds, Field Sparrows, and Lincoln's Sparrows. Watch along the road and in adjacent ponds for wood turtles and Blanding's turtles, both of which are specialties of Algonquin Park's east side. Typical birds along the road in summer (varying with the particular year) include Evening Grosbeak, Purple Finch, Pine Siskin, and Red Crossbill. Stops along the way may yield Solitary Vireos and the usual variety of Algonquin warbler species. The jack pine stands can be very productive of Spruce Grouse, especially in the early morning in the area between kilometre markers 62 and 70.

There are several campgrounds in Algonquin and three commercial lodges that take guests. Outside the park there are motels at Oxtongue Lake, Huntsville, Whitney, and Pembroke.

HALIBURTON COUNTY

Haliburton County, situated south of Algonquin, features scenic, rugged country, an abundance of lakes, and extensive forests. The county lacks larger population centres, and although it is served by three highways, all are slow, winding roads; the north of the county lacks roads completely. Highways 35 and 121 from the south are the main access routes, with the latter then bearing east across to Bancroft. **Cardiff** is on 121 at the boundary with Hastings County, and it has a *sewage lagoon*, situated south of the highway, and just south of the beginning of the Paudash Lake road (County Road 9).

The main area of interest, however, is the *Leslie M. Frost Natural Resources Centre*, situated about 12 km south of **Dorset** on Highway 35. This is on the boundary of Muskoka District, and the centre's 24,000 hectares encompasses crown land in both jurisdictions. It is an ideal location to become familiar with the bird life of the county, as it has access roads and a good network of hiking trails. The bird list of over 175 species includes an excellent mix of the woodland birds of the Great Lakes–St Lawrence Region. There is a naturalist on staff, and inquiries about birds are welcomed ([705] 766-2451). Organized groups of at least fifteen persons are invited to inquire well in advance about accommodation and activities at the centre. For individuals, the nearest accommodation is in either Dorset or Hall's Lake.

THE PEMBROKE AREA

Pembroke, a city of some 14,000 inhabitants on the Ottawa River, has far more of interest to birders than simply the access road to the east side of Algonquin. Starting in 1983, it became famous as the site of the largest swallow roost ever recorded in Ontario. The roost was estimated at 150,000 birds, and included all six eastern species, plus the Merlins which this huge concentration attracted. The birds occupied a grove of willows at the confluence of the *Muskrat* and *Ottawa Rivers*, with peak numbers about 15 minutes before sunset in late July through mid-August. Noted wildlife artist Neil Blackwell has painted the once-spectacular roost in the form of a large wall mural, the first of an acclaimed series, downtown at 243 Pembroke Street West. The roost is currently no longer active, but it could conceivably develop again in the future; and in any case, the viewing area is an outstanding vantage point for birding the two rivers. The waters here attract mergansers and goldeneyes until freeze-up. Loons, cormorants, geese, a variety of duck and possible shorebirds can also be expected, as well as ospreys, the local gulls, and migrants following the Ottawa River.

To reach this area, exit Highway 17 outside town northbound

onto Highway 41 and follow the signs to the Pembroke marina. Highway 41 finally becomes Mackay Street in town, intersecting Pembroke Street (Highway 148) after 4.2 km. Turn left on Pembroke and cross the bridge over the Muskrat River, then take the first right on Victoria. Drive one block to Lake Street, turn left and drive another block to Albert. Turn right here and cross the railroad tracks to a parking area for the marina and parkland west of the rivermouth. The swallows roosted in the willows on the opposite bank.

Southeast from Pembroke, 5.6 km on Highway 17 from the Highway 41 intersection, is County Road 24 signed to **Westmeath**, which is northeast from here along County Roads 24 and 12. On the way to Westmeath, the new *Westmeath Provincial Park* embraces a peninsula into the Ottawa River. At the date of writing, the park is not yet open, and the entrance remains a small, unmarked, gated road west off County Road 12 exactly 4.7 km from the intersection with County Road 21. Park at the entrance and walk in. The principal birding feature of the park is Bellows Bay, with extensive marshes at the south end. This is an important staging and resting area for waterfowl. There is also shorebird habitat on the sand beaches along the river. There is waterfowl hunting here in fall which will continue when the park opens.

Southeast 12.5 km from the 17/41 intersection, Highway 17 crosses the Muskrat River. *Mud Lake*, an important waterfowl area, lies to the west and is readily accessible by canoe from this point. There is also waterfowl hunting here in fall. There is a parking area on the south side of the highway just west of the bridge.

Northwest from Pembroke along Highway 17 from the Highway 41 intersection, at 13.4 km there is County Road 26 for Algonquin Park with access as described above, and at 4.7 km farther on is Black Bay Road. To the right this leads 4.2 km northeast to Laurentian Drive (County Road 25). A left turn there leads (3.1 km) to the junction of Victoria Street, where the county road turns left. Continue straight ahead here 0.9 km on Albert Street, which leads to River Road and *Petawawa Point*, a scenic waterfowl viewing area at the mouth of the Petawawa River. The waters here open relatively early in the spring.

Highway 17 now leaves the agriculture of the valley and

starts through the jack pine forests of the Canadian Forces Base Petawawa. This is the location in which Kirtland's Warblers were found in 1916. Occasional birds have been recorded here even as recently as the 1970s, and the species is always a remote possibility when passing through the area. Off-road access is prohibited without special permission, but possible suitable habitat occurs along the road beginning some 7 km northwest of the Black Bay Road.

Adjoining the base 35.5 km from the 17/41 intersection, is the *Petawawa National Forestry Institute*. With a fine diversity of habitats in the 100 square km research forest, and a bird list of over 140 species, the institute is well worth a visit at any time of year, except for the October-November hunting season. Visitors are welcomed, there is a visitor centre staffed in summer, an excellent checklist and habitat map, and biological scientists on staff. There is good year-round road and trail access. Among the breeding species are all three accipiters and twenty species of warbler.

THE NORTH BAY AREA

North Bay is a city of over 51,000 population at the east end of Lake Nipissing. There are several good birding areas in the vicinity. The waterfront between the government dock to the north and the LaVase River some 7 km south of town is especially good in fall. Earlier in the season shorebirds occur when habitat exists, and later grebes and diving ducks, including scoters, can be seen. There are many access points along the shoreline; however, across the downtown section of the city direct access to the waterfront is blocked by the railroad tracks. Memorial Drive is the road running west of the tracks, and it can be reached from the north via 9th Street, and from the south by turning west from Lakeshore Drive at Judge Avenue (the first lights after Lakeshore southbound crosses the railroad bridge), and then sharp right on to Memorial.

To reach the *Laurier Woods*, some 60 hectares of wetland and other habitats with good walking trails, leave the Highway 11/17 bypass at Fisher Street (Highway 17B; at the Information Centre). Drive west some 0.6 km to Laurier Avenue, the first street west of the light at Chippewa Street. Turn south (left) here and drive to the end. The woods are ahead across the Canadian Northland Railway tracks. This area is especially good for landbirds in migration, and Green Herons and Soras are among the array of breeding birds.

Callander is some 13 km south of North Bay on a bay of Lake Nipissing. However, the *sewage lagoons*, which can be very productive, are most easily reached from the south exit (the first northbound) of Highway 11B to North Bay (Lakeshore Drive). The latter heads west, but turn left almost immediately after the exit on to Lamorie Street, which is also called Pinewood Park Drive, and drive south some 3 km to the second road on the right – currently opposite a Viceroy Homes sales outlet. This rough dirt road runs west, crossing some old fields to the lagoons, 1 km from the highway. A 3 km trail also follows the concession line west from the end of the lagoon road to the lake. It passes through good warbler and woodpecker habitat, and ends at broad marshes and sandbars. The whole area can be rewarding. Note that the **Powassen** lagoons, some 15 km farther south again on Highway 11, are covered in chapter 15.

Mattawa is about 60 km **east of North Bay** on Highway 17. Samuel de Champlain Provincial Park is about two-thirds of the way along, and it has good forests typical of the area. At Mattawa itself the *sewage lagoons* are off Highway 17. At the point the highway turns right to follow the Ottawa River, turn left on Main Street, crossing the Mattawa River. Turn left just past the hospital on to Brydges Street. This follows the north bank of the river, and the lagoons are about 1.5 km along on the left.

Highway 17 continues **west from North Bay**, paralleling the north shore of Lake Nipissing, through Sturgeon Falls to Sudbury, also covered in chapter 15. The route is a pleasant one following the Veuve and Nepewassi rivers, with farmland alternating with forests of pine and poplar. Brewer's Blackbirds are as common on the farmland here as anywhere in the province.

Just west of Sturgeon Falls, and south of the highway, is **Cache Bay**. A drive south through town here leads to the dock and an extensive area of marshland to the west. This is readily accessible by boat, or can be viewed by telescope from the dock itself. An excellent range of typical marsh species have occurred, including rails, moorhen, Black Tern, and Marsh Wren. Turn off Highway 17 at Cache Bay and bear left on Cache Street. This leads south 1 km to Railway Street. Turn right there and drive 0.6 km to Dock Street on the left, which leads to the dock.

Farther west towards Sudbury the small communities of **Verner** and **Warren** have sewage lagoons which can yield waterfowl. At Verner turn left off 17 on to Highway 64. Drive 0.7 km, crossing the railroad and the river, to Olivier Street on the left. Turn here and drive another 0.7 km, and the long drive to the lagoon is on the right. The Warren lagoon is more accessible. Turn north off 17 on Highway 539 into town, and take the first right (Rutland Avenue, 0.1 km). Drive 0.4 km to the stop street at Warren Avenue. Turn right, and Warren ends almost at once at Mangan Avenue, which runs east along the railroad tracks, becoming a gravel road and curving north after 0.7 km to run alongside the lagoon, with the gate 0.4 km ahead. This lagoon can be good for waterfowl.

MAP 37   Northern Ontario

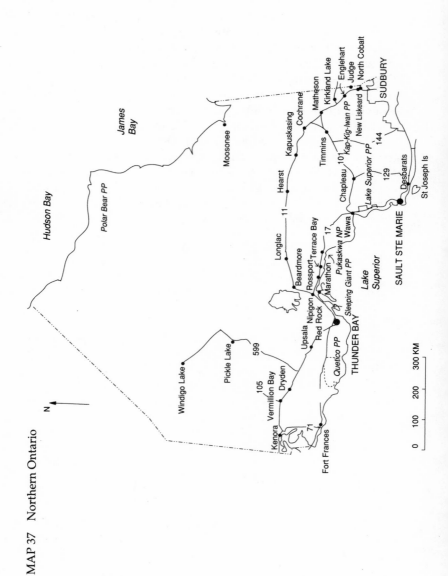

17 Northern Ontario

Northern Ontario as treated here is all of Ontario north of Lakes Huron and Superior, excluding Manitoulin Island, the Regional Municipality of Sudbury, and the area south of the line formed by Highways 6 and 17 between Little Current and Mattawa. It includes the District of Sudbury north of the Regional Municipality and Highway 17, and the District of Nipissing north of 17. The extreme western part of northern Ontario – the District of Rainy River west of Highway 71 – is dealt with in the next chapter.

The enormous size of this region can only be grasped when one travels across it. It is almost 1,600 km from North Bay in the east to Kenora in the west, and about 1,000 km from north to south. The westernmost administrative district alone, that of Kenora, is bigger than many European countries. Over much of this vast area there are no roads and few people. The tourist literature boasts of two time zones, three persons per square mile, and 400,000 lakes. Travel across this hinterland in summer is by airplane or canoe, usually both. Even highway travel can be daunting to those wishing a quick taste of the boreal forest; the sheer scale of the region largely precludes the casual visit.

The character of the north makes the traditional finding guide format problematic. As so often happens when suitable habitat abounds, birds that are everywhere can be difficult to find any-

where! Logging operations result in a constantly changing mosaic of habitats, which are fairly consistent when viewed on a
broad scale, but change with the forest succession at specific
sites. The approach used here will be to outline the broad picture and the species that will normally be encountered in the
breeding season, discuss some of the specialties of the region
and some points about finding them, and then touch briefly on
migration and the winter before proceeding with more detailed
coverage of main routes.

Birders usually travel to northern Ontario with specific objec-
tives in mind. Most arrive in the summer, and wish to see those
species that are rare or absent farther south, a goal that, unfortunately, can be difficult to achieve. A second objective, that of
seeing the array of boreal forest summer nesters (especially warblers) on their breeding grounds, is easy to accomplish with a
little time and a reasonably good ear. A relatively small but
growing number of birders now visit during migration periods,
drawn by the accounts of migrant concentrations and rarities,
mainly along the north shores of Lake Superior.

For many, birding in the north is incidental to other objec-
tives. Those bound for western Canada must cross the north to
get there, and will try to enrich their route with a good sam-
pling of northern species, but will probably be unable to com-
mit much time to birding off the Trans-Canada Highway. At
the other extreme is the wilderness canoeist for whom the north
is a destination, but the birding simply a part of the many
experiences of the canoe trip. Detail on such wilderness travel
is really beyond the scope of this guide. In fact, away from the
Hudson and James Bay coast, the vast majority of the birds
seen on such a trip are likely to be found more easily elsewhere.
On the other hand, for many miles the Trans-Canada Highway
routes are the only through roads. If one considers Highway 71
running north to the east of Rainy River as a linking road between Highways 11 and 17, these highways form two huge
loops, one west of Thunder Bay and the second between Nipigon
and North Bay. As all birders will use the Trans-Canada loops
to some degree, the text that follows describes these routes in
some detail.

The north is far from uniform. While forest dominates, there
are extensive areas of agriculture, huge water bodies, and rug-

ged topography. On a broader scale, there are four major forest regions represented, although only two are readily accessible by road. North of the highway network lies the Hudson Bay Lowland and, along the Hudson Bay coast, tundra.

The forests associated with the more southern parts of the settled north are still the mixed woodlands of the Great Lakes–St Lawrence described in earlier chapters. The change to boreal forest is most easily seen when driving through Lake Superior Provincial Park, where the maples in the south are gradually replaced by birch and spruce in the north end. The mixed forest extends east to the Clay Belt around New Liskeard, and reappears on the west of Lake Superior around Thunder Bay, and thence westwards to Kenora. These more northern sections often resemble the adjacent boreal forests more than the maple-dominated woodlands of the south. Aspens, birches, balsam fir, and spruces are widespread and the hardwoods seem relatively scarce. Nevertheless, there is enough diversity to attract many of the bird species of the mixed forest, for example Great Crested Flycatcher and Veery, together with enough of the boreal element to satisfy the typical northerners; together they give these forests the richest avifauna in the north.

The boreal forest also varies in its composition, and hence in its bird life. Along the north shore of Lake Superior jack pine alternates with spruces, balsam fir, birches, and aspen; but in the Clay Belt south and west of Cochrane stands of black spruce can dominate the scene for miles. Generally it is much less rich in its species composition than the forests to the south, with the trees listed above, together with tamarack and balsam poplar, comprising most of the forest cover. Rocky outcrops, small lakes, and open boggy areas are common, and open places develop a cover of shrubs such as alder, red osier dogwood, fire cherry, and mountain maple.

Achieving a representative day's list in the north calls for even more attention to habitat variations than in the south, and for different tactics. Here open country is at a premium, and birds that find conifers inhospitable tend to turn up in the townsites and along roads and railways. If these places are little used, so much the better, and if they form islands of fertility, as with sewage lagoons, that too is a bonus. Dumps, although lacking charm, can yield hawks, gulls, and ravens; and boat-launching ramps provide opportunities to get off the road and to view waterbodies that otherwise are often hidden behind screens of forest. For the forest birds themselves, changes in forest composition should be watched for, with each change bringing a different mix of bird species. Lakes abound, but usually have few birds. As in the Shield areas of southern Ontario, beaver dams can create the marshes that are often otherwise absent.

Significant areas of agriculture displace the unrelieved forest cover in the Clay Belts, which extend across the line of Highway 11 from Hearst to Cobalt. Other agricultural areas are north and east of Sault Ste Marie, and again around Thunder Bay and Dryden. Given the shortness of the growing season at these northerly latitudes, farming is usually confined to pasture and hay, with a limited amount of arable land. The farming appears more extensive from the highway than it really is, and the sideroads quickly lead back into forest; they provide excellent opportunities to sample bird life away from the busy highway.

The commoner birds that will be encountered (at least heard!) on a drive across the north in June would include the following species (asterisks indicate birds primarily associated with the Great Lakes–St Lawrence forest):

Common Loon	Ring-billed Gull
Great Blue Heron	Herring Gull
Canada Goose	Rock Dove
American Black Duck	Mourning Dove
Mallard	Belted Kingfisher
Blue-winged Teal	Yellow-bellied Sapsucker
Ring-necked Duck	Downy Woodpecker
Common Goldeneye	Hairy Woodpecker
Bufflehead	Northern Flicker
Osprey	Pileated Woodpecker
Northern Harrier	Olive-sided Flycatcher
Broad-winged Hawk	Alder Flycatcher
Red-tailed Hawk	Least Flycatcher
American Kestrel	Eastern Phoebe*
Ruffed Grouse	Great Crested Flycatcher*
Killdeer	Eastern Kingbird
Spotted Sandpiper	Tree Swallow

Cliff Swallow
Barn Swallow
Blue Jay
American Crow
Common Raven
Black-capped Chickadee
Red-breasted Nuthatch
Winter Wren
Golden-crowned Kinglet
Ruby-crowned Kinglet
Veery*
Swainson's Thrush
Hermit Thrush
American Robin
Gray Catbird*
Cedar Waxwing
European Starling
Solitary Vireo
Red-eyed Vireo
Tennessee Warbler
Nashville Warbler
Northern Parula
Yellow Warbler
Chestnut-sided Warbler
Magnolia Warbler
Yellow-rumped Warbler

Black-throated Green Warbler
Blackburnian Warbler
Black-and-white Warbler
American Redstart
Ovenbird
Northern Waterthrush
Mourning Warbler
Common Yellowthroat
Wilson's Warbler
Canada Warbler
Rose-breasted Grosbeak*
Chipping Sparrow
Savannah Sparrow
Song Sparrow
Lincoln's Sparrow
Swamp Sparrow
White-throated Sparrow
Dark-eyed Junco
Red-winged Blackbird
Common Grackle
Brown-headed Cowbird
Purple Finch
Pine Siskin
American Goldfinch
Evening Grosbeak
House Sparrow

A glance at this list will indicate that the typical northerners are not easily found in a fast drive across the north! Other species are present, but require a more concentrated effort (or good luck) to locate. These include other raptors, American Bittern, Common Snipe, Ruby-throated Hummingbird, Brown Creeper, Philadelphia Vireo, Cape May and Bay-breasted Warblers, and Rusty Blackbird. Many birds are quite localized and may be found once or twice on the trip, but not regularly – for example, the more southern species such as Eastern Phoebe and Bobolink, that reach the limits of their ranges across the north. Cliff Swallows are often the most usual swallow around settlements, with Tree Swallows abounding in the dead timber around beaver dams. Locating the various warbler species demands attention to their niches in the forest, as noted in the systematic list.

The most-wanted species in the north are those with ranges that can include the settled areas of northern Ontario but are scarce farther south in the breeding season. These are (asterisks here indicate species that are largely confined to the north):

Spruce Grouse	Yellow-bellied Flycatcher
Sandhill Crane	Gray Jay
Solitary Sandpiper	Boreal Chickadee
Great Gray Owl*	Palm Warbler
Boreal Owl*	Connecticut Warbler
Three-toed Woodpecker*	Pine Grosbeak*
Black-backed Woodpecker	crossbills

Unfortunately most of these are difficult to find even in the north. Indeed, quite apart from the millions of blackflies, boreal forest birding can be difficult, with species thinly distributed and difficult to see. Even the more common northerners – Gray Jay, Boreal Chickadee, and Black-backed Woodpecker – are often anything but easy to see without special effort at the times most persons visit the north. Sharp-tailed Grouse might also be added to this list, but is much easier to find in the Lake of the Woods area.

A further five species have ranges that reach the limits of the roads in the north, but generally will not be found along the Trans-Canada. These are:

Greater Yellowlegs	Orange-crowned Warbler
Bonaparte's Gull	Fox Sparrow
Northern Hawk-Owl*	

Indeed, some of these birds turn up along the Highway 11 corridor. I have encountered agitated Bonaparte's Gulls on Remi Lake and a singing Orange-crowned Warbler at the main intersection south of Cochrane, and others report similar experiences across this route. The birds are not reliable at such locations, although Atlas records indicate that the Bonaparte's Gull's range extends south of the highway in the Clay Belt.

To have a chance of finding these species, it is usually necessary to travel some of the roads that head north from the Trans-Canada. Only a couple of highways go north of 51°N, and none reach the north coast. The longest, the 292-km Highway 599 to Pickle Lake, is mentioned below and its 200 km gravel extension north to Windigo Lake is probably the only route where nesting Fox Sparrows are possible. These more remote highways, together with the logging roads off Highway 11, all provide opportunities to search out these more northern species, and also other northerners that are elusive along the major routes.

Timing is the key to finding many of these species. The grouse are easier to find outside the peak summer period; they often frequent the roadside verges of less travelled roads, but are still very difficult to spot. The owls are noisy and relatively active in April and early May but later become problematic. The residents generally – the two woodpeckers, Gray Jays, and Boreal Chickadees – are much easier to locate at the beginning of their breeding season, and even a change from an early June to later May visit can make a big difference in the visibility of these species, as indeed it can for such raptors as Broad-winged Hawk and Merlin. It's also before the blackflies reach their peak! The difference between late June and early July can also be dramatic. Song falls off rapidly, particularly later in the day, as the season progresses. Merlins are conspicuous again in August, when feeding young.

The nesting activity of finches such as crossbills is synchronized with the fruiting of the conifers on which they feed, which varies from year to year and place to place. Early in their nesting cycle they are noisy and conspicuous, but outside this unpredictable period they wander widely and finding them is rather a matter of chance. My own limited experience of Pine Grosbeak in summer outside the province is similar: birds early in their nesting cycle are conspicuous and sing loudly – reminiscent of a Purple Finch – but outside this period the species seems to be nomadic and to have a rather catholic range of diet, including a fondness for dandelion seeds! However, these observations seem inconsistent with some reports on Ontario birds, which are rare at best. Probably the only general advice possible on all the winter finches is to learn the call notes thoroughly and hope for the best.

Learning the songs and the preferred habitats is certainly the answer to locating the rarer warblers and Yellow-bellied Flycatchers. The latter's notes and song are rather thin and easy to overlook, and the bird itself is often quite low down in boggy openings among the conifers. The two warblers, both Palm and Connecticut, prefer open areas in bogs, although the latter species seems to have a range of suitable habitats. Along Highway 144 north of Sudbury I have found the species along the shrubby, boggy margins of small lakes, near Hearst birds occur in the brush bordering spruce forest, on Highway 17 around Upsala they favour the edges of open areas of sphagnum, while in the next chapter the birds are also found in aspen groves! Palm Warblers favour the tamarack edges bordering more open areas of sphagnum, but also occur in areas of young jack pine. Apparently the structure of the habitat is more important to these two birds than its plant composition.

The bulk of northern Ontario is inaccessible even by road. Hence the Hudson Bay Lowlands and the sea coast require special arrangements for visits. The second part of this account will deal briefly with these areas, and also with communities and roads not associated with the Highway 11-17 loops.

In *A Naturalist's Guide to Ontario* W.K.W. Baldwin characterizes the Hudson Bay Lowland as 'a vast peatland wilderness,' and points out that this huge area south of the coast comprises one-quarter of the land surface of the province. Even though the Atlas work expanded knowledge of northern Ontario's bird life enormously, there is relatively little information on the bird life of much of the Lowland. It is mainly a low-lying area of open bogs interspersed with stunted forests of black spruce and tamarack, although along the banks of the rivers quite vigorous well-grown forest occurs. Travel on foot here presents enormous difficulties, but canoe trips into the region are becoming more common. The Moose via the Missinaibi, Mattagami, or Abitibi rivers, and the Albany and the Winisk, are rivers that are popular with canoeists. To get a taste of this flat, desolate country by rail, see Moosonee.

North again, mainly around Cape Henrietta Maria, is a belt of tundra along the Hudson Bay coast itself. A large number of species are present in summer along the coast or on the adjacent lowlands that occur nowhere else in Ontario at that time, except as non-breeding stragglers from migration. These are:

Red-throated Loon
Pacific Loon
Tundra Swan
Snow Goose
Greater Scaup
Common Eider
Oldsquaw
Surf Scoter
White-winged Scoter
Rough-legged Hawk
Willow Ptarmigan
American Golden Plover
Semipalmated Plover
Lesser Yellowlegs
Whimbrel
Hudsonian Godwit
Marbled Godwit

Semipalmated Sandpiper
Least Sandpiper
Dunlin
Stilt Sandpiper
Short-billed Dowitcher
Red-necked Phalarope
Parasitic Jaeger
Arctic Tern
Gray-cheeked Thrush
American Pipit
Bohemian Waxwing
Blackpoll Warbler
American Tree Sparrow
White-crowned Sparrow
Lapland Longspur
Smith's Longspur
Common Redpoll

A number of other tundra and arctic species, such as King Eider, Sabine's Gull, Black Guillemot, Snowy Owl, and Snow Bunting, have been seen here in summer as well, but probably as non-breeders. Note that, of the above list, the Common Eider, Willow Ptarmigan, and Smith's Longspur can usually be seen in Ontario only in this area.

Until recently there has been little systematic coverage of migratory movements across the north. Opportunities for migration-watching abound. The southern end of the Sibley Peninsula has produced an outstanding assortment of rarities over the years, and a bird observatory is now established here. Heavy passage occurs along the northern Lake Superior shore-line, where enormous counts of Rough-legged Hawks and win-ter finches have been reported, and this entire area has acquired a name as a place where improbable rarities turn up. Later fall (October) appears to be the optimum time for such events. The area of Sault Ste Marie and the north end of Lake Timiskaming have also been identified as good for migrants.

Migration along the north coast, particularly the south end of James Bay, presents a wholly different dimension. It is recog-nized as one of North America's major fall staging grounds for shorebirds and waterfowl, and as a southern pocket of sea it should concentrate seabird migrants as well. The jaegers, Sabine's Gulls, and kittiwakes that appear at the south end of Lake Huron in late autumn likely originate here. Similarly the movement of Arctic Terns and some other species up the Ottawa River in spring may end at James Bay. But how these species get from south to north or vice versa – if in fact that is what occurs – remains to be established.

Northern winters are long – a month or more longer than in the south, with freeze-up in November and little amelioration until April – so most birds retreat from the region in that season. Grouse, ravens, Gray Jays, woodpeckers, and finches remain, with the odd goldeneye and merganser on open water. Noteworthy birds at this time include the owls, which start nesting activities early and whose calls build to a peak in March and April. Merlins and Sharp-tailed Grouse can be more conspicuous than usual at this time.

In concluding this introductory section, some caveats about northern travel may be in order. The blackflies in the north are legendary, and if they don't get you the mosquitoes will! Even with insect repellent, they can totally distract you from the business at hand. Ample supplies of fly repellent are essential, especially in June and July. Even on the major highways distances between communities and their associated services can be considerable, but venturing on to the more remote roads, especially bush roads, demands a vehicle in good mechanical condition, often ideally a four-wheel drive, as the conditions along such routes can be unpredictable and assistance a long way away. Similarly, venturing off the road, whether on foot or by canoe, demands appropriate equipment and survival skills. It is very easy to get lost in the bush, and the going can be arduous. Even on a short hike off the road a compass is essential, and hip-waders are usually necessary if venturing far into sphagnum bogs. It makes sense to contact the local Ministry of Natural Resources office before embarking on any ambitious trip, and non-residents of Ontario may need travel permits.

HIGHWAYS 11 AND 17

These two highways are very different from one other: in general Highway 17 is the preferred route. It is not only shorter and more scenic, but has a better mix of bird life. The more northerly route to Thunder Bay using Highway 11 via North Bay and Cochrane is about 1,000 km, much of it through the marginal farmland of the Clay Belts and associated stunted black spruce forest. Highway 17 is about 100 km shorter, and plays hide and seek with Lake Superior for much of the way. Because most travellers to Thunder Bay are likely to use Highway 17, it is covered first, and Highway 11 westbound appears at the end of the account.

West of Thunder Bay both routes have much to commend them. Highways 11 and 71 are about 600 km (longer if one makes the inevitable detour through Rainy River) to Kenora, while 17 is again about 100 km shorter, but wholly bypasses the fascinating areas at the south end of Lake of the Woods. I cannot visualize an Ontario birder with the time available wishing to do this, so here the highways west of Thunder Bay really are treated as a loop (west on Highway 11, east on 17).

HIGHWAY 17 WESTBOUND:
SUDBURY TO SAULT STE MARIE

The highway west of Sudbury runs through an area of rugged hills and bluffs covered by the mixed forests of the Great Lakes–St Lawrence region. For much of the distance to Sault Ste Marie the railway parallels the road, which soon passes through a series of small communities along the North Channel of Lake Huron. There is some mixed farming, which yields typical open-country species as well as Brewer's Blackbirds – the area is one of their main strongholds in the province. Some species, such as Red-headed Woodpecker and Purple Martin, reach their northern limits here. In spite of the agriculture along the road, the sideroads to the north quickly become forest roads, with the full range of mixed woodland warblers and other species. Vistas from the highway of the island-studded lake are few, but there is frequent access in the communities, and the marshes and open water along the lake can yield mergansers and other waterfowl, and an assortment of gulls and terns – mainly Ring-billed, with a few Herring Gulls, and Caspian and Common Terns. Bonaparte's Gulls appear on migration.

After Highway 6 heads south to Little Current and Manitoulin Island, it is some 40 km to the point at which Highway 17 itself starts to parallel the lake. In this section the Chutes Provincial Park is close to the road in **Massey**. The provincial parks and highway rest areas across the north – the latter recently elevated from disused gravel pits to delightful parkettes – provide the traveller with limited time an opportunity to sample habitats along the route. The first wetlands are between **Blind River** and **Iron Bridge**, where the river parallels the road and there are swampy sections and areas of marsh along the highway. Goldeneye and merganser are the usual duck on the river, and both Black Tern and Marsh Wren occur. There are more marshes at **Sowerby**.

The Sault Ste Marie area has a good population of Sandhill Cranes, and the traveller should be alert to the possibility of seeing these birds. Their distinctive bugling is often heard before the birds themselves are seen, and flight views as they leave or return to roosts are one of the most frequent ways the birds are encountered, but they may also sometimes be seen feeding in fields adjacent to the highway.

Continuing west, at **Thessalon** the alternative highway route from the north, Highway 129, intersects; it leads to Chapleau, and thence west to Wawa, and is the route to Wakami Lake Provincial Park, described below. The waterfront in Thessalon provides good vistas of the North Channel, with rocky islets offshore where Common Terns nest. To cover these turn left on to Highway 17B, which runs into town, eventually turning onto Main Street. At some 1.3 km from the main highway 17B turns right, but continue straight ahead here instead, and drive 0.1 km to Algoma Street on the left (the post office is on the corner). Turn left and drive to the dock (0.4 km), where there is waterfront viewing. Then return to follow 17B, turning left off Main Street. The road finally turns along the shoreline, past a beach where gulls and duck congregate, and then continues west to intersect with Highway 17 again.

Approaching **Bruce Mines** there are more marshes along the road (2.8 km east of Highway 638) and in town there is a small *sewage lagoon*. Turn north on Highway 638 and drive 1.2 km to the Trunk Road on the right. Turn, and then bear immediately left on a gravel road. The lagoon is on the right at 0.2 km and can be viewed from the road.

The fields just east of **Desbarats** are of interest. Just before the Desbarats sign on the highway, two small *sewage lagoons* are visible to the north across the railroad tracks. Entering the village, 0.5 km farther along, is Lake Huron Drive (coming east this road is just before the last of the marshes along the highway). It runs north 1 km to Government Road, which in turn runs east through some of the farmland north of the main highway. After about 3 km this road intersects with the Gordon Lake Road (at a stop sign), which leads back to the highway. The fields along these roads have been reliable locations for sighting Sandhill Cranes; search carefully, as the birds are often at the back of the fields, and can be difficult to see. Back along the highway there are marshes bordering the road for almost 1 km at the east end of town, and about 0.5 km farther, just past the high school, a sideroad leads south past more waterfront marshes to a boat launch.

Continuing westwards, **St Joseph Island** is south of Highway 17 on Highway 548. This highway, a gravel road for about half its length, circles the island, on which pastureland alternates with woodland. Sharp-tailed Grouse occur and Sandhill Cranes breed. Nesting sites are typically remote from roads, but the birds should be watched for feeding on neighbouring fields. The southwest end of the island is accessible by road and is a federal bird sanctuary and the historic site of Fort St Joseph. It should also be a migrant concentration point – we have seen accipiters flying across the river here. We would recommend a visit if you are birding around the Sault Ste Marie area, perhaps as part of a day on the island as a whole, since these places vary in quality with the status of migration. There are mixed woodlands and marshes at the point as well as open areas around the old fort itself.

The fastest way of getting there (it still takes 30–40 minutes) is to cross the bridge and take the right branch of Highway 548 towards Richard's Landing. A little over 7 km from the bridge the highway turns right and No. 10 Sideroad enters from the south. Turn on this sideroad and follow the paved road 12.5 km, the last section going west on P line to rejoin 548 again, now a gravel road. Continue south on 548, and drive straight ahead following the signs to the fort when the highway turns left. The road turns right at 4.2 km, then left, and right again. In all, the distance is about 38 km from the bridge.

SAULT STE MARIE

Back on the Trans-Canada, you are now approaching Sault
Ste Marie. The St Mary's River now parallels the road on the
south, and wooded hills appear to the north and west. If you
wish a side trip but do not want to wrestle with city traffic,
Hiawatha Park offers an alternative. To reach this park take
the Sault bypass (Black Road) north, and continue north when
the bypass turns left. Drive to the Old Garden River Road, a
T-intersection. Turn right and follow this road (it bears left to
become Landslide Road after about 1.4 km) to the park, which
is well marked on the corner of the 5th Line. There are the
usual amusements, but there is also an extensive area (Hiawatha
Highlands Conservation Area) of mixed woodlands with deep
ravines and a network of trails. The 5th Line leads west to
Highway 17. (Note that going this way you bypass the last
Sault service stations.)

Coming from the west, some 9 km south of the Highway 558
junction watch carefully for the 5th Line, left of the highway
(this sideroad is signposted to the Kinsmen's Park). Turn and
drive 3.8 km east to the point where the road bears sharply
right. The park is on the corner; turn left to the entrance. Leaving the park one can continue straight ahead, southwards instead of turning right to go back via the 5th Line. You will then
be on Landslide Road, which after about 2.5 km turns into
the Old Garden River Road. After about 1 km you arrive at a
Y-intersection where Old Garden River Road continues diagonally right and Black Road runs south. Turn on Black Road,
which after almost 2 km joins Highway 17 at the point it turns
east to bypass the city.

Sault Ste Marie has a deserved reputation as a migrant concentration area, and the St Mary's River downtown can provide good birding. As noted above, Highway 17 bypasses the
city around its northeast perimeter (see map 38). If you are
heading south (i.e., eastbound) continue straight ahead instead
of turning left on the bypass. The road eventually becomes
Church Street and angles southwest, to Queen Street East. Turn
right on Queen. Travellers heading west approach the city on
Wellington Street; continue past the bypass and drive to Pim
Street (about 2.8 km), which runs one way southwest, ending at
Queen Street. Turn right here.

MAP 38   Sault Ste Marie

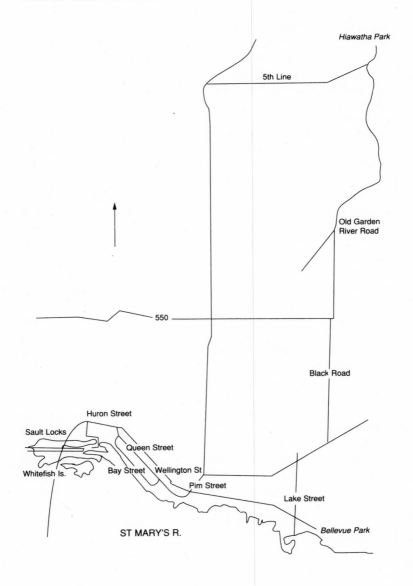

Drive west on Queen, and go eleven blocks to Huron Street. This is the well-marked access street for both the International Bridge and the *Sault Locks*. Turn left, following the signs to the locks. Drive to the end of Huron and bear left on Canal Drive, which leads (0.7 km) to the parking for the Canadian lock. This is no longer in use, and the island in the centre, called *Whitefish Island*, is readily accessible by walking across the lock gates. The island is wooded, with open areas, and the city maintains trails and boardwalks there. It is excellent for migrants; Veery and Yellow Warbler breed, and there are good views of the rapids at the west end. Access is also permitted to an adjacent southern section of island which is owned by an Indian band.

The open waters of the river host Common Goldeneye and Common Merganser in winter, and these, together with the local pigeons, may attract Gyrfalcons at that time. Bald Eagles also occur, but some perseverance may be necessary to see both species: scan the buildings and structures on both sides of the river. Bellevue Park, Station Mall at the foot of Bruce Street, and Whitefish Island are all good vantage points, but a boardwalk is under construction along the entire waterfront, and indeed these birds could turn up anywhere.

From the locks return to Queen Street and turn east. At the next block (Andrew) eastbound traffic is channelled south along Bay Street, and by keeping to the right-hand lane and bearing right one can continue east on Riverview Drive, which also affords excellent views of the river below the locks. Return to Bay and continue east. This street finally curves to rejoin Queen Street, which leads back to Highway 17 again via Church and Wellington – just follow the road signs, bearing left (north) on to Church Street to the intersection of the two roads.

To visit *Bellevue Park* continue east on Queen Street East and stay in the right lane when the Highway 17B traffic swings left. The park is at the corner of Lake Street about 3 km farther on. It too affords river views and is good for landbirds in migration. Lake Street runs north to 17B just west (0.8 km) of the bypass intersection at the east end of town.

West of the city two highways end at points near the mouth of the river. Migrant waterfowl may be viewed from the end of Highway 550 at *Gros Cap*, and Highway 565 leads south around the airport to *Pointe des Chênes Park*, a pleasant picnic and camping area on the river. There is possible waterfowl viewing here, migrant landbirds move along the shoreline, and blue-birds occur in the vicinity.

HIGHWAY 17 NORTH AND WEST OF SAULT STE MARIE

Driving north from Sault Ste Marie the road runs through mixed forest dominated by maples. The country along the route is substantially more rugged than that along Lake Huron, and after crossing the Goulais River the highway starts playing hide and seek with Lake Superior. Pines gradually become a more significant component of the forest, and rocky bluffs skirt the lakeshore. The *Batchawana Bay Road* (Highway 563, on the west) is short – 5.5 km – and has some potential as a migrant trap. At the end take the left branch of the road to the docks, and cover the surrounding shrubbery and field areas.

Lake Superior Provincial Park is an exceptional area from every point of view. It offers some of the most dramatic scenery to be seen on either of the northern Ontario Trans-Canada routes; it is fascinating botanically, the transition between mixed and boreal forest gradually occurring as one drives north; and it has a mixture of southern and northern bird species. There are ca-noe routes, nature and hiking trails, and an interpretive pro-gram in summer which can give assistance in locating birds.

In general, the northern species, such as Boreal Chickadee, are commoner in the north of the park, from Old Woman Bay north, and some southerners reach their northern limits in the area. At the south end of the park hardwoods still dominate and there's still time to record such species as Eastern Wood-Pewee, White-breasted Nuthatch, and Wood Thrush: they'll be much more difficult to locate farther north! In the Agawa Bay campground Merlins often nest, and Pine Warblers are regular.

The Frater Sideroad is the southernmost of three roads off the main highway. Its condition can be uncertain, but it leads to the Algoma Central Railroad track, where one can arrange to take a canoe up to bird the wild upper Sand River in the north-west of the park. Inquire at the park headquarters for further details. A little farther north the Awausee Lookout Trail has Black-throated Blue Warbler, and the lookout is a good spot for viewing raptors. After the Katherine Cove picnic area the highway turns inland for some 40 km. Two nature trails in this section can be worth while: the Orphan Lake Trail has a variety of habitats including hardwoods with more Black-throated Blues, and Scarlet Tanager; and the Trapper's Trail leads through a bog, with Olive-sided, Yellow-bellied, and Alder Flycatchers.

After about 20 km is the Mijinemungshing Road, the northernmost of the roads off the highway. It leads inland to the dock at Mijinemungshing Lake and canoe access to the excellent Mirimoki wetlands. A few kilometres north of here is the park headquarters, where one should check for up-to-date information. The lawns here have attracted migrants. Farther north again the Rabbit Blanket campground is good for finches.

The highway returns to the lake at the Old Woman Bay picnic area. The scenery here is spectacular, and shorebirds are possible in fall. The Nokomis Trail opposite leads through spruce forest and is good for Northern Parula. Finally the highway leaves the park, and crosses the *Michipicoten River*. The picnic area formerly located at this point has vanished, but there are still some parking areas along the riverbanks. Lincoln's Sparrows can be found here.

For an 11-km side trip to *Michipicoten Harbour*, turn left on Mission Road, 0.8 km north of the river crossing (driving south, this is 5.1 km south of the Highway 101 turn-off). The harbour itself is ugly, but the road en route passes through excellent habitat, and passerine movement along the shoreline occurs in migration times, with Bald Eagles and shorebirds possible near the rivermouth in fall. The much shorter road to the attractive *Magpie High Falls* is 3.4 km farther north (1.7 km south of the 101 turn-off) on the west of the road. It runs through heavy coniferous forest to the falls. The road is good for Hermit Thrushes.

The highway is now approaching **Wawa**. Here Highway 101 swings off to the east, passing through the town en route to Chapleau and Timmins. This offers an alternative route to Highway 17 southbound, via Highway 129. Highway 17 itself bypasses Wawa to the west, and here turns inland to wind through heavy forest en route to Heron Bay.

The main areas of interest in the Wawa area are the *sewage lagoons*. Going west, these are situated 1.2 km past the Highway 101 turn-off to town, and eastbound they are just past the

Magpie River bridge. Turn north on a gravel road (not the road
to the highway works yard, which is farther east) and the lagoons start about 0.5 km along where the road turns right. The
road runs around the two old lagoons (bear left at the fork
towards the golf course: continuing right leads into town). Behind the bank and high fence on the north at this point are two
newer lagoons, which can be viewed easily through the fence.
All these lagoons are exceptionally productive, with breeding
Gadwall and summering records of Ruddy Duck and Canvasback. The shrubby sections nearby along the river have American Bitterns and Lincoln's Sparrow, and Merlins hunt over the
entire area. In migration periods the trees along the river can be
excellent for landbird migrants. The KOA on the highway here
may not only be one of the most expensive campgrounds in the
neighbourhood but one of the best for birds anywhere!

Obatanga Provincial Park is 56 km from Wawa. The park
campground is set in tall conifers (Solitary Vireos nest) and has
an extensive network of canoe routes. Solitary Sandpipers occur.

At *White River* there are some ponds adjacent to the Information Centre on the south of the road, just west of the main
access to town. These can yield Blue-winged Teal and other
waterfowl. Some 17 km west of White River (50 km east of the
Heron Bay Road) is a smallish area of relatively new burn along
the highway, which is worth watching for woodpeckers.

By Heron Bay the highway is close to the lake again. The
road to the village is Highway 627, which also leads to
Pukaskwa National Park on the shoreline some 15 km to the
south. There are excellent trails here with an abundance of breeding birds, and Merlins breed in the campground. En route to
the park, the areas along the *Pic River* in the Heron Bay Indian
Reserve, some 12 km from Highway 17 (turn right on a rough
gravel road just before the Pic River bridge, and then bear right
when the road arrives at the river, 1.3 km in all) and the extensive dunes at the mouth of the river are good in migration, with
open country migrants such as longspurs.

Some 7 km farther west is **Marathon**, 5 km off Highway 17
via Highway 626, the largest community along this stretch of
shoreline. The townsite has yielded many migrants, including
shorebirds on the school playing fields and the golf course (the
latter 3 km from the highway on the way into town). The rail-

road, which parallels the highway and lakeshore through this section, also attracts birds; in fact, with the constant passage of bulk grain, the route has been likened to a thousand mile-long birdfeeder! The CPR line southeast from here has been exceptionally productive of rarities. It runs through open deciduous woodland along the lake, below a high ridge which channels landbird migrants. The most productive areas are along the first 4 km or so of line.

Some 19.2 km west of Marathon (2.7 km east of Neys) is a gravel road that leads to the railroad at the abandoned townsite of **Port Coldwell**, with a track to the lake. This open area can attract migrants and open country species such as longspurs, and migrant waterfowl are possible offshore.

The cooling influence of Lake Superior affects the forest composition, even to the extent of creating an alpine barren zone along the immediate shoreline, as in **Neys Provincial Park**. This fine park lies well below the highway at the mouth of Little Pic River, with sand beaches along the shoreline. There is good birding here both in summer and in migration periods, particularly in the campgrounds. Some 31 km west of Neys gate (19 km east of Airport Road at the east end of Terrace Bay) watch for a gravel sideroad which leads south about 2.4 km to the railroad line. West of here about 1 km along the tracks is another abandoned townsite, called **Jackfish**, along the shoreline. This has been a good site for vagrant landbirds: the open areas attract migrants, and there are views over the lake.

Just east of Terrace Bay is an extensive area of dwarf spruce along the highway. Terrace Bay has one of the few beaches along this section of the lake, at the mouth of the Aguasabon River. The road to it is south off the highway: turn on Kenogami Road 0.7 km west of the railroad bridge (0.6 km east of the Information Centre), then drive 0.7 km to Beach Road, turn and drive down the hill. This road passes the small sewage lagoon and the golf course. The whole area can yield interesting birds, especially in migration periods.

Continuing west, at 1.2 km from the Information Centre in Terrace Bay (some 10 km east of Schreiber) a paved road on the south leads to a generating station, where the warm water can attract waterfowl and gulls, particularly in winter. Like the other small communities along this stretch of Lake Superior, the streets and gardens of both Schreiber and Terrace Bay can yield migrants and open-country species that find the miles of forest inhospitable.

At **Schreiber** the railroad tracks are readily accessible both at the east end of town and along Brunswick Street. To reach the latter turn south on Winnipeg Street in the west section of town (past the cemetery and round the bend on Highway 17 westbound). Drive to the flashing stop light and turn right; then take the first left (Subway Street), drive under the railroad, then the first left on Winnipeg, then right along the tracks.

There is easy and frequent waterfront access to Nipigon Bay from east of **Rossport** (the townsite can be productive in migration periods) all the way to Nipigon, where Highway 11 joins 17 just east of the river. We have never observed much of note on the waters here, but the scenery is superb and it is a pleasant change from the forest. Close by Rossport is *Rainbow Falls Provincial Park*, with the birch-spruce habitats typical of this area. The Rossport campground section of this is also on the shore, and can yield migrants.

Red Rock is off the Trans-Canada on Highway 628. It is a noted place for rarities, and ideally in migration periods it may be worth while to cover the entire village on foot, particularly watching for active feeders and for birds on the lawns. Cover the rough grassland between the railway serving the paper plant and the waterfront, and the railway line to the west can also be productive. The waterfront itself, easily covered from the park there (Pull-a-log Park), can be good for duck, gulls, and shorebirds in migration, and the cliff ledges across the bay from here have nesting Peregrine Falcons.

West of Red Rock the highway becomes rather flat and uniformly forested until, near Hurkett, agriculture reappears for the first time on the Highway 17 route since Sault Ste Marie. The hamlet of **Hurkett** is located off the main highway on a loop road, Highway 582. At just over 3 km from either exit, a gravel road crosses the railway. This leads 1.4 km to the harbour, through an alder swale which has nesting Wilson's Warblers. The harbour can be very good for waterbirds in the spring, and Ospreys and Bald Eagles are frequent in the warmer months. *Hurkett Cove Conservation Area* is 3.1 km west of the west end of Highway 582 at the Wolf River Road intersection. The gravel sideroad on the south here leads 3.3 km to the area of water-front, alder swamp, and mixed forest that can be excellent in migration, and which provides a view over the waters of Black Bay. Waterfowl concentrate to the east and offshore, and there is a good mix of warblers in the woodlands, including North-ern Parula. Caspian Terns occur in summer, Bonaparte's Gulls sometimes gather on Black Bay in migration, and Parasitic Jaeger has been recorded – in July!

The country around Highway 11/17 between Hurkett and Thunder Bay is very rugged but patches of farmland continue to appear in the immediate vicinity of the road itself. The ham-let of **Dorion** is farther west. At 3.9 km from the Wolf River Road, in the centre of the village, a siteroad marked to the Community Centre/Anglican Church runs north. After about 1 km this passes through an area of open, often wet, fields which can attract gulls and shorebirds, and is another spot where rarities have turned up on occasion. Along the highway itself Brewer's Blackbirds nest under the power lines beside the road, near the end of the straight stretch of highway before the turn to Ouimet Canyon. This turn, to *Ouimet Canyon Provincial Park*, is some 5.6 km from Dorion. The park is to protect the spectacular canyon and the rare flora it harbours in its depth. It is worth seeing; and the 11 km road in passes more wet fields and wetlands. Between this siteroad and Pearl are some rock 'knobs' with scattered jack pines and spruce. Whip-poor-wills reach their northernmost limit here, and other species present include Olive-sided and Yellow-bellied Flycatchers and juncos. There are, however, no access roads.

The *Sleeping Giant Provincial Park* (formerly Sibley) turn-off is about 24 km from the canyon siteroad, 34 km from the north end of Thunder Bay, and the park itself is 38 km from the main highway, on a slow, winding secondary road (Highway 587) which is being upgraded at the time of writing. Neverthe-less, if you plan to visit here, it is a time-consuming detour. However, it is worth the time spent. It is a fascinating area for both plants and animals; be sure to get maps and bird and plant lists at the Lake Marie campsite gate (entrance fee). White-tailed deer and red fox are often encountered on the road. There are miles of hiking trails along the shoreline and up to the top of the bluffs, but there is no automobile access to views of Lake Superior in the park itself.

The park occupies most of the southern part of the peninsula, whose rugged cliffs form the famous Sleeping Giant that dominates the view from the Thunder Bay waterfront. The area is heavily forested, mainly with balsam fir, but also with major stands of white pine and swamps of black spruce and white cedar. It is on the boundary between the boreal and mixed forest regions. Hence it is excellent for the warblers of the coniferous forest: in all, twenty-seven species of warbler have been recorded (twenty nest) and Northern Parulas are common. Some more southern species can be found, and there are over two hundred species on the park checklist. The best birding areas within the park are *Pickerel Lake*, east of the highway – Olive-sided Flycatchers and Pine Warblers sometimes nest in the pines here – and the outlet of *Lake Marie Louise*, which is along the scenic drive to the west of the campground gatehouse. Peregrine Falcons nest on the cliffs of the Sleeping Giant, at the end of the peninsula.

At the southern end of the highway is the cottage community of *Silver Islet*, with open grassy areas and vistas of the lake. Migrants concentrate here during migration, the area representing one of the more accessible migrant traps along Lake Superior, and one of the best in the province. An astonishing assortment of rarities has been recorded, including Scott's Oriole, Chestnut-collared Longspur, and Black-throated Sparrow.

Southwest of here, at the foot of Thunder Cape itself, is the newly established *Thunder Cape Bird Observatory*, operating in both spring and fall. It is already making a name for itself as an exciting location for observing migration, and the province's first Violet-green Swallow recently appeared there. Visitors are welcome; however, access is via boat or an arduous hike of over three hours, so anyone planning to go should first inquire of the birders in Thunder Bay.

THUNDER BAY

This is the largest centre in northern Ontario, with a population of 110,000, and it has an active naturalists club that covers the Thunder Bay District as a whole. It publishes a useful checklist (*Checklist of the Birds of Thunder Bay District*), available from Thunder Bay Field Naturalists Club, Box 1073, Thunder Bay, Ontario P7C 4X8. One of the co-authors of this list is Nick Escott, who has provided most of the information for this section, and indeed contributed much to the chapter as a whole.

There are several interesting areas in and around the city itself. The first, **Boulevard Lake Park**, is the most accessible to the traveller and the only one that does not entail a major detour from the bypass route west via Highway 102. It is a popular city park, and very disturbed, but it does attract many migrants. Take the easternmost exit (i.e., the first travelling west) from Highway 11/17 to Thunder Bay (11B/17B, Hodder Avenue). Drive 3.2 km south to the point the road curves right to become Cumberland Avenue (see maps 39 and 40). Go across the light, cross the bridge, and turn (0.4 km) into a parking area in the park on the right. This is the south end of Boulevard Lake Park. Walk up the hill to the north and check the woods and shrubbery for migrant landbirds.

Continuing south on Cumberland, the Thunder Bay waterfront has become the best local birding area in fall through spring. **Marina Park** at the foot of Red River Road (the continuation into town of the Highway 102 bypass), is often good for duck spring and fall, and passerines in late fall, when there are fewer people about. A Townsend's Solitaire was here in December 1992, and stayed until a huge flock of Bohemian Waxwings annihilated its food supply of mountain ash berries.

Cumberland, as the main road paralleling the waterfront, merges into Water Street and eventually into Fort William Road. Watch all along the waterfront for Snowy Owls and Gyrfalcons in winter. Both species can be seen, the former at dusk, the latter in daytime. They hunt Rock Doves around the buildings of downtown Port Arthur, especially **Keskus Mall**, at Red River Road and Cumberland. Both should be watched for from here south along Fort William Road, which runs alongside the railroad tracks. The waterfront grain elevators are favourite perch sites for Gyrs, while the adjacent weed patches abound in sparrows in September and early October, including occasional rarities such as Golden-crowned Sparrow. The elevator slips attract duck and geese in the fall until freeze-up.

Just north of the Intercity Shopping Mall is the intersection with the Harbour Expressway. This road continues east into the harbour area as Main Street, and leads over a bridge to the Keefer Terminal. Just south of here along 10th Avenue is the

MAP 39   Thunder Bay North

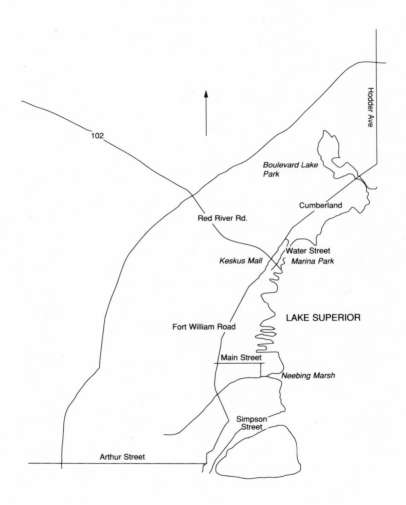

Neebing Marsh, reached by a paved path from a small parking area on the bank of the Neebing-McIntyre floodway. This is one of the few remaining grassy marshes on the waterfront, and is good for passerines and waterfowl spring and fall. Great Gray Owl has been seen here in winter.

Fort William Road eventually merges into Simpson Street, which finally turns west into Arthur Street, heading out past the airport (the short grass around the perimeter can yield open-country species) to become Highway 11/17 again.

Mission Island Marsh Conservation Area is the finest marsh in the Thunder Bay area. To reach it, from the corner of Arthur and May streets (just past the point Simpson turns west into Arthur) drive to the next light west on Arthur. This is Syndicate Avenue; turn left here and drive about 1 km to the next light, where New Vickers Street on the left crosses the river on a lift-bridge. This street merges into 106th Street, which leads east some 3 km to the conservation area. At the shore the main body of the wetland is to the south. This area is good for passerines, shorebirds, and waterfowl in spring and fall, and many un-usual species, such as American Avocet and American White Pelican, have been seen here. The wet grassy fields on the way in have Sedge Wrens and LeConte's Sparrows in the summer. Driving back over the lift-bridge, a left turn on Syndicate Avenue leads west and south through Westfort, past two old grain elevators on the banks of the Kaministiquia River (another good spot for Gyrfalcons in winter, peregrines at any season).

Chippewa Park is a productive area to the south of the city. Syndicate Avenue turns right on Francis Street: drive three blocks to Ford Street, turn left, and then bear right on Frederica. This leads to James Street (Highway 61B) and the Kaministiquia River swing bridge. Cross the bridge and continue 0.7 km to a T-intersection where 61B turns right. Turn left and follow the Chippewa Park signs 6.5 km to the park on the shore of Lake Superior. The park is worth covering for migrants, and both Cape May and Black-throated Green Warblers have nested. Off-shore here there is an extensive dredge dump area, comprising dikes and variably-filled cells. This is the city's best area for duck in spring, summer and fall. Many rarities have also been seen, including Smith's Longspur and Burrowing Owl. LeConte's Sparrows nest in the grassy fields, and a small colony of Yel-

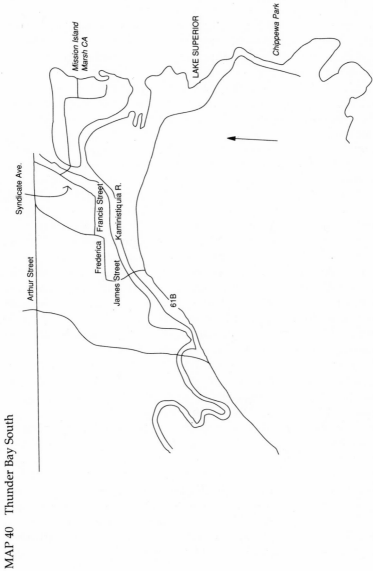

MAP 40 Thunder Bay South

low-headed Blackbirds is present most summers in the cattail marsh at the northeast corner of the landfill.

Bald Eagles are often seen in summer at Mission Island and Chippewa, and anywhere along the waterfront in spring and fall. Merlins are a common nesting species in Thunder Bay. There is always a pair in the vicinity of *Vickers Park* in Fort William, along Arthur Street, and this little park can also be good for migrants in the early morning, before the dogs and children arrive!

If you have more time and wish to visit some of the productive farming areas near Thunder Bay, a drive through Paipoonge Township can be worth while, and a pleasant change from forest birds. This area yields more southerly species such as Upland Sandpiper, Brown Thrasher, Bobolink, and Indigo Bunting, which are scarce across much of the north, but perhaps less exciting to the visitor from the south.

From Chippewa Park return to Highway 61B and continue on until it links up with Highway 61. The following drive is only one possible route to follow. The distances given are from point to point. From the 61B-61 intersection continue south past Loch Lomond Road and watch for some sewage lagoons on the left of the road (1.5 km) belonging to the *Thunder Bay Correctional Centre*, whose entrance is a short distance farther on. These lagoons can yield shorebirds and duck. (From here south to the intersection with Highway 130, the area west of Highway 61 is the *Slate River valley*. Any of the sideroads can yield interesting birds.) At 3.4 km turn west on Paipoonge 5 Sideroad. Continue to the next crossroad, which is Concession 2 (2.1 km). Turn right and check the river crossing and the wet area just beyond it (1.4 km). Then return, continuing south past 5 Sideroad, and watch for a wet area on the right (3.8 km) just before Highway 130 intersection (0.4 km). Turn right on Highway 130 and drive to the Kaministiquia River bridge (6.9 km). Park and check the river, particularly the path running down from the southeast side of the bridge, and also check the gravel pits nearby, where Northern Rough-winged Swallows have occurred. Highway 130 returns you to Highway 11/17 westbound.

An alternative road west – slow and rather rough – follows the north bank of the Kaministiquia from the village of **Rosslyn** to Stanley. From Highway 130 at the Kaministiquia bridge continue to the railroad crossing and turn left immediately on the far (north) side (1.6 km). This is the Harstone Road, which leads to the village of **Stanley** on Highway 588 (11.9 km; check the river south on 588 for waterfowl) and then continues about 3 km west to the hamlet of **Harstone**. There is excellent habitat throughout this route, but particularly around Harstone, where Eastern Bluebird and House Wren, and occasionally Warbling Vireo, occur. At Stanley you can turn north to return to Highway 11/17, just east of the **Kakabeka Falls**. Highway 588 runs some 45 km southwest from Stanley to *Whitefish Lake*, which is noteworthy as the only reliable nesting place for Red-necked Grebes in the area. The route is through more farms and mixed woodlands which have yielded many of Thunder Bay's records of southerly birds.

HIGHWAY 11 WEST FROM THUNDER BAY

Highway 11/17 continues west through mixed forest and farmland along the Kaministiquia River valley to **Shabaqua**, where 17 goes north and 11 turns left. The stretch of Highway 11 between here and Fort Frances is beautiful but relatively uniform in character. It runs through superb forests in rugged Shield country. The forests of this area are more diverse than any since the Lake Superior Provincial Park. Sugar maple and basswood reappear in forests dominated by white, red, and jack pines, together with white birches, balsam fir, and white spruce. However, this diversity is less apparent along the highway, where fine stands of boreal forest trees seem to dominate. There is one small patch of burn and several areas of recent logging along the route. Communities are scarce, and ones along the road even scarcer. This highway is one of the few places in the province where Great Gray Owls have been seen with some regularity along the road itself.

There is one major area of note. *Quetico Provincial Park* is a vast roadless wilderness area where travel is by canoe. There are two highway access points, the main one at the park's only highway campground at Dawson Trail. There is an excellent interpretive program here, and even if you do not propose to travel in the park, it is a good idea to contact the naturalists, who can often direct you to interesting locations. The other road, to the Nym Lake boat launch and headquarters complex some 29.5 km farther west, marked to Nym Lake and the Ministry of Natural Resources, can be productive; Yellow-bellied Flycatcher occurs in the bog along here. In Quetico the birds of the forests breed undisturbed. Some sixteen pairs of Bald Eagles nest every year and other raptors include Merlin and Osprey. Six species of owls occur in summer, and nests of five (Great Horned, Barred, Northern Hawk, Great Gray, and Northern Saw-whet) have been located. Both Three-toed and Black-backed woodpeckers are resident, and crossbills and Pine Siskins are usually present. Connecticut Warblers are regular summer residents along with twenty-one other warbler species. The owls are most vocal in early spring, and are not usually found at other times, although saw-whets sometimes nest in the tree cavities near the gatehouse.

As you approach **Fort Frances** you cross stretches of Rainy Lake and see more superb Shield scenery. The causeway across the lake here can be a good place for viewing Bald Eagles, and there is an eagle nest on an island to the south about halfway across. There are several lookout points on the north side of the road. West of Fort Frances you abruptly enter the agricultural areas described in the next chapter, and these continue along Highway 11 through to the Highway 71 turn-off, although this road is less interesting for the Lake of the Woods specialities than the areas farther west. The farmlands here have a distinctly western flavour, with Brewer's Blackbirds and Western Meadowlarks, and the entire area has an improbable – for Ontario – mix of bird life, with northern coniferous forest species side by side with such 'southerners' as Red-headed Woodpecker and Purple Martin.

A more productive alternative to Highway 11 here is to follow Highway 602 (River Road) westwards from Fort Frances. This road runs south from the west end of town, following Rainy River until it curves back up to rejoin Highway 11 at Emo. Along this road one should encounter a good mixture of the open-country species described in chapter 18. At **Emo**, some 35 km farther west, you have arrived back at Highway 11, 6 km east of its junction with 71. Before continuing west on 11, at the junction of 602 and 11, continue across the main highway to take the street that runs diagonally north and west past the Agricultural Society complex. At 0.5 km Adelaide Street runs north along the west side of the complex, and at its end (0.2 km) is the *sewage lagoon* drive. The south cell is readily visible from the road.

Farmland alternates with woods along the first 27 km of Highway 71 north, but after Finland one is once again in mixed forest, winding around past granite bluffs and small lakes, with periodic views of Lake of the Woods. Pelicans continue to occur along here, and indeed can sometimes be seen soaring over downtown Kenora. This country continues along Highway 17 west to Kenora.

Kenora has several attractive and well-signed parks overlooking the lake and river. However, it can be a time-consuming town to negotiate, and many persons will opt to use the 17A bypass. The highways continue through fine mixed forest similar to that described under the Highway 11 section past Quetico. There is a good mix of warblers, including Northern Parula; Bald Eagles should be watched for along the lakes, and Black-billed Magpies are possible at dumps.

HIGHWAY 17 EAST: KENORA TO THUNDER BAY

Going east from the Highway 71 intersection you will soon enter the large area of burn resulting from a major forest fire that crossed Highway 17 in 1980. This extends for some 30 km, as Highway 17 winds through the young growth in a countryside dotted with small lakes and rocky outcrops. The area should be good for more open-country birds for some time, although many of the characteristic forest species are present again. Farther east again the boreal forest reappears, as tall jack pine alternates with spruce and balsam fir, with pockets of aspen, and you will not encounter Great Lakes–St Lawrence forest again until almost at Shabaqua.

East of **Vermilion Bay** farmland appears along the highway, and continues for some 10 km east of **Dryden**, when it is largely replaced by second-growth forest to **Wabigoon**. There is further open country up Highway 105, running north from Vermilion Bay to **Red Lake**. These areas should be checked for open-country birds, including many of the same species listed in the next chapter for Rainy River. Black-billed Magpie,

Sedge Wren, Clay-colored and LeConte's Sparrow, Brewer's and Yellow-headed Blackbird, and Western Meadowlark all have occurred, although probably very locally. Mostly the farms yield Savannah Sparrows (the local accent can sound a little like a LeConte's) and Red-winged Blackbirds. When the forest resumes it is dominated by tall conifers through to Ignace, although extensive logging creates more variety and, as throughout the north, glorious stands of conifers along the road are often replaced by miles of clear cut just behind this screen. The heavy boreal forest yields all the usual warblers and northern birds.

The section from **English River** to **Upsala** has more areas of black spruce bog and small lakes. One such near English River has a pleasant roadside rest area where there should be Rusty Blackbirds and Lincoln's Sparrows. Black Spruce becomes more and more prominent around Upsala.

The largest single area of open bog along the road is some 20 km west of the village; in fact this is the only extensive area of muskeg along the entire Highway 17 route. It is also the only place on this route that we have seen Palm Warbler along the road, and Connecticut Warbler can be heard in the general area. However, the same species can be found at the edges of the heavy black spruce stands that dominate the highway east of the town, accessible by following some of the bush roads in the vicinity of the *Savannah River Resort*, and then walking out into the forest. This is prime Three-toed Woodpecker habitat, and Great Gray Owl has also been reported in the area. Persons choosing to leave the road in this way should, of course, be suitably equipped.

Near **Raith** the highway finally leaves the lowlands associated with Lac des Mille Lacs, and enters rather uniform rolling country with tall mixed forest. There is nothing else of particular note until Shabaqua, and the section thence to Nipigon is discussed above.

HIGHWAY 11 WESTBOUND: NORTH BAY TO NIPIGON

Highway 11 north of North Bay runs through mixed forests which gradually take on a more northern appearance after Tilden Lake. In the **Marten River** area there are fine stands of white pine, noted for their Hermit Thrushes. Marten River and Finlayson Point are pleasant provincial parks in this section.

At **Temagami** the *sewage lagoons* can be reached by turning east off the highway just south of the railway station on Ski Club Road. Follow this road 0.7 km to the end of the pavement, turn right, and drive a further 0.2 km, where the lagoons are straight ahead at a bend in the road. These are being upgraded at the time of writing and may lose some of their former attractiveness. Steven Road (sharp left off Ski Club Road, just over the tracks), and the Kanichee Mine Road (left off the highway 5 km north of town) are good areas to walk for warblers and other forest species.

North of **Latchford** the highway enters the mixed landscape of the Little Clay Belt, with farmland interspersed by mixed woodland. In the southern part of this area there are sewage lagoons at North Cobalt, New Liskeard, and Earlton. **North Cobalt** is east of the main highway. The small lagoon is not worth a special detour unless you are travelling on Highway 11B anyway. Follow it around to the junction of Highway 567 in town. Turn southeast onto 567 and proceed 1.6 km to Groom Drive on the right. Turn and drive 0.3 km; the lagoon is on the left. For the **New Liskeard** lagoon, continue north on Highway 11 to the junction of Highway 65. Just past this intersection (0.1 km) on the west is a gravel road, Dymond Road 3, which runs 0.6 km to dead-end at the lagoon, currently surrounded by a high fence.

Highway 65 itself runs northeast to the Quebec border. Some 23 km from its junction with Highway 11 is **Judge**, at the Blanche River crossing. In mid-April Canada Geese congregate in the wet fields south of here on both sides of the river, followed later in April by duck. The north end of Lake Temagami is noted for Brant in early June: I have no specific viewing areas to suggest, but the waterfront at Haileybury and New Liskeard gives excellent views of Wabi Bay, and farther north there are sideroads east off Highway 65 on the way to Judge.

Continuing north on Highway 11, the town of **Earlton** is just west of the highway, and the farmland around here is some of the most extensive along the entire route; watch for Brewer's Blackbirds as well as the more usual field species. Earlton sewage lagoon is rather difficult to reach. Follow the main street

(10 Avenue N) to 10th Street West. Turn west and drive about 1 km to a small cemetery on the north. The lagoon is at the back of this and to the west.

South of Englehart, a drive in to *Skeleton and Clear Lakes* off Highway 569 can be productive in summer. From Highway 11 drive 10 km east on Highway 569 to the point where it turns south. Turn north on a good gravel road, following it around for 5 km to a T-intersection at the top of a rise, where the road turns right. Turn left and drive 2.2 km to Clear Lake, then continue 2.1 km to the Clear and Skeleton Lake access points. On this route the highway crosses typical Clay Belt farmland, and the gravel roads run through excellent mixed woodland habitats. Osprey and Common Loons occur on the lakes and Common Ravens nest on the cliffs at Skeleton Lake. Watch for red foxes in the farm areas; they are common on the Little Clay Belt.

Back on the main highway again, the *Englehart lagoons* are probably the most productive ones in this region. They can be reached by turning east on First Street at the south end of town (0.5 km from the river bridge). Drive 1.1 km, crossing the tracks, to Lagoon Road. Turn left and drive 0.8 km to park at the far end of lagoons. The woodlands surrounding these yield sparrows and warblers – the shrubby areas have Lincoln's Sparrow – and the lagoons themselves waterbirds. Also at Englehart is the excellent *Kap-Kig-Iwan Provincial Park*. It follows the deep river valley and has a variety of habitats, some quite southern in character, at the north edge of the Hudson–St Lawrence forest. Some southern species, such as White-breasted Nuthatch and Northern Oriole, nest here at their northern limits.

The localities around **Kirkland Lake** are not worth a detour, but this rather populous area at the north end of the Little Clay Belt is a destination for many travellers. Highway 66 runs through Kirkland Lake to the Quebec border, and traverses some varied habitats. At the west limits of **Swastika** is the well-sign posted Culver Lake Park on the south. There are mixed habitats here, including a spruce swamp which is good for birds year-round. The river, 0.6 km farther east, often has a few waterfowl on the north of the road.

Continuing east towards Kirkland Lake, the mine slime deposits on the north entering town can attract shorebirds in season; and the town dump is on the south side of the highway 11.1 km from the railroad crossing at the east end of town. This attracts scavenging birds and can be particularly interesting in winter. East of **Larder Lake**,1.5 km from the Highway 624 junction, Station Road on the north passes through some good wetlands 0.5-1 km from the highway. Proceeding east a further 8 km, the highway itself passes some further areas of slime deposit to the south. Continuing along Highway 11, between **Kenogami Lake** and Matheson, the next area covered here, the agriculture becomes more limited and the road is more forested. This is now boreal forest, although it is more diverse than that farther north, and there are considerable stands of pine.

At **Matheson** turn east off Highway 11 onto Highway 101 east, and drive 0.7 km to the Black River bridge. Depending on water levels, there may be flats to the south where gulls and duck loiter, and the marshy edges of the river should be scanned for waterbirds. Return to Highway 11 and cross it, driving 0.6 km west to an old gravel pit on the right. Just east of this is a small pond, which also often has gulls and duck present. Highway 101 westbound to Timmins intersects with Highway 11 north of Matheson. However, those using Highway 144 from Sudbury as an alternative route to Highway 11 north will cut the corner by using Highway 67, which joins 11 farther north (see Timmins below).

The agricultural areas around **Iroquois Falls** alternate with extensive deciduous woodlands of birch and poplar, but north of here Highway 11 leaves the Little Clay Belt, and the 40 km between the intersection of Highway 578 and the town of Cochrane passes through areas of boreal forest with black spruce and tamarack bogs. The tall coniferous forest along here has yielded finches, including White-winged Crossbills, the more open areas Connecticut and Palm Warblers, and the bushy sections Lincoln's Sparrow.

Cochrane itself is in the Clay Belt proper. It is well situated for covering this area, and has a useful finding guide and annotated checklist available (see chapter 19). It also is a jumping-off point for flights into the James Bay goose camps and for the Ontario Northland Railway's Polar Bear Express to Moosonee. To the north of town is *Lillabelle Lake*, long noted for its prairie-like quality and bird life. In fact, it is sometimes difficult to believe one is in northern Ontario there! To reach it take Highway 579, which is the road running north into town from Highway 11 as the latter turns west. Follow 579, which itself turns west and then, outside town, north again. Continue north on Lillabelle Lake Road when Highway 579 again turns west. This road runs north 5 km to the north end of the lake, and then curves around the end. Just as the road starts this curve there is a concession road on the left that leads over the railroad tracks. There is a sizeable wetland 1.4 km along this road, with several species of duck possible on the pond there. Another good pond is just north of Lillabelle Lake, and it can be reached by walking north along the railroad tracks that parallel the main road for a short distance at this point. The poplar forest here can also be good for landbirds. Continue around the curve, where there is excellent lake viewing from the road. A further 2.8 km east is the next sideroad, Genier Road, now running south. Turn south, drive 2.5 km, and turn right on a sideroad just past Cochrane airport. This road leads to a seaplane base on the lake, and affords further views of its southeast end. Lake specialities include Red-necked Grebe, Ruddy and other duck, and Black Terns. Bonaparte's Gulls are regular, and good numbers of duck concentrate in spring and fall.

Return to the main road and continue south towards Cochrane. At 2.4 km is a crossroad: to the west this leads (about 1 km) to a sideroad on the south leading past the dump to the golf course. Behind the dump is a marsh where Pied-billed Grebe, American Bittern and Sora breed. This marsh offers the first open water in spring, when it becomes a concentration point for migrants. To the east of Genier Road, after a jog, the cross-road leads 0.2 km to the sewage lagoons. These are on the right, behind some garbage bins. They have yielded both duck and shorebirds in season. Genier Road itself leads back into town.

The open country around Cochrane is good for open-country species in migration. Rough-legged Hawk, Snowy and Short-eared Owls, and shorebirds can be found at this time. The area is perhaps most noteworthy for Sandhill Cranes, which stage on the fields in mid to late April and again in later August through September. Typically groups of ten to twenty birds occur, but flocks of up to two hundred have been recorded.

One of the better locations for finding Spruce Grouse near Cochrane is at Wally Creek. This area is some 20 km east of town on Highway 652. Watch for a small parking lot and a sign for the Wally Creek Drainage Project on the north of the road. From here a nature trail runs through the heart of a black spruce forest, where the grouse are common. A nesting platform for Great Gray Owl has also been erected within sight of the trail.

Clay Belt farmland lines the next 20 km of Highway 11. Typically this now consists of small fields, many often reverting to bush, alternating with areas of black spruce bog and willow-alder swamp. Forest is never far from view – generally at the back of the next field from the road. This farmland usually has a rather limited range of bird life; many of the familiar field birds farther south, such as meadowlarks, are rare or absent. Both Brewer's Blackbirds and Bobolinks can occur, and wetter sections should yield snipe. Much habitat seems suitable for LeConte's Sparrow, but there are very few records from this region. Sandhill Cranes are to be expected: watch the rear of the larger fields carefully for these birds, which can be hard to see.

Rivers and ponds add diversity, and a few have edges of cattail and sedge, which may yield American Bittern. The ponds may have a few duck, usually Mallards, but sometimes Blue-winged Teal and Lesser Scaup, although in general the sewage lagoons are far more productive. These may also yield American Wigeon, and possibly Wood Duck, Green-winged Teal, or American Black Duck, but the commonest duck of the area (and indeed across the north generally) is Common Goldeneye. Ring-necked Ducks prefer more wooded lakes, but may be present, and Hooded Mergansers (indeed all the mergansers) seem to prefer the rivers.

Some 15 km west of Cochrane is *Greenwater Provincial Park*, 14 km north of Highway 11. The park is situated on an esker overlooking a series of lakes surrounded by conifers. We have noted Solitary Sandpiper here, Ruffed Grouse are common, and Wilson's Warblers and Lincoln's Sparrows breed.

Between Cochrane and **Smooth Rock Falls** the character of the forest is similar to that south of Cochrane. This includes one of the best stretches of black spruce forest along either highway, and the proportion of tamarack is high. Listen for such species as Cape May, Palm, Bay-breasted, and Connecticut Warbler. The forests in this area also have populations of both Great Gray and Boreal Owls. Hope of finding them is slim, however, unless one comes in very early spring prepared to spend time tracing their calls. From Smooth Rock Falls to Hearst, and indeed for about 8 km east of there, much of the country along the road is again devoted to marginal agriculture.

Two small communities in this stretch boast sewage lagoons. The one at **Fauquier** is quite accessible, being behind the first houses on the north of the highway at the east end of town. To reach the lagoon at **Moonbeam**, take the first street north at the east end of town (Leonard Avenue), then right again at once onto Cimon Drive. Continue 0.4 km, when the road ends at René Brunelle Avenue; the lagoon is to the east.

At Moonbeam Highway 581 runs north 11 km to *Rene Brunelle Provincial Park*. The accessible parts of the park are set in a diverse second-growth forest on Remi Lake. It has yielded some interesting records, including Bonaparte's Gulls and Orange-crowned Warblers in summer, and it has a good diversity of breeding birds. It is unlikely that the gulls nest on Remi Lake itself, which is large and very disturbed, but it is possible that they do so on some of the smaller, less accessible lakes in the vicinity.

Kapuskasing is the largest community on Highway 11 between North Bay and Thunder Bay, and it has quite an extensive *sewage lagoon* complex. Entering town, turn north at the light at Brunelle Road (driving east, this is about 2 km from the bridge over the river), and continue past the arena to Brunetville Road. Turn right here, and the lagoons are on the right about 1 km along this road. Another small community with a sewage lagoon is **Val Rita**, west of Kapuskasing. The lagoon is also at the east end of town, hidden in a woodlot. Take the first street north entering the village, then the first right, and follow this street to its end, where the lagoon is on the right.

Entering **Hearst**, there are gravel roads on both sides of the Mattawishquia River crossing. That on the northwest side follows the river closely for some distance through pleasant mixed habitats, and waterfowl such as goldeneye and Hooded Merganser can be seen. For the Hearst *lagoon*, turn south at the light in the centre of town on Highway 583. Drive 1.4 km to the point the highway turns right. Turn left here on Gaspesie Street, past École Louisbourg, and drive 1.5 km to the next cross-road, Begin Road. Turn right (south) and continue 1 km to the long drive along the side of the lagoons on the right. These have been most productive of waterfowl.

Fushimi Lake Provincial Park, west of Hearst and 16 km north of the highway on a gravel road, has similar habitats to René Brunelle Park, but the forests have more coniferous species. There is a good mix of nesting birds and Bonaparte's Gulls have been recorded here too, but again the birds are more likely to nest on one of the smaller lakes adjacent.

Highway 11 west of Hearst, and especially west of the Highway 631 junction, enters a long stretch where the forest is unbroken by settlements. Initially the land continues flat and the forest composition is spruce, tamarack, and aspen, but west of the **Thunder Bay District line** the country becomes more rolling and jack pine, white birch, and balsam fir become more common. This is geographically the northernmost part of the highway, and the fine forest should be checked for the more northern species noted above.

The shore of Long Lake just west of **Longlac** is good for migrant shorebirds, and the marshes on the north of the highway there can yield waterfowl, Rusty Blackbirds, and the occasional Yellow-headed Blackbird. There is a colony of Common Terns on the lake. From Longlac to **Jellicoe** the highway passes through quite diverse boreal forest with a scattering of small lakes, each with its pair of loons or Ring-necked Ducks. North of Jellicoe the logging roads form a network going up to the CNR line; the more northerly roads of this area sometimes yield Sharp-tailed Grouse. Possible nesting species along these roads include Bonaparte's Gulls on the occasional shallow lake, and Greater Yellowlegs in roadside ditches.

Past Jellicoe spruce again becomes the main constituent of the forest, and this continues south and west to about Lake Nipigon Provincial Park. About 1 km before **Beardmore** Highway 580 runs some 13 km west to a campground on the shores of Lake Nipigon. The waters of this huge and beautiful lake usually seem empty, but American White Pelicans, Double-crested Cormorants, Bald Eagles, and Ospreys occur. Just outside Beardmore itself, immediately before the bridge crossing the river at beginning of town, the *sewage lagoons* are accessible by taking the gravel road on the west. Bear left almost at once, and again in 0.5 km; the lagoons are 0.5 km along on the left. There is some marsh vegetation here, and duck nest.

At Beardmore the highway curves more sharply southwards towards Nipigon and Lake Superior. South of the town *Lake Nipigon Provincial Park* is on an inlet of the lake, and a short hike provides views of the main lake to the northwest. The full expanse of Lake Nipigon is not visible from the highway at any point, but this now starts through the rugged country along the lake's southeast shoreline, prior to dropping down along the valley of the Nipigon River. Scenic, rolling country finally gives way to some of the most spectacular scenery along either Trans-Canada route, with steep bluffs bordering the road for almost 20 km. Finally the highway runs along Lake Helen for some 10 km, with mergansers and other waterfowl in the shallows, and Herring Gulls nesting on the rocky islets.

Just east of **Nipigon**, Highway 11 joins Highway 17 westbound along the north shore of Lake Superior. The two highways continue together as far as Shabaqua, some 50 km west of Thunder Bay, and the details on this stretch of road appear under the Highway 17 account.

OTHER AREAS IN THE NORTH

The routes just described do not cover the full network of major communication links in the north. Wawa and Iroquois Falls are linked by Highway 101, serving the communities of Chapleau, Foleyet, and the Timmins region. From this route Highways 129 to the west and 144 on the east both run south. The former provides an alternative route to Highway 17 through Sault Ste Marie, and Highway 144 from Sudbury is an a good alternative to the slow trip along Highway 11. Both highways have reputations as a good birding roads, and are less busy than the usual routes.

Chapleau, at the junction of Highways 101 and 129, has two noteworthy provincial parks nearby. *The Shoals*, west on 101 from the town, is outstanding for its northern wetland communities around the Prairie Bee River, and associated bird life. *Wakami Lake*, south off Highway 667, off 129 some 50 km southeast of Chapleau, is close to the boundary between the boreal and mixed forests, and has an excellent mix of bird life, including all the usual northern species. Yellow-bellied Flycatchers are common, and Northern Hawk-Owl and Solitary Sandpiper have occurred. The 65 km Height of Land Trail rings the lake, but a boat is probably the most effective way of seeing the park.

Highway 144 is one of our own favourite highways for northern birding. Once you are north of **Cartier** (and also past all the gas stations) the country is wild and there is excellent birding. We have noted Connecticut Warblers along here in heavy woodland beside the lakes – which is quite different habitat than is associated with this species elsewhere in the province. The best birding is south of **Gogama**.

Timmins is located towards the east end of Highway 101. It is the base for commercial air flights into the far north, but also has some good birding in the immediate vicinity. To the west in Mountjoy Township is a farm area that can be good for open-country birds, and Highway 576 leads some 15 km north to *Kamistokia Lake*, with a good mix of forest and wetland species, including Veery.

Highway 101 east from Timmins has a few lakes along the road, the best for birding being *Porcupine Lake*, about 9 km east of town and between South Porcupine and **Porcupine**. At the east end the river crosses the road, to enter the lake to the south, and there are extensive marshes on the north side. This is 0.3 km past the Cochrane-Temiskaming Resources Centre on the north of the road. *Bob's Lake* is just east of here, again on the south of the road. There is a small sewage lagoon near its outlet into Bob's Creek, at the southwest end of the lake. Between the junctions of Highways 610 and 67 along Highway 101 is a high bridge over the Rupertshouse River. A picnic area at the northeast end offers good views of the river, which may have waterbirds present.

Kettle Lakes Provincial Park is 3 km north on Highway 67 from its intersection with 101. The woodland and many small lakes here are good for birding, and Solitary Sandpipers occur.

The highways to such locations as Manitouwadge and Hornepayne all traverse forested lands and offer further opportunities to observe the birds of the northern forests.

PICKLE LAKE

Highway 599 to Pickle Lake is the farthest north it is possible to travel by road in Ontario. Pickle Lake itself is also served by Air Quebec. The highway is surfaced, and some 300 km long. At Pickle Lake a gravel road continues north some 237 km further to **Windigo Lake**, well beyond 52°N. Roy Smith drove this road in July 1985, and recorded eighty-seven species. The following notes are based on his account, as given in his article 'All Aboard for Pickle Lake.' in *Birdfinding in Canada* 7, no. 2 (1987): 8-11, and 7, no. 3 (1987): 20-22.

This road was lightly travelled and offered good boreal forest birding. There is gasoline at Pickle Lake and also at Windigo Lake, but it is expensive. Canoe access points and campsites are both reasonably plentiful. Roy Smith's article gives a useful table of physical features along the road, measured from the Thierry Mine Road turn-off, some 8 km north of Pickle Lake. Sites with potential for both camping and boat launching were identified at 19.3, 90.3, 102.5, 144.7, 162.9, 181.7, and 196.1 km. However, the up-to-date conditions of the route should be checked with the Ministry of Natural Resources before setting out.

The most interesting areas of the Windigo Lake road were some 70 km from Pickle Lake, beyond the Otoskwin River crossing. Least Flycatcher, Swainson's Thrush, Hermit Thrush, Tennessee Warbler, Nashville Warbler, Magnolia Warbler, Yellow-rumped Warbler, Ovenbird, and White-throated Sparrow were the commonest species on the route. Waterfowl were scarce and both Solitary and Spotted Sandpipers were seen regularly. Spruce Grouse and Gray Jays were quite frequent, but the other boreal specialties such as Boreal Chickadee and Black-backed and Three-toed Woodpeckers were rather elusive. Species not usually present farther south included Greater Yellowlegs, Bonaparte's Gull, Orange-crowned Warbler, Palm Warbler, and Fox Sparrow. The last two species were found in extensive tracts of young jack pine regeneration. One suggested area to investigate would be the section 82-86 km north of Pickle Lake, including the track to Lysander Lake.

THE NORTH COASTLINE

A trip to **Moosonee** is the easiest way to reach arctic tidewater, although the community itself is located some 20 km upriver from James Bay. From late June to the beginning of September the Ontario Northland Railway operates a daily excursion train, the Polar Bear Express, to Moosonee from Cochrane. At other times of year the train runs less regularly. There is free parking at Cochrane station and the train leaves at 8.30 a.m., the trip taking about four and a half hours. The return train leaves at 5.00 p.m., arriving in Cochrane at 9.20 p.m. There is no train on Fridays, and outside this period the train runs three times a week and the trip takes longer. For about half the journey the train crosses the huge muskeg of the Hudson Bay Lowland, and provides the only easy access to this area. It is desolate country, with miles of stunted black spruce bog; it is also fascinating, and you will be busy looking for Sandhill Cranes, Northern Hawk-Owls, and the more common species (such as bitterns and Red-tailed Hawks) that you can hope to see from the train.

At Moosonee there are several areas of note. The town itself, and the townsite of *Moose Factory* across the Moose River, yield open and edge habitats; west of the railway and airfield is boggy spruce woodland. *Tidewater Provincial Park* has trails in spruce forest, and the river itself has tide flats. Downriver there is *Shipsands Island*, which is noted as one of the best places to see LeConte's and Sharp-tailed Sparrows, and Yellow Rails. It, and the river mouth generally including the mainland just north of Shipsands, is a fine place for observing migration in progress – early September is a good time to visit for this purpose.

Species that have been reported from the Moosonee area in summer and not already mentioned above include Sharp-tailed Grouse, Arctic Tern, Marbled Godwit, Three-toed and Black-backed Woodpeckers, (Gray-cheeked Thrush), Northern Shrike, Orange-crowned Warbler, (Blackpoll Warbler), Fox and White-crowned Sparrows, Pine Grosbeak, and (Common Redpoll). This does not mean you will see even half of these because most of them are quite thinly distributed, and those in parentheses are likely not even regular in occurrence. Noteworthy among the commoner breeding birds are American Bittern, several species of duck, Northern Harrier, Common Snipe, Herring Gull, Alder Flycatcher, Tree Swallow, Gray Jay, Common Raven, Ruby-crowned Kinglet, Swainson's Thrush, Philadelphia Vireo, Tennessee Warbler, Yellow Warbler, Wilson's Warbler, and Lincoln's Sparrow. During migration it seems almost anything can turn up, as the coast is a major flyway in autumn for waterfowl, shorebirds, and such northern specialities as Gyrfalcons, and also seems to be the place that many misplaced southern, western, or even Asiatic species end up. Canada's first-ever Little Stint was noted in this area. There is a small but significant late autumn movement of true pelagic species along the shoreline as well.

More than casual observation of such movement entails something of an expedition, and locations on **Hannah Bay** east of the Moose estuary may be more suitable than the Moosonee area itself. The Cree Indians operate goose-hunting camps along the bay and can provide the expertise and facilities needed for a trip to such places as *Netitishi Point*, some 20 km east of the Moose. Knowledgeable guides are essential, as the waters of James Bay are hazardous and the coast is dangerous. Enormous numbers of shorebirds – principally Semipalmated Sandpipers and Red Knot – gather on the vast tide flats, and most of the North American population of Hudsonian Godwits is believed to assemble here. Other common shorebirds include American Golden Plover, yellowlegs, Whimbrel, Sanderling, and Pectoral Sandpiper. Major flights of Snow Geese and Brant occur, and Ross's Goose is an irregular visitor.

For less ambitious undertakings, travel across and down river is by hiring a Rupert's House canoe and Indian guide at the waterfront, and camping is possible on the mainland north of Shipsands, at Tidewater, and indeed on any suitable area of crown land. If you plan to camp at all, remember you will have to be wholly self-sufficient, and it is prudent to keep the Ministry of Natural Resources advised of your plans (non-residents of the province need a permit). There are also two lodges in town, operated by Ontario Northland. Trips at the height of the tourist season may present problems in lining up transportation, since all the Indians tend to be tied up running groups back and forth to Moose Factory, a more remunerative activity than taking one down the estuary! Further details on fares, schedules, and planning can be obtained from Ontario Northland Railway Services, 65 Front Street, Toronto, Ontario M5J 1E6; (416) 314-3750, or in Ontario only, 1-800-268-9281. For Tidewater Provincial Park, and wilderness travel information, contact Ministry of Natural Resources, Moosonee Area Office, Box 190, Moosonee, Ontario, P0L 1Y0; (705) 336-2987.

The Hudson Bay coast offers birders the enticing array of nesting species listed at the beginning of this chapter, and its potential for migration watching is virtually unknown. Just looking at the map suggests that points such as Cape Henrietta Maria could make some southern Ontario hot-spots look bland by comparison.

There are commercial flights via Air Quebec from Timmins to **Peawanuck** and **Fort Severn**, which are Indian villages near the coast along the Winisk and Severn rivers respectively. These can provide jumping-off points for expeditions to and along the coast. If you wish to visit areas far from these communities – the Cape Henrietta Maria sections of *Polar Bear Provincial Park*, for example, itself larger than the province's five southernmost counties put together – then you will have to charter your own aircraft and camp on the tundra. Although such trips are undertaken more and more frequently, it should be emphasized that they are not to be undertaken lightly. The coast is dangerous, and there are no readily accessible sources of assistance in an emergency. It is essential to make arrangements with the Ministry of Natural Resources prior to undertaking such an expedition, and if you plan to do much actual travelling on the ground you may be required to use the services of a guide. Cost, however, is probably the main factor inhibiting more visits to this region.

MAP 41   Rainy River and Lake of the Woods

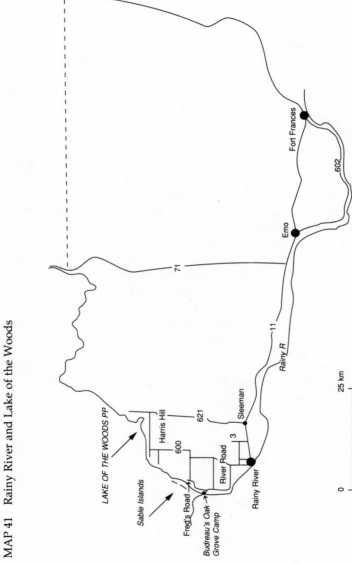

18 Rainy River and Lake of the Woods

West of Fort Frances the character of the landscape changes sharply from a rugged country of mixed forests and lakes to flat farmland interspersed with mixed bush. This southern corner of extreme western Ontario is not only remote from the rest of the province geographically; its bird life is very different as well. With average summer temperatures similar to those at Toronto, many southern birds which do not appear in most of the north do occur here. Poor drainage and severe winters produce boreal islands of black spruce bog, with associated northern birds. Most striking to the visitor from southern Ontario, however, is the presence of some prairie birds and other animals that are rare or absent elsewhere in the province. The marshes of Lake of the Woods are host to Yellow-headed Blackbird colonies, and Ontario's largest colony of American White Pelicans breeds on the lake's islands. Black-billed Magpies occur regularly, American Avocets and Western Kingbirds have nested, and Sprague's Pipits have been recorded.

The area's remoteness from the population centres of the south has meant that it has been poorly covered by birders, even though its unusual character and rich diversity was recognized as long ago as 1929. Not only do the breeding birds differ from those elsewhere in the province but the mix of migrants is quite different too. Much remains to be found out about the seasonal bird changes here; and many surprises still can be expected. Birding in the area has been described in detail in Dave Elder's

'A Birder's Guide to the Rainy River Area,' *Ontario Birds* 9, no. 1 (April 1991), on which most of the following is based, with gratitude.

The northern character of the area is strong, and the wooded areas have a similar, but richer, mix of species to those described for the rest of northern Ontario. Ravens are widespread, Black-backed and Three-toed Woodpeckers are elusive residents, and both Gray Jays and Boreal Chickadees occur. A number of species that are regular in summer in southern Ontario reappear in the extreme west of the province, or (asterisked below) north of the Minnesota border between Rainy River and Thunder Bay:

Wood Duck
Turkey Vulture
Mourning Dove*
Whip-poor-will* (rare)
Red-headed Woodpecker
Eastern Wood-Pewee*
Great Crested Flycatcher*
Purple Martin*
Northern Rough-winged
  Swallow* (rare)
White-breasted Nuthatch
House Wren*

Marsh Wren*
Wood Thrush
Gray Catbird*
Brown Thrasher*
Loggerhead Shrike (rare)
Yellow-throated Vireo
Warbling Vireo
Pine Warbler
Scarlet Tanager*
Indigo Bunting*
Northern Oriole*

Of these species, Loggerhead Shrikes do not appear to have been seen on visits in recent years. Two additional species, Eastern Screech-Owl and Golden-winged Warbler, have also been recorded and may sometimes breed.

The following species, mainly with western ranges, have been reported in larger numbers from this area in summer than from elsewhere in Ontario:

American White Pelican
Bald Eagle
Sharp-tailed Grouse
Yellow Rail
Sandhill Crane
Franklin's Gull (non-breeding)
Wilson's Phalarope
Short-eared Owl
Black-billed Magpie

Sedge Wren
Connecticut Warbler
Clay-colored Sparrow
LeConte's Sparrow
Sharp-tailed Sparrow
Western Meadowlark
Yellow-headed Blackbird
Brewer's Blackbird

The flora also has some western components, and Franklin's ground squirrel and white-tailed jack rabbit occur, their only Ontario stations.

Most naturalists' visits have been between mid-April and mid-October. The time of ice going out on Lake of the Woods appears to vary widely in May, but open water may occur along the channel between the mainland and the Sable Islands even when the rest of the lake is frozen. Information on the ice conditions at a specific time can be obtained from the Fort Frances District Office of the Ministry of Natural Resources.

Good waterfowl concentrations occur in April and early May, and there is hawk movement, including good numbers of Rough-legged Hawks. Sandhill Cranes can also be expected. Shorebirds in late May include both Marbled and Hudsonian Godwits, rare elsewhere in spring, and Harris's Sparrows can be looked for in sparrow flocks. June is the best period for breeding birds. By mid-July shorebirds are moving again, and large numbers are possible along the lakeshore in early August, when huge concentrations of Franklin's Gulls can occur in the Sable Islands channel. September brings hawk movement. By late September and early October flocks of Sandhill Cranes can be seen, and Harris's Sparrows can be relatively common in flocks of White-crowneds. Peak passerine movement is in May, and again in August and September. Western species, and northern birds that migrate principally through the prairies, have turned up much more frequently in this region than farther east, and with additional coverage many new records can be expected.

CAUTIONS AND HAZARDS

Most of the areas described here are private property; naturalists should use consideration and respect signs. Boating or canoeing on the Lake of the Woods can be hazardous, as it is a shallow, rough lake, full of dead-heads from logging days, and the weather can change abruptly. There are the familiar northern Ontario clouds of mosquitoes and blackflies, especially in June, when ticks can also abound in the wild rice and other vegetation. The area is indeed remote; accommodations are quite limited, and both motels and restaurants are scarce.

WHERE TO GO

There are two main highways to the Rainy River area. From the east Highway 11 from Thunder Bay crosses the southern portion of the region as far as the town of Rainy River. From the north the link with the Kenora area and the main Highway 17 Trans-Canada route is Highway 71, which ends at Highway 11 about halfway between Fort Frances and Rainy River. The main areas of interest are west of Highway 71 and north of 11, and all the areas described here lie south and west of Lake of the Woods Provincial Park and the main road between it and Sleeman on Highway 11(Highway 621). However, Highway 602 between Fort Frances and Emo, passing through similar habitat, is described in chapter 17; and it must be re-emphasized that the entire region is relatively poorly known, so other locations could be fruitful as well.

When driving on the roads of the area generally, a careful watch should be kept for Sandhill Cranes in open areas, including hay fields, and for both Long and Short-eared Owls in the evenings. Sharp-tailed Grouse and Black-billed Magpies can occur anywhere. Listen in summer for Connecticut Warblers in poplar woods, and in the farming and edge habitats watch and listen for Cliff Swallows, Eastern Bluebirds, Clay-colored Sparrows, and Brewer's Blackbirds. Most meadowlarks are Western, but the occasional Eastern is reported. Sedge Wrens and LeConte's Sparrows favour wet fields with a good growth of coarse grasses.

The first location is 3.3 km west of **Sleeman**, 6.6 km east of Rainy River, where Worthington Road 3 runs north over the railroad tracks. This has been one of the most productive roads in recent years, with Marbled Godwit, Western Kingbird, and Sprague's Pipit all recorded in the fields north of the tracks. Drive north to the first sideroad (1.6 km), and turn left. (This is Byrne's Road, although it is unmarked at this end.) Continue 6.6 km to Government Road, stopping regularly to watch and listen. Then turn left (south).

The *Rainy River sewage lagoons* are down a sideroad 1.3 km on the left. Coming from Rainy River, the lagoons can be reached by taking an odometer reading at the MTC Patrol Yard and Ontario Provincial Police Station on the south of the road as you enter town. Drive 0.7 km and turn north on Government Road. Drive 0.3 km and turn west on the gravel road which leads (0.5 km) to the lagoons. Soras and an excellent variety of shorebirds and ducks can be expected here in late May, and enormous numbers of Wilson's Phalaropes have been seen. Ruddy Ducks have bred, and Eared Grebes have occurred in early summer.

On returning to Government Road, a left-hand turn leads north on one of the more interesting sideroads, which joins Highway 600 after about 7 km. However, on the present route, turn left at 1.3 km on to Byrne's Road, and continue 1.6 km to Highway 600. Turn right on 600, which is the main highway through the areas of greatest interest. After 3.3 km turn west on to *River Road*. After about 4 km the overgrown fields on the south have had good numbers of Sedge Wrens and LeConte's Sparrows. In approximately 6 km from Highway 600, River Road reaches Rainy River itself. The oaks and hardwood bush here can be good for migrant landbirds, and the river for gulls and other waterfowl. Yellow-throated Vireos occur. River Road then continues northwards. At about 2.5 km from the river there is a microwave tower to the east, and an old barn opposite, where magpies nest. This is a good location to stop and cover the surrounding fields for grouse and cranes.

At 11.3 km from the highway, River Road crosses *Wilson Creek* and bears left. Cover the creek at this point, and west of here to its mouth at the river, for waterbirds and migrant landbirds. Wood Thrushes occur in the deciduous woodlands. The road running east from here is the Wilson Creek Road. The large fields along it are good for Sandhill Cranes and Sharp-tailed Grouse, as well as the other field species of the area. Then continue north on River Road 1.8 km to the sideroad to *Budreau's Oak Grove Camp*, which is 2.1 km west on the river, situated in delightful oak woodlands. The camp is an excellent spot for landbird migrants and has good views of the river. It is also one of the few places offering accommodation in this area (May to November). From here, continue north on River Road, which turns east and crosses McInnis Creek, then goes briefly north, and finally runs east again to rejoin Highway 600, some 30 km from the initial turn-off.

One of the areas currently good for Yellow Rails is in the

marsh north of the end of *Fred's Road*. This is the small sideroad on the north just after River Road turns east the second time. Drive 0.8 km to its end, and then left 0.1 km to a wet field on the right. (Do not block the entrance to the field.) Park and walk northwest towards the tall *Phragmites* visible at the far side, and continue into the marsh (the latter section of the walk is strenuous). Rails call most consistently in the evening. You will need rubber boots, a flashlight, and lots of insect repellent to walk into the marsh. It is also the home of Sedge Wrens, LeConte's Sparrows and, in the *Phragmites*, Sharp-tailed Sparrows. Yellow Rails, Sedge Wrens, and LeConte's Sparrows are fussy about water levels. Ideally the rails need about 15 cm of water, although the acceptable range of water depth seems to be between 3 and 30 cm. If the area is too wet or dry the birds should be sought in suitable habitat elsewhere.

South on Highway 600 there is a huge tamarack bog on the east and large fields on the west. These are habitat for Short-eared Owls in the evening, as well as Sandhill Cranes, grouse and Yellow-headed Blackbirds.

Highway 600 northbound runs a short distance east from its intersection with River Road and then turns north. The abandoned white school buildings of the almost invisible community of *Harris Hill* are 9.7 km from the intersection. A small dirt road here, Kreger's Road, which finally degenerates to little more than a cart track, runs west 5.2 km to the shore. The shoreline at this point opens on the channel between a line of sandy islands, the *Sable Islands*. These are excellent for shorebirds – Piping Plover, American Avocet, and Marbled Godwit all occur – and the channel between the two islands, normally joined by a sandbar, can yield pelicans, cormorants, duck, shorebirds, and gulls, including thousands of Franklin's Gulls in August. There are colonies of both Double-crested Cormorants and Common Terns on the lake, so these birds can occur in large numbers, as can Black Terns. Forster's Terns also should be looked for. The two ends are usually the most productive, and the long beaches on the lake side are undisturbed and are the best for walking. It is almost 10 km in all from end to end.

A boat can be launched here to visit the islands, or alternatively boats or canoes can be rented, or transportation arranged, at Oak Grove Camp or Windy Bay Lodge (below). Note the comments at the beginning of the chapter about the hazards of boating on the lake, and also note that the islands are very exposed.

The shoreline at Harris Hill is a flyway for hawks and passerines (watch for Bald Eagle and Osprey) and the oaks here are an excellent location for finding migrants. The marshes to the south have Yellow-headed Blackbirds, Sora and Yellow Rails, as well as Northern Harriers and Sandhill Crane. Sharp-tailed Sparrows can be found. In spite of its seeming remoteness, the land here is still private property and the visitor should use discretion.

Return to Highway 600 and continue north 1.7 to the next intersection, where the highway turns east. Continue north to the *Government Dock* (1.9 km, the road bears east), and once again cover the lake, the marshes to the west off Windy Point, and the woods for landbirds. At the point where the road curves right to the dock is Windy Bay Lodge, which is a second place offering accommodation, boats, and guide services (mid-May to October). Now return to the Highway 600 intersection and turn right (i.e., away from 600). This gravel road leads 3.8 km through good woodlands to a cottage area on the shore east of Budreau's Point (you pass a sideroad that goes right to the privately owned base of Windy Point). It is possible to follow a trail along a rocky ridge to Budreau's Point itself, which concentrates landbirds and gives good views of the lake; the woodlands at the beginning of the cottages also can be an excellent area for migrant concentrations.

From the above intersection Highway 600 runs east 11.6 km to cross Highway 621. Turn north on 621 and drive 4.6 km to *Lake of the Woods Provincial Park*. This park is to the west, on the lakeshore. There are Connecticut Warblers along the entrance road, and the Aspen campgrounds provide fine views of the shoreline north, and west to Windy Point. Look for pelicans, huge flocks of cormorants, as well as Bald Eagle and Osprey. Flocks of gulls gather at the mouth of the Little Grassy River immediately to the south, and the marshes associated with this probably will yield the wetland species that occur elsewhere in the region. There is a small colony of Yellow-headed Blackbirds here. The bog in the park has yielded both Palm Warbler and Gray-cheeked Thrush (probably a non-

19 For the Visitor

Getting Around

Public transportation outside cities in Ontario is rather limited, but there are bus, rail, and air links between major centres. Most international or transcontinental flights arrive at Toronto, the hub of the provincial transportation network. Cities with major airports are marked on the provincial road map.

Ontario's principal road network is the system of numbered Queen's highways, designated by a number in a shield topped by a crown. Most of these roads (those numbered to 99) are surfaced and of good all-weather quality, and the Queen Elizabeth Way and the 400 series are all major, divided, controlled-access highways. Other highways, numbered 100 and up, are secondary roads, and, in some cases, may be gravelled. In southern Ontario the numbered county and regional road systems (in grey on the current provincial road maps) are generally equal in quality to most of the main highways. These roads are sometimes designated as 'Regional Road XX' or 'County Road XX,' or sometimes by the name of the region or county in question, as in 'Durham Road XX.' Generally they are referred to in the text above simply as county or regional roads. The gravelled township roads are usually laid out in a grid pattern, and are called concession lines (or just lines) and sideroads, sequentially numbered. They can be in poor condition in winter and early spring, but are good for birding.

For further travel information, phone Ontario Travel toll-free at 1-800-ONTARIO (weekdays). Free material includes a travel guide, listings of accommodation and campgrounds, and a provincial road map. Be sure to get the road map, as most commercial maps do not give the county road numbers. The travel guide is useful as it tells you all the interesting things a tourist likes to know, and which I have almost ignored. In Toronto, the Toronto Transit Commission, at (416) 393-4636, has route information and a ride guide showing its subway and surface routes.

If you intend to do much birding in the province, more detailed maps will be of value. The Ministry of Transportation and Communications publishes a series of 1:250,000 maps that show the township road grids as well as the more major roads (available from the Map Office, Ministry of Transportation for Ontario, 1201 Wilson Ave., Downsview, Ontario, Canada, M3M 1J8). For even more detailed work the national topographic series, with maps on 1:50,000 and 1:25,000 scales, are invaluable. These are available from the Map Distribution Office, Department of Energy, Mines, and Resources, 615 Bruce Street, Ottawa, Canada, K1A 0E9, and from some local outlets. There is a charge for all the more detailed maps.

Accommodation

There are hotels in all the larger centres, and good to adequate motel accommodations over most of the province. Information on these is provided in the travel information referred to above. The accommodation booklet is arranged alphabetically by community.

The camping information is arranged similarly, but note that very few campgrounds are open year-round. Planning a camping trip after the Canadian Thanksgiving weekend (the second in October) or before the May 24 holiday weekend can be difficult for this reason. We have sometimes found the information in the campground directory unreliable in this regard, so write or phone to confirm. The provincial park campgrounds are infinitely superior to most private campgrounds from a naturalist's point of view, although they usually provide a more limited range of facilities. I have not attempted to mention all the provincial parks, but the Ministry of Natural Resources puts out a booklet listing them, and another giving information on rates, seasons, and the limited reserve camping arrangements. You can get these booklets from Ontario Travel as well on request.

If you are going to do much travelling in the province, some understanding of the parks systems will be useful. National and provincial parks range from huge, roadless wilderness areas to quite small campground parks, but most offer camping in good natural settings. Conservation areas are run by one or other of the thirty-nine Conservation Authorities across the province, each organized on a watershed basis. Their areas fill a regional park role, but include some extensive natural tracts of land with no public facilities, other developed areas with camping facilities similar to those in the provincial parks, and many smaller picnic and day-use areas. Some town and city parks (especially in Hamilton and Toronto) have good natural areas, but few have camping facilities.

Provincial parks and many conservation areas have entrance fees; currently the provincial parks charge $6.00 a vehicle for day use, and a seasonal pass is available. The Conservation Authorities vary in their fees, but are usually roughly similar to those of the province. Most urban parks are free, and many of the other parks do not collect fees in the off-season.

Finding Like Minds

The Federation of Ontario Naturalists (FON; 355 Lesmill Road, Don Mills, Ontario, Canada, M3B 2W8, phone [416] 444-8419) is the provincial naturalists' organization. It has member clubs in the following communities (some regional groups are not included; the name of the club is in the parentheses if it differs from the community which it serves): Barrie, Belleville, Brantford, Brighton (Presqu'ile), Brockville, Chalk River (Upper Ottawa Valley), Chatham, Cobourg (Willow Beach), Collingwood, Georgetown (Halton), Guelph, Hamilton, Huntsville, Ingersoll, Kingston, Kirkland Lake, Kitchener/Waterloo, Leamington (Sun Parlour), London, Manitoulin Island, Midland, Niagara Falls, North Bay (Nipissing), Oakville (South Peel), Orillia, Oshawa (Durham), Ottawa, Owen Sound, Parry Sound, Pembroke, Peterborough, Pickering, Port Hope (Willow Beach), Richmond Hill, St Catharines (Peninsula), St Thomas (West

Elgin), Sarnia (Lambton Wildlife), Sault Ste Marie, Simcoe (Norfolk), Stratford, Sudbury, Thunder Bay, Toronto, Walkerton, West Lorne, Windsor (Essex), Woodbridge (West Humber), Woodstock.

These groups vary considerably in their degree of activity. Most meet monthly from fall through spring, and often have field trips to good local areas. To contact them, check with the local library or write the Federation of Ontario Naturalists' head office. The FON'S magazine, *The Seasons*, emphasizes environmental matters, but the organization also offers a range of trips in the province, as does OFO and some freelance nature operators. The FON also publishes a provincial checklist jointly with the OFO.

The Ontario Field Ornithologists (OFO; Box 62014, Burlington Mall Postal Outlet, Burlington, Ontario L7R 4K2) sponsors the Ontario Bird Records Committee, and publishes a newsletter and *Ontario Birds*, a three times a year journal. The latter publishes the reports of the committee, and papers on a variety of other, mainly distributional, topics. It includes periodic Birding Site Guides, which will often serve to update and expand upon the information in this book. A second excellent periodical is *Birder's Journal* (8 Midtown Drive, Suite 289, Oshawa, Ontario L1J 8L2). It appears bimonthly, and includes current news on bird movements and occurrences in Ontario and Canada, and often has useful articles on identification in an Ontario context.

Other nature organizations in the province that are of interest to birders include the Canadian Nature Federation, 1 Nicholas Street, Suite 520, Ottawa, Ontario, Canada, K1N 7B7, whose program parallels that of the FON on a national level; and Long Point Bird Observatory, Box 160, Port Rowan, N0E 1M0, the latter covered in more detail in chapter 7. Directions to the National Museum of Sciences and the Royal Ontario Museum appear under the Ottawa and Toronto accounts respectively. There are many environmental and trail groups, but they are only peripherally interested in our subject.

For American Birding Association members the best reference for contacts – because it is updated fairly often, and indicates persons who are able to assist visiting birders – is the ABA Directory (PO Box 6599, Colorado Springs, CO 80934-6599,

USA). Local nature clubs can also, of course, often put people into contact with knowledgeable local birdwatchers.

It might be worth while repeating the ABA's rules of etiquette with regard to telephone calls. Try to call between 8:00 a.m. and 8.00 p.m. local time, and preferably between 7:00 and 8.00 p.m. Local callers might well follow the same advice: many of the people you will contact receive many requests for assistance and are glad to be of help, but to be awakened from a deep sleep at 11:15 p.m. by a call from a complete stranger who is planning a trip to Africa next year and would like some pointers strains hospitality to the breaking point! Many birders go to bed early, which is something to remember if you are a nighthawk yourself.

Telephone Numbers Giving Current Bird Sightings (Hot Lines)

Province-wide (519) 586-3959
Durham (905) 668-3070
Hamilton (905) 648-9537
London (519) 473-5853
Long Point (519) 586-3959
Ottawa (613) 761-1967
Point Pelee (519) 322-2371
Point Pelee/Windsor (519) 252-2473
Sault Ste Marie (705) 256-2790
Toronto (416) 350-3000, push button then enter 2293

Hazards Large and Small

Outside the major centres traffic can be agreeably light, but Highways 400 and 401 always seem to be busy, and the Queen Elizabeth Way is usually hectic. The northern Trans-Canada routes are very busy in summer, as are highways to the various cottage areas on weekends. From Hamilton east to Oshawa the lakeshore is heavily urbanized. Toronto itself is a typical big city (the conurbation exceeds 3 million) and Hamilton, London, and Ottawa are large urban areas as well.

Driving can be really hazardous in winter, and also in early spring and late fall, when the full gamut of icing conditions can be encountered. It you are coming in winter be prepared to deal with severe cold, and with all the problems, including exposure, this can create. Allow extra time in your travel plans to give you the option of 'waiting out' bad weather, which rarely lasts more than a couple of days in succession.

Ontario's large mammals are not dangerous provided you use common sense, which includes not feeding deer at the roadsides. One is unlikely even to see timber wolves or black bears, and unprovoked attacks on humans are extremely rare. Polar bears occur only along the north coast; they are very dangerous.

There is only one poisonous snake in Ontario, the Massasauga rattlesnake, which occurs along the southern Lake Huron–Georgian Bay shorelines and in places along Lake Erie. It is commonest in the Bruce Peninsula, where you can often find one in summer if you try. It is a small snake and not very aggressive, so not very dangerous, but be aware of it and listen for the buzzy, insect-like rattle. These snakes like dry mounds in boggy areas.

Ontario has its fair share of bugs. Mosquitoes are very common everywhere from late May through August or even later; and there are stable, deer, and moose flies and no-see-ums (midges). Blackflies are small black Simuliid flies that will accompany you in clouds in sunny areas, mainly in June. They abound all across the north and are expanding southwards; they are common in the Shield areas and in parts of the Bruce Peninsula. They like to get in around hat and wrist bands and the like, where they leave you dotted with little red spots which can itch unbearably for the following week. Liberal and frequent applications of insect repellant are needed to discourage these and other biting flies, which are all at their most abundant in June. In the extreme west, wood ticks are common at the same time of year (see chapter 18); otherwise ticks are not a very noticeable feature of the provincial scene, although recently lyme disease has been reported in the Long Point area, carried by the deer tick, so precautions should be taken there.

Poison ivy in Ontario is a sprawling groundcover, but climbing in the southwest. It is common in many of the best migration hot-spots, so if you are unfamiliar with its distinctive three leaflets and white berries learn to identify it. Any part of the plant can produce an irritating rash on contact.

Books That Will Help

The appropriate floras and the like are those covering north-eastern North America. I assume the reader will be familiar with these, and with the relevant popular field guides.

Basic National and Provincial References

Godfrey, W. Earl. *The Birds of Canada*. National Museums of Canada, 1986.

Cadman, M.D., P.F.J. Eagles and F.M. Helleiner. *Atlas of the Breeding Birds of Ontario*. University of Waterloo Press, 1987.

James, Ross D. *Annotated Checklist of the Birds of Ontario*. 2nd Ed. Royal Ontario Museum, 1991.

Peck, George K. and Ross D. James. *Breeding Birds of Ontario – Nidiology and Distribution*.
  Volume 1: Nonpasserines. Royal Ontario Museum, 1983.
  Volume 2: Passerines. Royal Ontario Museum, 1987.

Speirs, J. Murray. *Birds of Ontario. Volumes I and II*. Natural Heritage/Natural History Inc., 1985. (Use volume II, which is data-packed.)

Finding Guides

Goodwin, Clive E. *A Birdfinding Guide to the Toronto Region*. Rev. edition. The Goodwins, 1988.

Paleczny, Dan. *A Bird Finding Guide to the Cochrane Area*. Cochrane Naturalists Club, 1993. Available from Greenwater Provincial Park, P.O. Box 730, Cochrane, Ontario P0L 1C0.

Skevington, Jeff, Bev Collier, and Terrie Woodrow. *A Birding Guide to the Long Point Area*. Long Point Bird Observatory, 1990.

Regional Distributional Accounts

Beardslee, Clark S. and Harold D. Mitchell. *Birds of the Niagara Frontier Region*. Buffalo Museum of Natural Sciences, 1965.

Brewer, A.D. *The Birds of Wellington County*. Guelph Field Naturalists Club, 1977.

Devitt, O.E. *The Birds of Simcoe County, Ontario*. The Brereton Field Naturalists' Club, 1967.

Erskine, Anthony J. *Birds in Boreal Canada: Communities, Densities and Adaptations*. Canadian Wildlife Service, 1977.

Kelley, Alice H. *Birds of Southeastern Michigan and Southwestern Ontario*. Cranbrook Institute of Science, 1978.

LaForest, Steve M. *Birds of Presqu'ile Provincial Park*. The Friends of Presqu'ile, 1993.

Mills, Alex. *A Cottager's Guide to the Birds of Muskoka and Parry Sound*. Published by the author, 1981.

Nicholson, John C. *Birds of Sudbury District*. Published by the author, 1974.

– *The Birds of Manitoulin Island*. Published by the author, 1981.

Tozer, Ron. *Checklist and Seasonal Status of the Birds of Algonquin Provincial Park*. Friends of Algonquin Provincial Park, 1990.

*Sadler, Doug. *Our Heritage of Birds – Peterborough County in the Kawarthas*. Peterborough Field Naturalists, 1983.

Speirs, J. Murray. *Birds of Ontario County*. Federation of Ontario Naturalists, 1973–9.

*Sprague, R. Terry, and Ron D. Weir. *The Birds of Prince Edward County*. Kingston Field Naturalists, 1984.

Stirrett, George M. *The Birds of Point Pelee National Park*. Parks Canada, 1973 (contains four sections covering spring, summer, autumn, and winter).

Todd, W.E. Clyde. *Birds of the Labrador Peninsula*. University of Toronto Press, 1963 (includes parts of northeastern Ontario).

*Tozer, G. Ronald, and James M. Richards. *Birds of the Oshawa–Lake Scugog Region, Ontario*. Published by the authors, 1974.

*Weir, Ron D. *Birds of the Kingston Region*. Kingston Field Naturalists, distributed by the University of Toronto Press, 1989.

Most provincial parks have at least some form of bird checklist, and the same is true of many nature clubs. The quality and availability of these varies enormously, and a small fee is often charged for them; many of the better ones are mentioned in the appropriate sections of the text.

Books on Related Subjects

Banfield, A.W.F. *The Mammals of Canada*. University of Toronto Press, 1974.

Case, Frederick W. *Orchids of Western Great Lakes Region*. Cranbrook Institute of Science, 1964.

* Includes good sections on locations

Chapman, L.J., and D.F. Putman. *The Physiography of Southern Ontario.* University of Toronto Press, 1973.

Dore, William G., and J. McNeill. *Grasses of Ontario.* Agriculture Canada, 1980.

Groves, J. Walton. *Edible and Poisonous Mushrooms of Canada.* Agriculture Canada, 1962.

Holmes, Anthony M., Quimby F. Hess, Ronald R. Tasker, and Alan J. Hanks. *The Ontario Butterfly Atlas.* Toronto Entomologists Association, 1991.

Morton, J.K., and Joan M. Venn. *A Checklist of the Flora of Ontario – Vascular Plants.* University of Waterloo Biology Series No. 34, 1990.

Rowe, J.S. *Forest Regions of Canada.* Canadian Forestry Service, 1972.

Scoggan, H.J. *The Flora of Canada.* (4 vols). National Museum of Natural Sciences, 1978.

Soper, James H., and Margaret L. Heimburger. *Shrubs of Ontario.* Royal Ontario Museum, 1982.

Walshe, Shan. *Plants of Quetico and the Ontario Shield.* University of Toronto Press, 1980.

20 Systematic List

This list provides concise statements on the status of all species recorded in the province, with accompanying bar charts on the more regularly occurring ones. The coverage follows Ross D. James, *Annotated Checklist of the Birds of Ontario*, (Royal Ontario Museum 1991), with the addition of species that have been reliably reported since his list was published, to the end of 1992. A few later records have been included. These have been referred to as 'recent reports,' not to imply doubt as to their validity, but simply to identify them as awaiting the usual processes of review. The nomenclature has been updated to reflect the anticipated 1993 changes in the 39th Supplement to the American Ornithologists' Union's *Check-list of North American Birds* 6th edition (1983). For those species that have not been recorded in Ontario throughout the year, the outside dates for occurrence in the province appear in parenthesis.

The material is intended as a guide for the birder, not as a definitive statement of status: I have not undertaken the comprehensive review of literature necessary to ensure the latter. The statements and outside dates are based mainly on James above, and *American Birds* summaries over the years, supplemented by information from J. Murray Speirs, *Birds of Ontario*, volume 2 (Natural Heritage/Natural History, 1985), from the local publications listed in chapter 19, and from my own records. They should serve their purpose adequately.

The size of the province limits the utility of an undertaking of this nature and was the reason it was not undertaken in the first edition. On balance, however, I now feel that the help it might provide to the birder exceeds its potential for confusion, provided the user understands its limitations. The emphasis here is almost entirely on the south, as it is generally in the south that the earliest and latest dates have been recorded, and it receives the vast bulk of the coverage.

The bar charts are even more limited. They effectively apply *only* to the south, and will be most useful to observers along the lower Great Lakes. I have spent most of my life in Toronto, and the charts will inevitably reflect this bias, although I have referred freely to the seasonal lists covering Long Point and Kingston (*A Seasonal Checklist of the Birds of the Long Point Area* [LPBO, 1985]; and R.D.Weir: *Birds of the Kingston Area*) as some check against too parochial a slant. The north probably warrants two or three such charts in its own right, but must await the efforts of those with the requisite knowledge.

The list consists of two parts, which are complementary to one another. You should both read the text and refer to the chart. The text sometimes expands upon the categories shown in the chart, as in winter finches which are common some years but absent in others; and the chart may pinpoint periods where the text generalizes, as in the occurrences of wandering herons, which can appear over a fairly long period, but which sometimes 'clump' into particular periods.

Abundance criteria are necessarily subjective, and usually please no one. For the experienced local birder they often seem too conservative, while the visitor who fails to find species listed as regular tends to view them as overstated. Please remember that even common species can be missing on a given day, particularly in late summer and early fall when birds are harder to find, or during migration, when unfavourable weather conditions may lead to a general absence of birds. The categories also assume that habitat appropriate to the species will be visited. With these cautions, the following criteria have been used, with accompanying symbols in the charts:

Abundant – Usually widespread and easily found ██████████ on every field trip during the period.

Common – Usually widespread and normally easy to find on most field trips, but more localized and/or in smaller numbers than the preceding.

Fairly common – Seen regularly in suitable areas, but localized or usually in small numbers, or moving through quickly.

Uncommon – To be expected, and likely to be recorded on at least one or two trips in good habitat over the period, but scarce (or hard to find).

Rare but regular in specific areas – Refers to species that are rare (as defined below), but which occur significantly more predictably in certain localized areas.

Rare – Occurs annually (sometimes in small numbers) but can often be missed in the season even with regular field trips.

Occasional – Less than annual in occurrence, but still appearing with some regularity.

Exceptional – Has occurred, but not to be expected.

There may be enough detail below to eliminate confusion on other terminology. 'Resident' is used for a species that regularly spends either summer or winter or both in the province, while 'migrant' refers to species that occur regularly on migration. For rarer species, where the occurrences may or may not be part of a regular migratory pattern, the term 'visitor' is used. If a species' movements clearly seem to lack pattern, then the birds are described as 'wanderers'; at the extreme is a 'vagrant,' to describe a bird that turns up infrequently at widely scattered places and times.

LOONS AND GREBES

Red-throated Loon (*Gavia stellata*) – Breeds extreme N. Ontario (Hudson Bay and Cape Henrietta Maria). A regular but rare spring migrant on the lower Great Lakes (typically twenty to thirty birds total; but in 1993 found staging in mid-April, with

200 birds, along the Lake Huron shoreline from Point Clark northwards). Much more numerous in fall (total 50–150 birds), usually peaking Nov. 5–15, when substantial movements may occur on Lake Huron and along the Ottawa River. Smaller numbers (five to ten birds) are reported regularly in early winter into the first half of January, and occasional summering has occurred. Seen moving with Common Loons, when day-long counts have totalled 100 birds or more at locations such as Kettle Point, Sarnia, and Ottawa. Feeding birds and groups seem to occur most often on Lake Ontario, with Hamilton, Pickering, and Presqu'île being the most favoured locations.

Pacific Loon *(Gavia pacifica)* – Breeds extreme N. Ontario (Hudson Bay and Cape Henrietta Maria). An occasional migrant in both spring (Apr. 12–May 28; most May) and fall (Oct. 25–Dec. 26; most November) in southern Ontario. The majority of reports come from Pickering west to Hamilton on Lake Ontario, from Kettle Point on Lake Huron, and from Point Pelee. Possibly the species moves in very small numbers with the main flights of other loons; but the conditions under which these migrants are usually observed preclude critical examination, with the result that few sight records are accepted.

Common Loon *(Gavia immer)* – A fairly common nesting bird over most of the province, particularly on larger lakes; but scare or absent south and east of the Precambrian Shield and Bruce County, and thought to be declining on all more accessible waters. A common migrant on the Great Lakes and along the Ottawa River, more numerous in fall. Movements of thousands of birds can be counted from lookout points such as Kettle Point; and loose aggregations, sometimes totalling several hundred birds, concentrate along the lower Great Lakes shorelines (noteworthy viewing areas are Mississagi Light, MacGregor Point, southern Lake Simcoe, Whitby-Pickering, and the traditional concentration points). Occasional in winter north as far as open water exists.

Yellow-billed Loon *(Gavia adamsii)* – Exceptional (May 4–25).

Pied-billed Grebe *(Podilymbus podiceps)* – A rather uncommon and local nesting bird across southern Ontario, and north to the north shore of Lake Huron; much less common northwards,

	J	F	M	A	M	J	J	A	S	O	N	D
Red-throated Loon												
Common Loon												
Pied-billed Grebe												
Horned Grebe												
Red-necked Grebe												
Eared Grebe												
Northern Gannet												
American White Pelican												
Great Cormorant												
Double-crested C.												

and absent from most of northern Ontario. A fairly common migrant both in suitable wetlands and on the Great Lakes themselves; usually singly, but groups of up to thirty birds occur. A few remain into early winter. Most easily seen in the major wetlands along the lower Great Lakes.

Horned Grebe (*Podiceps auritus*) – Occasional in summer, a very infrequent breeder in both southern and (more regularly?) far northern Ontario. A common migrant, chiefly on Lake Huron and the lower Great Lakes, sometimes forming loose aggregations of 100–400 birds; but also widespread in ones and twos on smaller waterbodies. A few remain into early winter. Peak concentrations occur in April and mid-October to mid-November, when birds are widespread just offshore on the lower Lakes.

Red-necked Grebe (*Podiceps grisegena*) – A rare nesting bird, with a few widely scattered colonies across the province: Luther Marsh in southern Ontario, and Lillabelle and Whitefish lakes in the north are the best-known sites. Often a few birds will summer on Lake Ontario, with Pickering (off Cranberry Marsh), Port Credit (off Rattray Marsh), and Burlington the most usual locations. These same areas may host staging flocks (typically 100–300 birds, but to 3,000), also Mississagi Light and the shoreline of Lake Huron from Point Clark northward. A fairly common migrant on the Great Lakes, but often moving through rapidly (peaks late April; late October-early November). Occasional in winter.

Eared Grebe (*Podiceps nigricollis*) – Rare in migration, principally along the lower Great Lakes (only a couple of northern Ontario records, but a pair has been recorded on the Rainy River lagoons). Occasional at other times. Within these broad criteria appearances are widely scattered, although fall sightings (two to fourteen, September through November) typically out-number those in spring (one to eight in April–May), and a good number are seen on sewage lagoons.

Western Grebe (*Aechmophorus occidentalis*) – Earlier Ontario sightings of this species did not differentiate between Western and Clark's Grebe; however, it is likely that most or all the records were of this species. A pair has summered regularly on the Lake of the Woods since 1989. It is an occasional vagrant in southern Ontario in both spring (Apr. 5–May 27) and fall (Aug. 20–Dec. 4; most Oct. 6–Nov. 11). Fewer than one a year is re-ported, 75 per cent from Lake Ontario.

TUBE-NOSES THROUGH CORMORANTS

Northern Fulmar (*Fulmarus glacialis*) – Exceptional; possibly regular off the north coastline in fall (May 13; Oct. 19–Jan. 15).

Black-capped Petrel (*Pterodroma hasitata*) – Exceptional, prob-ably hurricane-blown (Jul. 19–Oct. 8).

Audubon's Shearwater (*Puffinus lherminieri*) – One record (Sept. 8).

Wilson's Storm-Petrel (*Oceanites oceanicus*) – Exceptional ('Spring'; Aug. 14).

Leach's Storm-Petrel (*Oceanodroma leucorhoa*) – Exceptional; however, the one north coast sight record suggests it should be watched for there (Jul. 19–Oct. 8).

Band-rumped Storm-Petrel (*Oceanodroma castro*) – One record (Aug. 28).

Northern Gannet (*Morus bassanus*) – An occasional to rare visi-tor, almost annual in occurrence since 1983, and mainly to the lower Great Lakes in later fall (Oct. 2–Dec. 8). There is a scatter-ing of inland records, some associated with the Ottawa River, and a sighting from the north coast. Most of the birds are young, and have appeared on Lake Ontario; some remaining as late as

Feb. 14, and there have been three or four in spring (May 4–Jun. 25). Van Wagner's Beach in an easterly gale has been the most consistent location for sighting these wanderers.

American White Pelican (*Pelecanus erythrorhynchos*) – Nests on Lake of the Woods and recently on Lake Nipigon. Non-breeding birds appear to wander widely, particularly in summer and early fall (Apr. 18–Jan. 13), and often remain in an area for extended periods. Being so conspicuous, they create great excitement wherever they appear: the lower Great Lakes, together with southern Lake Huron, have yielded most of these records. There have been up to a dozen such reports almost annually since 1979, although much duplication probably occurs.

Brown Pelican (*Pelecanus occidentalis*) – One record (Sept. 25), plus a recent report (Mar. 14).

Great Cormorant (*Phalacrocorax carbo*) – There have been one to three reports annually since 1978. The vast bulk of the sightings have been from Lake Ontario (one from Ottawa): birds are typically first seen in early winter but as early as Aug. 24, and perhaps overlooked earlier, and may remain into early spring, with sightings to May 22.

Double-crested Cormorant (*Phalacrocorax auritus*) – A common breeding bird on all the Great Lakes; it has increased dramatically in recent years, and huge flocks numbering thousands of birds (up to 10,000) are now being seen in the south. Isolated birds may appear on smaller lakes and along larger rivers, and north to James and Hudson Bay, although the species is rare away from large waterbodies. Migrants arrive in early April and leave in early November, but a few birds usually winter.

Anhinga (*Anhinga anhinga*) – One record (Sept. 7).

Magnificent Frigatebird (*Fregata magnificens*) – One record (Sept. 28).

BITTERNS, HERONS, AND ALLIES

American Bittern (*Botaurus lentiginosus*) – An uncommon and elusive migrant and summer resident, rarer in the north and in the southwest. There have been a few records in the late

December to early March period. Probably most easily located in spring, when they are calling, in the larger marshes along the lower Great Lakes, such as Pelee, Long Point, and Presqu'île.

Least Bittern (*Ixobrychus exilis*) – An uncommon and very elusive migrant and summer resident in the south (Apr. 19–Dec. 2), thought to be declining. Rare to occasional north of a line from Arnprior to Honey Harbour, except for scattered numbers in wetlands on the Bruce Peninsula and Manitoulin Island. It is probably easiest to find in the larger marshes along Lakes Erie and Ontario, and much easier to locate if the call is known.

Great Blue Heron (*Ardea herodias*) – A fairly common summer resident, usually forming large heronries to nest and ranging widely to feed, although it can be hard to find away from larger marshes. It is much less numerous northwards and absent in the far north. Birds are particularly common in fall when large numbers (200+) concentrate in marshes along the lower Great Lakes. A few winter in most years.

Great Egret (*Casmerodius albus*) – Nests in a few heronries in the southwest and in Bruce and Simcoe counties, occasionally elsewhere in the south (Luther Marsh). Foraging birds range widely to wetlands throughout the adjacent areas, and are relatively easy to find in Kent and Essex counties. Elsewhere the species is an uncommon to rare wanderer, mainly in early fall when the birds from the nesting colonies disperse. This is the commonest of the 'southern' herons in the province, and typically yields ten to twenty reports in both spring and fall (Mar. 23–Dec. 26) away from the southwest, usually along the lower Lakes, but also into northern Ontario as well.

Snowy Egret (*Egretta thula*) – One nesting record (Hamilton 1986). Otherwise a rare wanderer in spring (80%) and fall (20%; Apr. 17–Nov. 11); an average of five annually since 1970 with some increase in recent years to a high of seventeen. A few sometimes hang around into the summer; 85% of the birds have occurred along the lower Great Lakes, particularly in the southwest, and there are only three records from the north.

Little Blue Heron (*Egretta caerulea*) – A rare vagrant in spring (one to two annually; Apr. 3–Jun. 12; most May 4–Jun. 5); occasional in fall (zero to one annually; Jul. 13–Dec. 16; most Aug.

	J	F	M	A	M	J	J	A	S	O	N	D
American Bittern												
Least Bittern												
Great Blue Heron												
Great Egret												
Snowy Egret												
Cattle Egret												
Green Heron												
Black-cr. Night-Heron												

11–Sept. 26); 28% have occurred away from the lower Great Lakes, with at least three in the north.

Tricolored Heron (*Egretta tricolor*) – A rare vagrant in spring (one to two annually; Apr. 5–Jun. 24; most Apr. 29–Jun. 5); occasional in fall (some six records; Jul. 1–Sept. 22). Only 20% occur away from the lower Great Lakes, with one from the north. Almost half of the reports are from Rondeau, Long Point, and the marshes just east of Toronto.

Cattle Egret (*Bubulcus ibis*) – An occasional nesting bird in southern Ontario (to 1979). Otherwise a rare wanderer in spring (average eleven reports annually) and fall (average six reports annually; Apr. 8–Dec. 2), when flocks of as many as 112 birds have been sighted. Many birds linger well into or through the summer. Only 25% of the sightings have been away from the lower Great Lakes, and these include about a dozen records from the north.

Green Heron (*Butorides virescens*) – A common summer resident across most of southern Ontario, but rather uncommon to rare on the Precambrian Shield, with few records north of Lake Huron. It typically arrives and departs without fanfare (outside dates Apr. 7–Dec. 27). It favours more wooded wetlands.

Black-crowned Night-Heron (*Nycticorax nycticorax*) – Locally common in summer, nesting principally in large heronries along Lakes Huron, St Clair, Erie, and Ontario. There are only a few northern Ontario records. The birds are uncommon away from the vicinity of the heronries until midsummer, when they disperse up the rivers and into the marshes of southern Ontario and gather in day roosts (100+ birds), usually in wooded locations. Individuals often linger in these areas until early winter (yielding spurious late records of bitterns from the unwary). Birds have survived as late as Feb. 28, and the earliest migrants have been back by Mar. 4! Toronto, Hamilton, and Niagara Falls are among the more reliable locations for this species.

Yellow-crowned Night-Heron (*Nyctanassa violacea*) – A rare vagrant in spring (one to two annually; Mar. 31–Jun. 23; most Apr. 18–Jun. 2); occasional in fall (some ten records; Jul. 6–Oct. 4). Some 30% occur away from the lower Great Lakes, north to Ottawa, and almost 30% are reported from Pelee, Rondeau, and Long Point.

White Ibis (*Eudocimus albus*) – Exceptional (Sept. 27–Oct. 13).

Glossy Ibis (*Plegadis falcinellus;* includes *Plegadis spp.*) – A rare vagrant in spring (average three reports annually; Apr. 16–Jun. 30; most May 3–24) and fall (average one to two reports annually; Jul. 13–Nov. 7; most Sept. 12–Oct. 23). Some 40% of the sightings have been away from the lower Great Lakes, north and east to Grey County and Ottawa. Most earlier sightings of *Plegadis* ibis were considered to be this species, and to date there is no record of White-faced Ibis in the province.

Wood Stork (*Mycteria americana*) – Exceptional (May 11–17, Aug. 2–Nov. 9).

Greater Flamingo (*Phoenicopterus ruber*) – Some six records have all been judged escapees.

SWANS, GEESE, AND DUCKS

The spring waterfowl concentrations are among the birding highlights of the year. To eliminate constant repetition below, there follows a brief summary of their seasonal movements and distribution. Traditionally the main areas of concentration for wintering waterfowl have been, as ice permits, the west end of Lake Ontario (covered under Toronto) and the St Clair, Niagara, and St Lawrence rivers. Greater Scaup, Oldsquaw, Common Goldeneye, Bufflehead, and Common Merganser are the principal diving ducks present, with smaller numbers of other species. Since the invasion of zebra mussels into the Great Lakes, the western end of Lake Ontario has hosted enormous concentrations of birds in late winter, with huge flocks of scoters joining the wintering birds (see Greater Scaup, below).

Spring brings heavy movement as soon as – and sometimes even before – leads appear in the ice of the frozen bays. Long Point, Rondeau, and Presqu'ile bays are the best-known locations for huge concentrations of duck. The principal species present are scaup, Redhead, Canvasback, Ring-necked Duck, and American Wigeon, together with American Coot, and again with smaller numbers of other species. Numbers are usually at their peak in mid-March in the Long Point area and at the beginning of April at Presqu'ile, although conditions vary from year to year. Red-breasted Merganser stage at the same time, with the waters of Lake Erie off Pelee and Long Point among the best locales for them. Since the arrival of the mussels, Pelee has also become a major area of concentrations for migrant scaup and other species.

Northern Pintail and other dabbling duck are also moving, and seasonally flooded agricultural land, such as that associated with the South Nation River in eastern Ontario, and Minesing Swamp, attracts huge numbers, often associated with geese. There are, of course, a host of other areas with excellent waterfowl viewing opportunities.

Autumn passage is more prolonged, and does not result in the highly localized concentrations of spring, although large flocks of diving duck occur offshore in many of the same areas. The hunting season is usually from about Sept. 24 in the south, and many of the best-known localities are open to hunting.

Fulvous Whistling-Duck (*Dendrocygna bicolor*) – Occasional in migration periods (Apr. 7–Jun. 5; most May: Aug. 20–Dec. 8). Most of the twelve reports have been from the southwest and Lake Ontario, with two from extreme eastern Ontario.

Black-bellied Whistling-Duck (*Dendrocygna autumnalis*) – One record (Jun. 15–30, 1993).

Tundra Swan (*Cygnus columbianus*) – Nests along the Hudson Bay coastline; scattered birds occasionally in summer in southern wetlands. Vast flocks stage in the southwest in early spring (most Mar. 6–Apr. 2), principally at Long Point and on Lake St Clair, where counts of up to 20,000 birds have been recorded, and disperse out in small groups over the neighbouring countryside to feed. The fall movement is much less spectacular as

	J	F	M	A	M	J	J	A	S	O	N	D
Tundra Swan												
Mute Swan												
Snow Goose												
Great White-fronted Goose												
Brant												
Canada Goose												
Wood Duck												
Green-winged Teal												

there are no staging concentrations, but feeding groups can be found in the late fall across the southwest (mainly in Kent, Essex and Lambton counties; most Nov. 1–Dec. 3), and flocks moving generally southeastwards can be viewed from such locations as Kettle Point, Sarnia, Pelee, Rondeau, and Hawk Cliff. Elsewhere scattered birds and small flocks can sometimes be seen in the migration periods, mostly in spring and particularly along Lake Ontario. A few remain into winter, mainly at Long Point, where some numbers may be present.

Trumpeter Swan (*Cygnus buccinator*) – The Ontario Ministry of Natural Resources has been engaged in a limited reintroduction program for this species. A few of these birds now occur in the marshes and along the shoreline of western Lake Ontario, particularly around Toronto, at Wye Marsh (where breeding recently occurred), and on Lake Erie.

Mute Swan (*Cygnus olor*) – An increasingly common resident along western Lake Ontario, slowly expanding east, and west into Lake Erie. Birds turn up from time to time in other parts of the province, but the species is, of course, widely kept in captivity.

Greater White-fronted Goose (*Anser albifrons*) – A rare visitor during migration. Over 85% of the records are from spring, with over 60% in 1985 and 1989 alone. Excluding these two years, sightings average about three annually in spring (Mar. 8–May 5), and one to two in fall (Aug. 4–Nov. 29). There are at most six records for the winter period (Nov. 30–Mar. 7). Fewer than 20% of the sightings are away from the lower Great

Lakes and only some 5% in the north, which yielded the province's only summering record, at Thunder Bay.

Snow Goose (*Chen caerulescens*) – A colonial nester on the Hudson Bay coast. Staging and heavy migration occurs there and on James Bay, and counts of 1,000 or more are common from across northern Ontario, particularly in fall. Farther south it is an uncommon migrant with two areas of abundance. One is in the east, west to about Kingston and the Ottawa River, and the second is along the west shoreline of the Bruce Peninsula and through the southwest. Scattered birds can be found in most winters along the lower Great Lakes, usually with flocks of Canada Geese. Viewing areas for migrants include the west shoreline of Lake Huron south to Kettle Point in fall, as well as inland waters such as Fanshawe Dam. In spring numbers have occurred on Wolfe Island, and flocks of over 1,000 birds can gather along the South Nation River lowlands in the Riceville-Bourget area. Single birds and small groups are widespread in wetlands during migration periods.

Ross' Goose (*Chen rossii*) – Has nested in the extreme north, with Snow Geese. The small scattering of fall and early winter sightings in the south have always elicited heated debate as to the birds' origins. The current official view seems to favour escapees, always a strong possibility with rare waterfowl.

Brant (*Branta bernicla*) – Occasional in summer and winter. A fairly common migrant in the east (500–1,000 daily), west to Cobourg and Whitby and apparently following the line of the Ottawa River and along Lake Ontario. Much less common farther west, but smaller numbers possible all across the south, varying widely from year to year. There are relatively few northern reports away from the James and Hudson Bay coasts, where very heavy flights occur in mid-May and in later October.

Barnacle Goose (*Branta leucopsis*) – Occasional birds spring and fall (Mar. 28–Apr. 29; Oct. 15–Dec. 1); but, like Ross' Geese in the south, their pedigrees are difficult to establish and the official view currently favours escapees.

Canada Goose (*Branta canadensis*) – A widespread breeder in the Hudson Bay Lowland, and across the agricultural areas of

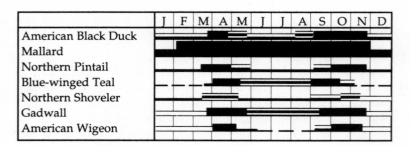

	J	F	M	A	M	J	J	A	S	O	N	D
American Black Duck												
Mallard												
Northern Pintail												
Blue-winged Teal												
Northern Shoveler												
Gadwall												
American Wigeon												

southern Ontario, mainly south of the Shield. The latter population originates from introduced stock, and is still expanding: Canadas are now common birds in the areas where most birders live, but are still rather rare on the Shield. Common in winter along the lower Great Lakes with occasional birds north to Ottawa and Manitoulin Island. Migrants are most numerous in the east (Port Hope to Ottawa; peak passage of up to 40,000 daily, Apr. 23–May 10 and Sept. 29–Nov. 7) and at Thunder Bay; but heavy flights do occur farther west in some years.

Wood Duck (*Aix sponsa*) – Fairly common but local in summer in wooded wetlands through southern Ontario, and north locally through the mixed forest region; absent from most of northern Ontario. A regular migrant spring (March) and fall (September), when its habitat tastes are more catholic. Fall counts of 100–400 birds have been recorded, but they are usually in rather small numbers. One or two usually winter along the lower Great Lakes and north to Algonquin Park.

Green-winged Teal (*Anas crecca*) – An uncommon bird in summer. In the more southern parts of Ontario the species is commonest in the Sudbury area and along the edge of the Canadian Shield. Northwards localized centres of abundance exist along the Hudson Bay Lowland and in the wetlands of agricultural areas. A common migrant (500+), with birds hanging around until freeze-up; small numbers winter regularly along the lower Great Lakes, and birds have occurred north to Sudbury and Thunder Bay. The Eurasian bird was reported annually in spring (once in October) prior to its merger into this species; subsequent reports have been only occasional, probably because few persons now look for them.

American Black Duck (*Anas rubripes*) – A widespread but declining breeder in the province, commoner in the north and east, but scarce in the far northwest and local in the southwest. A common migrant, forming large concentrations (7,000+) in areas such as Wolfe Island and Wildwood Reservoir. Fairly common in the winter on western Lake Ontario, and elsewhere along the lower Great Lakes as open water exists, with scattered birds north to Sudbury and Thunder Bay.

Mallard (*Anas platyrhynchos*) – A common summer resident, abundant in the south (where many originate from introduced stock) and on migration (10,000+). Common in winter on the lower Great Lakes and northwards as open water exists, to Sudbury and Thunder Bay.

Northern Pintail (*Anas acuta*) – A rare summer resident except on the Hudson Bay Lowland, where it is common. Locally common during migration, forming large spring concentrations (10,000+) in areas such as Minesing Swamp and the South Nation River lowlands – typically seasonally flooded agricultural land. A few birds will winter in the south, north and east to Peterborough, Ottawa, and Brockville.

Garganey (*Anas querquedula*) – Two records (Apr. 18–22 and May 12–15, 1993).

Blue-winged Teal (*Anas discors*) – A common summer resident in the south, becoming much less so on the Precambrian Shield, and absent over large areas of the far north. A common spring and early fall migrant (600+). Occasional in early winter, very rarely throughout the season, and northwards as open water exists to Sudbury and Sault Ste Marie.

Cinnamon Teal (*Anas cyanoptera*) – An occasional to rare wanderer in spring (Mar. 29–May 29), almost annual in recent years; there are a few old fall reports from 1953 and earlier, and a similar number of more recent summer sightings. The species has nested once. Almost half of the records since 1970 have been from northern Ontario, including three from Thunder Bay. All the other sightings were from the lower Great Lakes and the southwest.

Northern Shoveler (*Anas clypeata*) – A rare and local nesting

	J	F	M	A	M	J	J	A	S	O	N	D
Canvasback												
Redhead												
Ring-necked Duck												
Greater Scaup												
Lesser Scaup												
King Eider												
Harlequin Duck												

bird, mainly in the south and in the Sudbury area, but also at
Thunder Bay, the extreme west, and along the north coast. An
uncommon to locally common migrant in both spring and fall
(400+). A few birds try to winter along the lower Great Lakes,
east to Kingston. A small but reliable fall and early winter concentration is on Grenadier Pond in Toronto.

Gadwall (*Anas strepera*) – Formerly a rare migrant, this species
has rapidly expanded its numbers as a breeding bird since the
early 1970s. It is now a locally common nesting bird in the
south, and apparently still expanding northwards. It is a common migrant along the Great Lakes, less so inland and northwards. In winter, lower Great Lakes concentrations (500+) have
chiefly been along Lake Ontario between west Toronto and
Hamilton, but birds have occurred east to Ottawa and Cornwall.

Eurasian Wigeon (*Anas penelope*) – A rare visitor in spring (four
to five annually; Mar. 3–Jun. 23; most Mar. 25–May 12) and fall
(one to two annually; Aug. 2–Dec.18; most Sept. 26–Nov. 7).
Only 15% have occurred away from the lower Great Lakes,
including three in the north and six at Ottawa. There has been
some increase in spring sightings in particular since 1986, with
a high of sixteen in 1993, which may herald a change in status
for this species.

American Wigeon (*Anas americana*) – A common breeder along
the north coast, occasional farther south. It is common in migration, often locally abundant (up to 21,000), as at Long Point and
Presqu'île in spring. Winters regularly in small numbers along
the lower Great Lakes, and occasionally north and east to Barrie
and Ottawa.

Canvasback (*Aythya valisineria*) – Breeds in the extensive Lake

St Clair and Walpole Island marshes, at Rondeau and Luther Marsh, and isolated birds summer occasionally in other wetlands across the province. It is an uncommon spring migrant away from its traditional areas of concentration, notably at Wolfe Island, Presqu'île Park, and Long Point, where it can occur in thousands (10,000+). Birds occur more widely in fall, but are still rather uncommon. Large numbers usually winter on the St Clair River (Sombra), along the Niagara River, at Long Point, with smaller flocks and scattered individuals elsewhere along the lower Great Lakes as ice conditions permit; elsewhere there are a few records north to Barrie and Ottawa.

Redhead (*Aythya americana*) – Breeds very locally in some of the more extensive marshes in southern Ontario, particularly Lake St Clair, Walpole Island, and Long Point; isolated birds summer occasionally in other wetlands across the province. It parallels the Canvasback in occurring in thousands in traditional areas of concentration (10,000+), such as Presqu'île and particularly Long Point in spring migration and on the St Clair River in winter, but it is generally much more widespread than the Canvasback. Small flocks winter regularly along the lower Great Lakes, and winter birds have occurred north to Sault Ste Marie.

Ring-necked Duck (*Aythya collaris*) – This duck of woodland pools is a common breeder in central and northern Ontario, but is confined mainly to the Precambrian Shield in the south. Like other *Aythya* species, isolated birds will summer occasionally in more southerly wetlands, and breeding is established at Luther Marsh. In migration birds are widespread in suitable habitat, and large numbers (2,000+) gather with Canvasback and Redhead, and in the same locations, although fall concentrations seem to occur more to the east, with Ottawa (Shirleys Bay) particularly favoured. Wintering birds have been reported north to Thunder Bay, but it is only occasional anywhere in winter.

Tufted Duck (*Aythya fuligula*) – An occasional winter visitor. Most of the ten reports between 1981 and 1991 were from Hamilton's Windermere Basin, and plausibly most of these could all relate to a single bird: sightings were between Nov. 17 and Apr. 7. In 1993 there were up to seven reports (Dec. 14– May 29), but at least some of the birds were banded.

Greater Scaup (*Aythya marila*) – Breeds on the Hudson Bay coastline. Summering scaup records farther south usually pertain to the next species, but occasional Greaters occur as well, particularly in the north. An abundant migrant, one of the main constituents of the early spring *Aythya* spp. concentrations (27,000+), apparently more common in eastern Ontario, at least up to the 1990s. An abundant winter resident on the lower Great Lakes.

Since 1989 a decline in wintering numbers has occurred in the Toronto region, with an increase in birds (15,000+) at the western end of Lake Ontario. Exceptional numbers of other species have been present in the same area. It has been hypothesized that these birds were feeding on the introduced zebra mussels, which had expanded into Lake Ontario from Lake Erie. If so, the continuing expansion may well alter the distribution of waterfowl on the Great Lakes in the future.

Lesser Scaup (*Aythya affinis*) – A local summer resident in the north and west; occasional to rare as a breeding bird in the south, but non-breeders are regular in summer. An abundant migrant, particularly along the lower Great Lakes and in spring, apparently most numerous on Lake Erie (14,000+). A rare winter resident in the south, north occasionally to Sault Ste Marie. Winter scaup flocks, particularly those feeding in sheltered waters, often have one or two Lessers among them, while in Hamilton Bay and the southwest numbers can be considerably larger.

Scaup identification often tends to be problematical: the birds are frequently far off, bobbing up and down in the swell, or alternatively appear as inert dark lumps that refuse to do more than sleep for the duration of one's visit. Neither condition is conducive to precise observation, and the flocks are frequently 'called' on the basis of the one or two birds that are well seen, or 'because that's what we always get.' The comments here on the relative numbers and distribution of the two species should be read with this in mind!

Prior to the 1990s in the Toronto area, the first scaup to appear in fall were usually Lessers, and they seemed to comprise the bulk of the flocks until late October, when they became scarce. The reverse occurred in spring, and summering birds there usually proved to be this species. However, other authors do not totally agree with these generalizations, and it is my impression that the pattern changes somewhat from west to east along the lower Lakes. The situation in any event changed in the 1990s, when the Toronto concentrations largely vanished. This coincides with large increases in the numbers of migrants of both species on Lake Erie (Pelee), and parallels the changes in the distribution of other species described above.

Common Eider (*Somateria mollissima*) – Summers along Hudson and James Bay, with huge winter concentrations reported off Cape Henrietta Maria; no more than occasional elsewhere in the province. Apart from three summering records, from the Niagara River and Lake Ontario, all reports have been from late fall onwards (Sept. 25–Apr. 8; most Nov. 14–Jan. 6). Recent sightings away from the north coasts have averaged one every two years, almost all from the lower Great Lakes, and especially the eastern end of Lake Ontario; however, three birds were reported with the duck concentrations at the west end of the lake in 1992, on Mar. 26.

King Eider (*Somateria spectabilis*) – Breeding has been recorded on the Hudson Bay coastline. A rare and irregular late fall and winter visitor in the south (Aug. 7–Jun. 8; 90% Oct. 23–Feb. 28). The vast bulk of records are from Lake Ontario and the Niagara River, but there are a number from Lake Erie and southern Lake Huron, with isolated sightings north to Manitoulin and Capreol, and at least four from Ottawa. Prior to 1991, a normal year yielded three to six reports of this species, with above normal numbers (to twenty-five birds) in 1976, 1983, 1986–7, and 1990; and the best locations for finding them were Presqu'île and the Niagara River in late fall. In winter 1991–2, however, some thirty-three birds were present at the western end of Lake Ontario. They were associating with the large flocks of scoters there at that time, an apparent outcome of the spread of zebra mussels (see the Greater Scaup account).

Harlequin Duck (*Histrionicus histrionicus*) – A rare migrant on the Great Lakes and on the Ottawa River (six to twelve annually). A rare winter resident in the south; summering has occurred. The bulk of the records are between the beginning of October and the end of December, with wintering birds remaining as late as early April. There have been recent reports from Sault Ste Marie and Thunder Cape. Birds often return to

	J	F	M	A	M	J	J	A	S	O	N	D
Oldsquaw												
Black Scoter												
Surf Scoter												
White-winged Scoter												
Common Goldeneye												
Barrow's Goldeneye												
Bufflehead												
Hooded Merganser												
Common Merganser												
Red-breast. Merganser												
Ruddy Duck												

specific wintering sites for a number of consecutive years, particularly in the Toronto area.

Oldsquaw (*Clangula hyemalis*) – Breeds on the Hudson Bay coastline, and isolated birds will summer on the Great Lakes, where it is abundant in migration (16,000+). Birds will winter as far north as open water permits, but the main concentrations (to 10,000) are along the lower Great Lakes, where the flocks can be well out from shore. Spring departure is late, with birds usually remaining until late May.

Black Scoter (*Melanitta nigra*) – Summers in large numbers on Hudson and James Bay, with two or three summer sightings on the Great Lakes. An uncommon to rare migrant in the south, principally in fall (72% of all reports Sept. 14–Nov. 22) when large flocks of 1,000 or more have occurred. A rare wintering bird (20% of reports) with only a scattering of spring sightings annually. Most numerous in eastern Ontario, particularly Ottawa, Kingston, Presqu'île, although large flights also occur at Kettle Point. It is often in mixed flocks with the other two species of scoter.

Surf Scoter (*Melanitta perspicillata*) – A rare resident of the Hudson Bay Lowland and the north coast. Its movements and numbers in the south closely parallel those of the Black Scoter (65% of reports Oct. 1–Nov. 15), but it is more regular in spring (28% of reports Apr. 6–May 30) and much rarer in winter, with only 5% of the total reports. It occurs considerably more widely across the province than the Black, with a good number of inland reports, particularly around London (Strathroy).

White-winged Scoter (*Melanitta fusca*) – A rare resident of the Hudson Bay Lowland and the north coast, with scattered summer sightings across the south. A common late spring migrant (over 75% May 15–27), often in flocks of thousands (5,000+), but moving through quickly and often only seen in flight well out over the waters of the lower Lakes. Fairly common in fall (most Oct. 7–Nov. 28) and winter, but in much smaller numbers. In February of 1991–2, however, some 3,000 were present at the west end of Lake Ontario, with 13,000 recorded in the same period in 1993.

Common Goldeneye (*Bucephala clangula*) – An abundant breeding duck across northern Ontario, south to the north shoreline of Lake Huron and the Sudbury Region; usually present in the south in very small numbers during summer. An abundant winter resident on the Great Lakes and on inland waters wherever open water exists. Goldeneyes are usually present in relatively small numbers; however, in the late winter of 1991–2 an exceptional concentration of over 4,500 birds was present at the western end of Lake Ontario, with some 10,000 the following year.

Barrow's Goldeneye (*Bucephala islandica*) – A rare migrant and winter resident, often in flocks of Common Goldeneye. Usually there are five to fifteen reports annually (Oct. 11–May 7), with most migrants appearing Oct. 15–Nov. 30 and wintering birds leaving in late March and April. Some birds return to specific sites in successive years, as at Ottawa and Niagara Falls, but many sightings are for brief periods during the winter. Other favoured localities have been the Cornwall dam and the Sarnia area.

Bufflehead (*Bucephala albeola*) – Breeds in small numbers in the wooded wetlands across northern Ontario, and isolated birds and pairs are often located in the south during summer. A common winter resident and migrant (1,200+) on the Great Lakes and on inland waters across southern Ontario.

Smew (*Mergellus albellus*) – Two records, Niagara and Long

Point (Dec. 9–10, Jan. 17–Mar. 30).

Hooded Merganser (*Lophodytes cucullatus*) – A regular but local and retiring nesting bird, most widespread in the forested areas of the north. In southern Ontario it prefers wooded wetlands, and is most common on the Shield areas of eastern Ontario. It is a fairly common migrant (to 200), although relatively infrequent on the open waters of the Great Lakes. Birds regularly overwinter.

Common Merganser (*Mergus merganser*) – Widespread in summer north roughly of a line from Southampton to Ottawa, much less regular south of the line. A common migrant and winter resident (1,000–4,000, but to 40,000) along the lower Great Lakes, wintering as far north as open water permits.

Red-breasted Merganser (*Mergus serrator*) – A widespread nesting bird in the north, but farther south mainly confined to the shorelines of Georgian Bay and northern Lake Huron. An abundant migrant both spring and fall, forming huge flocks (60,000) on the lower Great Lakes. Its winter status seems to have changed since 1980, becoming more common; but it is still an uncommon bird on Lake Ontario, becoming more numerous to the south and west.

Ruddy Duck (*Oxyura jamaicensis*) – This species is never very common in the province. It is a local nesting bird in southwestern Ontario, is established at Luther Marsh, and elsewhere summers regularly at Cranberry Marsh and at various sewage lagoons. The latter are also among the best places for finding the birds on migration, although the marshes at Long Point and Pelee in spring are probably the most consistently reliable places to see the species (to 400 birds). There are frequent attempts to winter.

DIURNAL BIRDS OF PREY

Hawks are easiest to see in migration, when they follow shorelines and can be seen in numbers at several well-established observation points. In fall Holiday Beach and Hawk Cliff, both on Lake Erie, are the best known; in spring Beamer Point on Lake Ontario is the main locality. More detail on these flights, and their composition and timing, is given in the accounts of

Holiday Beach and Beamer respectively. It should not be thought, however, that these are the only locations where hawk movement can be seen. The key to the flights is that many hawks dislike flying over large bodies of water; any areas where the birds' movements are blocked by the Great Lakes are likely to provide hawk viewing in season. Hence, in fall Prince Edward is noteworthy on Lake Ontario, and the entire Lake Ontario shoreline, together with Lake Erie from Hawk Cliff west, can yield good viewing. In the north the Lake Superior shoreline in the Marathon area, Thunder Bay, and the east shoreline of the Lake of the Woods have all yielded good hawk movements.

Falcons and accipiters are less inhibited by water than the buteos. They will follow shorelines more closely, and the larger species in particular will strike out over the water if it appears to offer a more direct route to their destination. Hence there is a fall movement of falcons down the Bruce Peninsula, presumably island hopping from Manitoulin.

Black Vulture (*Coragyps atratus*) – Formerly an exceptional vagrant, this species has now been reported almost annually since 1979. Most have been in the extreme south, north to Lambton County and east to Milton and Campbellville, but there are two records farther east from Port Hope and Kaladar. Birds have been seen in all months except November, with 42% between June and August, although a number of recent records have been in early spring.

Turkey Vulture (*Cathartes aura*) – An increasingly common migrant and summer resident in the south and extreme west of the province, much less so in the forested areas of central and northern Ontario, although there are records of wandering birds north to the Hudson Bay coastline. Wintering attempts are also increasingly regular. Spring migration typically starts in early March, peaking at Beamer Point later in the month and in early April. The much heavier fall movements (3,000+ daily) along the lower Lakes peak in late September to early October.

Osprey (*Pandion haliaetus*) – This species has largely recovered from the decline of the 1960s, and now seems a regular but uncommon nesting bird across the north, and south through the Precambrian Shield. In the agricultural areas to the south and west of the Shield, it is confined to a few major wetlands. The Rideau

	J	F	M	A	M	J	J	A	S	O	N	D
Turkey Vulture												
Osprey												
Bald Eagle												
Northern Harrier												
Sharp-shinned Hawk												
Cooper's Hawk												
Northern Goshawk												
Red-shouldered Hawk												

and Muskoka lakes, together with Rice Lake, Lake Scugog, and Luther Marsh, are among the more accessible population centres in the south. A regular migrant in small numbers along the lower Lakes, especially in early fall. Exceptional in winter.

American Swallow-tailed Kite (*Elanoides forficatus*) – Occasional. Recorded in at least six years since 1978, with 75% of the sightings along Lake Erie from Long Point west (May 8–22, Aug. 16–Sept. 5). The other records scatter widely, as do a host of suggestive reports of this distinctive species that have never made it to the formal records!

Mississippi Kite (*Ictinia mississippiensis*) – Occasional. Recorded in at least six years in the last ten, with some 60% of the sightings from Point Pelee (May 9–28). The scattering of other reports includes the only one in fall (Sept. 19).

Bald Eagle (*Haliaeetus leucocephalus*) – Slowly recovering its Ontario numbers. Still a rare bird at any season, much more regular in the northwest. It has a limited stronghold in southern Ontario along western Lake Erie, with scattered pairs elsewhere. Outside the nesting season, birds are seen quite regularly at the Lake Erie hawk watches (September–October), while in winter the St Lawrence River (Ivy Lea) and the Petroglyphs are among the more predictable locations to see them.

Northern Harrier (*Circus cyaneus*) – A rather uncommon and localized breeding bird, favouring wetlands and old fields, and scarce or absent in large areas of the north. A common migrant, particularly in fall, and wintering in small numbers mainly along the lower Lakes.

Sharp-shinned Hawk (*Accipiter striatus*) – An uncommon breeding bird, favouring heavy coniferous woodland, becoming rarer northwards. The species is probably far more numerous in summer than the bar charts imply, but is very elusive and hence only occasionally encountered. Although likely much rarer in winter in absolute terms, it is more readily encountered then because of its habit of visiting feeders. The time to see it is in fall, when it follows the lower Great Lakes' shorelines westwards.

Cooper's Hawk (*Accipiter cooperii*) – Everything said about Sharp-shinned Hawks applies to this species too, except that this is a bird of southern Ontario, favouring deciduous and mixed forest, and is even less often seen (over a season hawk watches record some eight to ten Sharp-shins for every Cooper's). Proportionately more, however, seem to winter, so that a winter accipiter has at least a 50% chance of being this species. A fair proportion of the fall migrants, maybe as many as a half, pass through Point Pelee.

Northern Goshawk (*Accipiter gentilis*) – The Breeding Bird Atlas revealed that this species is commoner in the south than most observers thought, but it is still a rare and elusive bird in summer, and apparently absent from much of the north and southwest. It nests in coniferous woodland, including plantations. It is rare at other seasons as well, its actual numbers varying widely from year to year – its cycle seems to coincide with that of Ruffed Grouse, with a roughly ten-year interval between flights. The falls of 1963 and 1965, 1972–4, 1983, and 1990–2 were good, with 1991 and 1992 exceptional; and in the last decade 1988 and 1989 were poor and the other years seemed average. In good years, peak movement seems to occur in mid-April and mid-October.

Red-shouldered Hawk (*Buteo lineatus*) – An uncommon summer resident in deciduous woodlands in southern Ontario, particularly in the east, north to Lake Nipissing. Scattered pairs have nested farther north and west, and wandering birds have occurred north to the Severn River. It is commonest in areas of more extensive woodland, where it sometimes soars over the canopy in late spring, calling frequently. A fairly common mi-

	J	F	M	A	M	J	J	A	S	O	N	D
Broad-winged Hawk												
Red-tailed Hawk												
Rough-legged Hawk												
Golden Eagle												
American Kestrel												
Merlin												
Peregrine Falcon												
Gyrfalcon												

grant, especially at Beamer Point in the spring, and more generally in fall hawk flights. A few birds winter along the lower
Lakes.

Broad-winged Hawk (*Buteo platypterus*) – A hawk of mixed
forests, often seen sitting on roadside power lines and tree stubs
in such habitat, and in summer probably easiest to find on the
Shield. It is absent from the Hudson Bay Lowland and becomes
very scarce and local in the agricultural south. A common spring
and abundant early fall migrant, often in flocks of thousands
(10,000+), but these numbers are limited to the main migration
routes in ideal weather. Exceptional in winter.

Swainson's Hawk (*Buteo swainsoni*) – Has occurred almost
annually since 1975, with up to four sightings in a year. Some
60% of the reports are from fall (Sept. 5–Nov. 18, 73% of fall
records Sept. 5–Oct. 3); spring dates Apr. 10–May 25, with
most Apr. 27 on. As might be expected, most are seen at the
hawk lookouts (40% from Beamer Point and Hawk Cliff), and
along the lower Lakes, but a few are from the north (Moose
Factory) and the extreme west.

Red-tailed Hawk (*Buteo jamaicensis*) – Ontario's most conspicuous hawk, abundant year-round in the open country over most
of the south. It is much less common in the north, and in winter
north and east of the Toronto region. It is the main constituent
of the early spring and later fall hawk flights (April and October; to 1,500 daily).

Ferruginous Hawk (*Buteo regalis*) – One record (Mar. 17), plus
two spring 1992 reports.

Rough-legged Hawk (*Buteo lagopus*) – A rare summer resident of the extreme north. Elsewhere an irregular migrant and winter visitor, common in some years and almost absent in others, sometimes present throughout the winter in the south and sometimes moving straight through. Exceptional in summer. Heavy flights occur at roughly three to four year intervals, often with good numbers for two, rarely three, consecutive years. The most recent peaks were in the autumns of 1986 and 1987, and 1990 and 1991. Usually present on Wolfe Island in winter.

Golden Eagle (*Aquila chrysaetos*) – A very rare summer resident of extreme northern Ontario (the Sutton Ridges in the Hudson Bay Lowland). Southern Ontario nesting has been reported, one nest as recently as 1989. Otherwise a rare but increasingly regular fall migrant (peak dates Oct. 25–Nov. 12), less frequent in the spring and no more than occasional in summer. Every year yields a dozen or fewer wintering records, most regularly from the Petroglyphs and Algonquin Park.

Crested Caracara (*Caracara plancus*) – One very old record (Jul. 18).

American Kestrel (*Falco sparverius*) – A common nesting bird and migrant in the agricultural areas of the province, thinly distributed in more heavily forested regions. Its winter numbers in the south vary from relatively common to almost absent. This species, like the other falcons, follows the lower Great Lakes' shorelines in fall migration.

Merlin (*Falco columbarius*) – An uncommon breeding bird of coniferous woodlands in northern Ontario, and south very locally to the Bruce Peninsula and the southern Shield. Apparently absent from areas of heavy forest, and with only isolated pairs south of Pembroke and Parry Sound. A rare spring and uncommon fall migrant (peak dates Sept. 29–Oct. 9). Rare in winter.

Peregrine Falcon (*Falco peregrinus*) – Formerly a rare breeder in the province, it has now become more regular following a period of virtual absence at all seasons. Its migratory movements closely parallel those of the Merlin, and it also is rare in winter in the south. Its numbers continue to increase: I seem to see three or four Merlins for every Peregrine, and this ratio is still about right for winter, but in some years their reported migra-

	J	F	M	A	M	J	J	A	S	O	N	D
Gray Partridge												
Ring-necked Pheasant												
Ruffed Grouse												
Wild Turkey												
Northern Bobwhite												

tory numbers are now about equal (peak movement in the south, Sept. 27–Oct. 5).

Gyrfalcon (*Falco rusticolus*) – A rare winter visitor (Sept. 24–Apr. 20), perhaps more regular in the north, but less frequently reported from there due to limited coverage. There is an average of five to ten wintering reports annually but numbers vary from year to year. The winters of 1972–3, 1980–1, 1990–1, and particularly 1991–2 were banner ones for Gyrfalcon flights. Such records typically much exceed those in migration periods. Thunder Bay, Sault Ste Marie, Sudbury, and Ottawa all seem to get more than their fair share of Gyrfalcons.

Prairie Falcon (*Falco mexicanus*) – Records at Hamilton and Long Point likely escapees (September).

PARTRIDGES, PHEASANTS, GROUSE, AND QUAIL

Gray Partridge (*Perdix perdix*) – An uncommon resident of southeastern Ontario (mainly in the areas around Ottawa and Kingston and eastwards); the Niagara Peninsula and of adjacent parts of Hamilton-Wentworth, Haldimand-Norfolk, and Brant counties, with a tiny remnant population in Thunder Bay. Elusive and hard to find even in its limited range, but coveys will visit feedlots and barnyards in the winter, and are easiest to locate at that time.

Ring-necked Pheasant (*Phasianus colchicus*) – An uncommon resident of extreme southern Ontario, mainly south of latitude 44°N. Although it abounds in some suburban areas it has declined in recent years. Heard far more often than seen, it is most reliably found at feeding stations in the colder months. It is commonest in the southwest, particularly on Pelee Island.

Spruce Grouse (*Dendragapus canadensis*) – A resident in coniferous forests, widespread in the north, but extremely localized in southern Ontario, where Algonquin Provincial Park is its main centre of abundance. In spite of – and perhaps as a result of – its legendary tameness, the species is hard to locate even in places where it occurs. Algonquin, partly because of the experienced and helpful staff of naturalists there, continues to be the place to seek this species.

Willow Ptarmigan (*Lagopus lagopus*) – A resident of extreme northern Ontario, north of the tree line. The species is cyclic, and at very infrequent intervals – about every twenty years – it has wandered south, with scattered birds sometimes reaching southern Ontario.

Rock Ptarmigan (*Lagopus mutus*) – An irruptive species that appears very rarely along the north coast.

Ruffed Grouse (*Bonasa umbellus*) – A common resident in well-wooded areas throughout, favouring young second growth with poplar and birch. Populations in the north are cyclic, with lows around the end of each decade. Like all grouse it can be elusive, although the bird's drumming in spring reveals its presence. Most readily seen in the early summer, when females with broods can stage dramatic distraction displays.

Greater Prairie-Chicken (*Tympanuchus cupido*) – No recent records.

Sharp-tailed Grouse (*Tympanuchus phasianellus*) – A resident of peat bogs and brushy areas in the north, and of grassland habitats on Manitoulin Island, around Sault Ste Marie, and the Lake of the Woods. The northern race has staged very periodic irruptions in the past at roughly thirty-year intervals, the most recent being in 1932 and (much smaller) in 1967. There have been introduction attempts in the south, and a small population has been established for at least twenty years along the south shoreline of Prince Edward County, but the birds are extremely hard to find. They are most readily seen in the Rainy River area in spring and fall. Active leks are acknowledged as the best places to see this species, but peak lek activity tends to be in periods when birders are elsewhere!

Wild Turkey (*Meleagris gallopavo*) – In recent years there have been many attempts to reintroduce turkeys to their former range

	J	F	M	A	M	J	J	A	S	O	N	D
Yellow Rail												
King Rail												
Virginia Rail												
Sora												
Common Moorhen												
American Coot												
Sandhill Crane												

across southern Ontario, with the result that flocks are now present in wooded country from the Long Point area in the west and across the Oak Ridges Moraine north of Toronto and eastwards through to Campbellville and Stirling. The Hill Island population near Ivy Lea is the only one that has been established for more than a few years.

Northern Bobwhite (*Colinus virginianus*) – A rare and local resident of southwestern Ontario, particularly Middlesex, Lambton, and Kent counties and the Cambridge area, favouring brushy hedgerows. Bobwhites are hard to locate except by tracing their distinctive calls in spring: early mornings in late April may be best.

RAILS, GALLINULES, AND CRANES

Yellow Rail (*Coturnicops noveboracensis*) – A very rare and local summer resident in the south and around Lake of the Woods, but apparently common along the north coast. There have been small nesting populations in the Holland Marsh and in Richmond Marsh, but the most reliable areas for finding the species have been in the larger sedge and grass marshes of the Rainy River area – currently in the marsh at the end of Fred's Road. This species is most easily located by its distinctive calls, but actually seeing the birds is problematic, and they are rarely encountered away from their breeding marshes (present May 1–Oct. 29).

Black Rail (*Laterallus jamaicensis*) – Exceptional (lower Great Lakes, May 25–August).

King Rail (*Rallus elegans*) – An occasional summer resident, probably regular only in the marshes along Lake Erie and

Walpole Island. Rarely encountered away from the breeding grounds, and in the past most reliably seen at Point Pelee, but the birds there are subject to constant harassment (present Apr. 17–Oct. 20).

Virginia Rail (*Rallus limicola*) – Probably locally common in all wetlands across the south, much less numerous on the Shield, with only scattered nesting in northern Ontario, and occasional records north to Hudson Bay. Like all rails, it is very elusive, and needs special effort to find it, although the birds tend to be noisy in the evenings (present Mar. 3–October). There are a few wintering records every year.

Sora (*Porzana carolina*) – The easiest rail to find, but still easy to overlook. It is regular in marshy areas all across the south, although Atlas records imply it is a little less common there than the Virginia Rail, and it prefers deeper water. Soras are scattered across the north with nesting confirmed for the Hudson Bay coast. They are exceptional in winter to early January (mainly present Mar. 29–Nov. 16).

Purple Gallinule (*Porphyrula martinica*) – An occasional wanderer, with at least nine reports in the past twenty years. Apart from a Moosonee record, all have been in the south, with 70% along the lower Lakes and 60% in fall, but dates range from Apr. 22–Jul. 8 and Oct. 7–Dec. 31.

Common Moorhen (*Gallinula chloropus*) – A locally common but declining summer resident, mainly in wetlands south of the Shield. There are only a scattering of reports from northern Ontario. It is usually most conspicuous in early fall, when the greyish juveniles join the population and can be seen wandering around at the edges of the marsh vegetation. It is exceptional in winter to Jan. 18 (mainly present Apr. 7–Nov. 24).

American Coot (*Fulica americana*) – An uncommon summer resident in larger marshes south of the Shield, with scattered records farther north and in the west. It is a common migrant, and often abundant both spring and fall in favoured localities such as Long Point (10,000+). Large flocks will sometimes remain into early winter, but only scattered individuals attempt to remain past December (mainly present Mar. 5–Dec. 2).

Sandhill Crane (*Grus canadensis*) – A widely distributed summer resident in suitable habitat, mainly bogs, across the north and around Sault Ste Marie, and increasingly regular in the south in both migration and summer. The chart perhaps rather overstates the species' present abundance – it is still very rare in most of the south – but it is increasing steadily, and is now regular in summer on Manitoulin Island and the Bruce Peninsula, and at Ottawa and Long Point. Migrant sightings are mainly from the lower Great Lakes shoreline, with birds sometimes remaining into early winter, exceptionally later.

Whooping Crane (*Grus americana*) – No recent records.

SHOREBIRDS

In general shorebirds move through quickly in spring but have a protracted fall movement. Late spring birds can be seen well into June, while fall adults start to appear as early as the beginning of July, with peaks in late August and again in early October. Shorebird habitat is limited in the region, and largely dependent on Great Lakes' water levels. These are often high in the spring and early fall, resulting in only limited areas of mudflat in the lakeshore marshes. At these times, shorebird concentrations may be few and confined to wet fields and muddy areas. Spring shorebird flocks – Black-bellied Plover, Ruddy Turnstone, Whimbrel, and Dunlin – can regularly be seen flying along the Great Lakes shorelines.

The first fall shorebirds to arrive are typically Lesser Yellowlegs and Least Sandpiper, followed by Greater Yellowlegs and Semipalmated Sandpiper. Leasts and yellowlegs form the nucleus of the concentrations that develop later on mudflats, while Sanderlings, together with Semipalmated Sandpipers and Plovers, predominate on sand beaches. Feeding groups on areas of lakeshore algae are more mixed in composition, and as the season progresses these species are largely replaced by Dunlin, with smaller numbers of Pectoral Sandpipers and snipe. None of the birds is restricted to specific habitats, and other species, such as dowitchers, may also appear in numbers.

Black-bellied Plover (*Pluvialis squatarola*) – A common migrant both in spring, when flocks of thousands have occurred in May (to 13,000), and in smaller numbers with other shorebirds throughout fall; often on arable or short grass fields. Occasionally birds appear during the summer period (Mar. 25–Dec. 13). The onion fields at Pelee are one of the more reliable places for this species in spring.

American Golden-Plover (*Pluvialis dominica*) – A rare breeder along Hudson Bay. Elsewhere it appears as a migrant, its numbers varying widely from year to year. It should be regarded as uncommon, often appearing as one or two birds in a flock of Black-bellied, but flocks of up to 1200 have occurred in both spring and fall (Mar. 12–Dec. 16). Also occasional in summer.

Mongolian Plover (*Charadrius mongolus*) – One record (May 4).

Snowy Plover (*Charadrius alexandrinus*) – Exceptional (May 4–9).

Wilson's Plover (*Charadrius wilsonia*) – Exceptional (May 17–Jun. 2).

Semipalmated Plover (*Charadrius semipalmatus*) – Breeds on the Hudson and James Bay lowlands. One of the commonest shorebird migrants, usually in small numbers on beaches and mudflats (Apr. 19–Dec. 5). Birds often linger into the summer period.

Piping Plover (*Charadrius melodus*) – A few birds maintain a precarious toe-hold in the province on islands in Lake of the Woods, and there are scattered summer reports from beaches elsewhere in its former range. Otherwise the bird is now a rare migrant: typically there are two to five reports each spring, and one in fall (Apr. 18–Nov. 3).

Killdeer (*Charadrius vociferus*) – An abundant nesting bird, much less common in the north where habitat may be scarce. A common migrant, one of the first shorebirds to appear in spring, and often present well into December, but only exceptionally wintering successfully in the south.

American Oystercatcher (*Haematopus palliatus*) – Exceptional (May 22–Jul. 21, Nov. 2).

Black-necked Stilt (*Himantopus mexicanus*) – Occasional. Only three records prior to 1989, four since; with four from the

	J	F	M	A	M	J	J	A	S	O	N	D
Black-bellied Plover												
Am. Golden-Plover												
Semipalmated Plover												
Piping Plover												
Killdeer												
Greater Yellowlegs												
Lesser Yellowlegs												
Solitary Sandpiper												
Willet												

southwest, the rest from the north (May 19–Jun. 23; Sept. 1 and Oct. 14).

American Avocet (*Recurvirostra americana*) – Nesting has been recorded in the Rainy River area. A rare migrant, its appearances varying greatly from year to year. In recent years it has been seen most often in spring (up to seven reports annually, Apr. 20–Jun. 19), usually in ones and twos, but a flock of thirty-four has occurred. Formerly most frequent in fall (up to ten reports annually, Jul. 21–Dec. 11). Almost 70% of sightings are from the southwest, with the rest mainly along Lake Ontario and a scattering from the north.

Greater Yellowlegs (*Tringa melanoleuca*) – A widespread summer resident of the Hudson Bay Lowland, with some south to 50°N. Elsewhere a very common migrant, usually in much smaller numbers than the following species, with subtly different habitat preferences: yellowlegs feeding in deeper or moving water, or dashing around hysterically, are more likely to be this species! It averages an earlier arrival in spring and remains later in fall, although, because the Lesser is the commoner bird, the outside dates imply the opposite (Mar. 12–Dec. 6).

Lesser Yellowlegs (*Tringa flavipes*) – A summer resident of the Hudson Bay Lowland. Elsewhere a very common migrant (Mar. 6–Dec. 20), one of the most usual shorebirds on mudflats, both more frequent and much more numerous than the Greater, with birds occurring regularly in that ambiguous period we call summer.

Spotted Redshank (*Tringa erythropus*) – Exceptional (May 7, Jul. 19–25).

Solitary Sandpiper (*Tringa solitaria*) – An uncommon summer resident of the coniferous forests of northern Ontario, and an uncommon migrant elsewhere, favouring, but not confined to, more wooded wetlands. A shorebird along a woodland stream has a good chance of being this species (Apr. 5–Dec. 1).

Willet (*Catoptrophorus semipalmatus*) – A rare migrant, more common in spring (an average of thirty-one reports, Apr. 13–Jun. 29), when some large flocks of over twenty have occurred. The fall reports cover a much longer period (an average of eight reports, Jul. 7–Nov. 19). The vast majority of sightings are from the lower Great Lakes and the southwest, but there are a number from Thunder Bay and a scattering elsewhere.

Wandering Tattler (*Heteroscelus incanus*) – Exceptional (eastern Lake Erie, Jun. 8–Aug. 1).

Spotted Sandpiper (*Actitis macularia*) – The common nesting sandpiper of shorelines throughout, from farm ponds and river margins to the Great Lakes shorelines. Typically found in ones and twos. There are a handful of winter records (Mar. 27–Jan. 8).

Upland Sandpiper (*Bartramia longicauda*) – A widespread but elusive summer resident of grass and pastureland in southern Ontario, with small populations around Thunder Bay and Lake of the Woods. It is rarely seen in numbers, and disappears very early in the fall (Apr. 4–Oct. 21). Birds are most easily located in spring, where they are most conspicuous and their distinctive whistles can be heard. They are usually associated with areas of dry grassland and old fields, often standing on fenceposts, but are by no means confined to these habitats. The Carden Plain, southern Prince Edward County, and the fields around Pearson Airport are some of a host of good locations for them.

Eskimo Curlew (*Numenius borealis*) – No recent records.

Whimbrel (*Numenius phaeopus*) – A rare nesting bird along the Hudson Bay coast. Elsewhere a regular spring migrant along

	J	F	M	A	M	J	J	A	S	O	N	D
Spotted Sandpiper												
Upland Sandpiper												
Whimbrel												
Hudsonian Godwit												
Marbled Godwit												
Ruddy Turnstone												
Red Knot												
Sanderling												
Semipalmated Sandpiper												

the lower Great Lakes, often occurring in large flocks of up to 3,000 moving along the shoreline. Its main period of movement is usually limited to a few days around May 24, and hence it is easy to miss. The species is much less regular in fall, when large groups are most unusual and the infrequent sightings are usually of individual birds (May 3–Nov. 17).

Slender-billed Curlew (*Numenius tenuirostris*) – One record (October?).

Long-billed Curlew (*Numenius americanus*) – Exceptional (Oct. 17).

Hudsonian Godwit (*Limosa haemastica*) – A rare nesting bird along Hudson Bay, and a regular migrant along the north coast, commonest in fall. Elsewhere a rare spring migrant (Apr. 28–Jun. 12), exceptional in the summer, but much more frequently recorded in fall (Jul. 2–Nov. 15). Most likely in the marshes and along beaches of the lower Great Lakes, as at Pickering and Presqu'île, but also at Ottawa and on Manitoulin Island.

Marbled Godwit (*Limosa fedoa*) – At most a rare summer visitor to the north coast and the Lake of the Woods. Elsewhere a rare visitor in spring (two to eight reports annually, Apr. 12–Jun. 15), less common in fall (usually zero to four reports annually, Aug. 3–Nov. 13); exceptionally in larger numbers, as in fall 1988, and with summer sightings between the dates given. Much less common than the Hudsonian.

Ruddy Turnstone (*Arenaria interpres*) – A common migrant along the lower Great Lakes, much less common elsewhere. Spring migrants are usually in small flocks of up to 200, but in fall the species occurs as individuals scattered among other shorebirds (Apr. 18–Jan. 6). Very occasionally reported in summer and early winter.

Red Knot (*Calidris canutus*) – This species stages in large numbers along the north coast, but elsewhere is an uncommon migrant which mainly occurs along the lower Great Lakes. Like the Ruddy Turnstone, knots are often in small flocks in spring (but may be up to 1,000), and appear singly with other species in fall (May 4–Jun. 15, Jul. 15–Nov. 12). There are a half dozen summer records between the dates shown, and an old winter sighting (Jan. 2).

Sanderling (*Calidris alba*) – A regular spring and common fall migrant, rarely occurring away from the coast or Great Lakes beaches, and recorded very occasionally in early winter (Apr. 18–Dec. 28).

Semipalmated Sandpiper (*Calidris pusilla*) – Nests along the Hudson Bay coast. Elsewhere a common spring and abundant fall migrant (3,000+ birds) if suitable conditions exist: the commonest 'peep' (Apr. 25–Dec. 5).

Western Sandpiper (*Calidris mauri*) – A rare migrant. Much less regular in spring (zero to five records annually, May 3–Jun. 6) than fall, when there are two main periods of movement, one in late July and the second in early September (twenty to thirty records annually, Jul. 16–Dec. 13). There are a couple of summer records between the dates shown. Its exact status is difficult to determine, as the records imply a sharp increase in the mid 1980s, but this probably reflects the publication of better information on identification about that time rather than any actual change in numbers.

Little Stint (*Calidris minuta*) – One record (James Bay, Jul. 10), plus a recent report (Casselman, Jul. 25).

Least Sandpiper (*Calidris minutilla*) – A summer resident of the Hudson Bay Lowland, mainly along the coast. A common mi-

	J	F	M	A	M	J	J	A	S	O	N	D
Western Sandpiper												
Least Sandpiper												
White-rumped Sandpiper												
Baird's Sandpiper												
Pectoral Sandpiper												
Purple Sandpiper												
Dunlin												
Stilt Sandpiper												
Buff-breasted Sandpiper												

grant elsewhere, especially in the south. It is often the commonest 'peep' on smaller muddy areas, although rarely in large numbers (to 500), and is the first to return in fall (Apr. 5–Dec. 23).

White-rumped Sandpiper (*Calidris fuscicollis*) – A common migrant on the Hudson Bay coast. Elsewhere an uncommon late spring and fall migrant, mainly along the lower Great Lakes and on sewage lagoons (May 2–Dec. 8). Most reports are from fall, when it can be locally common when good habitat exists, particularly in late September and late October. Often most numerous at sewage lagoons, but regular in later fall at Presqu'île.

Baird's Sandpiper (*Calidris bairdii*) – A rare spring migrant (zero to four reports annually, May 4–Jun. 6, with isolated records Apr. 2–17 and Jun. 21). Uncommon in fall, usually most numerous early in the season (Jul. 10–Dec. 14). Perhaps most consistently present at Presqu'île in fall, often in small numbers to thirty.

Pectoral Sandpiper (*Calidris melanotos*) – At most a rare summer resident of the north coast. A fairly common spring migrant across the province, often appearing in flocks on wet grassy fields, particularly in the southwest, where counts of over 1,000 birds have been recorded. Common in fall, with an extended migration period that peaks in late August and again in October (Mar. 13–Dec. 4; isolated winter records to Jan. 1 in one year).

Sharp-tailed Sandpiper (*Calidris acuminata*) – Exceptional (Aug. 20–Dec. 5).

Purple Sandpiper (*Calidris maritima*) – An occasional spring (nine records, May 7–30) and rather rare fall migrant, exceptional in summer but often lingering into winter (ten to forty reports annually, Sept. 23–Mar. 7; a couple of late summer reports). It usually appears after most shorebirds have gone, and is as likely to occur in our area on a sandy beach as a rocky headland. Most regular at Niagara Falls, where it possibly winters on the rocks around the falls, but also annual at Presqu'île. Some flocks of up to 134 birds have occurred.

Dunlin (*Calidris alpina*) – Breeds on the Hudson Bay tundra. A very common migrant in the province in spring, often abundant in later fall (flocks to 7,000), and sometimes hanging on well into the winter (Mar. 28–Jun. 20, Jul. 24–Jan. 18).

Curlew Sandpiper (*Calidris ferruginea*) – One or two birds have been reported almost annually since 1984 (May 13–29, Jul. 18–Oct. 21). Almost all are from along the lower Lakes, 64% from fall, and 65% from the southwest.

Stilt Sandpiper (*Calidris himantopus*) – Breeds on the lowlands along Hudson Bay. A rare spring and uncommon fall migrant, mainly along the lower Lakes (Apr. 30–May 30, Jul. 1–Nov. 4, with less than six June reports). It is sometimes in substantial flocks up to fifty birds.

Buff-breasted Sandpiper (*Tryngites subruficollis*) – An occasional visitor in spring (seven records, May 13–Jun. 18), rare in fall (Jul. 9–Oct. 30), sometimes appearing in dryer sections of mudflats, sometimes on ploughed fields or pasture near the Great Lakes. It varies greatly in numbers from year to year, and although, like so many other shorebirds, it is most often seen along the lower Lakes, there are many northern records. The best locality for them over the years, often in numbers of up to 150 birds, has been the onion fields at Point Pelee, but also almost annual at Presqu'île.

Ruff (*Philomachus pugnax*) – Recorded annually since 1966, mainly in spring (zero to twelve reports annually, Apr. 13–Jun. 6). The number of sightings varies from year to year, but the period of spring occurrences has been broadly consistent (some years with many, some few) since about 1981. What does seem

	J	F	M	A	M	J	J	A	S	O	N	D
Short-billed Dowitcher												
Long-billed Dowitcher												
Common Snipe												
American Woodcock												
Wilson's Phalarope												
Red-necked Phalarope												
Red Phalarope												

to have changed is the period and the regularity with which fall birds are sighted; prior to 1984 most of the scattered reports were in the later fall (Sept. 10–Nov. 4), but in the last five years only one has been in this period, and the rest earlier (now one to three reports annually, Jun. 28–Aug. 23). Most sightings are from sewage lagoons in the south in May.

Short-billed Dowitcher (*Limnodromus griseus*) – A summer resident of the north coast. Elsewhere a common spring and fall migrant (flocks up to 150; Apr. 8–Dec. 1). Both *hendersoni* and *griseus* races occur, necessitating caution when identifying the next species.

Long-billed Dowitcher (*Limnodromus scolopaceus*) – An occasional spring migrant, recorded in some nine years since 1970 (Apr. 4–Jun. 1). Rare but regular in fall, with most after mid-August (thirty-five to forty-five reports annually; Jul. 13–Dec. 8).

Common Snipe (*Gallinago gallinago*) – A fairly common summer resident through most of the province, but scarce in the heavily agricultural southwest. In the south, it favours poorly drained fields with sedge cover, and is often associated with red osier dogwood tangles. It is a common fall migrant, although the spring movement is less pronounced. It will occasionally attempt to winter in the south close to patches of open water along creeks and in marshes. It is probably easiest to locate in spring when it perches on poles in between its display flights.

American Woodcock (*Scolopax minor*) – A fairly common summer resident across the south, less common in the more southerly parts of northern Ontario, north roughly to Highway 11. It is best located after dusk in early spring, when the birds are performing their display flights from areas of wet scrubland; sometimes they seem to be calling from every cedar bush. Relatively few are seen on migration, but it has strayed well north of its breeding range, and has attempted to winter in the south.

Wilson's Phalarope (*Phalaropus tricolor*) – A rare breeding bird, with nesting records from the Lake of the Woods area, the north coast, and from scattered localities in southern Ontario. Currently Luther Marsh, Amherst Island, and some of the sewage lagoons in eastern Ontario seem to be the most consistent locations for them in the nesting season. However, the species is a regular but uncommon migrant, especially in early fall, and is most easily found at that time (Apr. 4–Nov. 26). Rainy River lagoon can attract hundreds in mid-May; and fall migrants are often on sewage lagoons as well, but usually single birds, and more often on the shoreline than in the water.

Red-necked Phalarope (*Phalaropus lobatus*) – Nests along the Hudson Bay coast. Elsewhere a rare migrant, much less common in spring (three to eight reports annually, Apr. 12–Jun. 5) than fall, when some small flocks have been seen (thirty-five to forty-five reports annually; flocks of fifteen to thirty-five birds; Jun. 26–Nov. 14). Phalaropes are often seen on the occasional boat trips on the Great Lakes, but most turn up at sewage lagoons.

Red Phalarope (*Phalaropus fulicaria*) – A rare fall migrant (ten to thirty reports annually: most Aug. 25–Nov. 30; there are isolated May 9 and Jul. 28 dates), exceptionally remaining into early winter, with about a dozen December records (one to Jan. 6).

JAEGERS, GULLS, AND TERNS

Pomarine Jaeger (*Stercorarius pomarinus*) – Apart from a couple of late spring records in the south (May 24, Jun. 12) and nonbreeding birds along the north coast, this species is a rare fall migrant. It appears in the same areas as the following species, but later in the season, with birds occasionally sighted in the early winter (Aug. 27–Jan. 2).

Parasitic Jaeger (*Stercorarius parasiticus*) – A summer resident of the lowlands along Hudson Bay. Elsewhere a very infrequent spring (some ten records, Apr. 6–Jun. 18) and rare fall migrant, mainly along the lower Great Lakes and the Ottawa River, occasionally lingering into early winter (Jul. 30–Jan. 5, one report Feb. 11). Uncommon in fall off Sarnia and at the west end of Lake Ontario (Van Wagner's Beach and adjacent areas), where the birds can often be seen from shore, usually well out over the Lake, chasing gulls and one another.

Long-tailed Jaeger (*Stercorarius longicaudus*) – Possibly a rare migrant along the north coast. Recorded almost annually in the south since 1976 (Jun. 10–Oct. 28), mostly in September and October, with 60% from the lower Great Lakes. Exceptional numbers were reported in fall 1993 (ten reports, mainly from Van Wagner's Beach).

Laughing Gull (*Larus atricilla*) – A rare wanderer, occurring almost annually since 1971, varying widely both in numbers and season of occurrence. Almost all are seen on the lower Great Lakes, and May–June and August–September are the main months of appearance; however, birds have occurred in every month of the year. There were twenty-three fall reports in 1985, but five to ten annually are more usual, and the pattern of many sightings suggests one or two wandering birds appearing in heavily birded areas.

Franklin's Gull (*Larus pipixcan*) – A regular migrant and summering bird on Lake of the Woods. Elsewhere it is a rare migrant, most usual in fall and on the lower Great Lakes and the Niagara River, where it often occurs with Bonaparte's Gulls (ten to thirty reports annually; most Apr. 19–Jun. 9, Aug. 10–Dec. 1). There are occasional sightings in summer between the dates shown, and a few winter reports. Niagara in fall is probably the best place for them.

Little Gull (*Larus minutus*) – A rare breeding bird, apparently now established along the northern coast, and in a few scattered localities, notably Long Point, in the south. Since its first North American nesting at Oshawa, this rather unpredictable species has followed a pattern of nesting in a locality for a few years and then abandoning the site, and it is most readily seen outside the nesting period. It is a rather rare spring and fall migrant, most often along the lower Lakes where it can be locally common with small numbers wintering, usually at Long Point and along the Niagara River. The most consistently pro-

	J	F	M	A	M	J	J	A	S	O	N	D
Pomarine Jaeger												
Parasitic Jaeger												
Franklin's Gull												
Little Gull												
Co. Black-headed Gull												
Bonaparte's Gull												
Ring-billed Gull												
Herring Gull												
Iceland Gull												

ductive area at present is Long Point, especially in fall and early winter, but the Niagara region in later fall and winter is still good, and to the east Cornwall dam in fall may yield the species. It often occurs with Bonaparte's Gulls.

Common Black-headed Gull (*Larus ridibundus*) – Another species that turns up in Bonaparte's Gull flocks, this bird is a rare visitor, most frequent along the Niagara River in late fall and early winter. Elsewhere it is occasional in spring (zero to four reports annually, Mar. 19–Jun. 12) and rare in fall (one to four reports annually, Aug. 25–Nov. 30), mainly along the lower Great Lakes. A few birds have been seen in the summer period.

Bonaparte's Gull (*Larus philadelphia*) – This is the common small gull in Ontario. The species nests across northern Ontario. It occurs at all seasons, but is rare in winter away from the Niagara River, and may be absent even there late in the season. Summering birds on the Great Lakes are typically immatures, and may be numerous in some years and virtually absent in others. It is a common migrant, and can occur in huge numbers (100,000+) along the Niagara River and Lake Erie, and smaller numbers stage on Lake Simcoe.

Mew Gull (*Larus canus*) – Occasional. Some twelve reports, appearing almost annually since 1986, with 90% in the waters between Sarnia and Cornwall. It has been sighted in every month except, strangely, September, although 30% have been in October–November, and only one has been in the December–February period.

Ring-billed Gull (*Larus delawarensis*) – An abundant nesting bird on the Great Lakes, with smaller colonies on Lake Superior and a few places across the north. Very common in winter on the lower Great Lakes, rare farther north but possible where open water exists.

California Gull (*Larus californicus*) – Recorded almost annually (Mar. 11–Jan. 18) since an abortive breeding attempt in 1981–2, most regularly at Long Point, and with several reports each year in the 1990s. Most have occurred in the area south of a line between Sarnia in the west and Cornwall to the east, with the majority of reports May 2–Jun. 1 and Nov. 27–Dec. 20. At least one bird appeared in the Niagara River fall gull concentrations in 1992 and 1993. This species' rather abrupt change in status is puzzling, although hearsay reports were not infrequent prior to 1981.

Herring Gull (*Larus argentatus*) – An abundant migrant and winter visitor on the Great Lakes, less numerous but still common in summer, when it is a widespread breeding bird throughout the province. It occurs north in winter as far as open water permits.

Thayer's Gull (*Larus thayeri*) – James follows Godfrey in merging this bird with the Iceland Gull. The need to identify this plumage form remains, however, as it resembles the Herring Gull much more closely than do the other races of Iceland Gull. There have been at least ten to twenty reports over the winter annually in recent years, with smaller numbers in spring and fall, equivalent to some 10-20% of the current Iceland Gull sightings. A disproportionate number of reports come from Ottawa and the St Clair River, but this may be partly a reflection of observer effort. Otherwise its distribution closely parallels that of the Iceland Gull.

Iceland Gull (*Larus glaucoides*) – A rare to uncommon winter visitor on the lower Great Lakes and the major rivers, its numbers varying from year to year, with immature birds exceptionally remaining into and possibly throughout the summer. It is much rarer inland and northwards. The numbers of this species usually reach a peak around Christmas or in the early part of the New Year (and see Thayer's Gull above).

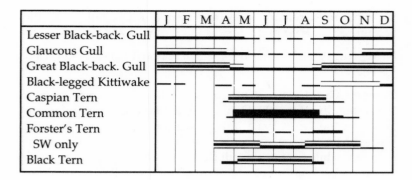

	J	F	M	A	M	J	J	A	S	O	N	D
Lesser Black-back. Gull												
Glaucous Gull												
Great Black-back. Gull												
Black-legged Kittiwake												
Caspian Tern												
Common Tern												
Forster's Tern												
SW only												
Black Tern												

Lesser Black-backed Gull (*Larus fuscus*) – An increasingly regular visitor in both migration periods and in winter. The increase in the number of sightings seems to have slowed in the last three years: there are now some thirty to forty seen in the fall period, fifteen to twenty overwinter, and twenty to thirty in spring, with relatively few seen over summer. The vast majority of the sightings are from the lower Great Lakes and from the traditional gull hot-spots such as Sarnia, Niagara (much the best place for them), and Ottawa.

Slaty-backed Gull (*Larus schistisagus*) – One recent report (Niagara, December 1992).

Glaucous Gull (*Larus hyperboreus*) – An uncommon winter visitor, much more numerous than the Iceland Gull, and more regular in the north and in summer, but otherwise paralleling its pattern of movements and distribution. Look for both species at Niagara in the very late fall and early winter.

Great Black-backed Gull (*Larus marinus*) – Fairly common in winter and in migration periods on the lower Great Lakes and the major rivers in the south (counts of 1,000+ in recent years); rather rare in summer, when it breeds locally on Lakes Ontario and Huron. Only occasional to rare inland and in the north.

Black-legged Kittiwake (*Rissa tridactyla*) – A rare but regular migrant and early winter visitor. There are a few late winter and spring records, with reports in all months, but under twenty between Jan. 30 and Aug. 18. The fall birds appear to move well out on Lake Huron and both of the lower Great Lakes, but are probably most reliably seen from Sarnia in late fall, or on the Niagara River then and later.

Ross' Gull (*Rhodostethia rosea*) – Exceptional (May 14–23, Dec. 11–Feb.21).

Sabine's Gull (*Xema sabini*) – A rare fall visitor (ten to twenty-five annually, Aug. 29–Dec. 13), but likely more regular offshore on the Great Lakes and along the north coast. In some years birds can be found in the fall gull concentrations at Niagara, while the Sarnia gull flight usually records one or two, and the west end of Lake Ontario and Cornwall dam are other places where birds are seen with some regularity. Sept. 25–Nov. 11 is probably the best period, with the probability improving towards November.

Ivory Gull (*Pagophila eburnea*) – An occasional late fall and winter vagrant (Nov. 22–Feb. 20), with some dozen reports in twenty years, half of them from northern Ontario. Most reports are in December, but otherwise there is no particular pattern to the sightings.

Caspian Tern (*Sterna caspia*) – A fairly common summer resident (Apr. 3–Nov. 2, one Dec. 1), nesting mainly along Lakes Ontario and Huron, and infrequent away from major water bodies. Summer records are regular north and west to Hudson Bay, Thunder Bay, and Lake of the Woods.

Royal Tern (*Sterna maxima*) – One record (Aug. 22).

Sandwich Tern (*Sterna sandvicensis*) – Exceptional (lower Great Lakes; Apr. 24–Jun. 25, Oct. 7).

Common Tern (*Sterna hirundo*) – A common migrant and summer resident where suitable nesting habitat exists (Apr. 5–Dec. 15). Fall concentrations of up to 100,000 have been recorded. Early spring sightings should carefully eliminate Forster's Tern.

Arctic Tern (*Sterna paradisaea*) – A summer resident of the north coast. A regular spring migrant at Ottawa (May 17–Jun. 15) and presumably elsewhere on the Ottawa River. There are a few scattered reports from fall and from elsewhere in the south (Apr. 24–Jul. 15, Sept. 4–Nov. 19).

Forster's Tern (*Sterna forsteri*) – A local nesting bird and regular migrant in the southwest (Mar. 21–Dec. 8), principally in the marshes at Rondeau, Long Point, and along Lake St Clair. Elsewhere this species may still be expanding its range, and there are regular sightings in the summer period in suitable marshes, including those of Lake of the Woods. In general, however, it is still a rather rare migrant, more common in fall than spring, when it appears earlier than the Common Tern (mainly Apr. 9–May 31; Sept. 12–Oct. 10).

Least Tern (*Sterna antillarum*) – One record (Jun. 26), plus a recent report (Jun. 9, 1993).

Sooty Tern (*Sterna fuscata*) – One record (Aug. 14).

White-winged Tern (*Chlidonias leucopterus*) – Exceptional in southwest (May 8–18, in 1991 and 1992).

Black Tern (*Chlidonias niger*) – A fairly common migrant and summer resident in marshes in the south (Apr. 19–Dec. 15); rarer in the north, but breeding locally there. Seriously declining; many former nesting sites are now no longer occupied.

Black Skimmer (*Rynchops niger*) – Exceptional (May 7, Jul. 19–25).

ALCIDS

Dovekie (*Alle alle*) – Exceptional (Oct. 23–Feb. 8).

Thick-billed Murre (*Uria lomvia*) – Exceptional; no recent records (Nov. 3–Feb. 28).

Razorbill (*Alca torda*) – Occasional: some six to seven reports in twenty years (most Oct. 14–Jan. 2, particularly November), 80% from Lake Ontario.

Black Guillemot (*Cepphus grylle*) – Rare on the north coast.

Marbled Murrelet (*Brachyramphus marmoratus*) – one recent report (Cornwall, Oct. 11–30, 1993).

Ancient Murrelet (*Synthliboramphus antiquus*) – Exceptional (Nov. 13–18).

	J	F	M	A	M	J	J	A	S	O	N	D
Rock Dove												
Mourning Dove												
Black-billed Cuckoo												
Yellow-billed Cuckoo												
Eastern Screech-Owl												
Great Horned Owl												
Snowy Owl												

Atlantic Puffin (*Fratercula arctica*) – Exceptional (October–Dec. 15).

PIGEONS THROUGH CUCKOOS

Rock Dove (*Columba livia*) – Abundant year-round in the agricultural south; mainly confined to settlements elsewhere.

Band-tailed Pigeon (*Columba fasciata*) – Exceptional (Aug. 30–Dec. 18).

White-winged Dove (*Zenaida asiatica*) – Exceptional (April, June, and December).

Mourning Dove (*Zenaida macroura*) – An abundant summer resident throughout the agricultural south, less common in similar areas northwards; scarce or absent in more forested areas. Wintering numbers have gradually increased in the south, and it is now often one of the more conspicuous winter birds there.

Inca Dove (*Columbina inca*) – One record (Oct. 19).

Common Ground-Dove (*Columbina passerina*) – One record (Oct. 29).

Black-billed Cuckoo (*Coccyzus erythropthalmus*) – An elusive and uncommon summer resident (Apr. 27–Nov. 11) widely distributed across the southern and central regions of Ontario, its range extending across the north of Lake Superior and west to Fort Frances. Numbers of this and the Yellow-billed Cuckoo are supposed to vary with the numbers of tent caterpillars, but these variations can be hard to detect. Both species are easy to miss; they prefer thickets and second growth, and are often most easily found in areas of marginal farmland. Immediately after arrival in late May the birds call persistently and move around more, but this period seems to last barely a week.

Yellow-billed Cuckoo (*Coccyzus americanus*) – This species is similar in its elusiveness and general behaviour to the Black-billed, but its distribution is confined to southern Ontario, and it is relatively rare even there, except in the southwest where it is probably the commoner of the two cuckoos (May 21– Nov. 12).

Groove-billed Ani (*Crotophaga sulcirostris*) – Exceptional (Oct. 9–Nov. 1).

OWLS

Barn Owl (*Tyto alba*) – An endangered nesting bird and now an occasional visitor to the south; formerly more common. This bird's foothold in the province is so precarious that it should be left alone.

Eastern Screech-Owl (*Otus asio*) – A widely distributed resident south of the Shield, present in wooded areas throughout but not usually seen unless the locations of roosting holes are known. Perhaps best located when calling at night, particularly in early spring and in fall. Mobbing by chickadees is often a lead to one of the smaller owls.

Great Horned Owl (*Bubo virginianus*) – A common resident through the south, less so northwards where it appears to be absent from areas of continuous forest. It prefers to roost high in pines and other conifers, but often uses nests in deciduous trees for breeding. It is then easy to locate by its distinctive ear-tufts, which are conspicuous when the bird is on the nest in late winter, although mobbing by jays and crows probably reveal more large owls than anything other than systematic searches. Following the pattern of other owls, northern races occasionally invade during the winter, as in 1954–5, 1969–70, and 1974–5.

Snowy Owl (*Nyctea scandiaca*) – A winter visitor, widespread in some years and rare in others, with birds very occasionally summering in the south. Flights are said to occur at four-year intervals but the timing fluctuates: in Ontario major flights have occurred in the winters of 1964–5, 1971–2, 1974–5 (moderate

	J	F	M	A	M	J	J	A	S	O	N	D
Northern Hawk-Owl	—	—	—								—	—	—
Barred Owl												
Great Gray Owl	—	—	—								—	—	—
Long-eared Owl												
Short-eared Owl												
Boreal Owl	—	—	—										
N. Saw-whet Owl	—	—	—	—	—	—	—	—	—	—	—	—

numbers), 1980–1, 1986–7, and 1991–2, giving intervals of four to six years. An 'echo' flight often follows in the year subsequent to a major movement, but a few birds seem to move south every fall. An unusually early and heavy flight developed in fall 1993. The birds appear in exposed locations, often along the lakeshores, and notably on Wolfe and Amherst islands, as well as Toronto's Eastern Headland.

Northern Hawk-Owl (*Surnia ulula*) – A resident of open coniferous forests in northern Ontario, south to the Kirkland Lake area, very rarely farther south. The species is thinly distributed and difficult to find in the breeding season. A few birds (usually under ten reports) appear south of the breeding range every winter, but very heavy movements occurred in the winters of 1962–3 and 1991–2, with well over one hundred birds seen each year. As usual in owl flights, birds appeared across northern Ontario a month or so before their arrival in the south, and the largest number of reports were from the east of the province. A diurnal owl favouring high perches, it can be quite conspicuous when present.

Burrowing Owl (*Speotyto cunicularia*) – Exceptional (Apr. 19–Jul. 1, Oct. 10–15).

Barred Owl (*Strix varia*) – An uncommon resident mainly in the central and Shield areas of southern Ontario. It favours more continuous forest than the Great Horned, and hence is largely absent from the heavily agricultural southwest. In some winters birds move south in numbers: 1968–9, 1970–1 and 1983–4 were such years, although, as with the Great Horned, such movements are difficult to detect because scattered birds occur regularly in winter away from the breeding range. Algonquin Park and other areas on the southern Shield in April are probably the best places to find this species.

Great Gray Owl (*Strix nebulosa*) – A rare resident of the boreal forests of northern Ontario, although it has nested as far south as Algonquin Park. A few birds wander south of the breeding range almost every winter, but invasions occur periodically, with well over one hundred birds seen in the winters of 1978–9, 1983–4 and 1991–2. Heavier than normal movements also occurred in 1965–6, 1969–70, 1973–4 and 1988–9, suggesting a three- to five-year cycle. Wintering birds are generally fairly conspicuous.

Long-eared Owl (*Asio otus*) – A rarely encountered resident of the province. It is most easily found in the south during winter when roosting birds concentrate in suitable areas, the numbers varying from year to year without much discernible pattern. Wintering roosts (ten to thirty birds) tend to be in low conifers or dense scrub near old fields where rodent concentrations are present, and conifers in country cemeteries are also used. Collections of pellets often identify active roosts. These are frequently deserted if there is undue disturbance, and harassment by birders can cause serious problems, as on Amherst and Wolfe islands. There is a regular migration, when birds occur along the shores of the Great Lakes, but the migrants are rarely visible by day.

Short-eared Owl (*Asio flammeus*) – A rare breeding bird in suitable habitat across the province, and hence absent from most of the forested north. It frequents marshes and open areas of marginal farmland, but its numbers and occurrences vary greatly. Amherst and Wolfe islands are among the most consistent localities for it. An uncommon migrant and winter visitor in the south, its numbers varying from year to year. It is most easily found in winter, when it often roosts near the previous species (ten to forty birds), although it is less regular in its appearances and usually favours more open areas such as airport perimeters and the Toronto Eastern Headland. Diurnal migration can sometimes be seen along the Great Lake shorelines.

Boreal Owl (*Aegolius funereus*) – A resident of coniferous forest in northern Ontario, with Atlas records south to the Sudbury area, but rarely reported except in winter and very early spring (late February–March), when the birds move in small numbers. This is one of the most sought-after of Ontario's owls, difficult to locate even in 'flight' years. These occur at irregular intervals, although there is some coincidence with Great Gray Owl movements: there were twenty or more sightings in the winters of 1962–3, 1977–8, 1983–4, and 1991–2. It is often found in areas being frequented by other wintering owl species.

Northern Saw-whet Owl (*Aegolius acadicus*) – A rare resident of forest land, mainly on the Shield in southern Ontario, but also occurring in the Thunder Bay and Rainy River areas. An uncommon spring migrant, more usual in fall, but requiring special effort to locate. It also occurs in winter, probably in small numbers across the south. Fall migrants stage along the shorelines of the lower Great Lakes in traditional areas, with the dogwood tangles of Toronto Islands being one of the best known. Spring (late February–March) birds often appear in areas where other owls are concentrated, and should be looked for in the tops of grape tangles in river scrub.

GOATSUCKERS THROUGH KINGFISHERS

Lesser Nighthawk (*Chordeiles acutipennis*) – One record (Apr. 29).

Common Nighthawk (*Chordeiles minor*) – An uncommon summer resident and spring migrant formerly much more common, more numerous in fall when it moves south in swirling flocks (up to 500 birds) in early evening (Apr. 2–Nov. 13). It used to be a characteristic bird of urban areas, but is now much less regular in these habitats.

Common Poorwill (*Phalaenoptilus nuttallii*) – One record (Jun. 4).

Chuck-will's-Widow (*Caprimulgus carolinensis*) – A rare summer visitor to southwestern Ontario, mainly at Rondeau and in the Long Point area (May 3–Jul. 31). Although birds have occurred east to Kingston (six records, one as early as Apr. 26), and a summering bird north to Manitoulin Island, reports away from the above stations and the Pelee area total fewer than ten.

Whip-poor-will (*Caprimulgus vociferus*) – An uncommon sum-

	J	F	M	A	M	J	J	A	S	O	N	D
Common Nighthawk												
Whip-poor-will												
Chimney Swift												
Ruby-thr. Hummingbird												
Belted Kingfisher												
Red-head. Woodpecker												
Red-bellied Woodpecker												

mer resident in wooded sections of southern Ontario, commoner on the Shield and north to the Sudbury area. It occurs more rarely along the Ontario border from Thunder Bay westwards, and north to Kirkland Lake. It is a regular but infrequently encountered migrant (Apr. 7–Nov. 5). Easy enough to locate when calling in the open wooded areas it favours, but it requires special effort to see even then, and is rarely found at other times.

Chimney Swift (*Chaetura pelagica*) – An common migrant and fairly common summer resident in the south (Apr. 2–Nov. 10, one Jan. 4 record), extending north to Kirkland Lake and, to the west, to Thunder Bay and Lake of the Woods. Its migration is particularly pronounced in fall when numbers often associate with migrating nighthawks. In summer the birds are largely confined to urban areas, where they may be locally very numerous, and are often absent away from towns.

Green Violetear (*Colibri thalassinus*) – One record (Jun. 30–Jul. 3).

Broad-billed Hummingbird (*Cynanthus latirostris*) – One record (Oct. 16–27).

Ruby-throated Hummingbird (*Archilocus colubris*) – A fairly common spring migrant, when it favours flowering gooseberry and currant shrubs, uncommon in summer in the south and north to about Highway 11, occasional farther north. In summer, particularly in the early part of the season, it makes heavy use of sapsucker sap pits. Common in fall, visiting jewelweed clumps (Apr. 12–Nov. 16).

Black-chinned Hummingbird (*Archilochus alexandri*) – One record (May 25–26).

Rufous Hummingbird *(Selasphorus rufus)* – *Selasphorus*-type hummingbirds, probably of this species, have been reported annually since 1983. The one or two records annually have been scattered widely across the province, the majority from feeders. Of these, 75% have been from fall, and as early as Aug. 25; however, over 30% are from September, and several of the fall birds have lingered, most with active human support, well into winter. The three summer reports were in the Jun. 30–Jul. 30 period.

Belted Kingfisher *(Ceryle alcyon)* – A common summer resident throughout most of Ontario, but becoming rarer in the north. Rare in winter in the south.

WOODPECKERS

Lewis' Woodpecker *(Melanerpes lewis)* – Exceptional (Feb. 6– Mar. 10, May 27, Oct. 27).

Red-headed Woodpecker *(Melanerpes erythrocephalus)* – A fairly common migrant and uncommon summer resident of southern Ontario, mainly south and west of a line from Midland to Brockville (the area to which the information in the occurrence chart applies). Occasional farther north, and rare in winter. The species favours open habitats, and particularly oak woodlands.

Red-bellied Woodpecker *(Melanerpes carolinus)* – A rare nesting bird in southwestern Ontario, mainly in Middlesex and Elgin counties westwards. East of this range the species occurs more irregularly, often at feeders in winter when it can become quite predictable, frequently in migration periods, and occasionally nesting. A series of warm winters in the 1980s allowed this species to consolidate its base in the province and appear more regularly across the south generally. If this warming trend continues, this increase can be expected to continue, but a couple of very cold winters could rapidly reverse it. The graph reflects this ambiguous situation. Probably most easy to find in the Long Point area.

Yellow-bellied Sapsucker *(Sphyrapicus varius)* – A common breeding bird across the more forested sections of the province, but uncommon to absent in summer across much of the south-

	J	F	M	A	M	J	J	A	S	O	N	D
Yellow-bellied Sapsucker												
Downy Woodpecker												
Hairy Woodpecker												
Three-toed Woodpecker												
Black-back. Woodpecker												
Common Flicker												
Pileated Woodpecker												

west. Common in migration, when it often frequents small pines. It is rare in early winter in the south, irregular later, north and east to Peterborough and Ottawa.

Downy Woodpecker (*Picoides pubescens*) – A common resident throughout most of Ontario, rare or absent only north of about 51°N.

Hairy Woodpecker (*Picoides villosus*) – A fairly common resident throughout the province except in the extreme north, but less common in the agricultural south, where it can be quite rare. There is a rather limited fall migration, and winter numbers – often the best time to see the species – vary from year to year.

Three-toed Woodpecker (*Picoides tridactylus*) – A rarely seen woodpecker of northern bogs. While it has bred near Kingston, its usual range lies north from Sudbury, and it is not often encountered even there. Birds appear in the south in most winters, averaging two to three sightings, principally in eastern Ontario, with Ottawa and Algonquin Park the most consistent locations. At irregular intervals, however, they move in larger numbers, with twenty birds or more appearing over a winter. Such flights seem to occur at six- to eight-year intervals, and sometimes for two or three winters in a row: 1956–7, 1963–6, 1974–5, 1980–1, and to a lesser extent 1985–7 were flight years. Both this and the Black-backed are very silent birds, and both are tame, making them easy to overlook. Their soft, persistent tapping seems as good a cue as any to their presence, and trees worked by them often have a distinctive scaled appearance.

Black-backed Woodpecker (*Picoides arcticus*) – A rarely seen woodpecker of coniferous forests, breeding south in small numbers to the Shield in southern Ontario, and particularly in Algonquin Park. This bird is commoner than the Three-toed, and favours drier forest and burns, but otherwise most of the things said about the last species apply to this also. Its movements parallel those of the Three-toed, although it appears in greater numbers, with its peaks involving seventy to eighty reports, and the 1980–1 flight extended into the next two winters as well.

Northern Flicker (*Colaptes auratus*) – An abundant migrant and summer visitor. Rare in winter in the south.

Pileated Woodpecker (*Dryocopus pileatus*) – An uncommon resident of woodlands throughout most of the province, becoming rarer in the north and absent in the Hudson Bay Lowland. It favours larger tracts of woodland, especially bottomlands with old trees and large snags. Heard far more often than it is seen, and most approachable on windy days.

TYRANT FLYCATCHERS

Olive-sided Flycatcher (*Contopus borealis*) – A fairly common summer resident of open spruce and tamarack bogs in the north, this species ranges down through the Shield areas of eastern Ontario, with a few birds in boggy areas on the Bruce Peninsula and elsewhere in the south. It is an uncommon late spring and early fall migrant (May 6–Oct. 5). On the breeding grounds it is noisy, and the calls locate the bird.

Western Wood-Pewee (*Contopus sordidulus*) – One record (Jun. 20; two song records have been questioned).

Eastern Wood-Pewee (*Contopus virens*) – A common migrant and summer resident in open mixed and deciduous forest in southern Ontario, becoming less common towards the northern limits of its range, which is roughly south of a line from Red Lake to Cochrane (Apr. 27–Nov. 27).

Yellow-bellied Flycatcher (*Empidonax flaviventris*) – An uncommon summer resident of coniferous forests in the north. This species ranges down very locally to the Shield areas of eastern

	J	F	M	A	M	J	J	A	S	O	N	D
Olive-sided Flycatcher												
Eastern Wood-Pewee												
Yellow-bellied Flycatcher												
Acadian Flycatcher												
Alder Flycatcher												
Willow Flycatcher												
Least Flycatcher												
Eastern Phoebe												
Great Crested Flycatcher												

Ontario, with a few on the Bruce Peninsula. It is a fairly common late spring and early fall migrant. Spring migrants can be persistent singers and provide the most satisfactory sightings, but are easy to overlook unless the calls are known (Apr. 25–Oct. 25).

Acadian Flycatcher (*Empidonax virescens*) – A rare and rather erratic summer resident in deciduous woodlands in the southwest, occasionally farther east. There are relatively few spring records from more eastern locales (May 6–Sept. 21). Rondeau has been one of the more consistent locations for this bird, but nesting locations are unpredictable, making Pelee in late May one of the better places to look for it.

Alder Flycatcher (*Empidonax alnorum*) – A common summer resident of northern Ontario, less numerous in the south and no more than local in the southwest. It favours alder bogs and wetter shrublands than the Willow, although both flycatchers sometimes seem to overlap. Common in migration, although records of non-singing birds are best assigned to the *traillii* complex (Apr. 25–Oct. 16).

Willow Flycatcher (*Empidonax traillii*) – A common summer resident of brushy areas, willow thickets, and well-grown hedgerows in southern Ontario. It ranges north to the Sudbury area, but most occur south of a line from Midland to Pembroke, and are uncommon on the Shield even in that area. It is probably also fairly common in migration, but most records of non-singing birds are combined with the last species (Apr. 20–?).

Least Flycatcher (*Empidonax minimus*) – A common migrant and common summer resident, but rare or absent on the Hudson Bay Lowland. It favours second growth woodlands (Apr. 8–Dec. 2).

Dusky Flycatcher (*Empidonax oberholseri*) – One recent report (Sept. 13, 1993).

Gray Flycatcher (*Empidonax wrightii*) – One record (Sept. 11), plus a recent report (Jun. 7, 1993).

Eastern Phoebe (*Sayornis phoebe*) – A common migrant and summer resident, north to the line of Highway 11; local northwards. It nests around buildings and under bridges. Occasional in early winter in the south, very rarely after December.

Say's Phoebe (*Sayornis saya*) – Occasional. Some nine reports, with six since 1980, lacking any geographic pattern. Apart from a bird which appeared on Oct. 6 and was kept alive until the following May, reports were all in the periods Apr. 18–May 11 and Jul. 31–Oct. 25, with 55% Sept. 1–Oct. 9.

Vermilion Flycatcher (*Pyrocephalus rubinus*) – Exceptional (Jul. 25, Oct. 29–Nov. 1).

Ash-throated Flycatcher (*Myiarchus cinerascens*) – Exceptional (May 20, Oct. 29–Nov. 25).

Great Crested Flycatcher (*Myiarchus crinitus*) – A common summer resident in the south, north to the Sudbury area and Lake Superior Provincial Park; and at Thunder Bay and in the Lake of the Woods area. Occasional farther north, and a common migrant (Apr. 20–Nov. 9).

Sulphur-bellied Flycatcher (*Myiodynastes luteiventris*) – One record (Sept. 28–Oct. 1).

Variegated Flycatcher (*Empidonomus varius*) – One recent report (Oct. 7–Nov. 6, 1993).

Cassin's Kingbird (*Tyrannus vociferans*) – Exceptional (Jun. 4, Sept. 16–Oct. 8).

Western Kingbird (*Tyrannus verticalis*) – A rare visitor and occasional breeder (once in the south), perhaps regular in the Rainy River area. Elsewhere there are some four to five reports

	J	F	M	A	M	J	J	A	S	O	N	D
Western Kingbird					▬			▬				
Eastern Kingbird					▬▬▬▬▬▬▬▬▬							
Horned Lark	▬▬▬▬▬▬▬▬▬▬▬▬▬▬▬▬▬▬▬▬▬▬											
Purple Martin				▬▬▬▬▬▬▬▬▬▬								
Tree Swallow				▬▬▬▬▬▬▬▬▬▬▬▬								
N. Rough-winged S.				▬▬▬▬▬▬▬▬▬▬								
Bank Swallow				▬▬▬▬▬▬▬▬▬▬								
Cliff Swallow				▬▬▬▬▬▬▬▬▬								
Barn Swallow					▬▬▬▬▬▬▬▬▬							

annually, with 80% from the south and over 60% in fall (May 17–Nov. 20). Long Point, Pelee, and the Toronto area report the most, but this may have more to do with the number of observers than of birds!

Eastern Kingbird (*Tyrannus tyrannus*) – A common migrant and summer resident, very common in the south but progressively rarer northwards, and rare or absent north of about 51°N (Apr. 6–Oct. 19).

Gray Kingbird (*Tyrannus dominicensis*) – Exceptional (Jul. 26, Oct. 29–31).

Scissor-tailed Flycatcher (*Tyrannus forficatus*) – A rare visitor, recorded almost annually since 1978. Over a quarter of the records have been in later May, with somewhat smaller numbers in June and October, with a scattering from July through September (Apr. 25–Nov. 22). Geographically almost a third of the sightings are from northern Ontario, and a disproportionate number in the south are from the Bruce Peninsula and adjacent areas: indeed, over 70% of the sightings are consistent with fall movements through Rainy River, along the north shore of Lake Superior, crossing the west end of Manitoulin and down through the Bruce, and then south, with the route reversed in spring.

Fork-tailed Flycatcher (*Tyrannus savana*) – One record (Oct. 28–30), plus a recent report (Sept. 29–30).

LARKS, SWALLOWS

Horned Lark (*Eremophila alpestris*) – A common summer resident of open country throughout, absent from forested areas. It winters in small numbers north at least to Sudbury, and to Lake Superior on occasion. It is one of the first birds to reappear in the spring, sometimes in large flocks (up to 1,000 birds) but can be hard to find in later summer.

Purple Martin (*Progne subis*) – A fairly common migrant and summer resident of southern Ontario, north to the north shore of Lake Huron; also in the Thunder Bay and Rainy River areas, but very local northwards. It is dependent on nest boxes, favouring those near waterbodies. Some large fall concentrations have occurred of up to 16,000 birds, notably along the Niagara River (Mar. 20–Oct. 26).

Tree Swallow (*Tachycineta bicolor*) – A common migrant and summer resident (Feb. 24–Dec. 22), the most widespread of the swallows in the province, favouring nest boxes and wetlands with dead trees, and the major constituent of large roosts of migratory swallows in early fall (August; up to 300,000 birds). These are typically in cattail marshes such as the Great Cataraqui Marshes and in Matchedash Bay, but tend to be deserted by the birds after a few years of regular use, as at Pembroke.

Violet-green Swallow (*Tachycineta thalassina*) – One record (Oct. 28–29).

Northern Rough-winged Swallow (*Stelgidopteryx serripennis*) – A fairly common swallow in the south, occurring mainly along watercourses; becoming rare northwards but recorded north to Cochrane, Thunder Bay, and in northwestern Ontario. Common in migration, it is less gregarious than the other swallows, but flocks of up to 700 birds have been reported (Mar. 16–Nov. 28, but with several winter records at London, to Jan. 6).

Bank Swallow (*Riparia riparia*) – A common migrant (Mar. 13–Nov. 16) and summer resident, when it is rather local and largely absent from much of the north, limited perhaps by the availability of nesting sites. The nesting colonies can be quite small, and sites are often abandoned after a few years. Migrant concentrations in mid-May and early August of up to 100,000 birds are regular, especially at Long Point.

Cliff Swallow (*Hirundo pyrrhonota*) – An uncommon migrant and local summer resident, when it nests almost entirely on man-made structures such as under eaves and bridges, and tends to forage very close to the breeding colony. Sites are usually abandoned after a few years. It is rare or largely absent north of the Highway 11 line, but is often relatively more numerous around populated areas in the north than it is farther south. It is rare in significant parts of the south, such as the Niagara Peninsula, Algonquin Park, and the counties of Lambton and Essex (Mar. 17–Nov. 2).

Cave Swallow (*Hirundo fulva*) – One record (Mar. 21).

Barn Swallow (*Hirundo rustica*) – The common swallow of the agricultural countryside, and quite common across the more settled parts of the north as well. A common migrant (Mar. 29–Jan. 21), sometimes forming large roosting flocks of up to 25,000 birds in early fall with other swallows.

JAYS, CROWS

Gray Jay (*Perisoreus canadensis*) – A common, but often elusive, resident of coniferous forests in the north. It extends south through the Shield in smaller numbers, with its centre of abundance there in Algonquin Park, where the birds are easier to find in the colder months. A few birds appear south of their breeding range in most winters, but occasionally a larger exodus occurs: the most recent was in 1986–7, but much larger movements occurred in 1961–2, 1964–5, 1972–3, and 1975–6.

Blue Jay (*Cyanocitta cristata*) – An abundant migrant and summer resident, north to about 51°N, becoming much less common northwards. It is fairly common in winter in the south, becoming uncommon as the season progresses. Enormous flights of jays of up to 50,000 a day move westwards along the lower Great Lakes in September, with a heavy, but less pronounced spring movement north and eastwards.

Clark's Nutcracker (*Nucifraga columbiana*) – Exceptional (Nov. 14–Jun. 19).

Black-billed Magpie (*Pica pica*) – A resident of the Rainy River area, rarely east to Atikokan. Occasional birds appear in the south, although most are judged escapees; however, the species also seems to stage infrequent fall and winter flights which

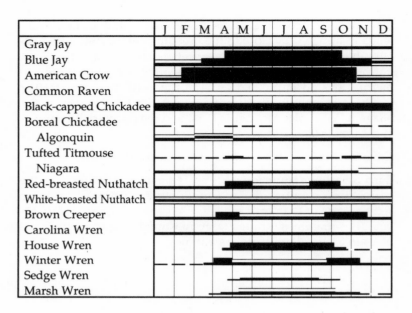

	J	F	M	A	M	J	J	A	S	O	N	D
Gray Jay												
Blue Jay												
American Crow												
Common Raven												
Black-capped Chickadee												
Boreal Chickadee												
Algonquin												
Tufted Titmouse												
Niagara												
Red-breasted Nuthatch												
White-breasted Nuthatch												
Brown Creeper												
Carolina Wren												
House Wren												
Winter Wren												
Sedge Wren												
Marsh Wren												

result in birds appearing east to Lake Superior, and a few southern records are associated with these movements.

Eurasian Jackdaw (*Corvus monedula*) – Exceptional (Apr. 13, Oct. 20).

American Crow (*Corvus brachyrhynchos*) – Abundant in migration and during summer, although much rarer north of 50°N. Common in the south in small numbers during winter, but increasing southwestwards, with Essex County roosts to 90,000 birds.

Fish Crow (*Corvus ossifragus*) – Exceptional (Apr. 21–May 20).

Common Raven (*Corvus corax*) – A common resident in the north, extending south in smaller numbers to a line roughly from Southampton to the Kingston area and then north to Ottawa, but expanding its range. An occasional visitor southwards, particularly in fall migration when it is now reported annually, usually during hawk flights (peak dates Sept. 28–Nov. 5).

TITMICE THROUGH CREEPERS

Black-capped Chickadee (*Parus atricapillus*) – A common resident of woodlands north to the Hudson Bay Lowland, but scarce in the extreme southwest. At irregular intervals – roughly every three years, with the most recent in 1990 and 1993 – there are huge flights (4,000+ daily) in October–November.

Carolina Chickadee (*Parus carolinensis*) – One record (May 18).

Boreal Chickadee (*Parus hudsonicus*) – An elusive resident of spruce forests in the north, extending south very locally to Algonquin Park, which is the best place for a southerner to see it. Elsewhere in the south it is an occasional visitor. The birds sometimes appear in numbers in fall, either as part of Black-capped Chickadee flights or alone, and isolated birds often winter subsequently in the south, and a few also stage return movements in spring. Particularly heavy fall flights occurred in 1951, 1972, 1975, 1981, and 1986, but the twenty-five-years to 1986 saw such movements at three to five-year intervals.

Tufted Titmouse (*Parus bicolor*) – A rare resident of the Niagara Peninsula and adjacent areas, most reliably seen visiting feeders in Niagara-on-the-Lake, less regular elsewhere in the southwest. The species has become better established during the warm winters of the 1980s, and scattered birds are now recorded annually in migration periods across the south, and winter regularly.

Red-breasted Nuthatch (*Sitta canadensis*) – A fairly common summer resident of coniferous woodlands, scarce or absent in the deciduous forest habitats of the southwest. A common migrant, its numbers varying greatly from year to year. Generally rare in winter in the south, but its numbers then also vary. A rather inconspicuous bird, more often heard than seen.

White-breasted Nuthatch (*Sitta carolinensis*) – A fairly common resident of mixed and deciduous woodland in the south, becoming scarce in the coniferous forest areas, and largely absent north of 48°N, except around Thunder Bay and Rainy River. Much less numerous in migration than the Red-breasted, but it stages periodic fall irruptions, at roughly six year intervals (most recently in 1989).

Brown Creeper (*Certhia americana*) – An uncommon and irregularly distributed summer resident, seemingly absent from much of the north and scarce or absent in much of the southwest. It is rather rare in winter in the south. A common migrant, when it is most easily seen; however, a familiarity with the brief song is a boon in locating otherwise elusive birds in summer.

WRENS

Rock Wren (*Salpinctes obsoletus*) – Exceptional (October–Mar. 5, and May 1–6).

Carolina Wren (*Thryothorus ludovicianus*) – A rare to uncommon resident in the southwest, currently expanding both its numbers and range into the rest of the south, with birds east to Kingston and Ottawa, and north to Parry Sound and Gravenhurst and occasionally even farther north. Two or three cold winters could reverse this trend, and the species barely survived in the province in the 1970s. Pelee continues to be the best place to see it.

Bewick's Wren (*Thryomanes bewickii*) – An occasional visitor in the south, with almost half the reports from Pelee, 28% from Long Point and Rondeau, and fewer than twelve away from the southwest, most of them from the Toronto region. Some 80% of the sightings are from spring (Apr. 1–May 26), with almost half of those in the first two weeks of May. The few fall reports are mainly in October (Sept. 17–Oct. 27). There is a scattering of other sightings, and indeed the bird was formerly more common: it was seen annually in the 1970s with substantially less coverage, and there were breeding attempts in the 1950s.

House Wren (*Troglodytes aedon*) – A common migrant and summer resident in the south, becoming rare on the Shield and largely absent north of the Sudbury area, except for stations at Thunder Bay and Rainy River. Occasional in early winter (Mar. 25–Jan. 23).

Winter Wren (*Troglodytes troglodytes*) – A common migrant and summer resident, local in summer in the south, where it favours cedar bogs, but rare in the southwest. Rare in the south in winter, most frequent then in the southwest.

Sedge Wren (*Cistothorus platensis*) – A widespread but elusive summer resident of grassy tangles and sedge meadows, mainly in the south and between Thunder Bay and Lake of the Woods, the best place to see them. The scattered small colonies in which these birds nest do not seem to persist, even when the habitat appears unchanged. The Atlas revealed the species as most widespread in areas of the Bruce Peninsula, Luther Marsh, and Kingston, and Long Point has been another consistent site for them. It is rarely encountered on migration (Apr. 21–Nov. 10), and there is one old winter record.

Marsh Wren (*Cistothorus palustris*) – A local summer resident in the south and in the Lake of the Woods area. It is usually in good numbers in larger cattail marshes, and is not often seen away from its nesting habitat (Mar. 15–Nov. 26, with isolated wintering records).

KINGLETS THROUGH THRUSHES

Golden-crowned Kinglet (*Regulus satrapa*) – A common summer resident of the coniferous forests of northern Ontario, local in the south with its centre of abundance on the Shield. It favours mature trees, and has widely colonized conifer plantations, as at Long Point. An abundant migrant, and uncommon in winter in the south.

Ruby-crowned Kinglet (*Regulus calendula*) – A very common summer resident of coniferous forests of northern Ontario, less common than the Golden-crowned in the south. It does not seem to adapt to planted conifers, and occurs mainly on the Shield. An abundant migrant, occasional in the south in winter.

Blue-gray Gnatcatcher (*Polioptila caerulea*) – A rare to uncommon summer resident in the south, north roughly to a line from Southampton to Ottawa, but mainly in the southwest, where it can be locally common (as at Pelee) and along Lake Ontario. It is rare northwards and rare to uncommon on migration (Apr. 11–May 23, Sept. 2–Nov. 8), with the occasional bird lingering into early winter (to Feb. 12). A familiarity with its thin, peevish notes is a major aid in locating this species.

Siberian Rubythroat (*Luscinia calliope*) – One record (Dec. 26, dead).

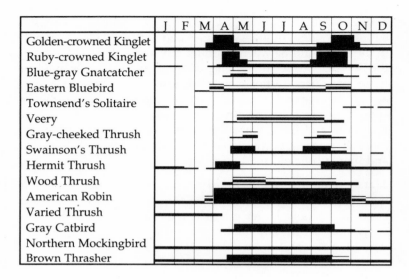

	J	F	M	A	M	J	J	A	S	O	N	D
Golden-crowned Kinglet												
Ruby-crowned Kinglet												
Blue-gray Gnatcatcher												
Eastern Bluebird												
Townsend's Solitaire												
Veery												
Gray-cheeked Thrush												
Swainson's Thrush												
Hermit Thrush												
Wood Thrush												
American Robin												
Varied Thrush												
Gray Catbird												
Northern Mockingbird												
Brown Thrasher												

Northern Wheatear (*Oenanthe oenanthe*) – An occasional visitor, possibly regular on the Hudson and James Bay coasts, where summer birds have been recorded. Of the records south of Hudson Bay, 60% are from the east, with some three-quarters of those associated with a line along the James Bay coast to Moosonee and then south to follow the Ottawa River. Over 85% of the sightings are from fall (Aug. 26–Oct. 18). The other records are scattered both in terms of date (Mar. 19–Jul. 2) and location.

Eastern Bluebird (*Sialia sialis*) – An uncommon migrant and summer resident, absent both from areas of intensive cultivation and extensive forest, and from about 50°N. It is commonest in areas of marginal farmland, especially where nest boxes exist. Rare in the south in winter.

Mountain Bluebird (*Sialia currucoides*) – An occasional visitor. Appearances are about evenly divided between north and south, and some 70% are in fall and early winter (Sept. 26–Dec. 29, one Jan. 24–Mar. 20). The few spring records are mainly in April (Mar. 31–May 20).

Townsend's Solitaire (*Myadestes townsendi*) – A rare winter visitor (Sept. 18–May 10), mainly from the Hamilton area east, with

Toronto yielding more than its share. Birds have tended to remain in one locality for some time, and favour buckthorn fruit.

Veery (*Catharus fuscescens*) – A fairly common migrant and summer resident in wet woodlands, to about 50°N (Apr. 21–Nov. 28, one Dec. 27).

Gray-cheeked Thrush (*Catharus minimus*) – Rare in summer in the extreme north; elsewhere an uncommon – or perhaps simply under-reported – migrant (Apr. 22–Nov. 7). There are three or four winter records (to Dec. 23).

Swainson's Thrush (*Catharus ustulatus*) – A common summer resident of coniferous woodlands in the north, in smaller numbers south, roughly to a line from Southampton to Ottawa. Very local farther south and absent from the southwest. A very common migrant (Mar. 3–Nov. 5), lingering occasionally into early winter (to Jan. 21).

Hermit Thrush (*Catharus guttatus*) – A common summer resident in the north, its distribution similar to Swainson's, but extending farther south and east, where it often occurs in older pine plantations. A very common migrant, and isolated birds winter regularly in the south.

Wood Thrush (*Hylocichla mustelina*) – A widespread nesting bird of deciduous and mixed woodlands in southern Ontario, north to New Liskeard and Lake Superior Provincial Park, becoming uncommon northwards, and probably declining. An uncommon migrant (Apr. 14–Nov. 14), with only a couple of winter records (to Dec. 30).

Eurasian Blackbird (*Turdus merula*) – One disputed record.

Fieldfare (*Turdus pilaris*) – Exceptional (Jan. 1–May 24).

American Robin (*Turdus migratorius*) – An abundant migrant and summer resident, becoming much less common northwards. Wintering birds are regular, sometimes in numbers in the south, occasional farther north.

Varied Thrush (*Ixoreus naevius*) – A rare winter visitor, with about ten reports annually (Sept. 26–May 20, but a few later, to Jul. 17). Single birds often appear in a location and winter there, seeming to favour heavy coniferous cover near feeders. Appearances are rather evenly spread geographically with the most in the Toronto area, perhaps partly a reflection of the number of observers and feeders there in winter.

THRASHERS THROUGH PIPITS

Gray Catbird (*Dumetella carolinensis*) – A common migrant and summer resident of brushy habitats in the south, becoming less common towards Lake Nipissing, and then north in small numbers to Kirkland Lake and Kenora. It is rare in winter in the south.

Northern Mockingbird (*Mimus polyglottos*) – An uncommon resident of the Niagara Peninsula, the best area in which to find it. Elsewhere a rare visitor, which occasionally will winter or summer in a locality. It has become established in very small numbers in scattered locations across the province, as at Kingston, Ottawa, and Sudbury. Most wanderers typically appear in May (Apr. 28-May 29) and less frequently in later fall (Oct. 26–Nov. 26). It likes *multiflora* rose plantings.

Sage Thrasher (*Oreoscoptes montanus*) – Exceptional (Apr. 27–Jun. 4, Jul. 21, Oct. 20).

Brown Thrasher (*Toxostoma rufum*) – A common migrant and summer resident in old field and edge habitats in the south, north in small numbers to Kirkland Lake and Kenora. A few birds usually winter in the south.

American Pipit (*Anthus rubescens*) – A summer resident of the Hudson Bay coast. Elsewhere a rare spring and common fall migrant (Mar. 16–Jun. 8, Jul. 27–Dec. 7). Exceptional in winter (most to Jan. 15, a few later).

Sprague's Pipit (*Anthus spragueii*) – Exceptional in the north, but breeding season records of apparently territorial birds near Rainy River suggest it may occur more regularly there (May–Jul. 6).

WAXWINGS THROUGH VIREOS

Bohemian Waxwing (*Bombycilla garrulus*) – A rare summer resident in extreme northern Ontario, with a few summer records

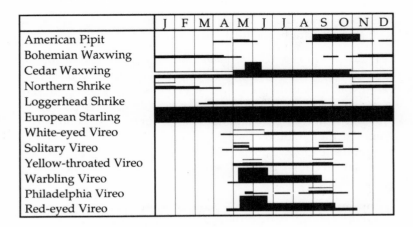

	J	F	M	A	M	J	J	A	S	O	N	D
American Pipit												
Bohemian Waxwing												
Cedar Waxwing												
Northern Shrike												
Loggerhead Shrike												
European Starling												
White-eyed Vireo												
Solitary Vireo												
Yellow-throated Vireo												
Warbling Vireo												
Philadelphia Vireo												
Red-eyed Vireo												

elsewhere across the north. Elsewhere in Ontario an irregular winter visitor which appears to have become more common over the past twenty years (Sept. 17–May 12). It is reported annually, often as single birds in flocks of Cedar Waxwings, but sometimes in sizeable flocks, and in the south favours mountain ash and *multiflora* rose plantings. Flight years occur at roughly three- to four-year intervals (most recently, 1975–6, 1980–1, 1985–6, 1989–90 and 1993–4). The birds appear most regularly in the north and east of the province, and one of the more reliable places for this species has been the Ottawa area.

Cedar Waxwing (*Bombycilla cedrorum*) – A very common migrant and summer resident, uncommon in winter in the south, when numbers vary greatly depending on the berry crop. Winter birds in particular rove the countryside in small flocks, concentrating in any area where they locate good supplies of food. Spring birds are one of the latest migrants to return.

Phainopepla (*Phainopepla nitens*) – Exceptional (Dec. 27– Mar. 1).

Northern Shrike (*Lanius excubitor*) – A rare breeding bird in the extreme north. Elsewhere an uncommon fall migrant and winter visitor (Sept. 10–May 2, with a few later in the north), often becoming much scarcer after the end of the year. The birds range widely over open country, sitting high in treetops, and frequently stage attacks on birds at feeders. Numbers vary from year to year, with flights at roughly four- to five-year intervals (most recently, 1976–7, 1981–2, 1986–7 and 1990–1) often with an 'echo' flight the following year.

Loggerhead Shrike (*Lanius ludovicianus*) – A rare and declining migrant and summer resident in the south, considered endangered, and now only occasional elsewhere (Feb. 18–Dec. 27, but very few good records after September). It favours poor pastureland with well-grown thorn bushes, but is largely gone from much former habitat. Its remaining strongholds are in the Kingston and Ottawa areas, with smaller numbers on the Carden plain and in Grey County. Possible nesting birds should be left undisturbed.

European Starling (*Sturnus vulgaris*) – Abundant year-round through most of the south, becoming rarer in forested areas and in the north, where it winters in larger communities.

White-eyed Vireo (*Vireo griseus*) – A rare summer resident of brushy edge habitats in southwestern Ontario, principally at Rondeau and Pelee, and easiest to find there in spring when it is singing. A rare migrant elsewhere in the province, mainly in May (Apr. 7–Nov. 18, with three or four records to Dec. 29).

Bell's Vireo (*Vireo bellii*) – An occasional spring visitor at Pelee (May 6–22, one Jun. 23), appearing at two- or three-year intervals, but less regular since 1986. There have been a few reports elsewhere in the south, east to Presqu'ile.

Black-capped Vireo (*Vireo atricapillus*) – One record (Apr. 27).

Solitary Vireo (*Vireo solitarius*) – A common summer resident of the taller coniferous forests of northern Ontario, rarer to the south, where it is mainly confined to the Shield. It also uses mature coniferous plantations, as across the Oak Ridges Moraine and in the St Williams area. A fairly common migrant in very small numbers (Mar. 31–Nov. 27, one Dec. 12).

Yellow-throated Vireo (*Vireo flavifrons*) – A rather rare migrant and summer resident in the south (Apr. 18–Nov. 3) occurring in stands and groves of mature deciduous trees. Rondeau, the Halton County Forest, and the forests north of Kingston are among the established localities for this bird, and early mornings in late May are probably the best times to locate it.

Warbling Vireo (*Vireo gilvus*) – A very common migrant and summer resident in the south, north to Sudbury and Sault Ste Marie, and in the Rainy River area (Apr. 23–Nov. 19). It favours open woodland, parkland, and gardens with deciduous trees.

Philadelphia Vireo (*Vireo philadelphicus*) – A summer resident, uncommon in the north and favouring aspen groves, but absent on the Hudson Bay Lowland; very easy to overlook due to its song's close similarity to that of the Red-eyed. It is very local in the south, mainly on the Shield, and is an uncommon migrant (Apr. 21–Nov. 10).

Red-eyed Vireo (*Vireo olivaceus*) – A very common migrant and summer resident in broad-leaved and mixed woodlands almost throughout; less common northwards, where it favours aspen groves (Apr. 9–Nov. 16).

WOOD-WARBLERS

There is a distinct sequence to the spring warbler migration, starting with Yellow-rumped and Pine, followed by Palm, Yellow, and Black-and-White Warblers and Northern Waterthrush; with American Redstart, Wilson's, Canada, and Bay-breasted appearing towards the end, followed by Mourning, Connecticut, and Blackpoll Warblers. Females seem to average about a week later in arrival than males. These patterns are difficult to portray in the bar charts, and in any case in any given year are often distorted by the weather. Their existence, however, often accounts for the seeming variations in the relative abundance of species from one year to another, because weather conditions can create good concentrations early in May in one year and later in another, with the result that different species are seen.

Blue-winged Warbler (*Vermivora pinus*) – A rare migrant and summer resident in the south (Apr. 19–Nov. 4, one Dec. 2). Most occur in the southwest, with a few east to the Kingston area, with the main centre of abundance in an area roughly bounded by Tillsonburg, Woodstock, Cambridge, Hamilton, and Long Point. Exceptional in the north. This species continues to expand its numbers and range at the expense of the Golden-

	J	F	M	A	M	J	J	A	S	O	N	D
Blue-winged Warbler					▬			▬				
Golden-winged Warbler					▬			▬				
Tennessee Warbler					▬			▬	▬			
Orange-crowned Warbler					▪					▬		
Nashville Warbler				▪	▬				▬	▬		
Northern Parula					▬					▬		
Yellow Warbler					▬					▬		
Chestnut-sided Warbler					▬					▬		
Magnolia Warbler					▬				▬			

winged Warbler, notably in Oxford County, and may eventually replace the latter across its present range. Both favour brushy edges and old field habitats and often do not sing for long, so finding them requires early visits, both in the day and the season.

Golden-winged Warbler (*Vermivora chrysoptera*) – A rare migrant and local summer resident in the south (Apr. 21–Oct. 27), inhabiting the same areas in the southwest as the Blue-winged and being displaced by it, but also widespread in suitable habitat north at least to Sudbury, and particularly numerous in the abandoned farmland along the southern edge of the Shield. Of the two hybrids with the Blue-winged, Brewster's are regular, but Lawrence's are exceedingly rare.

Tennessee Warbler (*Vermivora peregrina*) – A common summer resident of mixed and edge habitats in northern Ontario, south to the Sudbury area. Farther south the species is uncommon through the Algonquin area, with only scattered birds elsewhere, although singing individuals wander throughout the south well into the nesting season. A common migrant (Apr. 18–Nov. 17). This species, with Cape May Warbler and Bay-breasted Warbler, is capable of increasing its numbers explosively during periods of spruce budworm outbreak; hence its abundance varies dramatically, and it is currently in decline after a number of years of abundance.

Orange-crowned Warbler (*Vermivora celata*) – A local summer resident of the boreal forest, mainly north of 52°N, favouring shrubby areas and open woodland. Elsewhere a rare spring and uncommon later fall migrant, occasional in early winter (Apr. 20–Dec. 28, one to Jan. 26).

Nashville Warbler (*Vermivora ruficapilla*) – A very common migrant, and a common breeding bird in dense second-growth coniferous woodland across the north, south through the Shield, and then locally west to a line roughly from the Pinery to Long Point. Occasional in early winter (Apr. 3–Jan. 6).

Virginia's Warbler (*Vermivora virginiae*) – Exceptional (May 3–16, all Pelee area).

Northern Parula (*Parula americana*) – An uncommon migrant, rare and local in summer (Apr. 14–Nov. 28). It favours spruce draped in *Usnea* lichen, rare commodities in southern Ontario. In the north, birds are most common along Lake Superior and thence westwards to Fort Frances; in the south, Algonquin is the main stronghold, with smaller numbers on the Bruce and Manitoulin Island.

Yellow Warbler (*Dendroica petechia*) – A common migrant and summer resident in shrubby areas throughout: one of the commonest warblers. There are a couple of December records, but generally it is one of the first warblers to leave (Apr. 27–Nov. 19, two to Jan. 6).

Chestnut-sided Warbler (*Dendroica pensylvanica*) – A common summer resident north to about 51°N and south across the Shield, but local elsewhere in the south. It favours shrubby deciduous growth along forest edges. A common migrant (Apr. 17–Nov. 23).

Magnolia Warbler (*Dendroica magnolia*) – A very common summer resident in the north, south more locally across the Shield. Very local elsewhere in the south, but it favours coniferous forest edge, and will utilize mature coniferous plantations. A very common migrant (Apr. 18–Nov. 18, a couple to Dec. 5).

Cape May Warbler (*Dendroica tigrina*) – An uncommon migrant, and summer resident of mature coniferous forest in northern Ontario where spruce budworm is plentiful. It extends south to the Algonquin area, and is occasional in early winter (Apr. 18–Dec. 27). Like the Tennesseee, this species' abundance varies dramatically.

	J	F	M	A	M	J	J	A	S	O	N	D
Cape May Warbler												
Black-throated Blue W.												
Yellow-rumped Warbler												
Black-throated Green W.												
Blackburnian Warbler												
Pine Warbler												
Prairie Warbler												
Palm Warbler												
Bay-breasted Warbler												

Black-throated Blue Warbler (*Dendroica caerulescens*) – A fairly common summer resident on the Shield north to about 49°N, very local elsewhere in the south. It favours understorey shrubs in deciduous woodland. A fairly common migrant (Apr. 26– Nov. 25; one to Dec. 16).

Yellow-rumped Warbler (*Dendroica coronata*) – A very common summer resident of conifers in the north, south in smaller numbers to a line roughly from Goderich to Kingston; and very local in the rest of the south. An often abundant migrant, the first to arrive in spring and moving in numbers long after most other warblers have left in fall (Apr. 1–Nov. 15). Wintering attempts are almost annual, and occasionally successful.

The Western Audubon's race appears almost annually, with about 30% of the reports from Pelee. Birds appear mainly in the spring, averaging later than the Myrtle race (Apr. 6–May 29), with only a few fall (Oct. 22–Nov. 13) and winter records (Dec. 1–Jan. 31).

Black-throated Gray Warbler (*Dendroica nigrescens*) – An occasional visitor, almost half the reports from the Toronto area (May 3–Jun. 17, Aug. 11–Jan. 6).

Townsend's Warbler (*Dendroica townsendi*) – An occasional visitor, almost all in the southwest (Apr. 23–May 19).

Hermit Warbler (*Dendroica occidentalis*) – Exceptional (Apr. 30– May 23, Sept. 10).

Black-throated Green Warbler (*Dendroica virens*) – A common summer resident in northern Ontario, north to about 52°N, south more locally across the Shield and in the Bruce Peninsula. Its distribution through the rest of the south is limited by the availability of suitable habitat, usually well-grown coniferous forest, although it occurs in mixed stands as well, where it favours pines. A very common migrant (Apr. 17–Nov. 11).

Blackburnian Warbler (*Dendroica fusca*) – A fairly common summer resident of northern Ontario, north to at least 50°N, extending south more locally across the Shield and in the Bruce Peninsula. Its habitat and distribution are very similar to that of the Black-throated Green, but it forages in the upper branches of the conifers. A fairly common migrant (Apr. 23–Nov. 11, one Jan. 8–9).

Yellow-throated Warbler (*Dendroica dominica*) – A very rare visitor, with one to twelve reports annually. Occurrences fall into two clear groups: spring birds, which occur in a relatively limited period (Apr. 9–May 22, most in May), and area, with over 85% in the southwest and over half of those from Pelee, account for over three-quarters of the reports. The other quarter are from fall and winter (Jul. 8–Jan. 5, but over 80% Oct. 14 or later), and here the reports are scattered at random across the province, and many of the birds appeared at feeders and stayed for a week or more.

Pine Warbler (*Dendroica pinus*) – A very local nesting bird in old pines and mature pine plantations, mainly across the south, but north to Sudbury, Lake Superior Provincial Park, Thunder Bay, and Kenora. An uncommon spring migrant, arriving as early as the Yellow-rumped Warbler and not so confined to pines then as it is at other times, but much less frequently seen in fall (Mar. 13–Nov. 29). It has occasionally wintered, and occurs almost annually in early winter. It can be a hard bird to find, most easy to locate by song in later spring on the breeding grounds.

Kirtland's Warbler (*Dendroica kirtlandii*) – An occasional visitor. Most reports (48%) are from spring, and along the lower Great Lakes (May 9–Jun. 1). The species formerly bred in southern Ontario, and some 32% of records relate to sightings over the years in the breeding season, most relating to apparently territorial birds, including some in the last decade in areas of young jack pine. There are a small number of fall reports (Aug. 20–Oct. 2).

Prairie Warbler (*Dendroica discolor*) – A rare migrant and summer resident in very localized areas in the south, favouring scrubby habitats in rocky or sandy terrain (Apr. 27–Oct. 22). Populations are centred along the rocky eastern shorelines of Georgian Bay and in the Rideau Lakes area, with outlying stations in the Long Point area and the Pinery Provincial Park. One 1993 report from the north.

Palm Warbler (*Dendroica palmarum*) – A summer resident of the margins of northern bogs, mainly north of 50°N. There are a few summer records from the extremely limited bog habitat in southern Ontario. A fairly common migrant, favouring more open country than do the other warbler species (Mar. 1–Nov. 23); occasional in early winter (to Jan. 31). Birds of the yellow race are reported annually in migration.

Bay-breasted Warbler (*Dendroica castanea*) – A summer resident of northern Ontario, favouring mature conifers. It enters the south very locally along the Ottawa Valley and across the Shield. Like the Tennessee Warbler, this is a budworm specialist, and its abundance varies accordingly. In recent years – ones of budworm abundance – it has been a fairly common spring and very common fall migrant (Apr. 28–Dec. 3).

Blackpoll Warbler (*Dendroica striata*) – A summer resident of the northern treeline. The occasional singing bird will linger well into summer south of its breeding range; otherwise it is a common migrant, the latest of the warblers to arrive in spring, and hence easy to miss unless the song is known (Apr. 27–Dec. 2).

Cerulean Warbler (*Dendroica cerulea*) – A rare summer resident in mature deciduous woodlands, north to a line roughly from Wiarton to Brockville. The species has a very localized breeding range within the area given, with its largest populations in the Long Point and Rideau Lakes areas and smaller numbers at Rondeau and Minesing. A rare migrant, much more regular in spring than in fall, when it leaves early in the season (Apr. 18–Oct. 27).

Black-and-white Warbler (*Mniotilta varia*) – A fairly common

	J	F	M	A	M	J	J	A	S	O	N	D
Blackpoll Warbler						▬		▬	▬			
Cerulean Warbler					▬▬		▬	▬				
Black-and-white W.				▬▬▬					▬			
American Redstart					▬▬▬				▬▬			
Prothonotary Warbler				▬▬			—	—	—			
Worm-eating Warbler					—		—	—				
Ovenbird				▬▬▬				▬▬▬	▬			

summer resident, mainly in mixed woodlands and appearing to favour cedar woods in the south. Largely absent from the southwest and the far north. A very common migrant (Mar. 24–Nov. 17), with two winter records, one to early February.

American Redstart (*Setophaga ruticilla*) – A common summer resident of woodland edges and second growth, local south of the Shield and absent from the far north. A common migrant (Apr. 29–Nov. 28, one to Dec. 12).

Prothonotary Warbler (*Protonotaria citrea*) – A rare and very localized summer resident in wooded wetlands in the southwest, the main centres at Rondeau and Long Point, with birds also at Pelee and the Pinery and occasional nestings east to Hamilton. A rare migrant with about twenty to thirty reports annually, almost all in spring in the southwest. There are usually one to three sightings annually elsewhere (Apr. 17–Oct. 23).

Worm-eating Warbler (*Helmitheros vermivorus*) – A rare visitor in spring in the southwest (Apr. 19–Jun. 7, mostly at Pelee), much more rarely east along Lake Ontario; occasional in the same areas in fall (Jul. 1, Jul. 23–Oct. 23), more regular in the past decade. There are usually ten to thirty reports annually, but only two to three away from the southwest, including three (total) from Ottawa. This species seems to be planning to nest here if it is not already doing so. There are a few summer season sightings, and there is a relatively recent pattern of early fall sightings (55% from Aug. 6–Sept. 4).

Swainson's Warbler (*Limnothlypis swainsonii*) – Exceptional (May 6–22).

Ovenbird (*Seiurus aurocapillus*) – A common summer resident of dense woodlands, more local in the southwest and absent in the far north. A common migrant (Apr. 19–Nov. 19), occasional in early winter (to Jan. 4, one to Feb. 28).

Northern Waterthrush (*Seiurus noveboracensis*) – A common summer resident of woodland pools, more local in the southwest and absent in the extreme south. A common migrant (Apr. 5–Nov. 30), occasional in early winter (to Jan. 6, one throughout).

Louisiana Waterthrush (*Seiurus motacilla*) – A rare and very localized summer resident, along streams in forested areas. It occurs mainly in the southwest, but its largest populations are in the Long Point and Rideau Lakes areas, and smaller numbers along the Niagara Escarpment. A rare migrant, regular at Pelee and much more usual in spring than in fall, with the Toronto area of High Park yielding most of the records away from the main range (Mar. 28–Sept. 30). Probably easiest to find at Pelee in spring, or in the Long Point area in the nesting season.

Kentucky Warbler (*Oporornis formosus*) – A rare visitor in spring in the southwest (fifteen to thirty-five reports annually, Apr. 22–Jun. 17, mostly at Pelee, and usually in the second half of May), much more rarely east along Lake Ontario (two to four annually) with the bulk of the sightings from the Toronto area. There have been at least four reports of apparently territorial males (1966 and 1981–6) but no confirmed nesting. Very occasional in fall (Aug. 12–Oct. 25).

Connecticut Warbler (*Oporornis agilis*) – A local and extremely elusive summer resident of northern Ontario, from Sudbury, where it occurs in bogs, to the Rainy River area, where it occurs in open poplar woodland and can sometimes even be seen! A late, uncommon and extremely elusive spring migrant, even less often seen in fall when it is no longer singing (Apr. 2–Sept. 29). Pelee in the third week in May is reputedly the surest place to see this bird, but a familiarity with the song will reveal it elsewhere in this period. Rainy River is the best place for breeding season sightings.

Mourning Warbler (*Oporornis philadelphia*) – Another elusive late spring migrant and summer resident, but a persistent singer that responds well to pishing, and a fairly common bird of

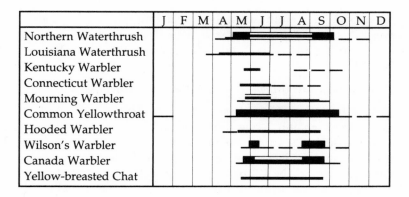

	J	F	M	A	M	J	J	A	S	O	N	D
Northern Waterthrush												
Louisiana Waterthrush												
Kentucky Warbler												
Connecticut Warbler												
Mourning Warbler												
Common Yellowthroat												
Hooded Warbler												
Wilson's Warbler												
Canada Warbler												
Yellow-breasted Chat												

brushy tangles along watercourses and raspberry cane thickets. It is absent in the far north and local in the south, but is easiest to find in the breeding season rather than on migration, when it is often silent (Apr. 30–Oct. 25).

MacGillivray's Warbler (*Oporornis tolmiei*) – One record (May 20).

Common Yellowthroat (*Geothlypis trichas*) – A very common migrant and summer resident in brushy and wet areas, absent only in the far north (May 2–Nov. 26). It is almost annual in early winter, occasional later.

Hooded Warbler (*Wilsonia citrina*) – A rare summer resident in hardwood forests, mainly in the Long Point area, but also elsewhere in the southwest (occasionally farther east) and singing birds reported north and east to Ottawa and Manitoulin. A rare migrant, mainly along the lower Great Lakes and mainly in spring (Apr. 6–Nov. 27). Pelee in May is the still best place to see this species, and in the nesting season the Long Point area is now probably the best area for it.

Wilson's Warbler (*Wilsonia pusilla*) – A fairly common summer resident of wetland scrub in coniferous forests in the north. It occurs south to the Sudbury area with isolated records elsewhere in the south. A common migrant, moving late in spring and early in fall (Apr. 16–Nov. 20; exceptionally later, to Jan. 7).

Canada Warbler (*Wilsonia canadensis*) – A rather uncommon summer resident in wet woodlands, most numerous north to

about 50°N and south across the Shield, and scarce in the southwest. A fairly common but rather skulking migrant, moving
late in spring and early in fall, and hence easy to miss (May 1–
Nov. 22).

Painted Redstart (*Myioborus pictus*) – One record (Nov. 9).

Yellow-breasted Chat (*Icteria virens*) – A rare summer resident
in the south, mainly along Lake Erie and in the Niagara Peninsula, favouring shrubby tangles in old field habitats. A rare
migrant, mainly in spring in the southwest and along Lake
Ontario (Apr. 25–Nov. 16, very occasionally in winter, to Jan.
8). Pelee is a reliable location for this species, which is easiest to
locate by its calls.

TANAGERS

Summer Tanager (*Piranga rubra*) – A rare visitor (three to fifteen or more annually; Apr. 19–May 28, Sept. 7–Nov. 25), mainly
in spring and in the southwest, where 85% of the reports originate, with most of the remainder along Lake Ontario. There
have been occasional summering records, associated with years
of exceptionally heavy spring movements (1972–3, 1979, 1984–
6, and 1990–2). There are also early wintering records in three
years, to Jan. 1. Pelee in May is the most likely place for this
species.

Scarlet Tanager (*Piranga olivacea*) – A fairly common summer
resident in mixed and deciduous forest, most numerous in the
Shield areas of eastern Ontario, and north in smaller numbers
roughly to the Highway 11 line. It frequents the upper canopy
of the forest, and its distinctive call note is often the first clue to
its presence. A fairly common migrant (Apr. 19–Nov. 25, two
early winter, to Feb. 5).

Western Tanager (*Piranga ludoviciana*) – An occasional visitor
in migration periods (Apr. 27–May 27; Aug. 3–Nov. 22), with at
least four winter reports (to February). Apart from a group of
North Bay sightings, there are only some three fall records, the
scattered reports being mainly in spring, and along the lower
Great Lakes. A high percentage of putative sightings do not
receive records committee approval, as the Scarlet Tanager can
exhibit wingbars as well.

	J	F	M	A	M	J	J	A	S	O	N	D
Summer Tanager												
Scarlet Tanager												
Northern Cardinal												
Rose-breasted Grosbeak												
Indigo Bunting												
Dickcissel												
Rufous-sided Towhee												
American Tree Sparrow												

CARDINALS, GROSBEAKS, AND ALLIES

Northern Cardinal (*Cardinalis cardinalis*) – A very common resident of edge habitats in the southwest and along Lake Ontario, decreasing rapidly to the east and north, but slowly expanding its range.

Rose-breasted Grosbeak (*Pheucticus ludovicianus*) – A common summer resident in deciduous woodlots and mixed woodland, north roughly to the Highway 11 line. A very common migrant (Apr. 15–Nov. 22); occasional in early winter, exceptionally throughout.

Black-headed Grosbeak (*Pheucticus melanocephalus*) – A very occasional visitor; there are four May records and three late fall and winter. Four of the sightings were from the Thunder Bay area.

Blue Grosbeak (*Guiraca caerulea*) – A very rare spring visitor (Apr. 22–Jul. 30). Over 80% of the reports are in May, and 62% from Long Point, Rondeau, and Pelee (alone, almost half). The remaining records are more typical of vagrancy, being scattered across the province and representing the bulk of the later dates. A high percentage of sightings do not receive records committee approval.

Lazuli Bunting (*Passerina amoena*) – Exceptional (May 10–Jun. 18).

Indigo Bunting (*Passerina cyanea*) – A common summer resident of deciduous woodland edges, becoming scarcer northwards but present across the north of Lake Superior and west to Kenora. A fairly common spring and uncommon fall migrant (Apr. 20–Oct. 28); occasional in early winter, exceptionally throughout.

Painted Bunting (*Passerina ciris*) – Exceptional, with debates about possible escapees (Apr. 29–Jun. 4).

Dickcissel (*Spiza americana*) – Only Red Crossbill is more erratic in its Ontario appearances than this species. Migrants are most regular in the southwest, particularly at Pelee (Apr. 7–May 28, Aug. 12–Nov. 30) and are sometimes most numerous in spring (zero to five reports annually), sometimes in fall (zero to ten reports annually). Birds winter almost annually, usually joining House Sparrow flocks at feeders. Territorial and nesting birds, sometimes in small numbers, usually follow periodic spring influxes, and are perhaps associated with prairie droughts (most recently 1963, 1972, and 1988). Both summer and winter records are quite scattered, with the larger number of summer birds in the extreme southwest and in the Bruce Peninsula, and winter birds reported most often in the Toronto area.

EMBERIZINE FINCHES AND SPARROWS

Green-tailed Towhee (*Pipilo chlorurus*) – Exceptional (October–Apr. 24).

Rufous-sided Towhee (*Pipilo erythrophthalmus*) – An uncommon migrant and summer resident in the south, north roughly to a line from Midland to Prescott, then much more locally north to the Sudbury area. It favours brushy areas, typically in old field habitats. It winters regularly in small numbers.

Bachman's Sparrow (*Aimophila aestivalis*) – Exceptional: almost annual in May to 1966, none since.

Cassin's Sparrow (*Aimophila cassinii*) – Exceptional (May 7–23, Aug. 15–Oct. 17).

American Tree Sparrow (*Spizella arborea*) – A summer resident of the north coasts. Elsewhere a common migrant and fairly common winter resident in southern Ontario (Sept. 14–Jun. 10, later in the north), favouring open bottomlands and willow scrub.

Chipping Sparrow (*Spizella passerina*) – A very common migrant and summer resident, less common in the north, favouring open park-like habitats and well-established gardens as well as woodland edges (Mar. 31–Nov. 23). Rare in early winter, occasionally throughout. Like most sparrows, much harder to find once it has ceased singing.

Clay-colored Sparrow (*Spizella pallida*) – A rare and very local summer resident, colonizing young coniferous plantations for a period when the trees are about 3 metres high, but also occurring in scrubby, old field habitats similar to those on the prairies. In the south, Simcoe and Prince Edward counties, Lake Scugog, Ottawa, and Sudbury have good populations, with Thunder Bay and Rainy River in the north. A rare migrant (May 9–Oct. 26). It is much more common in the Rainy River area than elsewhere.

Brewer's Sparrow (*Spizella breweri*) – One disputed record (Mar. 25).

Field Sparrow (*Spizella pusilla*) – An uncommon migrant and local nesting bird in the south, north roughly to a line from Parry Sound to Pembroke, but scarce northwards, and with a few as far as Sudbury and Manitoulin Island (Mar. 25–Nov. 29). It favours old fields with mature shrubs. Individuals occur regularly in winter, often with American Tree Sparrow flocks.

Vesper Sparrow (*Pooecetes gramineus*) – A fairly common migrant and summer resident, north to Kirkland Lake and Kenora, but much less common northwards and on the Shield. It favours open country with undisturbed grassy areas and trees nearby for singing perches (Mar. 13–Nov. 28). Rare to occasional in the south in winter.

Lark Sparrow (*Chondestes grammacus*) – An occasional summer resident, favouring open habitats with scattered trees. Formerly summer birds were reported, sometimes nesting, at two- to five-year intervals, at a variety of locations, but most often near Long Point. A rare visitor in migration, principally along the lower Great Lakes (two to eight reports annually; Apr. 6–May 31, Aug. 8–Dec. 4, a couple later, to Mar. 22).

Black-throated Sparrow (*Amphispiza bilineata*) – One record (Oct. 2–3).

	J	F	M	A	M	J	J	A	S	O	N	D
Chipping Sparrow												
Clay-colored Sparrow												
Field Sparrow												
Vesper Sparrow												
Savannah Sparrow												
Grasshopper Sparrow												
Henslow's Sparrow												
Le Conte's Sparrow												
Sharp-tailed Sparrow												

Lark Bunting (*Calamospiza melanocorys*) – An occasional visitor, reported less than annually from across the province. Seen in every month except November (most Apr. 6–May 25, Aug. 29–Oct. 21). There is one wintering record.

Savannah Sparrow (*Passerculus sandwichensis*) – A common migrant and abundant summer resident in open country throughout, but scarce on the Shield and in the north due to lack of habitat (Mar. 5–Nov. 22). Rare in early winter in the south, occasionally throughout the season. The common sparrow of agricultural areas everywhere.

Grasshopper Sparrow (*Ammodramus savannarum*) – An elusive and uncommon summer resident of southern Ontario and the Rainy River area. The species, which occurs mainly south of the Shield, has declined in recent years. The birds mainly favour areas of thin grassland and typically use mullein stalks as song posts; however, fields with heavier ground cover seem acceptable as well, as long as song perches are available. The species is rarely seen outside the breeding season (Apr. 7–Nov. 11; two in winter, Dec. 12 and Jan. 18 on).

Henslow's Sparrow (*Ammodramus henslowii*) – A very rare and declining summer resident, considered endangered in Ontario. Breeding birds survived in the Kingston and Luther Marsh areas, with possibly a few scattered stations elsewhere in the south. However, a 1993 survey only located a single breeding pair in the province. The birds favoured old fields with a dense ground cover of such plants as asters and goldenrods, and formerly used the moist depressions in abandoned fields frequented by the last species. Rarely seen outside the breeding season, perhaps most reliably at Pelee in early May (Apr. 14–Dec. 3).

Le Conte's Sparrow (*Ammodramus leconteii*) – A very rare and elusive summer resident, mainly in the north; regular and quite widespread along the James Bay coast and in the Rainy River area, where they can be easy to locate when singing, with other populations near Thunder Bay, and possibly around Dryden and New Liskeard. In the south, birds have occurred in the Luther Marsh area and occasionally elsewhere. Birds in summer are typically associated with sedge marshes and wet fields, but in migration they can appear in (or, more usually, disappear into) any grassy or brushy tangles; like Henslow's, they have been most reliable at Pelee in late April and early May, less often in October, but are rarely seen outside the breeding season (Apr. 10–Nov. 7).

Sharp-tailed Sparrow (*Ammodramus caudacutus*) – A regular summer resident of marshes on James Bay and along the Lake of the Woods. Elsewhere a rare migrant, mainly in fall in tangles and beds of Beggar's ticks or cattails in the larger marshes along the lower Great Lakes, but rarely seen without the special effort of ploughing through dense marsh vegetation (twenty to thirty reports annually; Apr. 25–Jun. 19, Aug. 2–Nov. 30 one to Dec. 21). Dundas Marsh and the marshes east of Toronto are areas where the species has been found fairly regularly, perhaps most often in October.

Fox Sparrow (*Passerella iliaca*) – A summer resident of dense bush in northern Ontario, mainly north of 50°N. Elsewhere an uncommon migrant favouring woodland edges. It moves through our area very quickly, and hence is easily missed (Mar. 7–May 25, Aug. 30–Nov. 30; most the second halves of April and October). Occasional in winter.

Song Sparrow (*Melospiza melodia*) – An abundant migrant and summer resident, less common in the north. Rare in winter in the south, but becoming commoner west of Toronto.

Lincoln's Sparrow (*Melospiza lincolnii*) – A common summer resident of bog margins and brushy areas in the north, south

	J	F	M	A	M	J	J	A	S	O	N	D
Fox Sparrow												
Song Sparrow												
Lincoln's Sparrow												
Swamp Sparrow												
White-throated Sparrow												
White-crowned S.												
Harris' Sparrow												
Dark-eyed Junco												
Lapland Longspur												
Snow Bunting												

very locally across the Shield and in a few pockets of suitable habitat farther south (Luther Marsh, Wainfleet Bog). A fairly common but retiring migrant, favouring heavy cover (Apr. 9–Nov. 19). Occasional in early winter in the south, exceptionally throughout the season.

Swamp Sparrow (*Melospiza georgiana*) – A common migrant and summer resident in marshes and wetlands (Mar. 22–Nov. 29). Rare in winter in the south, when it can often be found among cattails.

White-throated Sparrow (*Zonotrichia albicollis*) – A common summer resident of forest edges, more local in the agricultural south, and largely absent west of a line from Long Point to the Pinery. An often abundant migrant, the common migrant sparrow of woodlots and along woodland edges (Mar. 22–Nov. 24). Rare in winter, becoming commoner southwestwards.

Golden-crowned Sparrow (*Zonotrichia atricapilla*) – An occasional, almost annual, visitor since 1982 (one Jan. 1–20, two Apr. 16–May 4, the rest Sept. 24–Nov. 11). Three of the nine reports are from the Toronto area.

White-crowned Sparrow (*Zonotrichia leucophrys*) – A summer resident of open shrubby areas near the northern coasts. Elsewhere a common migrant, favouring more open habitats than the White-throated, but often occurring with it in edge areas (Mar. 2–Jun. 23, Aug. 16–Nov. 30). It is rare in winter.

Harris' Sparrow (*Zonotrichia querula*) – A rare summer resident of extreme northwestern Ontario, and an uncommon migrant from the Thunder Bay area west. Elsewhere a rare visitor in migration periods (two to four annually; Mar. 26–May 24, Sept. 11–Nov. 22), occasional in winter.

Dark-eyed Junco (*Junco hyemalis*) – A common summer resident in northern Ontario, south more locally across the Shield, and very rare and local south of it. It colonizes burns and second growth. A very common migrant and common winter resident in the south, favouring open woodland and edge habitats. Occasionally individuals of western races can be found in junco flocks.

Lapland Longspur (*Calcarius lapponicus*) – A summer resident along the north coast. Elsewhere a rather rare fall migrant, but sometimes occurring in numbers; less regular in spring (Sept. 11–May 31). In migration, birds are often along the shorelines of the Great Lakes, and in winter individuals can be found in flocks of Snow Buntings, appearing as smaller, darker birds.

Smith's Longspur (*Calcarius pictus*) – A summer resident along the north coast. Elsewhere an occasional visitor in migration, perhaps regular along western Lake Superior (Apr. 19–May 22, Sept. 23–Nov. 2).

Chestnut-collared Longspur (*Calcarius ornatus*) – Exceptional (Apr. 17–May 2).

Snow Bunting (*Plectrophenax nivalis*) – Rare in summer along the north coast, occasional elsewhere. A fairly common migrant, often following the Great Lakes shorelines (Mar. 1–May 5, Aug. 26–Nov. 20). Less common in winter and mainly in the south, sometimes in huge (5000+) flocks, often visiting manured fields.

BLACKBIRDS, ORIOLES, AND ALLIES

Bobolink (*Dolichonyx oryzivorus*) – A common summer resident in the south, rarer northwards to Cochrane and Kenora, favouring fields with dense grass. A common migrant, but easy to miss in fall unless the calls are known (Apr. 3–Nov. 22, one Dec. 20).

Red-winged Blackbird (*Agelaius phoeniceus*) – An abundant mi-

	J	F	M	A	M	J	J	A	S	O	N	D
Bobolink												
Red-winged Blackbird												
Eastern Meadowlark												
Western Meadowlark												
Yellow-head. Blackbird												
Rusty Blackbird												
Brewer's Blackbird												

grant and summer resident, nesting in grassland as well as marshes, but scarce north of 50°N. In fall, the birds concentrate in huge numbers in cornfields, and may be absent elsewhere. Individuals are regular in winter, common in the southwest, feeding at corn cribs, but becoming progressively rarer to the east and north.

Eastern Meadowlark (*Sturnella magna*) – A common summer resident of fields in the south, mainly south of the Shield but occurring north to Timmins and Rainy River. A common but inconspicuous migrant, sometimes very difficult to find in fall. Rare in winter.

Western Meadowlark (*Sturnella neglecta*) – A common summer resident of the Rainy River area, and eastward in small numbers to Thunder Bay. In the south, it is rare and very local in summer on Manitoulin Island and west of the Shield, with its best numbers in Grey, Bruce, and Simcoe counties. The Atlas suggests the largest numbers are in the open country around Chesley. A rare migrant, almost all in spring (five to twelve reports annually; Mar. 17–May 24, Oct. 10–Nov. 24). Formerly thought to be regular in winter, but I know of none in the last decade at least.

Yellow-headed Blackbird (*Xanthocephalus xanthocephalus*) – A summer resident in western Ontario, mainly in the cattail marshes of Lake of the Woods, and in very small numbers eastwards to Thunder Bay. A second population exists in extreme southwestern Ontario around Lake St Clair and near Amherstburg. Both populations appear to be expanding slowly. Elsewhere it is a rare migrant, mainly in spring (Mar. 9–Jun. 2, Aug. 13–Nov. 2) which winters almost annually in the south.

Like other blackbirds, outside the breeding season it is most likely to be found associating with mixed blackbird flocks.

Rusty Blackbird (*Euphagus carolinus*) – An uncommon summer resident of brushy wetlands in the north, south in smaller numbers through the Algonquin area, and extremely locally elsewhere in the south. A fairly common migrant, but tending to move through our area quickly (Apr. 19–Nov. 22; most in late April and late October). Rare in winter, but more numerous in the southwest.

Brewer's Blackbird (*Euphagus cyanocephalus*) – A rather uncommon summer resident of open field areas in western Ontario, east to Thunder Bay, of the agricultural country between Sault Ste Marie and North Bay, and of Manitoulin Island and the Bruce Peninsula. The species also nests in a few other widely separated areas in the south, but such colonies have not usually persisted for long. It is a rare migrant (Mar. 30–May 29, Sept. 19–Nov. 30) which will winter in small numbers in the southwest, occasionally elsewhere. The Bruce Peninsula has been the only consistent area for this species in the south, although even there the colonies move around from year to year.

Great-tailed Grackle (*Quiscalus mexicanus*) – Two records (Oct. 7–Jan. 6).

Common Grackle (*Quiscalus quiscula*) – An abundant migrant and summer resident, less common northwards and absent from much of the Hudson Bay Lowland. In fall the birds concentrate in large numbers with Red-winged Blackbirds in cornfields, and may be absent elsewhere. Individuals are regular in winter, common in the southwest, but becoming progressively rarer to the east and north.

Brown-headed Cowbird (*Molothrus ater*) – A very common migrant and summer resident in the agricultural south, much less numerous northwards, but present in more disturbed areas throughout. Like the Common Grackle, it concentrates in cornfields in fall, with a similar pattern of distribution in winter.

Orchard Oriole (*Icterus spurius*) – A rare migrant and summer resident in open, park-like settings south of the Shield, mainly in the southwest and along western Lake Ontario (Apr. 25–May

25, Aug. 5–Sept. 25). Birds are usual at most of the migration concentration points along the lower Great Lakes in mid-May, particularly at Pelee.

Hooded Oriole (*Icterus cucullatus*) – One record (May 19–20).

Northern Oriole (*Icterus galbula*) – A common migrant and summer resident in the south, much less common northwards but still regular in areas of deciduous woodland from Kenora to Thunder Bay, and north of Sudbury and Sault Ste Marie (Apr. 11–Oct. 31). Very rare in the south in winter, mainly in the southwest and to mid-January. Bullock's race is an occasional visitor (Apr. 1–Jun. 2, Oct. 31–Jan. 3).

Scott's Oriole (*Icterus parisorum*) – One record (Nov. 1).

FRINGILLINE AND CARDUELINE FINCHES

Brambling (*Fringilla montifringilla*) – Exceptional (Oct. 23–Apr. 11; two from Atikokan).

Gray-crowned Rosy-Finch (*Leucosticte tephrocotis*) – Exceptional (Nov. 3–Mar. 31).

Pine Grosbeak (*Pinicola enucleator*) – A rare and local resident in the north, appearing unpredictably in the south in winter time, sometimes in moderate numbers (Sept. 4–May 25). In flight years, birds typically appear first in the north and east; the southwest may fail to record any except in the heaviest movements, which in recent years have occurred in 1965–6, 1971–2, 1977–8, 1983–4, and 1989–90. In spite of this apparent regularity, patterns of appearance are very irregular from year to year and are difficult to analyse because of wide variations in numbers from one area to another, doubtless reflecting fluctations in the availability of food supplies (a lack of pattern shared with other winter finches). In the south, this species seems to favour soft fruits, such as mountain ash and woody nightshade.

Purple Finch (*Carpodacus purpureus*) – A fairly common summer resident north of a line from Ottawa to Southampton, rare to the south and in the far north, and favouring coniferous forest. A fairly common migrant which also winters, most often in the southwest, and often appears in large numbers like other

	J	F	M	A	M	J	J	A	S	O	N	D
Common Grackle												
Brown-headed Cowbird												
Orchard Oriole												
Northern Oriole												
Pine Grosbeak												
Purple Finch												
House Finch												

winter finches, as in 1974–5, 1980–1, and 1984–5. Their winter diet seems quite varied; I have found them feeding on burdocks as frequently as anything else!

Cassin's Finch (*Carpodacus cassinii*) – One record (Aug. 13).

House Finch (*Carpodacus mexicanus*) – A recent (1972) immigrant to our area, still expanding its range outward from the Niagara Peninsula, and now a fairly common to abundant resident in urban areas north at present to Port Elgin, Orillia, Peterborough, Smith's Falls, and Ottawa (although apparently still largely absent from large areas even within this region), and in smaller numbers as far as Sudbury and Sault Ste Marie.

Red Crossbill (*Loxia curvirostra*) – A rare and erratic nomad with a life cycle wholly geared to the availability of the conifer seeds upon which it feeds (see Lumsden and Smith's discussion on crossbills on pp. 572–3 of the Atlas). The Ontario race nests irregularly from Sandy Lake to Cochrane southwards, probably but very rarely at least as far as Long Point and Kingston when good cone crops, mainly pines, are available; and breeding behaviour has been reported any time between at least March and August. The species also stages periodic irruptions like other winter finches, appearing in large numbers and feeding on conifers. Some four to five different races from across the continent may be involved in these flights, and as different races are thought to favour different species of conifer, the timing of their flights and their behaviour when here can vary greatly. In some cases the birds appeared in fall and went straight through, in others the flight did not even begin until early spring. Noteworthy flight years have been 1960–1, 1963–4, 1969–70, 1973, 1984–5, and 1988–9.

	J	F	M	A	M	J	J	A	S	O	N	D
Red Crossbill												
White-winged Crossbill												
Common Redpoll												
Hoary Redpoll												
Pine Siskin												
American Goldfinch												
Evening Grosbeak												
House Sparrow												

White-winged Crossbill (*Loxia leucoptera*) – An uncommon resident of the boreal forest that is rather more predictable than the Red Crossbill, but has a similar lifestyle. It has nested south to the Algonquin area, and in flight years occasionally as far south as Long Point. Irruptions occurred in 1963–4, 1965–6, 1971–2, 1980–1, 1984–5, and 1988–9, but a few appear every winter. The pattern of movement is usually similar to that described for Pine Grosbeak, and it favours spruce, hemlock, and other small-coned conifers.

Common Redpoll (*Carduelis flammea*) – A summer resident along the north coasts. Elsewhere it is an irregular migrant, especially in the north, but often in small numbers in the south in late fall, even in years when no winter flight develops (Sept. 27–May 30). Redpolls are the classic winter finch, abundant in some years and absent in others. Widespread flights occurred in 1969–70, 1977–78, 1980–1, 1985–6, 1988, and 1993–4, often with an echo flight the next year. The pattern of movement is usually similar to that described for Pine Grosbeaks, but unlike that species and the crossbills, these birds will visit feeders in numbers and forage over open fields, as well as feeding on birch and conifer fruits. A few can be found in most winters, usually associating with goldfinches or siskins, and even in flight years flocks are often mixed.

Hoary Redpoll (*Carduelis hornemanni*) – The Atlas recorded a few summer birds along Hudson Bay. Otherwise an occasional winter visitor in flocks of other redpolls, most regular in the north (Oct. 24–Apr. 30). There have been up to 120 reports in the south in heavy irruption winters, which do not always coincide with those of the last species. Good years include 1968–9, 1973–4, 1977–8, 1981–2, 1985–6, and 1988–90.

Pine Siskin (*Carduelis pinus*) – A common summer resident in the north, much less numerous in the far north and in the south across the Shield; rare and erratic farther south, typically nesting in widely scattered areas following good flight winters. It is the most regular of the winter finches, usually common in winter, and often very common at feeders. Favoured foods include white cedar, yellow birch, and hemlock.

Lesser Goldfinch (*Carduelis psaltria*) – One record (Aug. 10).

American Goldfinch (*Carduelis tristis*) – A common migrant and summer resident, north to at least 50°N, but much rarer in, or absent from, areas of heavy forest. Uncommon to fairly common in winter in the south, concentrating at feeders.

Evening Grosbeak (*Coccothraustes vespertinus*) – A fairly common summer resident in the north, north to Pickle Lake and Moosonee, and southwards in smaller numbers across the Shield, with summer records irregularly southwards, extending to a line from Southampton to Simcoe. During the 1970s, this species irrupted in huge numbers even when other winter finches stayed home, and birds were regular in migration even in years when no flight developed, with a few to be found every winter. With the decline of the spruce budworm outbreaks, the species has become much less common in the south.

House Sparrow (*Passer domesticus*) – Abundant year-round in urban areas and around dwellings, but much less common in northern communities, where winter mortality can be high.

Appendix   Scientific Names of Mammal, Reptile, and Plant Species Mentioned in the Text

Bear, black *Ursus americanus*
Bear, polar *Ursus maritimus*
Beaver *Castor canadensis*
Deer, white-tailed *Odocoileus virginianus*
Fox, red *Vulpes vulpes*
Ground squirrel, Franklin's *Spermophilus franklinii*
Rabbit, white-tailed jack *Lepus townsendii*
Massasauga *Sistrurus catenatus*
Moose *Alces alces*
Squirrel, gray *Sciurus carolinensis*
Turtle, Blanding's *Emydoidea blandingi*
Turtle, wood *Clemmys insculpta*
Wolf, timber *Canis lupus*

Alder *Alnus* spp., mainly *incana*
Apple *Pyrus malus*
Ash, blue *Fraxinus quadrangulata*
Ash, mountain *Sorbus* spp.
Ash, prickly *Zanthoxylum americanum*
Aspen *Populus* spp., mainly *tremuloides*

aster *Aster* spp.
Basswood *Tilia americana*
Beech, American *Fagus grandifolia*
Beggar's Ticks *Bidens* spp.
Birch, silver *Betula papyrifera*
Birch, yellow *Betula alleghaniensis*
Buckthorn *Rhamnus cathartica*
Burdock *Arctium* spp.
Buttonbush *Cephalanthus occidentalis*
Cattail *Typha* spp.
Cedar, red *Juniperus virginiana*
Cedar, white *Thuja occidentalis*
Cherry, choke *Prunus virginiana*
Cherry, fire *Prunus pensylvanica*
Cottonwood *Populus deltoides*
currants *Ribes* spp., mainly *americanum* and *triste*
Dandelion *Taraxacum officinale*
Dogwood, red osier *Cornus sericea*
Fir, balsam *Abies balsamea*
goldenrod *Solidago* spp.

gooseberries *Ribes* spp., mainly
  cynosbati
grape *Vitis* spp.
Hackberry *Celtis occidentalis*
hawkweeds *Hieracium* spp.
hawthorns *Crataegus* spp.
Hemlock *Tsuga canadensis*
Hickories *Carya* spp.
Ivy, poison *Toxicodendron radicans*
jewelweed *Impatiens* spp. mainly
  capensis
Juneberry *Amelanchier* spp.
Juniper *Juniperus communis*
Maple, Manitoba *Acer negundo*
Maple, red *Acer rubrum*
Maple, sugar *Acer saccharum*
maples *Acer* spp.
Mulberry, red *Morus rubra*
Mullein *Verbascum thapsus*
Nightshade, woody *Solanum*
  dulcamara

Oak, black *Quercus velutina*
Oak, red *Quercus rubra*
oaks *Quercus* spp.
Pitcher plant *Sarracenia purpurea*
Pine, jack *Pinus banksiana*
Pine, red *Pinus resinosa*
Pine, white *Pinus strobus*
Poplar, balsam *Populus*
  balsamifera
poplars *Populus* spp.
roses *Rosa* spp.
Sassafras *Sassafras albidum*
sedges mainly *Carex* spp.
Spicebush *Lindera benzoin*
Spruce, black *Picea mariana*
Spruce, white *Picea glauca*
Sumac *Rhus* spp., mainly
  typhina
Tamarack *Larix laricina*
Tulip-tree *Liriodendron tulipifera*
willows *Salix* spp.

Mammal names from A.W. Banfield, *The Mammals of Canada* (National Museum of Canada 1974); plant names from H.A. Gleason and A. Cronquist, *Manual of Vascular Plants of Northeastern United States and Adjacent Canada*, 2nd. ed, (New York Botanical Garden 1991).

Index

Long Point Harbour 238
Long Point Provincial Park 111,
    113–14, 370, 376
Long Sault Parkway 256
Long Swamp 253
Longlac 329
Longspur, Chestnut-collared 237,
    313, 441
Longspur, Lapland 33, 56, 70, 80,
    230, 299, 309, 310, 440, 441
Longspur, Smith's 299, 316, 441
longspurs 309, 310
Loon, Common 18, 30, 73, 80, 81,
    85, 88, 97, 112, 132, 136, 180,
    194, 195, 197, 200, 216, 237, 240,
    257, 266, 268, 276, 281, 285, 294,
    324, 329, 358, 359
Loon, Pacific 73, 299, 358
Loon, Red-throated 30, 73, 80,
    186, 195, 257, 299, 357, 359
Loon, Yellow-billed 358
loons 46, 68, 74, 89, 117, 143, 185,
    220, 223, 251, 311
Low Island 273
Lowbanks 121
Lucan 102
Luther Marsh 17, 22, 125, 132–5,
    359, 362, 371, 376, 378, 395, 419,
    440
Lynde Creek 195, 197, 205
Lynde Shores Conservation Area
    195

Macauley Mountain Conserva-
    tion Area 235
MacGregor Point Provincial Park
    81, 358
MacPherson Park 80
Madoc 214, 244
Magpie High Falls 308

Magpie, Black-billed 321, 337,
    338, 340, 341, 415
Mahon Tract 167
Malden Centre 53, 56
Mallard 17, 70, 101, 130, 132, 136,
    143, 178, 180, 219, 240, 294, 327,
    368, 369
Mallorytown 242
Mallorytown Landing 243
Manchester 199
Manitoulin Island 11, 13, 14, 22,
    30, 78, 261, 272–6, 291, 301
Manitouwadge 331
Manitowaning 273
Manotick 252
Maple 206
Mar 86, 90
Marathon 32, 309–10, 377
Marie Curtis Park 184
Marilyn Bell Park 188
Marina Park 314
Mariner's Memorial Park 237
Mark S. Burnham Provincial Park
    211
Marmora 214, 244
Marten River Provincial Park
    322–3
Martin, Purple 22, 134, 141, 301,
    320, 338, 413, 414
Martindale Pond 150
Martyrs' Shrine 267
Marysville 232
Massena 257
Massey 302
Matchedash Bay 268, 414
Matheson 325
Mattawa 288, 291
Mazinaw Rock 244
McGeachy Pond Conservation
    Area 48